Freedom, Union, and Power

Freedom, Union, and Power

Lincoln and His Party during the Civil War

by

MICHAEL S. GREEN

Fordham University Press
New York
2004

The North's Civil War, No. 27
ISSN 1089-8719

Library of Congress Cataloging-in-Publication Data

Green, Michael S.
Freedom, union, and power : Lincoln and his party during the Civil War / by Michael S. Green. — 1st ed.
p. cm. — (The North's Civil War, ISSN 1089-8719 ; no. 27)
Includes bibliographical references and index.
ISBN 0-8232-2275-6 (alk. paper)
1. United States—Politics and government—1861–1865. 2. Lincoln, Abraham, 1809–1865—Political and social views. 3. Republican Party (U.S. : 1854–)—History—19th century. 4. Political culture—United States—History—19th century. 5. Political science—United States—History—19th century. 6. United States—Intellectual life—1783–1865. I. Title. II. Series.
E456.G75 2004
973.7'1—dc22 2003018679

Printed in the United States of America
07 06 05 04 03 5 4 3 2 1
First edition

To Mom
For Dad

CONTENTS

ABBREVIATIONS USED IN THE NOTES

CG	*Congressional Globe*
CR	Department of Manuscripts and University Archives, Cornell University Libraries, Cornell University
CU	Department of Rare Books and Manuscripts, Butler Library, Columbia University
CW	Roy P. Basler, Marion Dolores Platt, and Lloyd A. Dunlap, eds., *The Collected Works of Abraham Lincoln*, 9 vols. New Brunswick, N.J.: Rutgers University Press, 1953–55.
HL	The Henry E. Huntington Library, San Marino, California
HSP	Historical Society of Pennsylvania, Philadelphia
HU	Houghton Library, Harvard University
IU	Lilly Library, Indiana University
LC	Manuscript Division, Library of Congress
MHS	Massachusetts Historical Society
NHHS	New Hampshire Historical Society
NJHS	New Jersey Historical Society
NYHS	New York Historical Society
NYPL	Manuscript Division, New York Public Library
OR	*Official Record of the War between the States*
SP	The Papers of Charles Sumner, Microfilm Edition
UR	Department of Rare Books and Manuscripts, Rush Rhees Library, University of Rochester

PREFACE AND ACKNOWLEDGMENTS

This book began as a dissertation proposal to examine the ideology of the Republican party during the Civil War: what its leaders believed and how those beliefs manifested themselves in word and deed. Several years, many computer disks, and a couple of file cabinets later, I have found a great deal of agreement between the diverse members of this organization. I also found much disagreement, but less over the ends to be pursued than over the means of pursuing them. No one who has studied the politics of the Civil War era would be likely to deny that Republicans sometimes fought one another with what strikes us today as a surprising amount of vitriol. After all, not only did they belong to the same political party, but they were waging a war for the nation's survival; they might have been expected to sublimate petty political hatreds for the sake of a higher cause. However, they spilled most of this venom over how to fight and win the war, or elections, or appointments—not over whether even to try to win them, or what winning them might mean.

Consequently, what follows is an attempt to offer insight into the Republican party's mind, from its victory in the election of 1860 until the death of Abraham Lincoln. It is not a history of the Republican party during the Civil War, although much of that history is necessarily discussed here. It is not a history of the Cabinet, Congress, or Lincoln or any other individual, although elements of that creep into the text and certain prominent Republicans receive more attention than others. Nor is it a statistical study of the peaks and valleys of the party, citing an array of quantification and regression analysis to prove its point. I have benefited greatly from such works, and they underpin some of the conclusions that follow, but the appearance of any statistics in the pages that follow is purely accidental.

Lincoln emerges here as the central figure in his party, and I mean that in two ways. As president he was the only Republican answerable to a national constituency—or, given the circumstances, it might be more accurate to say that he was answerable to a sectional or regional constituency. He had to balance the views and personalities of radicals, moderates, and conservatives. However, as one whose views were evolving, Lincoln provides us with a useful yardstick by which to measure his fellow Republicans. That Lincoln disliked slavery should be beyond argument. Whether he opposed it enough to eliminate it is harder to determine—he made no such noises as he became president, but ultimately he sought its abolition through a constitutional amendment.

Other Republicans tended to be more set in their ways, on all sides of the spectrum. The masterful way in which Lincoln managed to weave between radicals and conservatives, and cleave them, is at the heart of this work. Even as brilliant a politician as Lincoln never could have managed this feat without a set of beliefs that he shared with others and that they, in turn, shared among themselves. Many may argue that he did not achieve this nearly as well as I think he did, but even they must agree that Republicans managed to hang together during the war. This point merely underscores the importance of this ideology, and hence the need to study it. I hope that this book fulfills that need.

The limitations of space and sanity have circumscribed this study in some ways and expanded it in others. I have tried to avoid historiographic debates, except in some footnotes and in occasional textual references. I have not delved into foreign policy or dealt in great detail with the give-and-take of legislation and certain other aspects of Republican activity. To a small degree I wanted to avoid replicating, in too great detail, several recent studies that have considered such matters. When I have dealt with these issues, I have tried to do so in the context of the party's ideology.

What follows may strike some as fitting the mold of traditional history, and some may believe that *mold* is an appropriate word to describe traditional history. I disagree. The study of political and intellectual history remains important to understanding our past, present, and future. Whatever criticisms of government have crept into our discourse in the twentieth and twenty-first centuries, leaders are still expected to lead, or at least to reflect the ideas of the public they have been elected or chosen to represent. What Republicans did during the Civil War was undeniably an outgrowth of what they heard from their constituents, friends, and colleagues. Ultimately, though, the party's elected officials were the ones who took action and elaborated on their action. Their words and related deeds form the core of this book.

Many readers turn to the acknowledgments to see who is mentioned, how sappy an author may be, and whether the list is as long as the Manhattan telephone directory. I plead guilty to all of these charges.

Completing this book affords me an opportunity to thank friends and family who have tolerated, encouraged, and supported me throughout this long—overlong—process. For the length of the process and any errors that follow, I am to blame; after all, had I listened to them, there would have been no errors.

I was wise enough to listen to librarians. I am especially indebted to those at Columbia University; the Huntington Library; the Lilly Library at Indiana University; the Library of Congress; the New York Public Library; the New York Historical Society; the University of Rochester; Cornell University; Yale University; the New Hampshire Historical Society; the Historical Society of Pennsylvania; Harvard University; the University of Nevada, Las Vegas; and the Community College of Southern Nevada.

The staff at Fordham University Press has been unfailingly helpful. I would like especially to thank Paul A. Cimbala, a professor of history at Fordham and the editor of the series in which this volume appears. He took me in hand while I was still a graduate student and has been a constant source of encouragement, prodding, and ideas. The staff at Fordham University Press has been a joy to work with.

Several groups provided much-needed and much-appreciated financial support. Thanks to the Fletcher Jones and Michael J. Connell Foundations, I was able to spend three glorious months at the Huntington Library. The Ball Brothers Foundation made it possible for me to mine the holdings of the Lilly Library at Indiana University. The Dunning Fund for travel in the Columbia University history department enabled me to travel to conferences to present some of my findings, and fellowships from that institution made it possible for me to go there in the first place.

My fellow Columbia graduate students, in history and other areas, provided friendship and sustenance. For true friendship—and lodging—I am exceptionally indebted to Yanek Mieczkowski and his parents, Bogdan and Seiko; Bob Dobie and his parents, Bob and Marge; and Ted and Pamela Stanford. In and out of the classroom, I have profited from knowing and working with Leah Arroyo, Jon Birnbaum, Alana Erickson Coble, Walter Friedman, Kevin Kenny, Ed O'Donnell, and Craig Wilder.

The time I spent at the Huntington was among the most intellectually and spiritually rewarding I have ever spent. That was due to the efforts of Martin Ridge and his successor in charge of research, Robert Ritchie, and to the friends I made there: Thomas Cox, Karen Lystra, Wilbur Miller, Andrew Rolle, and Paul Zall. Discussions with Daniel Walker Howe and Mark Summers greatly affected my work. I developed a friendship there with Stanley, Janet, and Scott Hirshson, and am glad I did.

I never would have been a history major if a high school teacher named Phil Cook had not demanded that I participate in a speech contest. It led to my hiring at the *Valley Times,* a newspaper that was an educational institution in its own right. Bruce Hasley and Sue Volek, Bob and Linda Faiss, Ken and Kerrie White, Lew and Shirley Shupe, Marilee Joyce, Mark Brown, and Terry and Jenny Care became friends through that experience, and better friends through other experiences.

While earning my bachelor's and master's degrees at the University of Nevada, Las Vegas (UNLV), I studied with a fine group of professors. Andy Fry and Gene Moehring taught me a great deal about writing and historical thought. Going to UNLV introduced me to Charles and Joan Adams, Felicia Campbell, and Tom Wright and Dina Titus. Through Professor Moehring, I was able to meet Hans Trefousse, whose advice meant a lot.

The experience of going to graduate school at Columbia was enormously rewarding in so many ways, not the least of which was my exposure to scholars who built upon what I learned at UNLV and made me much better for it. John Garraty and David Cannadine set wonderful examples of scholarship and kindness. James Shenton and Josh Freeman opened my eyes to previously shadowy areas of historiography. Alden Vaughan introduced me to new ways of thinking about race, and his good nature as a mentor and a member of my orals committee will be with me always. Eric McKitrick oversaw my master's essay and my work as a teaching assistant, talked to me at length about both, was exceptionally kind to a young practitioner, and—to the surprise of no one who has read his work or knew him—constantly gave me so much to think about.

The members of the dissertation committee, Daryl Scott, Jim Caraley, and Robert Erikson, were exceedingly kind in helping me to steer this work to completion. I would like especially to thank Elizabeth Blackmar, for whom I was a teaching assistant and who served on my prospectus committee and as chair of the dissertation committee. Her kindness and rigorous analysis were wonderful, and wonderful examples.

I was hired and became a tenured professor of history at the Community College of Southern Nevada (CCSN) while pursuing this doctorate. I am blessed to have a wonderful group of colleagues who make my place of work both pleasant and intellectually exciting. In particular, two historians there, DeAnna Beachley and John Hollitz, read parts of this dissertation; if that did not demonstrate their friendship and talent, nothing could, and their criticisms went above and beyond the call.

My students deserve thanks. From the time I was a teaching assistant at UNLV and then at Columbia, and throughout my years as an instructor at UNLV and CCSN, they insisted on being able to understand what I was saying. This forced me to say it better. Also, Andy Fry gave me the chance to offer a junior-level class on Abraham Lincoln. In there and in my constitutional history survey at CCSN, students heard some of the ideas presented here and, with fangs bared and malevolent delight, critiqued several chapters.

I am grateful that while I teach at a community college, my colleagues at the university appreciate that we not only prepare students for them but also remain active scholars. In addition to those already mentioned, I am indebted to David Tanenhaus of the UNLV history department for his comments on Chapter 6. This chapter also benefited from my work preparing the history of the law firm of Lionel Sawyer and Collins, whose attorneys and staff were and remain friends and guides to the world of law.

I presented some of my findings before the Organization of American Historians. I would like to thank Paul Finkelman, Donald Nieman, and James Rawley for offering their thoughts on my work. Eugene Berwanger and Harold Hyman have provided important encouragement.

Two others who read this were Wang Xi, a Columbia friend who is now an associate professor of history at Indiana University of Pennsylvania, and Michael Vorenberg, another Huntington fellow who is now an assistant professor of history at Brown University. They saved me from many an imprecision, their sharing of their research for their own important and superb works saved me much time, and their friendship has saved me from much more; I also am grateful to Jin Pang, Dan Wang, and Katie and Emma Vorenberg for letting their guys devote so much more time to me than I deserved, and for giving me space to sleep.

Many friends and family members sustained and nagged me to finish. They know, I hope, how important they are. To list any would be to insult anyone I leave off the list, but a few deserve special notice, and the others would agree: Sara and Ralph Denton and their family, and Michael Epling and Mary Lou Foley, who made possible a most important acknowledgment below. My aunt and uncle Irene and Joseph Calca always lifted my spirits.

Several people who contributed greatly to my life and this dissertation did not live to see it completed. I am honored to have known them and to pay tribute to them here. My aunt and uncle Dora and Leo Robbins provided me with warmth and a family to visit in New York. Their (and my) family—Donna and Morton Gettenberg, Diane and Bruce Robbins, Ellen and Todd Gettenberg, and Sandy and Evan Gettenberg—carry on their tradition, and I am grateful to and for them all.

Bob Brown hired me to work at his newspaper when I was a teenager; had he not done so, I might never have become a historian. He and Adam Yacenda, his predecessor at the *Valley Times,* taught me much about politics and ideology, without my or their knowing it.

Ralph Roske made me a history major, then a historian. He showed me that historians should take their craft seriously, but not themselves. He taught me by his example as a caring adviser, and it is a pleasure not only to acknowledge that but also to try to follow his example. His family, especially Rosemary Roske, has done much to ensure that I do.

Gary Elliott was a better friend than anyone is entitled to have. As students at UNLV, then as colleagues at CCSN, we shared more ideas and conspiracies than I thought possible. If he had been here to read this, it would have been a much better work, and Debbie Elliott and Kim Hooper, his wife and daughter, would have tolerated his taking the time to read it.

Four special people deserve special attention:

Those familiar with Eric Foner and his work know that he is brilliant and sets an example for his students that we can only hope to emulate. However, I owe him more. When I arrived in New York the first time I had lived away from home, I was scared to death. He showed me more kindness than I suspect he realized. I went to New York to learn from him; I learned more than I thought possible. He has been encouraging or tough when necessary, and a model and exemplar at all times.

This dissertation was almost completed when Deborah Young entered my life. I discovered the pleasure of sharing her with a dynamic and fun group of family and friends who have enriched my existence. She discovered that she had to share me not only with a similar group, but with stacks of paper and piles of disks. Not only did she not complain; she encouraged—perhaps a better word is prodded—me to finish. She even agreed to share the rest of our lives together. Her good cheer, caring, sensitivity, and love have inspired me in countless ways, not just to finish this work. I can no more express my appreciation for her contribution to my writing, my sanity, and my life than I can express my love.

The dedication of this dissertation reflects gratitude and guilt. Robert and Marsha Green dedicated their lives to me and tolerated my work and the expenses it caused, financially and psychically, beyond any reasonable expectation. Her proofreading of the early drafts, and his proofreading of the later ones, saved me from many a typographical error and considerable fuzziness of writing. They gave me what their parents, Armand and Helen Green and Louis and Florence Greene, gave to them. They had faith in me, and to say that I am proud to have rewarded that faith is an understatement. Unfortunately, my mother died before I finished. I will always regret that, but not her love and common sense, nor my father's unfailing kindness and decency. To her memory and his continued importance and influence in my life, this work is dedicated.

INTRODUCTION

No aspect of the Civil War, except for the fighting of it, has received as much attention from historians as the political developments that caused the war and shaped its effects. In the decades before and following the war, the second party system collapsed and the third party system began—and, after many controversies and convolutions, it still survives today. A sectional, minority party won the presidency, then struggled to become a national majority party and survived to enjoy great success, even as it and the nation changed. When one region elected the president, the other dissolved the Union rather than accept the result. That president's party doubted him enough to threaten his administration's survival and his renomination for a second term, even during the nation's bloodiest war. When the tide turned he won reelection, assuring freedom for about four million slaves as well as the redefinition of a nation and its mission. And with victory near, assassination made Abraham Lincoln a martyr.

These plot threads of the Civil War have prompted endless efforts to weave a coherent whole and endless explorations of those threads. A slew of publications shows the unflagging interest of both historians and the public in the Civil War. And, despite the increasing emphasis among historians on looking at the past "from the bottom up," students of the subject have heeded Eric Hobsbawm's entreaty to examine the "history of society." Recent scholarship has extended well beyond the life and times of a great man or group. Biographies have probed the lives of prominent figures and their times. Studies of public policy and the party's economic vision have explained what Republicans did to win the war and remake the nation. Examinations of Lincoln's words and deeds have demonstrated how he broadened the war into "a new birth of freedom," denied freedom to some of his foes, and refused to support full freedom for those whom the war freed from bondage. Other works on Northerners in military and political battles have analyzed why they fought and reelected the man who sent them to fight.

One scholar has even called one year of the war, 1863, the turning point in the nation's history.[1]

These and many other studies have examined the war as a whole or the roles played by its participants—individual or collective actions and events. While previous works about the Civil War have acknowledged the importance of ideology in general, they have failed to examine the party's ideology fully or demonstrate how it affected Republican actions. This study is meant to fill that void. What follows, then, is an examination of what Richard Hofstadter described in *The American Political Tradition* as a "central faith" that unites a group or an organization—an analysis of how the party's core beliefs shaped the conduct of the Civil War and the nation that fought it. Those beliefs are captured in three words that stand both separately and together: freedom, union, and power.[2]

When Republicans debated emancipation, criticized generals, shaped legislation, and sniped at one another or their opponents, they acted on what they believed—an ideology. This term requires elaboration. In his study of the party's antebellum thought, Eric Foner defined ideology as a "system of beliefs, values, fears, prejudices, reflexes, and commitments—in sum, [a] social consciousness." Many scholars have used different and invariably more complex, elaborate, or sociological definitions, and these have much to recommend them. However, it is possible to become too bogged down in semantics, and unwittingly impose present-day standards. Ideology, beliefs, viewpoint, and mindset are, at bottom, similar terms to reflect what people think. To suggest that a group united under a party banner may seem anachronistic when modern political parties appear to be nonideological. If anything, the willingness of two regions to go to war, and the partisan and personal arguments that continued in both regions after they went to war, demonstrate the existence of a unifying process of thought—in the case of the Northern Republicans, who often battled over preferment and place, an ideology of freedom, union, and power.[3]

This begs the question of where this ideology came from. The issue is not whether it was based on the party's antebellum attitudes, mixed with the necessities the war created; that should be obvious enough. Rather, was this an ideology the party shared and its members accepted, or did the members create it? Of course, since neither a political party nor an ideology is an independent entity capable of existing on its own, freedom, union, and power are ideas that Republicans, voicing them independently, grew to understand as a common cause. Naturally, some placed a greater premium on preserving freedom, or saving the Union, or retaining power, than did others, and those differences will become apparent in the pages that follow. But to try to quantify these individuals and their views seems frivolous. Whatever their disagreements and failings, they survived the war's duration as a party, and that party had a core system of beliefs.

Some of those beliefs have received attention in the recent or distant past from students of the antebellum era and the war. Almost any study of the Civil War addresses race and emancipation, but few tie them to how the Republican free labor ideology changed during the war. In their superb works on secession, David Potter and Kenneth Stampp drew no connection to the party's adjustment to responsibility and its relationship to the beliefs of its members, nor have biographers of the key players linked their actions to a shared ideology. Military historians have turned their attention from generals to foot soldiers and African Americans hoping to be soldiers, but not to how Republicans saw the leaders, battles, and battlers. Potter, Eric McKitrick, Michael Holt, and Mark Neely addressed the role of political parties in the Union, but not how Republican views of those parties fit into their ideas about the Union and the Constitution. Studies of the national quest for law and order, and the Supreme Court's role in it, have never stressed how the party's mind-set affected the court's reshaping. What little has been written about the war in the West has focused on the few battles fought there or on certain individuals, but not on Republican views of that region and its future. Republican policies toward the South and Reconstruction have won ample notice, but the same cannot be said for what motivated those policies.

None of these subjects can be properly understood without an appreciation of the ideology that affected them. And what makes this study all the more important is that many of the works that have described and analyzed an ideological slant remain useful for the wealth of information they provide, but their explanations—the irrational hatred that radicals allegedly felt toward the South, for example—have often been consigned to the interpretive scrap heap.[4]

One problem is that these subjects have been examined through one of two prisms: the party's antebellum ideology and development, or the war. As writers ranging from historians to novelists have been fond of pointing out, the war undeniably was a turning point, central to the American experience—an effect of one part of the nation's history and a cause of the other. Thus, while the Civil War is inseparable from the rest of American history, it is also a separate event, unlike anything before or since. Its uniqueness adds to its attractiveness as a subject for inquiry, but that inquiry has yet to extend sufficiently to the political mind. What and how Republicans thought about those subjects merits examination and analysis—not through separate prisms, but through the party's wartime ideology, the combined result of what Republicans believed and did before the war, and what the war itself forced them to believe and to do.[5]

The works of Foner, a Hofstadter student, have done much to reveal the Republican mind-set. Indeed, two of Foner's books might be called intellectual bookends to this study. The first, *Free Soil, Free Labor, Free Men,* depicted an activist party struggling with the failings of society and itself. Concluding with the party rising to power late in 1860 and early in 1861, Foner wrote that "its identification with the aspirations of the farmers, small entrepreneurs, and craftsmen of northern society . . . gave the Republican ideology much of its dynamic, progressive, and optimistic quality. Yet paradoxically, at the time of its greatest success, the seeds of the later failure of that ideology were already present." How those seeds sprouted is central to the other book, *Reconstruction: America's Unfinished Revolution,* which began by examining the Emancipation Proclamation of 1 January 1863 but placed far more emphasis on the rise and fall of Reconstruction in the late 1860s and 1870s. Near the end of this work, Foner noted "how closely the Civil War era had tied the new industrial bourgeoisie to the Republican party and national state," and how the immediate failure of Reconstruction could be linked to "the weakening of Northern resolve, itself a consequence of social and political changes that undermined the free labor and egalitarian precepts at the heart of Reconstruction policy."[6]

Even the most cursory reading of these two books makes clear that the party that went into the war and the party that came out of it differed in important ways. Other studies have explained the activities of political parties during the Republican ascent of the 1850s, Northern opposition to the "slave power" in the same period and fears of its revival, and how the party and the government evolved, for better or for worse, in the decade after the war. Yet none of that changes Foner's fundamental point, which is inseparable from that of the first book and crucial to the second one: during the Civil War years, the free labor ideology was a critical part of the Republican ethos.[7]

However, crucial questions about that ethos remain. Perhaps the most tantalizing are those that ask how and why that ethos changed, and why any such changes mattered. A simple answer is that Republicans were the prewar party of reform and the postwar party of laissez-faire. But the constitutional amendments and laws that they passed were revolutionary, changing the nation forever. Thus, the answer must be more complex. Their belief in the free labor ideology before the war is apparent; that they achieved their goals during and after the war is more problematic. Even if it had done no more than free four million slaves, the Civil War would have been the largest, if bloodiest, reform movement in the nation's history, culminating an era in which many reform movements began and some prospered. It also recast the role of government in American society and led to the creation of a new nation and a new West, with railroads and homesteaders. By changing the Supreme Court's composition, the Civil War altered the third federal branch, the judiciary. It shaped political discourse and the relationship between the political parties for decades to come. While these changes affected and reflected Republican thinking, they also flowed from the circumstances of the time. That time was unique to American history, and the views of the party in power must be examined from that perspective.[8]

Inevitably, Foner and his work greatly influenced this study. Not only are the ideological ties evident, but many of the same politicians and thinkers were important to the party before and during the war as well as after. Indeed, these Republicans and their actions have received so much more attention from historians than their common mind-set in part because the cast of characters is almost Shakespearean in scope: the foppish and intellectual Charles Sumner; the Rabelaisian and cunning William Seward; the ominous and unwavering Thaddeus Stevens; the sincere and ambitious Salmon Chase; and, underestimated at first yet eventually towering above them all, the brooding, methodical, poetic, and shrewd Abraham Lincoln. Each has been the subject of much study. Together they seem even more than the sum of their parts: their party, what it believed, and what they accomplished.

Their actions and their motivations are inseparable, just as political ideology, political culture, and public policy are inseparable.

Thus, while this work examines how their beliefs and accomplishments were inextricably linked, it must also study their personalities and rivalries. Their ambition for power, and sometimes their desire to achieve it at another's expense, prompted pitched battles over office and policy. Their political activities could have torn them asunder—and, it may be argued, eventually did. But that happened after the war, thanks both to new issues and to new circumstances that affected older issues. During the war, even when they were at loggerheads—and that was surprisingly often—Republicans held together, however tenuously.

A recent study by Mark Neely illuminated the need for this work. In lamenting the absence of a sequel to Foner's analysis of antebellum party ideology, Neely deemed it "not possible simply to extend Foner's scheme for understanding the antebellum Republicans forward into Lincoln's presidency because the Civil War made much of the original Republican outlook, like its platform, irrelevant." But Republicans believed in a whiggish form of activist government; if anything, the Civil War forced them to go beyond their original goals but certainly not to dismiss them. Their belief in free labor and the connotations of freedom that went with it—the slogan "free soil, free labor, free men" is evidence of that—surely remained critical as they writhed over the question of what to do about slavery and when to do it, and as they celebrated the soldiers who won the physical battle for what they had fought for politically and intellectually.[9]

Clearly, the Civil War required Republicans to understand that "[t]he dogmas of the quiet past, are inadequate to the stormy present. . . . As our case is new, so we must think anew, and act anew," as Lincoln wrote. But that hardly implied a state of ideological tabula rasa, for Lincoln or for anyone else, when the guns started firing at Fort Sumter. How Republicans reacted to these events was rooted in what had happened before the war and in what they thought of it.[10]

It is important to understand what united them in their cause: it was a common ideology. In many ways, their differences revealed their similarities: despite their ambitions and hatreds they stayed united, and that unity flowed from shared beliefs. What Republicans believed in the period between when they won the presidency in 1860 and when the first Republican president died in 1865—the years of the Civil War—

is crucial to understanding the war and the nation that the war made. Yet historical knowledge of this ideology is akin to Lincoln's description of General William Tecumseh Sherman's march to the sea. While Sherman was cut off from his communications, Lincoln responded to a serenade at the White House and told the crowd, "We all know where he went in at, but I can't tell where he will come out at." We know where Republicans went into the war. Hindsight tells us where they came out. What they did in between is the focus of this study.[11]

Notes

1. The Hobsbawm quotation is in Eric Foner, *Politics and Ideology in the Age of the Civil War* (New York: Oxford University Press, 1980), 6. Recent biographies include David Herbert Donald, *Lincoln* (New York: Simon and Schuster, 1995); James A. Rawley, *Abraham Lincoln and a Nation Worth Fighting For* (Chicago: Harlan Davidson, 1996); Allen C. Guelzo, *Abraham Lincoln: Redeemer President* (Grand Rapids, Mich.: William B. Eerdmans Publishing, 1999); William E. Gienapp, *Abraham Lincoln and Civil War America: A Biography* (New York: Oxford University Press, 2002); John Niven, *Salmon P. Chase: A Biography* (New York: Oxford University Press, 1995); and Hans L. Trefousse, *Thaddeus Stevens: Nineteenth-Century Egalitarian* (Chapel Hill: University of North Carolina Press, 1996). On wartime policies, see Phillip S. Paludan, *The Presidency of Abraham Lincoln* (Lawrence: University Press of Kansas, 1994); Heather Cox Richardson, *The Greatest Nation of the Earth: Republican Economic Policies during the Civil War* (Cambridge: Harvard University Press, 1997); Paul A. Cimbala and Randall M. Miller, eds., *An Uncommon Time: The Civil War and the Northern Home Front* (New York: Fordham University Press, 2002); Melinda Lawson, *Patriot Fires: Forging a New American Nationalism in the Civil War* (Lawrence: University Press of Kansas, 2002). On Lincoln, freedom, and law, see Eric Foner, *The Story of American Freedom* (New York: W. W. Norton, 1998); Xi Wang, *The Trial of Democracy: Black Suffrage and Northern Republicans, 1860–1910* (Athens: University of Georgia Press, 1997); George Anastaplo, *Abraham Lincoln: A Constitutional Biography* (Lanham, Md.: Rowman and Littlefield, 1999); William C. Harris, *With Charity for All: Lincoln and the Restoration of the Union* (Lexington: University Press of Kentucky, 1999); Garry Wills, *Lincoln at Gettysburg: The Words That Remade America* (New York: Simon and Schuster, 1992); and Mark E. Neely Jr., *The Fate of Liberty: Abraham Lincoln and Civil Liberties* (New York: Oxford University Press, 1991). On the military and politics, see Earl Hess, *Liberty, Virtue, and Progress: Northerners and*

Their War for the Union, 2d. ed (New York: Fordham University Press, 1997); James M. McPherson, *What They Fought For: 1861–1865* (Baton Rouge: Louisiana State University Press, 1994); McPherson, *For Cause and Comrades: Why Men Fought in the Civil War* (New York: Oxford University Press, 1997); David E. Long, *The Jewel of Liberty: Abraham Lincoln's Reelection and the End of Slavery* (Mechanicsburg, Pa.: Stackpole Books, 1994); John C. Waugh, *Reelecting Lincoln: The Battle for the 1864 Presidency* (New York: Crown Books, 1997); Lerone Bennett Jr., *Forced into Glory: Abraham Lincoln's White Dream* (Chicago: Johnson, 1999); James M. McPherson, ed., *"We Cannot Escape History": Lincoln and the Last Best Hope of Earth* (Urbana: University of Illinois Press, 1995); and Mark E. Neely Jr., *The Union Divided: Party Conflict in the Civil War North* (Cambridge: Harvard University Press, 2002). See also Joseph E. Stevens, *1863: The Rebirth of a Nation* (New York: Bantam Books, 1999). The war's continuing popularity is easily borne out by the presence on the *New York Times* best-seller list of Donald, *Lincoln;* and Geoffrey C. Ward, Ric Burns, and Ken Burns, *The Civil War: An Illustrated History* (New York: Alfred A. Knopf, 1990), based on the popular Public Broadcasting System documentary, which was repeated in the fall of 2002.

2. Richard Hofstadter, *The American Political Tradition and the Men Who Made It* (New York: Alfred A. Knopf, 1948), ix, viii.

3. Eric Foner, *Free Soil, Free Labor, Free Men: The Ideology of the Republican Party before the Civil War* (New York: Oxford University Press, 1995), 4–5; Barbara J. Fields, "Slavery, Race, and Ideology in the United States of America," *New Left Review* 181, no. 3 (May–June 1990): 95–118; and Alden T. Vaughan, *Roots of American Racism: Essays on the Colonial Experience* (New York: Oxford University Press, 1995), 167–74.

4. See note 1, above, and the following: David M. Potter, *Lincoln and His Party during the Secession Crisis* (New Haven: Yale University Press, 1942); Kenneth M. Stampp, *And the War Came: The North and the Secession Crisis, 1860–1861* (Baton Rouge: Louisiana State University Press, 1950); Allan Frank, *With Ballot and Bayonet: The Political Socialization of American Civil War Soldiers* (Athens: University of Georgia Press, 1998); David M. Potter, "Jefferson Davis and the Political Factors in Confederate Defeat," in David Herbert Donald, ed., *Why the North Won the Civil War* (Baton Rouge: Louisiana State University Press, 1960), 91–112; Eric L. McKitrick, "Party Politics and the Union and Confederate War Efforts," in William N. Chambers and Walter Dean Burnham, eds., *The American Party Systems: Stages of Political Development* (New York: Oxford University Press, 1967), 117–51; Michael F. Holt, "Abraham Lincoln and the Politics of Union," in John L. Thomas, ed., *Abraham Lincoln and the American Political Tradition* (Amherst: University of Massachusetts Press, 1986), 111–41; Phillip S.

Paludan, *A Covenant with Death: The Constitution, Law, and Equality in the Civil War Era* (Urbana: University of Illinois Press, 1975); David M. Silver, *Lincoln's Supreme Court* (Urbana: University of Illinois Press, 1956); James G. Randall, *Constitutional Problems under Lincoln,* rev. ed. (Urbana: University of Illinois Press, 1951); Harold M. Hyman, *A More Perfect Union: The Impact of the Civil War and Reconstruction on the Constitution* (New York: Alfred A. Knopf, 1973); Mark E. Brandon, *Free in the World: American Slavery and Constitutional Failure* (Princeton: Princeton University Press, 1998); Eric Foner, *Reconstruction: America's Unfinished Revolution, 1863–1877* (New York: Harper and Row, 1988); Brooks D. Simpson, *The Reconstruction Presidents* (Lawrence: University Press of Kansas, 1998).

5. On the war's centrality to the overall American experience, see, for example, James M. McPherson, *Ordeal by Fire: The Civil War and Reconstruction* (New York: Alfred A. Knopf, 1982), vii; Foner, *The Story of American Freedom,* 95–113; Eric Foner and Olivia Mahoney, *A House Divided: America in the Age of Lincoln* (New York: Chicago Historical Society and W. W. Norton, 1990), ix and *passim;* Ward, Burns, and Burns, *The Civil War,* 264, 269.

6. Foner, *Free Soil,* 316; Foner, *Reconstruction,* 584, 603.

7. Foner, *Free Soil;* William E. Gienapp, *The Origins of the Republican Party, 1852–1856* (New York: Oxford University Press, 1987); Michael F. Holt, *The Rise and Fall of the American Whig Party: Jacksonian Politics and the Onset of the Civil War* (New York: Oxford University Press, 1999); Tyler Anbinder, *Nativism and Slavery: The Northern Know Nothings and the Politics of the 1850s* (New York: Oxford University Press, 1992). See also Foner, *Reconstruction;* Wang, *The Trial of Democracy;* Mark W. Summers, *Railroads, Reconstruction, and the Gospel of Prosperity: Aid under the Radical Republicans, 1865–1877* (Princeton: Princeton University Press, 1984).

8. On the revolutionary nature of the Civil War and Reconstruction era, see Foner, *Reconstruction, passim,* and James M. McPherson, *Abraham Lincoln and the Second American Revolution* (New York: Oxford University Press, 1991). On reform movements of the time, see Ronald G. Walters, *American Reformers, 1815–1860* (New York: Hill and Wang, 1978).

9. Neely, *The Union Divided,* especially 143.

10. "Annual Message to Congress," 1 December 1862, in Roy P. Basler, ed., *The Collected Works of Abraham Lincoln,* 9 vols. (New Brunswick: Rutgers University Press, 1953–55), vol. 5, 537. Hereafter *CW.*

11. "Response to a Serenade," 6 December 1864, *New York Tribune,* 8 December 1864, in *CW,* vol. 8, 154.

1

Freedom, Union, and Power: The Civil War Republican Party

NO TWO MEN could have been more alike and more different than Charles Sumner and William Pitt Fessenden. Both were Republican senators from New England. Both rebelled against their previous parties and joined the Republicans. Both chaired key committees where their talents shone—Sumner headed Foreign Relations, with his knowledge of and connections to Europe; Fessenden led Finance, with his cautious and analytical mind. Both could be difficult to deal with: Sumner reveled in his intellectual superiority, and his idealism and self-absorption only grew worse after his caning by Preston Brooks in 1856; Fessenden turned dyspeptic when egos and debate detracted from completing the job at hand. And each captured his party's competing views. Fessenden said, "I have been taught since I have been in public life to consider it a matter of proper statesmanship, when we aim at an object which we think is valuable and important, if that object . . . is unattainable, to get as much of it and come as near it as we may be able to do." Sumner said, "A moral principle cannot be compromised."[1]

The differences between Sumner and Fessenden, between principle and pragmatism, represent and reflect the Republican party's ideological transformation during the Civil War. The party of "free soil, free labor, free men" retained its antebellum commitment to freedom, but events prompted a redefinition, in some cases a reordering, of its beliefs. Victory in the 1860 presidential election, the South's subsequent secession, and the accompanying Republican takeover of Congress made Republicans the ruling party, responsible for restoring a Union that some of them occasionally had considered unworthy of salvation. The depth of the party's commitment to the Union varied, although its members almost unanimously agreed that it should be preserved, if only to end the South's reliance upon slavery. To radicals like Sumner, the Union mattered as a means to freedom, the broadly defined end they sought during the party's brief antebellum life; believers in abolitionism, or verging on it, they hoped for the yoke of slavery to be removed from African Americans—and thus from all Americans.

To moderates and conservatives like Fessenden and most of the party's leaders, freedom was important, but preserving the Union came first. If preservation required freedom, that was an added benefit. But if ending slavery would hurt the Union cause more than it would help it, freedom would have to wait. From what they considered their pragmatic perspective, the eventual destruction of slavery was possible only if the country remained together; a separate Southern republic would protect the institution. This required them to think and talk about freedom, union, and power; not only did they vary in their degree of commitment to one or another of these, but circumstances often required them to reexamine their priorities and preferences. During the war, "free soil" and "free labor" remained articulated Republican goals, but achieving them would take much more than waving a wand or passing a law. If this had been unclear to Republicans when they had been in opposition, it became apparent when they assumed power.[2]

Thus, responsibility or governance is crucial to understanding the party's wartime mind-set. Now that Republicans wielded power, they faced a series of questions. What was the extent of their power? Who among them should and would exercise it? Which branch of government—not only among the executive and legislative branches of the federal government, but also the states—had more of it, and when was it best to use it? At the heart of these related questions lay still more issues, many similarly connected. This newfound power could be used to grant freedom—and, paradoxically, to impose it by executive or legislative fiat. However, it also could and would enable Republicans to save the Union. Republicans had to resolve for themselves and for the country's sake what government could do and what it should do; the answers, often to their displeasure, might vary greatly. More difficult still for them, freedom, union, and power sometimes fit neatly together, but at other times one might prove more important than another, forcing them to select and reorder priorities. Freedom, union, and power were not just issues or concepts. They were the central ideology and theme, commingled, contradictory, and often combustible, of the Republican party during the Civil War.

The 1850s: Freedom from Power

Further complicating the Republican ascent to power was that before the war, their plight had been so much simpler. While they quickly gained support and success, they remained a national minority, with the freedom to object to the majority and freedom from responsibility for the policies to which they objected. The Republican party had been born in the mid-1850s in the wake of two events: the Whig party's dissolution and the introduction of the Kansas-Nebraska Act. The Whigs, created in response to the rise of Andrew Jackson, could elect only two presidents, both of whom died in office and left a deeply divided party as their legacy. Those ruptures concerned many issues, including slavery. Northern and Southern Whigs split even within their regions over their stand on Pennsylvania Democrat David Wilmot's proviso against slavery in territory acquired in the Mexican-American War, and over the introduction and passage of the Compromise of 1850. And even the preeminent historian of the Whigs has argued that the force that drove them tended to be what Democrats did or might have done, not their own depth of commitment. In the early 1850s, lacking much of an ideology at its center or leaders of any magnetism to represent and unify it, the Whig party simply collapsed.[3]

Hastening the Whigs' death was the increasing tendency of the North and South to entrench over slavery. By passing a bill to allow Kansas and Nebraska to vote on whether to allow slavery in those territories, Senator Stephen Douglas effectively sought to repeal the Missouri Compromise. In removing that line, Democratic leaders drew another—in the sand. By making the Kansas-Nebraska Act a party issue, they almost guaranteed that their Northern anti-slavery followers would abandon them, and they did, joining with politically homeless Northern Whigs and the staunch but small Free-Soil party to form a new organization, the Republicans. The new party sought to stop the spread of slavery into new territories and to secure both the ultimate triumph of free labor over slave labor and the political power that represented slavery and sought to perpetuate it. They did so on principle, believing in the rightness of their cause and that their views would appeal to the electorate, and on the political ground that Democrats were in thrall to the slave power.[4]

However, Republicans remained in the opposition, and seemed unlikely to escape the opposition anytime soon. Their first presidential nominee, John C. Frémont, won fame and popularity for his exploits as an explorer, but he was too radically anti-slavery to appeal to Northern Democrats who might have been enticed into leaving their party to vote for the son-in-law of Democratic anti-slavery legend Thomas Hart Benton. Nor did Frémont attract conservative Whigs, who tended to prefer the nativist American or Know-Nothing party and its unwillingness to take a stand against slavery. Democrat James Buchanan won the presidency in 1856, and his party solidified its majorities in the House and Senate. With an almost completely supportive Supreme Court added to the mix, it made for the kind of Democratic supermajority, sympathetic or at least neutral toward proslavery interests, to which the South had grown accustomed. But Frémont ran strongly enough to make Republicans optimistic about the future, provided that they found an appealingly moderate candidate. In the meantime, their minority status enabled them to plan ahead, attack their opponents, and refine and repeat their message.[5]

That Republican message had been evolving from the beginnings of the second party system in the late 1820s and early 1830s. Even before they became Republicans, the party's early leaders insisted that the North's political economy and social culture of free labor were far superior to the South's dependence and insistence upon slave labor. They reminded the Northern majority of the Southern disdain for free labor and determination to spread slave power, no matter what the cost. And that message gained in resonance as the Democratic majority divided and the South overplayed its hand. Aghast at the corruption of his concept of "popular sovereignty" in Kansas and at the weak reed in the White House who was ready to accept that territory's pro-slavery constitution, Douglas broke with Buchanan. While the chasm between Northern and Southern Democrats widened, Republicans maintained a drumbeat against them and the Supreme Court over *Dred Scott v. Sandford.* Never before had the slave power conspiracy that Republicans decried seemed greater or more powerful; never before had its hostility toward free labor seemed more obvious; and rarely did they miss an opportunity to argue that Democrats were in its grasp. With gains in the 1858 midterm voting, Republican chances improved in the 1860 presidential election.

But with success came a price: after attacking the leadership of Buchanan and other Democrats—or the lack of it—Republicans would have to do more than just trumpet an ideology of freedom. They would have to act on it, governing a country in which the residents of its Southern half and a substantial minority of its Northern half were openly hostile to Republican beliefs. Spreading free soil would require holding the Union together and exercising just enough power just wisely enough; the issue for Republicans would be not whether to do this, but how best to do this.[6]

The combination of Democratic divisions and Republican gains rightly convinced the newer party of its chances of electing a president in 1860. This prompted yet another bow to political reality, but not at the expense of ideological purity. In 1856, Republicans chose Frémont over William Seward and Salmon Chase, both more experienced politically and more important in defining the party and its ethos. In 1858, they flirted with backing Douglas against Abraham Lincoln in the Senate race in Illinois—not because they accepted popular sovereignty as a solution to the issue of slavery in the territories, but because the "Little Giant" had split with Buchanan and they thought that perhaps the enemy of their enemy could be their friend. In those cases, they implicitly admitted that they might sacrifice at least some of their beliefs for the sake of victory—that a commitment to union and the possibilities of power compensated for a lesser commitment to freedom.

That was unnecessary in 1860, but again Republicans looked past their more prominent founding fathers. They turned instead to Lincoln, not because they saw his greatness but because it was the politically smart thing to do. Whether radically, moderately, or conservatively anti-slavery, all Republicans could claim him as their own—partly because he was less known than other candidates whose names were bandied about, partly because his record offered something for each wing of the party. He believed in the party's commitment to free labor, but he admired Henry Clay and his brand of nationalistic Whiggery enough to put the Union above all else. Lincoln's views might reassure the wavering Northern voters whom Republicans hoped to gain and, if he took office, prove less threatening to the hostile South. In either case he offered the potential for broader appeal than Seward and Chase, whom even some Republicans considered too radical on slavery. And since Republicans had assailed Democrats as unethical, a candidate they could call "Honest Abe" seemed less corruptible than Seward and less ambitious than Chase. Perhaps Lincoln would exercise power more prudently and deferentially than leaders who were more successful and possibly more self-centered. His more moderate appeal, a majority of population in the North, and divisions in the Democratic party assured that Americans would have the opportunity to find out whether that would be the case.[7]

The Politics of Responsibility

Obviously, Lincoln and his presidency turned out differently than his party expected, and both the country and Republicans changed accordingly. While free labor remained at the party's core, the evolving ideology linking freedom, union, and power absorbed what had been at the center of the antebellum party. This wartime ideology might be likened to a flow chart. Guaranteeing freedom, preserving union, and wielding power all proved important—indeed, inseparable. However, Republicans varied as to which one mattered more. And each of these categories flowed into one another, with subtle and not-so-subtle gradations.

For all Americans, North and South, freedom was fraught with complex meanings. While defining freedom has always been problematic, the problem was compounded for Republicans. Eric Foner wrote, "With the Union's triumph, freedom truly defined the nation's existence." When Representative James Garfield of Ohio asked in 1865, "What is freedom?" his answer concerned how much freedom former slaves should enjoy. This suggested that the abolitionists whom Republicans had once scored for going too far had actually been right: freedom could be defined only by resorting to slavery as its antithesis. But Republicans were in a struggle to save the Union and expand their party, both of which might be in danger if they seemed interested only in the plight of the slave. Thus, they attacked slavery on economic, political, and social grounds rather than for moral reasons. At the same time, empowerment forced Republicans to devote less attention to thought and more to action. Before the war, they had little opportunity to turn their plans into reality. The war gave them that chance but deprived them of the time to articulate their ideas as fully as they once had—perhaps to the detriment of historians analyzing them, but to the benefit of themselves and the society they sought to change.[8]

While Republicans believed in freedom, any analysis of their thought makes clear that they had in mind a white man's freedom. As usual, Lincoln captured the essence of his party's views. In his annual message late in 1862, he suggested a constitutional amendment for the gradual abolition of slavery. It was a striking, contradictory moment: the first president elected on the grounds that he opposed slavery proposed to end it, but only over the course of several decades. He concluded, "In *giving* freedom to the *slave,* we *assure* freedom to the free." To Republicans, slavery had grown from a regionally confined wrong, a blot on the national escutcheon, to a disease that threatened to kill the republic; the way to cure the disease was to get rid of it. Whether Lincoln divulged his real feelings or engaged in salesmanship—probably both—his motivation had more to do with freeing whites from the threat of disunion than with freeing blacks from oppression. That was understandable, even commendable to many, and no doubt necessary. But Republicans had long since made clear that their devotion to free labor had far more to do with how slavery affected white workers than with how it affected the black slaves themselves. By reducing slaves beyond their already secondary level to a tertiary one, Republicans assigned additional tiers and meanings to freedom. For them to differ over this issue, then, was natural; they had created the differences.[9]

Within the party, each wing fought for what it believed each tier of freedom to mean. Radicals, or what would now be described as the party's left, often advocated equal rights for blacks, including suffrage. Theodore Tilton, whose abolitionism grew more fashionable as bodies and expenses piled up, called the war "a struggle for social equality, for rights, for justice, for freedom." More mainstream Republicans agreed. The *Chicago Tribune,* whose editors were more radical than Lincoln yet still saw their paper as his organ, said, "Liberty or slavery must rule in this Republic." William Evarts, a New York lawyer with conservative leanings, expected the war and the party to "secure this continent to liberty." Republicans used liberty and freedom interchangeably, but what the radical Tilton, the moderately radical *Tribune* editors, and the moderately conservative Evarts meant by those words differed. Generalizations are dangerous, but the desire for emancipation and black civil rights clearly narrowed from the radical to the conservative ends of the party spectrum.[10]

On the issue of union, the party reversed course: the more conservative the Republican, the stronger the unionism. Abolitionist John

Jay, linked to the nation's heritage through his grandfather and to the party through the radicals with whom he plotted strategy, said, "If we cannot have liberty and union in any new readjustment, I go for liberty in that union. The Union is a great blessing—but it is not the greatest of blessings." These sentiments were private, but he wrote them to the unswervingly radical Sumner, an abolitionist who said, "Freedom national—slavery sectional." Once the bane of conservative Whigs, who considered him too anti-slavery for their and the nation's good, *Albany Evening Journal* editor and New York political boss Thurlow Weed revealed his conservative stripes during the war. The day after Lincoln's election, he told his readers, "Fidelity to the Union is a practical, present, live question. It means something." During the war, he objected as radicals and moderates seemed to frame it as a fight for freedom rather than, or ahead of, union.

This divergence should be no surprise: conservative Republicans tended to be former Democrats or, especially, Whigs, and were more committed to party loyalty than were radicals, who had often been on the fringes of the second party system. Yet with divergence came convergence. Amid all of their carping and threats to leave the party, all were Republicans and remained so. Thus, as freedom and union competed in the Republican mind for primacy, they had the effect of keeping party members together out of a shared belief in both of them and out of a shared desire to win their private battle for what they preferred. Freedom-loving or union-loving—actually, both—the question was of degree; they were not mutually exclusive.[11]

Indeed, in the question of degree lies the danger of trying to place Republicans in neat categories, for they defy easy categorization. In the midst of great events they retained their fundamental beliefs, but they varied in when and how they stressed them. Horace Greeley saw himself as many historians have also seen him: as a radical reformer at heart. But he also wanted to be a political player, and he was one—thanks to the massive circulation of his daily *Tribune* in New York City and his weekly *Tribune* across the North—if often an inept one. Partly out of his own desire for power, partly out of intellectual inconsistency, he weaved between radical and conservative, and thus between differences in emphasis. Greeley called the Union "a reality . . . a vital force, and not a mere aggregation, like a Fourth of July gathering or a sleighing and supper party." That was an editorial writer's flippant way of saying that the Union and the Constitution were more than a confederation to be tossed aside whenever some of its members disliked its provisions. Yet the same Greeley insisted in the winter of 1860–61 that the Union would be better off without the slave-holding South, and in the summer of 1862 that Lincoln must put freedom above all else by emancipating the slaves at once—and in the summer of 1861 that for the sake of the Union, the Union army must attack the rebel army. To say that Greeley was unique in countless ways, even in this way, is no exaggeration; but it is equally correct to say that other, more grounded Republicans varied in the importance they attached to freedom and union according to the circumstances of the moment.[12]

While the dialogue over freedom and union may seem like the debate over the chicken and the egg, a mere semantic issue, this much was clear: all Republicans confronted questions about the power to enforce their goals, and about which goals should take priority. Again, their views varied across the ideological spectrum, with Lincoln as a central point. To radicals he was too methodical, too willing to concede to conservatives, too easy to manipulate—or, more accurately, for others to manipulate, since their efforts failed. To conservatives he seemed too easy for radicals to manipulate, too susceptible to their entreaties. This stamped him not only as a superior politician, but as a classic moderate. And members of that group often viewed Lincoln according to how much he agreed with them on a particular issue. As radicals concluded that he sought to slow their efforts in behalf of civil rights and refused to take their advice unquestioningly on everything from his Cabinet to his generals, they insisted on legislative superiority, much as the Whigs had in battling Andrew Jackson.

While conservatives often found Lincoln perplexing, even aggravating, to them he became a bastion against the fanatical left—to use his phrase, their last best hope. This only increased their regret when he seemed to shift toward accepting radical views. The irony was that the conservatives for whom Lincoln served this purpose included old Democrats who had reveled in Jacksonian decisiveness and bemoaned the absence of it in lesser lights such as Franklin Pierce and James Buchanan, as well as old Whigs who spent much of their political lives rebuking strong executive government.[13]

Beyond the issue of which branch of the party and which branch of the government could wield more power, Republicans had to figure out what that power meant. Lyman Trumbull, a moderate former Democrat from Illinois, told a radical fellow senator, Ohio's Benjamin Wade, "With power comes responsibility, and we must now prepare to take it." Yet at times they recoiled from power, questioning whether they even wanted it. Depressed over criticism, Seward hoped soon to "leave public life . . . to rest during what remains of life free from the suspicions and jealousies of enemies and the reproofs of friends." Across the Capitol and across the party's spectrum, Sumner, a Seward admirer turned Seward hater, lamented that job hunters filled his days now that he headed the Foreign Relations Committee. He confessed to preferring the opposition: "I am now to see the experiences of power, and I do not like them." Yet Republicans, as Trumbull suggested, took that power—and grew to like it. Asked what became of a bill he opposed, Sumner replied, "It still sleeps . . . in my committee room." Several party members agreed: simply to oppose the majority was easy; becoming the majority or ruling party, taking power, and understanding its uses were harder, but increasingly satisfying. For some Republicans, adapting from the obstructionist tendencies that an opposition often demonstrates proved difficult. In each case it was an important part of their evolving ethos.[14]

Republicans found their ability to turn their ideals into reality deeply satisfying; how closely related—indeed, intertwined—they understood those ideas to be is especially striking. Freedom, union, and power were central ideas to them, not just a historian's construct. Henry Winter Davis, an ex-Whig and Know-Nothing en route to radicalism, captured the party's essence when he called its goal "liberty guarded by power." Less prominent and less pithy Republicans agreed. Governor Austin Blair of Michigan said, "It has been demonstrated beyond cavil, that freedom is the best basis of power." William Buckingham, his Connecticut counterpart, hailed "our national emblem of liberty, union, and power." From radical to conservative, Republicans had to acclimate themselves to the problems and perks of power, and with that acclimation came an understanding: while the power to act meant the possibility of success, power itself was part of their ideology. The debate over how to use it and who would use it resembled the one over freedom and union.[15]

Yet the tenets of their ideology were so clearly inseparable that Republicans had to address the contradictions those tenets created. In warning Wade about the meaning of responsibility, Trumbull added, "The success of Mr. Lincoln's administration depends in my judgment on his prudently but firmly carrying out the principles on which he has been elected, without pandering to cliques or factions from any quarter." Other Republicans agreed. Senator James Doolittle of Wisconsin warned Trumbull that the party had won only the presidency and would take over Congress only through running an honest, efficient administration that did all it could to turn Republican promises into reality. All three senators belonged to factions: Wade was a radical ex-Whig, Trumbull a moderate ex-Democrat with radical leanings, Doolittle a conservative ex-Democrat. While they shared the principles on which Lincoln had been elected, as Trumbull said, they disagreed over which issue mattered more at a certain time, how much to do about it, and which branch of government should do it. For them to differ over the degrees of importance attached to freedom, union, and power was neither unnatural nor unusual, then or later.[16]

However, these differences bring into sharp relief the importance of the party's ideology as a unifying force. Disputes that seemed ideological—to Republicans then and historians since—were actually rooted in pure partisan politics. Lincoln's argument in behalf of emancipation that "we cannot escape history" might just as easily have explained support for or criticism of his policies. Individually and collectively, Republicans had a history and no intention of forgetting it. In New York, Greeley and his followers were more radical than the Seward-Weed machine, but their battles also reflected how they had first united and then divided as leaders of New York's anti-slavery Whigs. In Maryland, Davis veered toward radicalism while the Blair family led the conservatives. But Davis had been a Whig, and the Blairs had been as Democratic as it was possible to be. That these men remained in the same party shows their ambition and their ability to raise pettiness and partisanship to an art form. It also demonstrates that, at least in wartime, their shared convictions outweighed their shared hatreds. They could belong to the same political organization because the stakes were so great, they and the other members of that organization constantly adjusted their views to the needs of the moment, and in the end those views were more alike than different.[17]

Part of that adjustment included coming to grips with a genuinely puzzling result of the interplay between freedom, union, and power:

how much power was necessary to preserve freedom and union? The question can be stated another way: how much freedom might be surrendered to save the Union and enable the government to use its power to do so? To use power to protect the Union would, Republicans thought, assure peace and with it freedom. But using power to excess would violate not only their commitment to freedom, but perhaps also the Constitution. According to *North American Review* editor Andrew Peabody, the Constitution "claims our allegiance because it is law and order—the only government possible for us, the only bond of peace and beneficent relations by which our nation can be held together," or else the result would be "disintegration and anarchy." A week after the firing on Fort Sumter, a New York union meeting's organizers invited "[a]ll good citizens who prize liberty with order, over usurpation and anarchy." George Sumner, who shared his brother Charles's radicalism, may have said it best. After telling New York conservative Hamilton Fish that he was "educated in the most rigid respect for law and good Government," he recalled a speech in which he had called conservatism "the guardian of order, of law, and of *instituted* liberty." Not only were law and order critical to liberty, but the ensuing freedom was agreed to, not imposed.[18]

The other contradictory impulses reflected in this ideology involved history—how Republicans viewed it and their place in it. Both Union and rebel leaders claimed the founding fathers as their own. To Southerners, their cause was for the Constitution: the right to be left alone to pursue their interests was, as Gordon Wood showed, crucial to the revolutionary generation. Southerners considered themselves squarely in that tradition. So did Northerners, who saw free labor as the path to the kind of freedom—financial, political, and intellectual—that Jefferson had in mind. They too claimed to fight for the government of the fathers. In his almost biblical second inaugural address, Lincoln said, "It may seem strange that any men should dare to ask a just God's assistance in wringing their bread from the sweat of other men's faces; but let us judge not that we be not judged." Of course, Lincoln and the North judged both the rebels and themselves; otherwise there would have been no war and could have been no government, no politics, no policy. Their judgment was for freedom and union, and was reflected in the power they used to impose it.[19]

However, Republicans worried about how they would be judged in light of those they claimed to emulate. Not only were they conscious of John Winthrop's warning two centuries earlier that they were as "a citty *[sic]* upon a hill"; they believed it. Surveying European views of the young republic, writer J. Ross Browne said, "There has never existed and never can exist again, a combination of circumstances so favorable to the practical working of a republican system of government as in the United States. If it fails there after the experience of nearly a century, . . . then truly is freedom at an end." Ambrose Burnside, a general of dubious ability but great unionism, summed up the Republican party's view in calling the war "pre-eminently a 'Providential Revulsion,' brought about for the purpose of creating a great revolution in our social system and . . . we are but instruments in the hands of God for the accomplishment of this great work." It is neither a study in mass psychology nor an allusion to mass paranoia to say that Republicans thought they were being watched—by their constituents, by others unborn, and by those who had built the country that they now sought to save.[20]

Indeed, Republicans watched themselves because they understood James Bryce's axiom even before he coined it: power tends to corrupt, and absolute power tends to corrupt absolutely. Bernard Bailyn has shown how the colonists felt that power made England susceptible to corruption and insensitive to liberty. Wanting freedom and union to survive, Republicans feared the effect of their power on that survival. When Congress met in 1861, Lincoln said, "Must a government, of necessity, be too *strong* for the liberties of its own people, or too *weak* to maintain its own existence?" The answer to that question vexed the party, for personal and ideological reasons. While some Republicans thought in political terms based on which politician or branch seemed more influential at the time, many believed in the primacy of one branch, executive or legislative. Whatever their reasons for admiring or doubting others, even if they could be blind to their faults, Republicans sought purity in themselves, the government, and the people. They found it hard to come by. Rivalries and habits that had been decades in the making refused to die, even with the Union's life at stake.[21]

Republicans also had to be careful to avoid an identity crisis. While some historians have called the party a coalition united by collective hatred, others have argued, as David Herbert Donald did, that Lincoln was really a Whig; or, as William McFeely did, that Ulysses Grant was the first true Republican president. One problem with understanding Republicans has been that during the war, their party ceased to exist. Reconstituting themselves as the Union party enabled them to woo Democrats and old Whigs, but created doubts later about just how Republican the Republicans were. Yet the party remained, for the most part, the party it had been in the 1850s. Republican ideology was another matter. During the 1860s, of necessity, it changed because the stakes were greater; circumstances demanded adaptation. The Union party may have been a political wolf in Republican sheep's clothing, a way to win broader support than the party of their name and reputation would have received. Yet the terminology was apt. Preserving the Union became at least as important as, and for some more important than, perpetuating freedom.

George Boutwell, a Massachusetts radical who had often been unhappy with the progress toward emancipation, recalled that Republicans "became the party of the Union; and . . . with Mr. Lincoln at its head, it was from first to last the only political organization in the country that consistently, persistently, and without qualification of purpose . . . met, every demand of the enemies of the government. . . . He struggled first for the Union, and then for the overthrow of slavery as the only formidable enemy of the Union."[22]

BURYING THE PARTY WITH LINCOLN

This confluence of freedom, union, and power, with their varying degrees of emphasis, ended with the war. When John Wilkes Booth killed Lincoln, he killed the Civil War party. For all of their arguing over how to win the war and win the peace, Lincoln and the radicals disagreed over means, not ends. At heart a states-rights, racist Jacksonian Democrat, Andrew Johnson reacted accordingly when more nationalistic Republicans sought to protect freedmen's rights and remake the South; he sought different ends from the Republicans. To say the party then splintered is to misstate or overstate the case. Most who had been Republican remained Republican. Those who broke with the party tended to be the most conservative Republicans: the Blairs, whose Southern background made them loathe to accept the radical idea that the South needed to be remade, saw the South as having a problem, a disease to be cured, not as a sick society in need of a total refurbishing; Seward, who always put unionism first, saw the party system as swinging too far in either direction as the war ended. Once more the issues changed, meaning not the end of the Republican party's reason for existence, but the need for another redefinition or refinement to suit national issues and the national temper.[23]

That adaptation had prompted the creation of the Union party during the war, but the needs of the party and the nation before and after the war were different. What worked for the party from 1854 to 1860, and then after 1865, could not be the same as what worked for the party during the war. Two Massachusetts writers crystallized the issue: Henry Adams found that daily happenings "at another time would be the event of a year, perhaps of a life," and George Ticknor saw a "great gulf between what happened before in our century and what has happened since. . . . It does not seem to me as if I were living in the country in which I was born." Before the war Republicans had been the party of freedom, seeking power; after the war they were the party in power, seeking freedom. During the war, the Union had to be preserved. Republicans accomplished that. They were committed to expanding freedom and exercising power in ways that suited each other.[24]

That those ways had to suit each other suggests that Republicans might differ in how they defined the terms they used, and they did. The party had no choice but to change during the war, but could and did choose what to believe. The ideology of freedom, union, and power was central to the theory and practice that made the victory and remade the nation. It also proved central to the tragedy that the party's wartime political problems could have foretold. The need to preserve the Union no longer existed as it had when the war ended; the dream of spreading freedom turned into a reality, but created new questions about the nature of that freedom; the acquisition of political power and the behavior of their opponents forced Republicans into a different kind of governance from what they had anticipated, and into adopting views and habits that could and would prove hard to change. Ironically, then, the ideology examined in this study, the ideology that was the Republican lodestar during the war, was in large part its eventual undoing.

Notes

1. Michael Les Benedict, *A Compromise of Principle: Congressional Republicans and Reconstruction, 1863–1869* (New York: W. W. Norton, 1974), frontispiece. On these two men, see David Herbert Donald, *Charles Sumner and the Coming of the Civil War* (New York: Alfred A. Knopf, 1960); Donald, *Charles Sumner and the Rights of Man* (New York: Alfred A. Knopf, 1970); and Charles Jellison, *Fessenden of Maine: Civil War Senator* (Syracuse, N.Y.: Syracuse University Press, 1962).

2. On the changes and troubles of the Republican party during the secession winter, see Potter, *Lincoln and His Party;* Stampp, *And the War Came;* Kenneth M. Stampp, *The Imperiled Union: Essays on the Background of the Civil War* (New York: Oxford University Press, 1980), 163–90; Paludan, *The Presidency of Abraham Lincoln,* 21–68. On the importance and relationship of unionism and compromise, see Peter B. Knupfer, *The Union As It Was: Constitutional Unionism and Sectional Compromise, 1787–1861* (Chapel Hill: University of North Carolina Press, 1991).

3. Holt, *The Rise and Fall of the American Whig Party,* makes the point in several places about the reactive nature of the Whigs, especially at xiii and 951–54. See also Daniel Walker Howe, *The Political Culture of the American Whigs* (Chicago: University of Chicago Press, 1979).

4. On the Republicans, see Foner, *Free Soil;* Foner, *Politics and Ideology,* 15–53; and Gienapp, *The Origins of the Republican Party.*

5. On the 1856 election's participants and meaning, see Kenneth M. Stampp, *America in 1857: A Nation on the Brink* (New York: Oxford University Press, 1990), 3–67; David M. Potter, *The Impending Crisis: 1848–1861* (New York: Harper and Row, 1976), 225–67; Andrew F. Rolle, *John Charles Frémont: Character as Destiny* (Norman: University of Oklahoma Press, 1991), 162–77; Roy F. Nichols, *The Disruption of American Democracy* (New York: Free Press, 1948), 17–103; Tyler G. Anbinder, *Nativism and Slavery: The Northern Know Nothings and the Politics of the 1850s* (New York: Oxford University Press, 1992).

6. Foner, *Free Soil,* 73–102; Richard Hofstadter, *The Paranoid Style in American Politics and Other Essays* (New York: Vintage Books, 1967), 3–41; David Brion Davis, *The Slave Power Conspiracy and the Paranoid Style* (Baton Rouge: Louisiana State University Press, 1969); Don E. Fehrenbacher, *The Dred Scott Case: Its Significance in American Law and Politics* (New York: Oxford University Press, 1978); Potter, *The Impending Crisis,* 267–404; Donald, *Lincoln,* 196–229; Neely, *The Union Divided,* 57–59.

7. Foner, *Free Soil, Free Labor, Free Men,* 211–18; Donald, *Lincoln,* 230–56; Reinhard H. Luthin, *The First Lincoln Campaign* (Cambridge: Harvard

University Press, 1944). See also Mark W. Summers, *The Plundering Generation: Corruption and the Crisis of the Union, 1849–1861* (New York: Oxford University Press, 1987).

8. Foner, *The Story of American Freedom,* 100.

9. "Annual Message to Congress," 1 December 1862, in *CW,* vol. 5, 518–37, at 537; Foner, *The Story of American Freedom;* and Edmund S. Morgan, *American Slavery, American Freedom: The Ordeal of Colonial Virginia* (New York: Oxford University Press, 1975).

10. *The Independent,* 25 June 1863, in Victor B. Howard, *Religion and the Radical Republican Movement, 1860–1870* (Lexington: University of Kentucky Press, 1982), 52; *Chicago Tribune,* 23 April 1861, in Jay Monaghan, *The Man Who Elected Lincoln* (Indianapolis, Ind.: Bobbs-Merrill, 1956), 227; *New York Herald,* 24 December 1861, in Chester L. Barrows, *William M. Evarts: Lawyer, Diplomat, Statesman* (Chapel Hill: University of North Carolina Press, 1941), 107. An excellent analysis of the party's commitment to civil rights in this period is Wang, *The Trial of Democracy,* especially 7–23. See also Michael Vorenberg, *Final Freedom: The Civil War, the End of Slavery, and the Thirteenth Amendment* (Cambridge: Cambridge University Press, 2001).

11. John Jay to Charles Sumner, Katonah, 4 February 1861, the Papers of Charles Sumner, Microfilm Edition (henceforth SP), Reel 21; *Albany Evening Journal,* 7 November 1860, in Glyndon G. Van Deusen, *Thurlow Weed: Wizard of the Lobby* (Boston: Little, Brown, 1947), 266 and *passim.* On Sumner, see Donald, *Charles Sumner and the Coming of the Civil War,* and Donald, *Charles Sumner and the Rights of Man.* On the seeds of this unionism, see Foner, *Free Soil,* 103–225.

12. *The Independent,* 18 April 1861 and 16 May 1861; Glyndon G. Van Deusen, *Horace Greeley: Nineteenth-Century Crusader* (Philadelphia: University of Pennsylvania Press, 1953), 262–63 and *passim.* See also Harlan Horner, *Lincoln and Greeley* (Urbana: University of Illinois Press, 1953); and Jeter Allen Isely, *Horace Greeley and the Republican Party, 1853–1861* (Princeton: Princeton University Press, 1947).

13. Foner, *Free Soil,* 103–225. On the radicals, see Hans L. Trefousse, *The Radical Republicans: Lincoln's Vanguard for Racial Justice* (New York: Alfred A. Knopf, 1969). Conservatives have yet to receive a full treatment. See John Niven, *Gideon Welles: Lincoln's Secretary of the Navy* (New York: Oxford University Press, 1973); and Maurice G. Baxter, *Orville H. Browning: Lincoln's Friend and Critic* (Bloomington: Indiana University Press, 1957).

14. Lyman Trumbull to Benjamin F. Wade, Springfield, 9 November 1860, Benjamin F. Wade Papers, Manuscript Division (Wade ms), Reel 2, LC; Hans L. Trefousse, "The Republican Party: 1854–1864," in Arthur M. Schlesinger Jr., ed., *History of U.S. Political Parties,* 4 vols. (New York: Chelsea

House, 1973), 1161; Norman B. Ferris, *The Trent Affair: A Diplomatic Crisis* (Knoxville: University of Tennessee Press, 1977); Sumner to Henry Wadsworth Longfellow, Washington, 16 March and 7 April 1861, SP, Series II, Reel 74; Sumner to Hamilton Fish, Washington, 16 March 1861, ibid.; Sumner to Francis Lieber, Washington, 13 April and 4 May 1864, ibid., Series I, Reel 64; Allen G. Bogue, *The Earnest Men: Republicans of the Civil War Senate* (Ithaca: Cornell University Press, 1961), 61; Donald, *Charles Sumner and the Rights of Man,* 12; Zachariah Chandler to Letitia Chandler, Washington, 22 January 1863, Zachariah Chandler Papers, Microfilm Edition, Manuscript Division (Chandler ms), LC; *Congressional Globe,* 37th Congress, 2d session (henceforth *CG*) 37, 2, 9 January 1862, 248 (Senator Jacob Collamer); Richard H. Sewell, *John P. Hale and the Politics of Abolition* (Cambridge: Harvard University Press, 1965), 197–99.

15. Gerald S. Henig, *Henry Winter Davis: Antebellum and Civil War Congressman from Maryland* (New York: Twayne, 1973), 246; George N. Fuller, ed., *Messages of the Governors of Michigan,* 2 vols. (Lansing: Michigan Historical Commission, 1926), vol. 2, 495–96; Samuel G. Buckingham, *The Life of William A. Buckingham: The War Governor of Connecticut* (Springfield, Mass.: W. F. Adams Company, 1894), 361. See also John Austin Stevens Jr. to Chauncey Depew, New York, 15 May 1863, John Austin Stevens Papers (John Austin Stevens ms), NYHS.

16. Trumbull to Wade, Springfield, 9 November 1860, Wade ms, Reel 2, LC; James R. Doolittle to Trumbull, Racine, 10 November 1860, Lyman Trumbull Papers, Microfilm Edition, Manuscript Division (Trumbull ms), Reel 6, LC. Doolittle still awaits an in-depth biography. On his two colleagues, see Hans L. Trefousse, *Benjamin Franklin Wade: Radical Republican from Ohio* (New York: Twayne, 1963); and Ralph J. Roske, *His Own Counsel: The Life and Times of Lyman Trumbull* (Reno: University of Nevada Press, 1979).

17. On Maryland, see Jean H. Baker, *The Politics of Continuity: Maryland Political Parties from 1858 to 1870* (Baltimore: Johns Hopkins University Press, 1973). On New York, see Glyndon G. Van Deusen's trilogy: *Greeley; Thurlow Weed;* and *William Henry Seward* (New York: Oxford University Press, 1967).

18. Phillip S. Paludan, *A Covenant with Death: The Constitution, Law and Equality in the Civil War Era* (Urbana: University of Illinois Press, 1975), 28; Margaret A. Clapp, *Forgotten First Citizen: John Bigelow* (Boston: Little, Brown, 1947), 145; George Sumner to Fish, New York, 7 May 1861, Hamilton Fish Papers, Manuscript Division (Fish ms), LC. For similar views, see also *The Independent,* 18 April 1861, in Van Deusen, *Greeley,* 270; Williston H. Lofton, "Northern Labor and the Negro during the Civil War,"

Journal of Negro History 34, no. 4 (July 1949): 270–71; "A Song on Our Country and Her Flag. By Francis Lieber. Written in 1861, after the Raising of the Flag on Columbia College, New York. Printed by the Students," in Lieber to Sumner, New York, ca. 1861, SP, Series II, Reel 75.

19. Gordon S. Wood, *The Radicalism of the American Revolution* (New York: Vintage Books, 1991), *passim;* "Second Inaugural Address," 4 March 1865, in *CW,* vol. 8, 332–33. On Northern views, see Foner, *Free Soil.*

20. Perry Miller and Thomas H. Johnson, eds., *The Puritans: A Sourcebook of Their Writings,* 2 vols. (New York: Harper and Row, 1938), vol. 1, 199; Milton H. Shutes, *Lincoln and California* (Stanford: Stanford University Press, 1943), 56–57; Ambrose E. Burnside to L. B. Wyman, New York, 29 January 1864, "Autographs Presented to the Brooklyn and Long Island Fair by L. B. Wyman, February 22, 1864," New Jersey Historical Society (NJHS); Horatio J. Perry to William H. Seward, Madrid, 22 November 1864, No. 144, U.S. Dept. of State, *Foreign Affairs 1865,* 4 vols. (Washington, D.C.: Government Printing Office, 1866), vol. 2, 467–68.

21. "Message to Congress in Special Session," 4 July 1861, in *CW,* vol. 4, 421–41, at 426. On Maryland, see Baker, *The Politics of Continuity.* See Bernard Bailyn, *The Ideological Origins of the American Revolution* (Cambridge: Harvard University Press, 1967); Stanley Elkins and Eric L. McKitrick, *The Age of Federalism: Birth of the Republic, 1788–1800* (New York: Oxford University Press, 1993).

22. Allen Thorndike Rice, ed., *Reminiscences of Abraham Lincoln by Distinguished Men of His Time* (New York: North American Publishing Company, 1886), 348. On the Union party, see William Frank Zornow, *Lincoln and the Party Divided* (Norman: University of Oklahoma Press, 1954). On the party as coalition, see Foner, *Free Soil,* 316. On Republican presidents, see David Herbert Donald, *Lincoln Reconsidered: Essays on the Civil War Era,* 3d ed. (New York: Vintage Books, 2001), 133–47; William S. McFeely, *Grant: A Biography* (New York: W. W. Norton, 1981).

23. On political parties at the war's end, see LaWanda Cox and John H. Cox, *Politics, Principle, and Prejudice, 1865–1866: Dilemma of Reconstruction America* (New York: Macmillan, 1963). On Johnson, see Eric L. McKitrick, *Andrew Johnson and Reconstruction* (Chicago: University of Chicago Press, 1960); and Hans L. Trefousse, *Andrew Johnson: A Biography* (New York: Norton, 1989). On the Blairs, see William E. Smith, *The Francis Preston Blair Family in Politics,* 2 vols. (New York: Macmillan, 1933); and Elbert B. Smith, *Francis Preston Blair* (New York: Free Press, 1980).

24. James M. McPherson, *Battle Cry of Freedom: The Civil War Era* (New York: Oxford University Press, 1988), vii, 861.

2

Free Labor, Freed Labor, and Free Capital

IN THE WINTER of 1861, Abraham Lincoln sent his first annual message to Congress. Between a lack of military success and what he called "unprecedented political troubles," he seemed to have little good news to report. Nor did the prose soar with the turns of phrase that glittered in many of Lincoln's later pronouncements as president. He recited a litany of government actions that would serve as a precursor to one of the most activist administrations, executive and legislative alike, in the nation's history. He defended the choice of George McClellan as general-in-chief and sought to assuage concerns about how the "Little Napoleon" displaced the legendary Winfield Scott, part of broader Republican concerns about whether the military could be trusted to accept civilian authority. These subjects were intimately related to the party's ideology but, in this case, seemed to matter far less to Lincoln than trying to provide some meaning for or understanding of the war, in addition to the quest for the preservation of the Union itself. Then he launched into an analysis of free labor that opened a window into the Republican mind. These words revealed him for what he was: the lynchpin or centerpiece of his party's thought. They also demonstrated the beginnings of the evolution of the party's ideology and the circumstances that helped to create it.[1]

Lincoln's commentary began with an attack on those who were, in his and his party's mind, at war and at odds with their free labor ideology. He accused the South and its sympathizers of waging "a war upon the first principle of popular government—the rights of the people," a view that he later expressed with more majesty at Gettysburg. Charging rebel leaders with limiting the consent of the governed in order to free themselves to pursue their own ends, he indulged in what might be called a leaden, halfhearted attempt at demagoguery: "Monarchy itself is sometimes hinted at as a possible refuge from the power of the people." These views were related, he felt, to another difference between North and South. The Confederacy sought "to place *capital* on an equal footing with, if not above *labor,* in the structure of government," he said. "It is assumed that labor is available only in connexion with capital; that nobody labors unless somebody else, owning capital, somehow by the use of it, induces him to labor." Those who accepted this notion accepted, by extension, that "all laborers are either *hired* laborers, or what we call slaves. And further it is assumed that whoever is once a hired laborer, is fixed in that condition for life." For Lincoln to say this, and thus denigrate the Southern economy and ideology, was nothing new; he and his fellow Republicans had offered similar arguments long before they had even belonged to the same party.[2]

While his defense of free labor was similarly old hat, it was an unusual subject for a president to address in an annual message. "Labor is prior to, and independent of, capital. Capital is only the fruit of labor, and could never have existed if labor had not first existed. Labor is the superior of capital, and deserves much the higher consideration," he wrote. Not that capital lacked the right to protection; besides, "there is, and probably always will be, a relation between labor and capital, producing mutual benefits." More important, labor and capital might unite the two warring regions. "In most of the southern States, a majority of the whole people of all colors are neither slaves nor masters; while in the northern a large majority are neither hirers nor hired," he said, pointing out that "a considerable number of persons mingle their own labor with capital—that is, they labor with their own hands, and also buy or hire others to labor for them." Nor should a Northern laborer consider his status permanent. "Many independent men everywhere in these States, a few years back in their lives, were hired laborers. The prudent, penniless beginner in the world, labors for wages awhile, saves a surplus with which to buy tools or land for himself; then labors on his own account," he said. "This is the just, and generous, and prosperous system which opens the way to all. . . . No men living are more worthy to be trusted than those who toil up from poverty—none less inclined to take, or touch, aught which they have not honestly earned."[3]

This statement is of inestimable importance to understanding the Republican mind during the Civil War. It offers great insight into Lincoln, whose office logically stamped him as the most important Republican of that period. First, in more ways than one, he described himself: the son of a man he saw as improvident, Lincoln was the laborer who worked hard and saved wisely to turn himself into a Horatio Alger story long before Alger began writing. As historians from Gabor Boritt to Heather Cox Richardson have asserted, Lincoln and other Republicans had an economic vision, whether it was the realization of "the American dream" or the creation of a great nation. The road to that success was paved with a free labor ideology and by free laborers with the ability and incentive to rise above their level, not by advocates of and for slave labor, whose economic system seemed so obviously rooted in disgust with labor and laborers.[4]

Lincoln's presidential-sounding exegesis on labor and capital compares in significant ways with the pre-presidential Lincoln, whose thinking may have been less crystallized. In 1859, more than two years earlier, he gave an almost verbatim address to the Wisconsin State Agricultural Society. For a politician to offer such bromides to that kind of audience was as natural as it was for a president to lecture his nation of constituents on what they were fighting for and against. Yet two other examples of his writing from that year reveal what might be called the prehistory of this portion of his first annual message. Shortly before his Wisconsin speech, jotting a note to himself, Lincoln distinguished more clearly between Northern and Southern attitudes toward labor and defined himself more clearly, if modestly, as the exemplar of free labor: "We know, Southern men declare that their slaves are better off than hired laborers amongst us. How little they *know,* whereof they *speak!* There is no permanent class of hired laborers amongst us. Twenty five years ago, I was a hired laborer. The hired laborer of yesterday labors on his own account to-day; and will hire others to labor for him to-morrow. . . . Free labor has the inspiration of hope; pure slavery has no hope." To Boston Republicans honoring Jefferson's birthday earlier that year, Lincoln said, "The democracy of to-day hold [*sic*] the *liberty* of one man to be absolutely nothing, when in conflict with another man's right of *property.* Republicans, on the contrary, are for both the *man* and the *dollar;* but in cases of conflict, the man *before* the dollar."[5]

Irony was hardly Lincoln's rhetorical stock in trade, yet this message, especially in the light of his earlier pronouncements, was fraught with it. While he may have shared, if to a lesser degree, Jefferson's tendency to temper his private inclinations when voicing them in public, he recycled some of the material from 1859—but not the part about putting the man ahead of the dollar. The precepts that he articulated in 1859 and 1861 were similar, but the circumstances under which he wrote them had changed dramatically. Republicans evolved not by choice, but because they were fighting for the nation's survival. That evolution fostered policies that changed the party's ethos. Perhaps most important, the cause of those changes, the war and the need to win it, forced Republicans to refine and redefine what they meant by free labor and, at times, to put capital above labor.

Yet at the risk of seeming contradictory, this rethinking actually had a limited effect on Republican views. What seemed to have been a transformation of the party and its ideology was more of a transformation of the issues and people with which that ideology was concerned. While believing in the principle of freedom, the party faced seemingly unrelated matters. Saving the Union, assuming political power, and preserving both entered into Republican thought, altering the importance of free labor. In many ways, this proved more damaging to the party and the country than a mere change of mind: where Republicans changed, they adjusted not only to power but to an unanticipated war; where they remained the same, the world around them changed enough to disconnect their views from the realities they needed to confront after the Union's restoration.

Forgetting the Past, Forging the Future

In the Northern society of individual producers, entrepreneurs, and small-scale industrialists in which Republicans campaigned for office in 1860, the free labor ideology as the party defined it was an almost ideal message. During the Civil War the government became more active in everyday life, industry grew larger, and national and international trends were almost inescapable, even for those only remotely involved in market capitalism. Granted, the war merely sped up this process rather than creating it, but financing the war required Republicans to turn to large-scale businesses and financiers. The legislative and executive branches, and state governors, argued that cooperation between business and government would foster unity that would prove beneficial to the party and the country, especially when they were trying to quell an insurrection.

They were right, and this affected the policies the party pursued in power. Lincoln had been a successful lawyer and was a living shrine to free labor and its possibilities; now he ran a government whose salvation required massive production of ammunition, massive amounts of men to go to work for that government shooting the ammunition, massive railroad and military projects to assure that men and munitions could go where needed, and massive infusions of capital to pay for it all. Chase had been a successful lawyer and politician, another monument to free labor; now he oversaw a treasury whose depletion, by his predecessors and by the war, required him to work closely with leading bankers and bond dealers. Seward had been perhaps the most successful Republican politician of the 1850s, and an architect and admirer of the party's free labor ideology; now he dealt with foreign governments concerned mainly with the balance of power and the flow of goods and resources to their large producers.[6]

One reality of the party's past was that the free labor ideology never had been the exclusive intellectual property of that party, or even that of its members when they had belonged to its predecessors. Rather, a belief in free labor permeated much of the North late in the eighteenth century and throughout the nineteenth century. At the same time, any possible support for free labor in the South faded as the region, for reasons ranging from a desire for social control to a knee-jerk reaction to Northern criticism, deepened its commitment to maintaining slavery. With the lines drawn so clearly, historians who have emphasized the importance of free labor, especially for the Republican party's birth and rise, at times have seemed to critics to miss the point. After all, even advocates of popular sovereignty could concede the superiority of free labor if they wished, and the pro-slavery forces could implicitly do so by endorsing the superiority of free laborers with the claim, stated or not, that blacks were inferior to whites.[7]

Ultimately, the Northern case for free labor and against slavery rested largely on the idea of equality of opportunity. According to politicians, editors, and thinkers, free labor generated greater profits than slave labor; with those profits came a better standard of living for all of society. In turn, slavery created an undemocratic class or caste system that smelled suspiciously of aristocracy, which Northerners believed the founding fathers to have fought the revolution to escape. As for the social costs, Northerners claimed that the idea of equality was what

Jefferson had in mind when he wrote that all men are created equal; if they ultimately proved unequal, that was because some worked harder or happened to have better luck than others, not because they were born into slavery or a system in which slaves did their work for them. However much other Northerners shared their belief in free labor, only Republicans ran for office on the mantra that free labor was best for the nation's politics, economy, and society. While they designed their platform to appeal to as many people and interests as possible, they gained in support with each election in the 1850s, culminating in winning the presidency in 1860, without hiding their belief in free labor or its logical concomitant, that slavery and its labor system were inferior.[8]

Indeed, a comparison of their public and private pronouncements from the 1850s and the 1860s reveals little difference on certain key points. For one, Republicans continually exalted labor. Dignity was the issue, said the *San Francisco Bulletin.* It praised the Emancipation Proclamation, on which most contemporaries and historians focused in relation to slavery and military policy, because it "dignifies labor, ennobles humanity, and honors God, and it enables us to accept the Declaration of Independence without mental reservations." As the reference to the Declaration suggests, the freedom of and right to labor could be seen as part of a higher national calling, inseparable from the republic itself. Governor John Andrew of Massachusetts, a moderate who mingled with all wings of the party, explained to an agricultural organization that the war was being fought to "protect the printing press, the plough, the anchor, the loom, the cradle, the fireside and the altar, the rights of Labor, the earnings of industry, the security and the peace of Home," a litany that connected labor, in capital letters, to home and church. The religious underpinnings were even more apparent to conservative Thurlow Weed, who believed in "the divine law that by the sweat of a man's brow shall he earn his bread. . . . In our country thousands of poor boys, by industry, honesty, and ambition, have not only acquired wealth, but become useful and honored citizens." By linking work to home and church, Republicans showed that labor held as high a place in their eyes as it was possible to occupy.[9]

Republicans also insisted that free labor simply outperformed slave labor, not because slave labor was black—although most of them believed in white supremacy—but because free laborers were free.

Supervising contrabands in the Mississippi Valley and running the embryonic origins of the Freedmen's Bureau, John Eaton concluded that while free black laborers were mostly unfit or too young to fight, "Even with this crippled body of workers, free labor could be compared not unfavorably with slave labor." When Senator James Lane reported early in 1863 that his state of Kansas was trying to grow cotton without slavery, he added that "our people are ambitious to prove that this commodity, heretofore grown exclusively by slave labor, can more successfully and more profitably be raised by free labor." Later that year, Horace Greeley continued a trend he and other Republican editors had begun in the 1850s, publishing statistics in his *New York Tribune* that proved free labor to be more productive and profitable than slave labor. Writer Edward Atkinson devoted an entire pamphlet to proving that free laborers grew cotton more cheaply than slaves.[10]

Others were more subtle. For example, Secretary of State William Henry Seward told one of his diplomats that many Southerners were emigrating to western territories—a sign, he felt, that the war was proving even to defenders of slavery the value of free labor, financial and otherwise. To say that Republicans believed in the more modern political concept that people vote their pocketbooks would be to overstate the case and understate their other precepts; clearly, though, they understood and saw a link between slavery and economic dislocation and decline.[11]

In keeping with their belief in their own system, Republicans were also more concerned about what free labor meant for their race, not for blacks. Adam Gurowski, a Polish count whose angry radicalism relegated him to the party's fringe, expected the war to "uproot domestic oligarchy, based upon living on the labor of an enslaved man; it has to put a stop to the moral, intellectual, and physical servitude of both, of whites and of colored." Moderates and conservatives showed less interest in elevating freedmen; they wanted to aid those already presumed free to economic independence and a proper appreciation of republicanism—both lowercase and with a capital R. "The liberation of the negro slave will be the redemption of the poor white man," said the *Sacramento Union,* a devoutly Republican western newspaper, "and will raise him to that standard of political excellence which will enable him to guard his birthright of freedom against the encroachments of aristocratic privilege."[12]

Indeed, the Republican commitment to free labor often focused more on the individual than on the institution. Republicans made no bones about opposing slavery, but were far more concerned with those who sought to protect it. Rather than emphasizing slavery as a moral wrong or focusing all of their arguments on it as an economic ill, they preferred to stress to wartime voters that slavery instead enabled the South to maintain an aristocracy based wholly on wealth and privilege, and thus antithetical to everything presumed to be American. Worse, they said, their political opponents in the North aided the South in creating and maintaining its own version of feudalism. John Bigelow, a *New York Evening Post* editor whose party loyalty and moderation won him a diplomatic appointment to Paris, called the war "a struggle between free and slave labor, between the aristocratic or privileged element in our government and the democratic. The two cannot live in peace together. . . . We have gone so far as to draw the sword in defence of the democratic element and the aristocracy have drawn theirs in favor of the privileged element." Not only did these views echo those of other Republicans, they were addressed to Weed. As Bigelow's own words showed, the party boss was in many ways the quintessential Republican who worked hard to become rich and powerful. Weed also sounded more conservative as the war went on, blanching at the kind of social revolution that other Republicans sought when they demanded the end of slavery—the kind of social revolution that Bigelow implicitly suggested.[13]

Whether or not they realized it, a revolution that would alter Southern society was exactly what Republicans proposed when they advocated free labor and attacked slavery and the world it created. In 1864 the *Chicago Tribune,* whose editors tended to be more radical in private than in public, stated the issue in terms regional and partisan. In the South, "labor has been degraded, the laborer left untaught, and the doctrine that capital should own, sell, lash, and if resisted shoot or burn labor" left the South "without a free religion, free speech, free press or free schools. . . . In the regenerated Union the free school, a free press, and free speech will be enjoyed by all without asking the leave of some adjacent owner of a thousand slaves." Republicans varied as to how to throttle the slave power or the lengths to which they would go. A few Republicans would divide the aristocracy's land, but at issue was how: Thaddeus Stevens, whose hatred for slavery and slave owners may have been matched by his desire to protect industry, wanted blacks to take over plantation lands; the *Ohio State Journal* expected poor whites to become the South's dominant landowners. But most Republicans thought more broadly: the Southern aristocracy had to be relieved of its regional power or convinced that it could no longer have national power. In the confines of his diary, conservative New York attorney George Templeton Strong captured his party's view of the South when he imagined how rebels addressed the rich:

> Your place and your duty require you to own the poor man that works for you, to convert him (so far as you can) into a chattel and a brute, to appropriate the fruit of his labor (giving him in return such sustenance as will keep him in working order) to treat him as you treat your oxen and your mules, and to deny him every privilege and faculty of which he can be deprived by the legislation of tyrannous, selfish, wicked men. By all means give him Christian teaching, but remember that his wife and his children belong to you and not to him. It is your right and your duty to sell them off whenever you can thereby make money. Such is the true relation between capital and labor, rich and poor.[14]

Yet Republicans hoped that the South could be convinced that the slave system was a failure. If only the rebels could see that they could prosper without slavery, free labor would be the agent and beneficiary of any change. During the war Republicans looked for signs of an adjustment in attitude and, as hindsight shows, overstated any progress they saw. In 1862, a Republican visitor to Arkansas and Tennessee reported that local slave owners planned to work out labor contracts with slaves whom Union armies had turned into freedmen. The same correspondent detected an understanding among the planters that they would have to accommodate themselves to a different system, because these laborers were necessary to their economic success. Representative William Kelley of Pennsylvania predicted that all Southerners would benefit from the creation of a force of free laborers: with free blacks paying taxes, whites could build schools and improve industry. The South would provide Republicans with a laboratory for government activism that would rejuvenate a region they deemed desperately in need of help. Once Southerners saw the benefits of remaking their society, they would heartily accept free labor and perhaps even acknowledge the error of their ways.[15]

However, Republicans saw the benefits as likely to be for whites only. Blacks barely figured into the Republican equation, and when they did they were an ancillary concern at best. After Lincoln announced the Preliminary Emancipation Proclamation, a Republican editor warned, "Emancipate labor and you place him immediately in conflict with the more energetic and shrewd Caucasian, and to save himself from the competition and rivalry, in which he is certain to be beaten, he will move gradually away into other regions, and leave this a white man's country." According to Representative John Kasson, an Iowa moderate, banning slavery in the territories meant that those areas would be "forever free to the white man without competition with slave labor." The idea that former slaves could compete with white laborers, or might migrate into the North and West to try to do so, seems to have struck Republicans as impossible, if the idea struck them at all.[16]

Nor were Republicans consistent or even sure about what slave labor would do when it became free. After the final Proclamation, the usually moderate-to-conservative *New York Times* doubted that the freedmen would easily adapt to a new form of labor. Its editors warned that "they must be compelled to do it—not by brute force nor by being owned like cattle and denied every human right, but by just and equal laws—such laws as in every community control and forbid vagrancy, mendicancy and all shapes by which idle vagabondage preys upon thrift and industry." Setting aside that one of the first post-Proclamation comments from a leading Republican voice was a stark harbinger of the postwar black codes with which Southerners virtually reinstituted slavery, it was as though the writer had realized in mid-sentence that compulsory free labor was slavery, but never awoke to the oxymoronic racism in his argument. By contrast, John Eaton sought to run the Union's free labor experiment on Mississippi plantations with as much color-blindness and as great a commitment to equality as he could muster. Early in 1864, hoping for "the elevation of the race," he reported finding the freedmen able, dedicated, and quiet, but "no one can mark out the exact steps in the progress of a race." He advocated martial law, with the War Department running any government programs to promote free labor. His intentions were good, even honorable, but seemingly the opposite of what he claimed to believe.[17]

If Republicans seemed inconsistent about the racial and social effects of free labor, they never doubted its superiority—in other words, its economic benefits, and how other benefits would follow. Sure in their conviction that slave labor lagged behind free labor in output and uplift and dragged the South down with it, they remained dedicated to the flip side of that argument: free labor elevated the North in every imaginable way. This belief, so central to uniting one-time Whigs, Democrats, Know-Nothings, and Free-Soilers in a Republican party founded on the premise that free labor would triumph over all, proved critical to the Northern victory in the Civil War. It provided a foundation upon which Northerners could fight the war, for while Southerners could justifiably claim to be defending their homes against the North, Northerners could claim with equal justification that they fought to protect themselves from slavery and its economic and societal destructiveness. Both regions fought for a way of life, and therein lies the importance of the free labor ideology.[18]

ALTERING THE FREE LABOR IDEOLOGY

Yet its importance, and thus Republican uncertainty and inconsistency about it, also lies elsewhere: in how the free labor ideology changed during the war, dooming itself to become something it had never been. During the war, the belief in free labor gradually became part of a broader belief in freedom, union, and power. Republicans had to redefine and refine exactly how free labor fit into the overall scheme of things. Free labor became part of their idea of what freedom meant—for example, free speech and the freedom that comes with and from an ordered society, both of which obviously had weighed on Republican minds but occupied less important places than free labor in the party's rhetorical spectrum. For Republicans, freedom became linked more closely than ever to unionism and the need to win support for fighting the war, especially from Northerners belonging to a different party or less committed to free labor. Freedom and union increasingly were, in the Republican mind, a unit. One was impossible without the other, but the possibility of conflict between them existed. That would force Republicans to choose, and thus to balance free labor and freedom itself against the needs and importance of the Union and an assessment of their own powers to save the Union. To do what they had to do—assure freedom, save the Union, and stay in power—Republicans had to shift their emphasis according to circumstance. Once they started doing so, it became easier—indeed, for the fate of free labor, too easy.

The tumble began when Republicans confronted the issue that Lincoln described in 1859: whether the man came ahead of the dollar, and whether labor was superior to capital. For a moderate such as Lincoln to suggest that both were true suggests a possible Republican consensus on the issue, a middle ground of the kind he so successfully occupied during the war. But in the end, just as the war forced Republicans to change their outlook and priorities, it affected their attitudes toward labor and capital. On 21 April 1861, Wendell Phillips addressed a Boston rally. An unrepentant abolitionist, critical of Lincoln and other Republicans who declined to advocate or engineer immediate emancipation, Phillips hardly represents the average Republican, except in his ideas about free labor. He expected a war "between barbarism and civilization, between a North that *thinks* and is the nineteenth century" and a South that "*dreams*" and "is the thirteenth or fourteenth century—baron and serf, noble and slave." His point of view exemplified the party's charges that the South sought to perpetuate an aristocracy rooted in slavery. He said, "I know what the sewing-machine and reaping machine and ideas and types and school houses cannot do, the muskets of Illinois and Massachusetts can finish up," and "I know that free speech, free soil, school houses and ballot boxes are a pyramid on its broadest base," signifying his belief that the war would create a new nation or at least a new South. Then, as he urged an eight-hour workday and deprecated strikes, Phillips struck a different note: "Capital and labor are not enemies but friends," he said, and "they cannot lead a separate life." Besides, capital was just "crystallized labor," and labor "but capital dissolved and become active." They were interdependent, and his home state proved it. "Massachusetts workingmen" made their state a "treasure house of capital. They have covered it with roads, dotted it with cities; they have filled it with schoolhouses, they have joined it to the markets of the world."[19]

Other Republicans, as radical as Phillips or more moderate, linked labor and capital in a continuum to prosperity and the freedom in which they deeply believed. Not only abolitionists argued that labor and capital were inseparable; Republicans believed that how they intermingled made the American republic unique. Because "the largest individual liberty of action consistent with due security to life and property will give the largest national production, other things being equal," wrote John Lothrop Motley, a historian from Massachusetts serving as minister to Vienna, "in the United States the same amount of capital, land, and labor yields more wealth than can be expected in any European country." While Motley combined an argument in favor of linking labor and capital with an assault on aristocracy, less historically inclined Republicans shared his sense that European leaders felt more of an affinity with the Confederacy than with the Union. In the minds of Republicans, labor and capital could work together in the North because labor could be a part of capital; in the South, they had to be at odds because capital owned labor.[20]

Disputes between capital and labor in the North were the last thing Republicans wanted. After all, they needed a united front to bring the South to heel. This guided their approach in creating the Cabinet and the Union party, and their debates over how quickly and how far to move against slavery. If political and social issues were part of the equation in uniting the North for war, the economy would surely be at least as crucial, if not more so. Just as the firing on Fort Sumter unified the North, it united capital and labor in a common cause: union. Addressing the House as it began its first wartime session on 4 July 1861, Speaker Galusha Grow, a Pennsylvania radical, saw unity everywhere he looked. "The merchant, the banker, and the tradesman, with an alacrity unparalleled, proffer their all at the altar of their country, while from the counter, the workshop, and the plow, brave hearts and stout arms, leaving their tasks unfinished, rush to the tented field." The war required Republicans to redefine their commitment to freedom in light of the need to preserve the Union; no longer could they advocate free labor as a total panacea. Accordingly, free laborers would adapt and work for the Union with those they labored for and with.[21]

Nearly two years later, the Republican effort to link capital and labor took another tack more redolent of Phillips's words than of Lincoln's. By early 1863, the Northern war effort was foundering: the Army of the Potomac had suffered a crushing defeat at Fredericksburg; even if he was more in control than he appeared, Grant seemed thoroughly flummoxed at Vicksburg; and Republicans had lost a few congressional seats and the key governorship of New York in the recent elections. In an effort to deal with the economic effects and requirements of the war, and in a throwback to the party's

Whiggish roots, Congress debated creating a national banking system so that the war could be more easily and competently financed. John Sherman, once of the House Ways and Means Committee and now on the Senate Finance Committee, argued that the measure would "make a community of interest between the stockholders of banks, the people, and the Government," and "by the passage of this bill you will harmonize these interests, so that every stockholder, every mechanic, every laborer who holds one of these notes will be interested in the Government—not in a local bank, but in the Government of the United States." Labor and capital would work together, Republicans hoped, not just in their interest but in the interest of the government and thus of the country as a whole.[22]

Yet as any Republican knew, self-interest was unavoidable. The national interest, the party believed, required winning the war and thus preserving the Union. This required, in turn, the kind of assistance that only large industry could provide. If the North had an obvious advantage over the South, it lay with the North's industrialization—the greater speed with which it had happened and the greater extent to which it had spread. As the party in opposition in the second half of the 1850s, Republicans had tried to straddle the fence: extolling laborers and their ability to become independent entrepreneurs, yet appealing to business leaders on issues such as the tariff. To have concentrated exclusively on slavery would undoubtedly have inspired the financial community to consider Republicans the sort of radical reformers not to be trusted with government power; some businessmen already felt that way, in some cases for fiscal reasons and in others because they simply disagreed with the party's message. But the party's quick electoral success reflected its success in appealing to labor and capital, uniting them in fact as it united them in spirit.[23]

Winning the war, though, demanded different priorities. Republicans could and sometimes did consider anyone willing to fight or support the fight for the Union an ally or advocate of free labor. The sinews of war required not just men, but machines and money. Thus, the party cozied up to businessmen, especially railroad and bank operators, who could aid the war effort and bankroll Republicans and their policies. In turn, businessmen benefited by showing their loyalty, always to the Union and often to the party. To complete this vicious but successful circle, Republicans welcomed business efforts to cultivate them, creating a conundrum that outlasted the war: if the interests of labor and capital proved incompatible, where would Republican loyalties lie?

At the time of Lincoln's election in November 1860, Republicans were ambivalent about the business community, believing that their free labor appeal made them seem too radical for that more conservative group's taste. Nor did the party expect support from merchants if they sensed a risk to any profits from the South. As one Republican said, "We owe a debt of gratitude to the laboring classes who gave us this victory, not to the mass of the merchants . . . frightened by the cry of wolf." Where the party ran poorly that fall, its members blamed businessmen: in New York City they succumbed to Southern threats of secession in case of a Republican victory; in New Jersey Democrats won due to "corporation influence," a railroad that "runs through it and twirls it around like a skewer." Even Lincoln, who had represented large businesses as an Illinois lawyer, noted, "I am not insensible to any commercial or financial depression that may exist; but nothing is to be gained by fawning around the 'respectable scoundrels' who got it up. Let them go to work and repair the mischief of their own making; and then perhaps they will be less greedy to do the like again."[24]

As secession became a reality, Republicans voiced little interest in the financial community's plight. When representatives of industry begged for compromise, even Republicans willing to concede some points saw the requests as rooted more in money than in principle. Across the North, they noticed that many who suggested appeasing the South came from cities where the financial community wielded influence, not small towns or rural areas. It reminded them of the importance of the free labor ideology and which tier of society offered them more support. Greeley's *Tribune* compared merchants with "common people" who had "a wider range of vision than the shelves of dry goods and warehouses of cotton and groceries." The *Chicago Tribune* was critical: "Chicago has not yet descended to the dead level of New York. Cotton has not usurped the functions of Conscience; Pork has not conquered Patriotism; Lard has not dethroned Loyalty; nor have Cut Meats amended the Constitution." Seward-Weed loyalist James Nye expressed the attitude that Republicans, especially radicals, developed toward business. When told, "A merchant says that his business is gone," Nye shot back, "Well, let it go."[25]

What Kenneth Stampp called the "paradox of the propertied classes" was clear: continued profits required the status quo, so they preferred concessions; but to concede political power was to concede economic power, both of which the North, or so Republicans felt, had fairly won. The *New York Times* captured the inconsistency: "It is not easy to say what evils would follow a dissolution of the Union,—but they could scarcely be more serious than the general fear of that event has already caused to our business interests." Senator Zachariah Chandler of Michigan, a successful merchant, agreed that deciding the issue would help business, despite his own losses. Amid fears that the South would repudiate its debts, amid the gyrations of eastern markets, businessmen reported panic, bankruptcies, retrenchment, or reductions, among consumers and themselves.[26]

Thus, despite their displeasure, Republicans tried to be sympathetic. They saw that continued success required them to win over the myriad blocs that comprised the financial community. Even an abolitionist such as Phillips contended that a unionist ideology relied on "the clink of coin—the whistle of spindles, the dust of trade." In Pennsylvania, the citadel of protection on which many felt the election hinged, a Republican explained the need to broaden their appeal by telling radical Thaddeus Stevens, "We now, as we ever have, recognized in you a bold, fearless advocate of Freedom, Constitutional Right, and Protection of the Industrial Interests of Pennsylvania." Seeking to persuade business that the party could be trusted, Republicans predicted that Lincoln would promote prosperity, trumpeted the North's economic superiority, and denigrated the Southern economy. A free labor ideology had finally attracted enough believers to win the White House in a plurality; to hold power, they would have to assure the employers of free labor that they would see profits in the process.[27]

In February 1861, when seventy Republicans and twenty businessmen dined together in Washington, the courtship's effects were obvious, not only for those present but also for the party's ideology. A merchant asked, "Shall we . . . stand upon a platform made some time ago in view of facts when then existed, and which have ceased to exist now; or . . . yield some fair concession, without any sacrifice of principle?" Most Republicans wished them well and promised to listen to ideas about compromise, which was more than many of them had previously been inclined to do. Galusha Grow, the lone dissenter, argued that since the merchants saw the Union as "only a co-partnership for mutual mercantile advantages," they were "in some degree responsible for the present troubles." Many Republicans agreed, but the "co-partnership" for "mutual advantages" would not be between Northern and Southern capitalists. Rather, the party and businessmen were merging in a mutual dependence all too familiar to business and all too new to Republicans. Businessmen needed stability and support from government to function profitably, which meant currying favor with Republicans; the party needed financial stability and support for the government to function properly, which meant currying favor with business. The move away from the free labor ideology and toward one that mixed freedom, union, and power resembled the underlying point of that merchant's query: whether to change with the times and circumstances.[28]

During the war, Republicans followed through on their 1860 platform plank in favor of a transcontinental railroad. Even businessmen not noted for scruple shared Republican beliefs—Central Pacific builders Charles Crocker, Leland Stanford, Mark Hopkins, and Collis Huntington met through party activities—but others concentrated on buttering up whoever could help them. When Union Pacific officials asked several of Lincoln's Cabinet ministers to help raise money for a corporate reorganization, Postmaster General Montgomery Blair and Secretary of the Interior John Usher issued a public letter in their behalf. Usher, whose department chose railroad construction inspectors, received ten thousand shares of Union Pacific stock worth $500,000, and other politicians similarly benefited. He and Caleb Smith, his predecessor, worked closely with New York railroad lawyer and Democrat Samuel Tilden, whose business connections aided Republicans in building the line, despite their political differences. After the war, railroad executive Thomas Scott, a former War Department aide, sought to meet with Stevens about the Union Pacific's eastern division because "your friends in Pennsylvania have become interested in the enterprise and will make it a success." Knowing how to go beyond patronage or profit to discuss what appealed to the Republican mind, Scott described the project as "now on a sound basis" and en route to becoming "a good road to develop our Western territories," which Republicans such as Stevens (and Scott) hoped to fill with loyal free-soilers and free laborers.[29]

Another ardent advocate of free labor, Horace Greeley, also developed close ties to railroad capitalists. Fervently in favor of a transcontinental line to transport free laborers who would spread the Republican gospel, Greeley became an official "consulting agent" to the Union Pacific. This linked him to lobbyists and builders and made him an ally of Cornelius Vanderbilt Jr. They shared a commitment to the party and mutual animus toward New Jersey's Camden and Amboy railroad monopoly: Greeley hated its political power, while Vanderbilt was unhappy that the monopoly belonged to someone else. They cultivated one another accordingly. In Vanderbilt, Greeley found a strong and wealthy business supporter of Republicans and their views; in Greeley, Vanderbilt found a friend, mentor, and publicist. Greeley called Vanderbilt "about the only rich man's son among us who is a Republican." For his part, trying to impress his father without relying wholly on the family fortune, Vanderbilt obtained loans from Greeley, keeping them secret and telling the editor that if his plans succeeded, "the advantage both pecuniary and otherwise can hardly be estimated." More important, Vanderbilt turned politically active, lobbying for Greeley's friend Schuyler Colfax in his campaign to become Speaker of the House. In its own way this represented a harbinger of what railroad executives would do in decades to come, when they sought to control political parties rather than be a part of them.[30]

The question of whether their exposure to railroad builders corrupted Republicans is problematic. Besides, not only were they quick to deny any change in their attitude, but none of them entered the party or the war with an absolutely clean slate; as politicians, lawyers, and businessmen, they had dealt with financial elites, whatever their views. Still, hypocrisy or rationalization occasionally resonated in their words and views: declining a pass to use the railroad as a state legislator because "I cannot conceive that any member of the New York Legislature as such has any claims on any railroad company in the state for such favors," Ezra Cornell said, "On account of our telegraph contracts and connections I shall be happy to receive a pass, as such a pass I could use, without feeling less than a man."[31]

A recipient of railroad largesse, Elihu Washburne of Illinois welcomed a House probe of such gifts, calling railroads "perfectly lawless in their dealings with the Government as well as with individuals." In reply, Stevens mixed humor with an explanation of Republican beliefs. "I do not rise to defend the railroads, having no free tickets whatever, although I do not say that I should have rejected any if they had been offered me." This was met with a laugh. More seriously, Stevens would "go for any number of railroads that capitalists will make with their own capital, whether it be between this [city] and New York, or Philadelphia, or Boston, or anywhere else. So long as they ask no appropriation in money or bonds from this Government, I will go for one or for twenty railroads, for all monopolies of that kind I look upon as injurious to the interests of the country." He captured his party's feelings: winning the war and building a better Union required Republicans to work with railroad interests. A few free passes were unlikely to divert Republicans from seeking the spread of freedom and union.[32]

Nor would the Republican party change, at least not on its face, due to the need for banks to finance and underwrite the government leading the fight for freedom and union. The party born to celebrate free labor still did so, and hailed bankers for contributing to the capital that employed free labor. When he spoke of the harmony of interests between bankers and workers, Sherman also spoke for those lobbying for passage of the bill to create a national banking system and thus bolster financial institutions: Lincoln, that onetime laborer whose legal practice in Illinois included what might be called the nascent field of corporate law; Salmon Chase, the Treasury secretary whom many saw then and now as the architect of the free labor ideology; and Jay Cooke, the Philadelphia investor working closely with Chase in running his department. Not yet the Speaker, Colfax, an Indiana publisher, took the opportunity "to render my homage to the banks for their patriotism at that trying hour. They acted like corporations that had souls." Republicans continued to celebrate the workers' sacrifices and bond purchases, but showed more appreciation for bankers, brokers, and bond sellers whose investments, they felt, fended off the Union's collapse. For workers, Republicans offered rhetoric; for financiers they provided legislation, which would aid laborers—an embryonic form of trickle-down economics. To promote freedom and union, they found, demanded a union of their own with investment capital.[33]

In addressing the hoary issue of the tariff, Republicans also showed how their ethos evolved. Granted, they had debated protectionist and revenue-raising tariffs long before they had been part of that party, but during the war Republicans increasingly tied protectionism to free labor. Representative Justin Morrill of Vermont, the architect and namesake of the 1862 protectionist tariff, declared, "We are a nation of producers, and one of the paramount duties of legislators is to see that producers are profitably employed and have a market for their products." That market, logically enough, would be free laborers, and labor leaders agreed that protection from abroad and fair competition at home aided workers. By contrast, said Maine's James G. Blaine, "the protectionist claims that his theory of revenue preserves the newer nations from being devoured by the older, and offers to human labor a shield against the exactions of capital." Seeking the exemption of some steam machinery from the usual tariff limits, New York's Giles Hotchkiss told the House that he preferred "labor-saving machines" to "importing the laborers. . . . Our mechanics will doubtless improve upon the machines sent from Europe, when they have those machines here in actual operation."[34]

Many historians have pointed out the importance of wartime economic issues. The Republican party was indeed a conglomeration of interests, a coalition of men interested in more than just slavery, expected to take stands on railroads, banks, and tariffs that would be compatible with those of the parties from which they had migrated. Whatever they did, of course, they would bear in mind the needs and views of their constituents, including rich and poor, capitalist and laborer. While taking power enabled them to enact their principles, or at least try to do so, the war also forced them to view these matters through a different prism. If campaigning for the right to govern the Union and then governing it were two different activities, the same could be said of governing the Union and winning a war to preserve it. Each demanded a different approach.

Campaigning for the right to govern the Union gave Republicans an opportunity to spread their gospel of free labor, and they took advantage of it. This was politically expedient, because many voters were or hoped to be self-sufficient individualists, as independent entrepreneurs or Jeffersonian yeomen. For Republicans to attack the South's system of slave labor as unfair for the free laborer appealed to these voters for obvious reasons; for Republicans to advocate such programs as railroad-building, federal banking, and tariff protection would entice fewer of them but would reach a significant number nonetheless.

Yet Republicans showed no myopia. They remained committed to free labor. As the war neared its end, Phillips stated the case, as he had at the beginning. "Wealth sees the ballot in the hands of poverty, and knows that its gold and its roof depend upon the use made of that ballot, and wealth hurries to put intelligence on one side and religion on the other of the baby footsteps that will one day find their way to the ballot," he said. "That is the essence of democratic institutions. It mortgages wealth and learning and strength to lift up the poor man's cradle." As he put it more pithily on another occasion, "Mr. Cash is a more efficient master than Mr. Lash. I defy a million men, having got comfort and leisure, not to improve."[35]

While Phillips's abolitionism struck many moderates and conservatives as somewhere between unreasonable and insane, he spoke for the party. Republicans believed in what he said, and that their policies would elevate rich and poor alike, economically and morally. Yet linking labor and capital presented a potential problem: What if their interests were somehow in conflict, and Republicans had to choose, to use Lincoln's phrase, between the man and the dollar? Their economic policies and running a war machine allied Republicans more closely than ever with large financial interests whose beneficence reminded them of the importance of unity between labor and capital. Citizen soldiers might buy bonds and fight for the government that guaranteed their value, but the most important—or at least the most noticeable—aid came from bankers and financial titans. Thanks to the war, the large-scale entrepreneur, who seemed to feed off the free laborer, fed the government's and Union's needs in their time of crisis. Thus, while Republicans viewed labor just as favorably, they tended to view capital more favorably than before.

The implications of this subtle shift were significant for the present and the future. During the war Republicans wanted to help industry because they needed one another: the party needed business to finance the war, business needed the Republicans to assure that government policies would help it grow. This symbiotic relationship would continue after the war, but with a crucial difference: Republicans no longer needed to preserve the Union or spread free labor, since the Union was preserved and slavery was dead. Two-thirds of the party's wartime needs, as expressed by its wartime ideology, had been met. The final third was power. Republicans sought it before the war, exercised it during the war, and wished to retain it after the war.

The Civil War not only restored a South with an elephantine memory and no love for free labor, but it helped and built a Republican relationship with large railroad companies, financial firms, and industrial producers. When the war was over, these companies wanted to maintain the spirit of cooperation so that they could protect their interests, which were simple and understandable: to do their business and keep their profits.

From Free Labor to Freedom, Union, and Power

To perpetuate their vision of freedom and the Union, Republicans wanted to keep power. That meant continuing their spirit of cooperation. But the smaller corporations and the government of 1860 became bigger and more powerful during the war. What Lincoln's administration did with and for businessmen, it did with a velvet glove, not an iron fist. In a sense Republicans created a monster and, like Dr. Frankenstein, had to figure out how to deal with it. The answer lay in the free labor ideology and the freedom it entailed: the Republican belief that the individual should be allowed to pursue economic self-sufficiency and independence. Republicans had long argued that all men should be free and equal to do as they pleased: to enjoy the freedom to labor. After the war Republicans offered that freedom, but they could hardly, in the same breath, deny the same freedom to those who had succeeded and amassed fortunes.

The ties between freedom, union, and power were clear to Republicans, but they understood that these words had many meanings; for the sake of their party's success, they had been wise to understand them. Republicans did more during the war than legislate against slavery and the South. Charles Sumner introduced a bill to reform the civil service system and eliminate the "spoils system" that had always been part of the nation's political life. With "the scale of business now and the universal interests involved," he noted the need for "trained men. 'Rotation in office' is proper enough—in the political posts, where political direction is determined, but absurd in the machinery of Administration." The significance of this statement is what it included and who said it. It included an awareness that the scope of the federal government, and the industry and corporations it dealt with, had grown during the war. The author of those words, Sumner, often seemed to colleagues and constituents to be caught up entirely in issues of slavery and diplomacy. The proposal reflected his reformist views, but it also signified his awareness that the country, and how it did business, had changed.[36]

In acting and thinking as they did, Republicans could hearken to two documents written in 1776. In the first and most obvious, the Declaration of Independence, they understood Jefferson to be arguing that all men were created with equal opportunity. That was the essence of free labor: it meant the right to pursue opportunities, to reap the fruits of their self-interest. That year, another student of Enlightenment rationalism published *The Wealth of Nations.* When Adam Smith espoused laissez-faire, he described a kind of freedom both like and unlike Jefferson's. Both argued for equality of opportunity, which Republicans had supported all along. If some outperformed others, that was normal, even common, in Jefferson's and Smith's time, in Lincoln's, and afterward.[37]

Whether Jefferson would have supported or even tolerated the laissez-faire approach of the late nineteenth century is no more knowable than how Lincoln and other Republican leaders such as Seward, Chase, Sumner, or Stevens would have responded. Some of the party's more prominent early figures left power or redirected their energies, intentionally or not. Others, including Stevens and William Pitt Fessenden, died before the postwar era became known as the Gilded Age. Not only can we never know what they would have done, but a new or different generation of Republicans had risen to the leadership. Just as James Madison and Alexander Hamilton, for example, had come of age during the Revolution and differed with some of their elders regarding the issue of a strong central government, those who took the party's reins after the war had different political experiences from Republican leaders before and during the war. The leadership and the circumstances changed, while the free labor ideology survived.

These changes were unavoidable and unfortunate. For Republicans, the free labor ideology marked both the best and the worst of their thought. Its greatness lay in its goal: to aid labor, white or black. Its failing lay in the achievement of its goal: to aid labor, white or black, by making it free to compete with one another. The problem was that the competition would be almost wholly unfettered, and that the creation of a free labor society accompanied the creation of a large-scale industrial society rooted in the idea that labor and capital would cooperate. For the government to cooperate as well was natural. Given the war's effects, it was equally natural for those who were in charge of the government—or wanted to be—to gravitate toward capital and capitalists and to allow the same kind of unfettered competition.

That is the final irony of Lincoln's meditations on labor and capital. When he first wrote, in 1859, another significant figure was writing words that would greatly affect his times: Charles Darwin. In the late nineteenth century some thinkers applied his theories, or more accurately a variant of them, to American society with crushing results. When Social Darwinists explained and supported laissez-faire on the grounds that only the fittest survived, they had only a short step to take from the antebellum Republican ideology of free labor. Out of political calculation and belief, Republicans would seek equality of opportunity; capital asked for no less. Free labor became the freedom to labor, and neither the Republican party nor the nation would ever be the same.[38]

Notes

1. "Annual Message to Congress," 3 December 1861, in *CW,* vol. 5, 35–53, at 35.

2. Ibid., 51–52. On the Republican view of the South, see Foner, *Free Soil,* 40–72; and Richard H. Abbott, *The Republican Party and the South: The First Southern Strategy, 1855–1877* (Chapel Hill: University of North Carolina Press, 1986).

3. "Annual Message to Congress," *CW,* vol. 5, 52–53.

4. Gabor Boritt, *Lincoln and the Economics of the American Dream* (Memphis: Memphis State University Press, 1978); Richardson, *The Greatest Nation of the Earth;* Stewart Winger, "Lincoln's Economics and the American Dream: A Reappraisal," *Journal of the Abraham Lincoln Association* 22 (2001): 51–80. On Lincoln and his view of his father, see Donald, *Lincoln,* especially 32–33, 152.

5. "Address before the Wisconsin State Agricultural Society, Milwaukee, Wisconsin," 30 September 1859, in *CW,* vol. 3, 471–82, at 478; "Fragment on Free Labor," ca. 17 September 1859, in ibid., 462–63; Lincoln to Henry L. Pierce and others, Springfield, 6 April 1859, in ibid., 374–76.

6. Neely, *The Union Divided,* 142–52, argues that Republicans actually lost confidence in capitalism for a while. While evidence of doubts certainly exists, the long-term Republican ideology reflected growing confidence.

7. Foner, *Free Soil,* ix-xxxix.

8. Ibid, and *passim.*

9. Shutes, *Lincoln and California,* 75–76; John A. Andrew, "An Address Delivered before the New England Agricultural Society, on Hampden Park, Springfield, Mass., September 9, 1864" (Boston: Wright and Potter, 1864), 21–22; Thurlow Weed Barnes and Harriet A. Weed, *Life of Thurlow Weed, Including His Autobiography and a Memoir* (Boston: Houghton Mifflin, 1884), 7.

10. John Eaton, *Grant, Lincoln and the Freedmen* (New York: Negro Universities Press, 1969), 217, 119–20, 205; *CG,* 37, 3, 2 February 1863, 669; *New York Tribune,* 12 November 1863; Edward Atkinson, "Cheap Cotton by Free Labor: By a Cotton Manufacturer" (Boston: A. Williams and Co. 1861), *passim.*

11. William Henry Seward to William L. Dayton, No. 518, Washington, 4 April 1864, U.S. Department of State, *Foreign Affairs 1864* (Washington, D.C.: Government Printing Office, 1865), vol. 3, 59–60; Foner, *Free Soil,* 11–72.

12. LeRoy H. Fischer, *Lincoln's Gadfly, Adam Gurowski* (Norman: University of Oklahoma Press, 1964), 233; *Sacramento Union,* 11 November 1864.

13. John Bigelow to Thurlow Weed, Paris, 15 August 1862, Weed ms, Department of Rare Books and Manuscripts, Rush Rhees Library, University of Rochester (UR). See also Van Deusen, *Thurlow Weed;* Clapp, *Forgotten First Citizen.*

14. *Chicago Tribune,* 28 September 1864; *Ohio State Journal,* 19 December 1864; Foner, *Politics and Ideology,* 128–49. See Wendell Phillips to Benjamin F. Butler, Boston, 13 December 1863, in Jessie A. Marshall, ed., *Private and Official Correspondence of General Benjamin F. Butler during the Period of the Civil War,* 5 vols. (Norwood, Mass: Plimpton Press, 1917), vol. 3, 206–7; Allan Nevins and Milton Halsey Thomas, eds., *The Diary of George Templeton Strong,* 4 vols. (New York: Macmillan, 1952), vol. 3, 11 September 1863, 256–57.

15. *Ohio State Journal,* 9 December 1862; William D. Kelley, "Speeches of Hon. William D. Kelley. Replies of the Hon. William D. Kelley to George Northrop, Esq., in the Joint Debate in the Fourth Congressional District" (Philadelphia: Collins, 1864), 59; *CG,* 37, 3, 21 February 1863, 143.

16. *Ohio State Journal,* 15 October 1862; Edward Younger, *John A. Kasson: Politics and Diplomacy from Lincoln to McKinley* (Iowa City: University of Iowa Press, 1955), 136–37.

17. *New York Times,* 3 January 1863; John Eaton to "Dear Sir," Vicksburg, 6 February 1864, in Thomas D. Eliot to Sumner, n.p., 7 March 1864, Reel 30, SP.

18. McPherson, *For Cause and Comrades,* addresses some of these issues.

19. James Brewer Stewart, *Wendell Phillips: Liberty's Hero* (Baton Rouge: Louisiana State University Press, 1986), 222–23, 262–63.

20. John Lothrop Motley to William Hunter, No. 111, Vienna, 27 June 1865, *Foreign Affairs 1865,* vol. 3, 29–30. On European views of the war, see David Paul Crook, *The North, the South, and the Powers* (New York: John Wiley and Sons, 1974); Philip S. Foner, *British Labor and the American Civil War* (New York: Holmes and Meier, 1981); Howard Jones, *Abraham Lincoln and a New Birth of Freedom: The Union and Slavery in the Diplomacy of the Civil War* (Lincoln: University of Nebraska Press, 1999).

21. *CG,* 37, 1, 4 July 1861, 4–5.

22. *CG,* 37, 3, 10 February 1863, 843.

23. Three books are indispensable to understanding the North's industrial state in this period: Emerson D. Fite, *Social and Industrial Conditions in the North during the Civil War* (New York: P. Smith, 1930); Robert V. Bruce, *Lincoln and the Tools of War* (Indianapolis, Ind.: Bobbs-Merrill, 1956); and Phillip S. Paludan, *"A People's Contest": The Union and the Civil War, 1861–1865* (New York: Harper and Row, 1988).

24. See the *New York Times, New York Tribune,* and *New York Evening Post* for November 1860 on this issue; Phillip S. Foner, *Business and Slavery: The New York Merchants and the Irrepressible Conflict* (Chapel Hill: University of North Carolina Press, 1941), 206, 224; John Bigelow to William Hargreaves, New York, 10 November 1860, John Bigelow Papers (Bigelow ms), Box 1, Manuscript Division, New York Public Library (NYPL); Quincy, 8 November 1860, Adams Diary, Adams Family Papers, Microfilm Edition (Adams Family ms), I, Reel 75, Massachusetts Historical Society (MHS); Lincoln to Truman Smith, Springfield, 10 November 1860, in *CW,* vol. 4, 138.

25. *New York Tribune,* 31 January and 2 February 1861; *Chicago Tribune,* 15 February 1861, in Stampp, *And the War Came,* 145; DeAlva S. Alexander, *A Political History of the State of New York,* 3 vols. (New York: Henry Holt and Company, 1906–9), vol. 2, 337–38; Potter, *Lincoln and His Party,* 127; *New York Times,* 15 February 1861. See also Foner, *Business and Slavery,* 252–64.

26. Stampp, *And the War Came,* 200–201; *New York Times,* 7 December 1860; Chandler to Trumbull, 17 November 1860, Trumbull ms, Reel 7, LC; John Trible to Trumbull, Alton, 18 December 1860, ibid.; George Opdyke to Trumbull, New York, 17 December 1860, ibid.; George Livermore to Sumner, Boston, 12 December 1860, in Reel 21, SP; *Boston Daily Atlas and Bee,* 3 December 1860, in Perkins, ed., *Northern Editorials on Secession,* 2 vols

(Washington: American Historical Association, 1942), 566; Foner, *Business and Slavery,* 214–16.

27. Bruce Levine, *Half Slave and Half Free: The Roots of Civil War* (New York: Hill and Wang, 1992), 229–32; Robert Harper et al., to Thaddeus Stevens, Gettysburg, 9 November 1860, Thaddeus Stevens Papers (Thaddeus Stevens ms), Box 1, LC; W. H. Osborn to Nathaniel Banks, New York, 12 November 1860, Nathaniel P. Banks Papers (Banks ms), Box 13, LC; Stampp, *And the War Came,* 215, 226.

28. *Philadelphia Press,* 24 February 1861, in Foner, *Business and Slavery,* 255–58.

29. George T. Clark, *Leland Stanford, War Governor of California, Railroad Builder, and Founder of Stanford University* (Stanford: Stanford University Press, 1931), 174–75; Elmo R. Richardson and Alan W. Farley, *John Palmer Usher* (Lawrence: University Press of Kansas, 1960), 55–56; Thomas A. Scott to Stevens, Philadelphia, 30 November 1865, Stevens ms, Box 3, LC.

30. Horace Greeley to Schuyler Colfax, New York, 29 November 1864, Horace Greeley Papers (Greeley ms), Box 6, Folder 14, NYPL; ibid., 1 July 1863; Cornelius Vanderbilt Jr. to Greeley, Hartford, 1 March 1863, 12 August 1863, and 16 April 1864, Greeley ms, Box 7, LC. On the railroad and Greeley, see Sam Hallett to Greeley, New York, 10 June 1863, ibid.; ibid., 9 January 1865, Box 6. On the Camden and Amboy, see Greeley to Sumner, New York, 26 June 1864, Reel 31, SP; J. R. Freese to Joseph P. Bradley, Trenton, 16 January 1865, Bradley ms, Series I, Part B, Folder 2, NJHS; *CG,* 38, 1, 7 April 1864, 1467 (Representative Frederick Woodbridge of Vermont). On Colfax, see Vanderbilt to Colfax, Hartford, 28 June, 6 August, and 28 September 1863, Schuyler Colfax Papers, Personal Miscellaneous (Colfax ms), NYPL; Willard H. Smith, *Schuyler Colfax: The Changing Fortunes of a Political Idol* (Indianapolis, Ind.: Indiana Historical Bureau, 1952), 183–84.

31. Ezra Cornell to Nathaniel Marsh, Albany, 7 March 1862, Ezra Cornell Papers, No. 1-1-1, Box 21, Folder 6 (Cornell ms), Department of Manuscripts and University Archives, Cornell University Libraries, Cornell University (CR).

32. H. A. Risley to Elihu B. Washburne, Washington, 17 February [1863?], Elihu Washburne Papers (Elihu Washburne ms), Volume 30, LC; *CG,* 38, 1, 6 January 1864, 111. Other examples of Republicans welcoming passes include Seward to George A. Dedman, Washington, 4 and 5 January 1862, William Henry Seward Papers (Seward ms), Personal Miscellaneous, NYPL; Gideon Welles to George Tucker, Washington, 3 January 1862, Gideon Welles Papers (Welles ms), Box 1, ibid.; W. Reynolds to Henry S. Lane, Lafayette, 16 January 1861, typescript, Henry S. Lane Papers (Lane ms), Lilly Library, Indiana University (IU).

33. *CG,* 37, 3, 27 February 1863, 1353. See Paludan, *"A People's Contest,"* 122–23; Jeannette P. Nichols, "John Sherman," in Kenneth W. Wheeler, ed., *For the Union: Ohio Leaders in the Civil War* (Columbus: Ohio State University Press, 1968), 405; Sherman to William T. Sherman, Mansfield, 20 March 1863, William T. Sherman Papers (William T. Sherman ms), LC, ibid., 411; Henry Cooke to Jay Cooke, 23 January 1863, in Ellis P. Oberholtzer, *Jay Cooke: Financier of the Civil War,* 2 vols. (Philadelphia: G. W. Jacobs, 1907), vol. 1, 332–33.

34. *CG,* 38, 1, 27 January 1864, 377 (Morrill); Paludan, *"A People's Contest,"* 130; James G. Blaine, *Twenty Years of Congress,* 2 vols. (Norwich: Henry Bill Publishing Company, 1884–86), vol. 1, 213–14; *CG,* 38, 1, 4 June 1864, 2750 (Representative Giles Hotchkiss of New York); A. B. Stone, J. E. Williams, H. B. Payne, A. Pope, W. B. Castle, and Daniel P. Rhodes to Justin Morrill, Cleveland, 10 August 1865, Justin S. Morrill Papers (Morrill ms), Box 7, 14 June 1864 to 19 October 1865, LC; Morrill to the Society for the Protection of American Industry, Stratford, 4 September 1865, ibid. On Morrill, see William B. Parker, *The Life and Public Services of Justin Smith Morrill* (Boston: Houghton Mifflin, 1924); Coy F. Cross II, *Justin Smith Morrill: Father of the Land-Grant Colleges* (East Lansing: Michigan State University Press, 1999).

35. *The Liberator,* 17 February 1865, in Stewart, *Wendell Phillips,* 257, 262.

36. Sumner to Lieber, Washington, 15 May 1864, Series I, Reel 64, SP.

37. Wood, *The Radicalism of the American Revolution;* Adam Smith, *An Inquiry into the Nature and Causes of the Wealth of Nations* (New York: Modern Library, 1937).

38. Richard Hofstadter, *Social Darwinism in American Thought,* rev. ed. (Boston: Beacon Press, 1955).

3

The Great Secession Winter and the Politics of Power and Responsibility

"A MEMORABLE DAY," conservative Republican George Templeton Strong wrote on 6 November 1860, election day. "We do not know yet for what." Abraham Lincoln knew, telling reporters, "Well, boys, your troubles are over, mine have just begun." In six years his party had vaulted from sectional opponents to the presidency. Its call for freedom, combined with other planks and a divided opposition, had produced a victory that made Republicans responsible for governing the Union. But first came the winter of Southern secession and Republican discontent. By 4 March 1861, when Lincoln took office, seven states had seceded and formed the Confederacy. For four months Republicans endured a frustrating preparation for responsibility, with everything they did subject to scrutiny. Victory and secession forced them into new stands on the future of slavery and the Union, and to redefine and refine their ideology and purpose.[1]

This preparation for responsibility exasperated Republicans, but that winter midwifed the Civil War party and its redefined ideology. During six years on the outside looking in, they had insisted on spreading ideas of free soil and free labor. During the four months they had spent partway in, trying to fill some of the vacuum left by President James Buchanan's irresolution and the South's departure, the dominant themes of their wartime ideology—freedom, union, and power—came to the fore. If the growth of freedom was needed to preserve the Union as the framers had designed it, the Union was even more crucial to preserving freedom. The party's power, then and later, was needed to save the Union, whether or not that Union stood for freedom as strongly as its new leaders did. In years to come, they sought to resolve that contradiction. To have a Union there must be freedom; to have freedom there must be a Union; to have both, there must be power to preserve and protect them. While it was less obvious than it would become, Republicans increasingly saw freedom, union, and power as complementary strands of a coherent ideology.[2]

The awareness and coherence developed over four years of war, but that winter provided a kind of laboratory for them to experiment with ideas of how they would use their power. At the same time, their quest to spread their beliefs about freedom and its implications (not just free soil and free labor but, for example, the freedom of thought and discussion that the South had denied anti-slavery forces) appeared endangered. Publicly and privately, Republican leaders wrestled with the meaning of events not just for the country but for their party. Ultimately, they also fought one another for power. The party's unelected leader, William Henry Seward, sought intellectual and political influence. He contributed to the party's evolution, while the elected but less familiar leader, Abraham Lincoln, became the most articulate voice of freedom, union, and power.

Power was a word that Republicans had grown accustomed to using in connection with others. They had elected a Speaker of the House and won several statehouses but were ignored or scorned at the White House, in the Senate, and on the Supreme Court. Few Republican leaders had held key jobs when they had belonged to other parties. Those of Democratic ancestry had been too anti-slavery for administrations led by the likes of Buchanan or Franklin Pierce. Even Whig refugees who had tasted power during their former party's two terms in the presidency had had little time to savor the sensation. Inexperience led Republicans to make mistakes, but meant that they approached their responsibilities without bad habits to unlearn. They could take their stand against Buchanan without having to answer whether they could do better than the incumbent; there simply was no way to know.

Acclimating to Victory

With their victory in 1860 came the opportunity for Republicans to mull what it meant. Their attitude varied from giddiness at their success to disdain for doomsaying opponents. Surely it was the apogee of "the cause of free speech and free labor" for them and for a nation slow to agree that slavery contradicted freedom. Relieved that Northerners had awakened to the moral decay they blamed on Southern rule, Republicans hailed them for voting against slavery and standing up to Southern threats to secede. John Nicolay, Lincoln's secretary, expressed a common wonderment: "I can scarcely realize that, after . . . so many defeats, I am at last rejoicing in a triumph which only two years ago we hardly dared dream about." Having dreamed far longer, Wendell Phillips spoke for abolitionists: "For the first time in our history, the slave has chosen a President."[3]

While this rhetoric went beyond that of any Republican stalwart, slavery had been decisive in the election, and the party saw a mandate to act against it. Those who called 6 November "a day of jubilee" were more prescient than they imagined. "At length the first of the great wishes of my life is accomplished," Salmon Chase said. "The slave power is overthrown. When will the other, namely the denationalization of slavery and . . . initiation of emancipation by state action, be realized?" Given how early-nineteenth-century religious revivals influenced abolitionism, and reform movements affected the party's birth and growth, it should be unsurprising that Republican responses to victory resonated with missionary zeal. They saw the election as providential for the Union. Whether conservative or radical, of Democratic or Whig origin, Republicans felt that winning the presidency opened a long-closed window to reform—or restored values they considered inherent in the Constitution. As Carl Schurz told Lincoln, "Yours . . . is the greatest mission that ever fell to the lot of mortal man: the restoration of original principles in the model Republic of the world." The nation, they believed, had fallen prey to an indecent system, denuding the government of the respectability that its people demanded and deserved. Republicans saw themselves as the Union's salvation.[4]

However optimistic and zealous they were, Republicans failed to sense that saving the Union would go beyond the metaphysical to the physical. Rather than restoring the Union of the fathers, they faced the challenge of rebuilding a Union riven by secession. Undeniably, Republicans began the long winter with their eyes open; victory did nothing to mitigate their view of Southerners as mad with power. William Cullen Bryant, the poet whose *New York Evening Post* spoke for Democrats turned radicals, said, "At our feet lies the carcass of that great oligarchy which has so long held the South silent through submission and fear; and has ruled the North through the treachery of northern men; and has tyrannized equally over both." Other radicals vented their spleen, with William Lloyd Garrison fuming at "bloody-minded tyrants . . . insane from . . . their lust of power and rule, their hatred of free institutions." From a different perspective, Charles Francis Adams, more conservative than radical, more analytical than emotional, saw that Southerners were interested only in "power. They must control the Government or . . . leave it."[5]

Yet most Republicans doubted that the South would leave the Union rather than give up power. The reasons varied: optimism, misjudging the Southern psyche, and a tendency to liken Southerners to the boy who cried wolf. After all, they had threatened to secede before, and then backed off even when the North met only some of their demands. "We are not prophets if the result . . . does not settle disunion," the unprophetic *Chicago Tribune* said, predicting no war and no problem with enforcing the law. Even as perspicacious a realist as Lyman Trumbull, the moderately radical senator from Illinois, expected Southerners to calm down once Republicans showed their ability to grasp the levers of power. Others expected "fire-eaters," the most rabidly secessionist Southerners, to fall silent when they realized that the South lacked the transportation and markets to survive on its own. Most Republicans agreed that the South hoped to frighten them into concessions to assure continued Southern dominance in Washington. In the minds of Republicans, their new power and responsibility meant that caving in was out of the question.[6]

Confident in Northern firmness and Southern bluster, and dubious about unfounded threats, Republicans underestimated Southern resolve and overestimated Southern unionism. Lincoln saw the fire-eaters as few, and doubted that Southerners would squander the patronage jobs that seceding from the Union would cost them. Party leaders such as Seward dismissed disunionism as temporary. Former Democrats Chase and Frank Blair—once allies, later enemies; one an Ohio radical, the other a border state conservative—agreed that Republicans should go about their business and ignore, as Blair put it, "the compromisers and the disunion twaddle." For politicians with only limited exposure to most of the Southern people, such attitudes might be dismissed as naive; for Blair, who had been in the trenches or much closer to them, to offer such advice suggests that Republicans adopted the languid attitude that they had heard it all before.[7]

However, Republicans occupied an unhappy position. They had won, but they had won little: the presidency remained weaker than it had been and would become, especially, many presumed, with an ex-Whig in the office. Nor would they easily retain it: no president since Andrew Jackson had won two terms; no party in the last two decades had kept the White House for consecutive terms except Democrats Pierce and Buchanan, who set an example that no Republican wished to emulate. Republicans believed that too much time in power had corrupted Democrats. They were more confident in their own honesty than in their ability to avoid the divisiveness that holding power can create or worsen. Thus, one of their first goals was to blunt intramural disputes. Worried New Yorkers begged state party boss Thurlow Weed to reconcile with radical *New York Tribune* editor Horace Greeley, and Ohioans urged Chase and Ben Wade to mend differences born of ambition for the Senate and control of the state party. Responsibility and power made it important for Republicans to get along; their minority status made it more so. As one ally warned Senator John Hale of New Hampshire, "Our enemies will be on the alert to take any advantage."[8]

While common fears of failure and disunity united Republicans, so did common hopes. Considering themselves the framers' heirs, they hoped to destroy the opposition, as Jeffersonians sought to do to Federalism. This was especially true of Democrats whom slavery drove into the Republican fold. Chase foresaw "a truly democratic party, which will control the Government," maybe permanently. Befitting Jacksonians who found their old party untrue to their cause, the Blairs' St. Louis organ separated democracy and Democracy: "The sovereignty of the people rising in awful majesty has overwhelmed the minions of oligarchical tyranny and slavery propagandism. The fiat has gone forth which transfers the sceptre from the . . . recreant and degenerate Democracy to another power." However unrealistic their claims, Republicans considered the Democratic party treasonous, if not to the country then certainly to its own precepts.[9]

Their views of opponents North and South stiffened Republicans' resolve to stay true to their ideology, which resonated well enough with Northern voters to elect them. But that ideology addressed what kinds of freedom should exist in the Union, from free soil to free speech, and not the Union's existence. Admitting that "we can even now have Union, but it is not so clear that we can have Union and Liberty. The object of the Union was to secure the blessings of Liberty," one Republican feared that "the Union might be preserved by measures . . . false to its original object." For others liberty was secondary, the Union primary. New York's conservative *Courier and Enquirer* caught this belief: "We love the Union, because at home and abroad, collectively and individually, it gives us character as a nation and as citizens of the Great Republic . . . [it] will make us the greatest, richest, and most powerful people on the face of the earth." Whether those ideas could unify Northerners worried Maryland's Henry Winter Davis: "The South has always been able, by its one common interest, to impose on the divided North its policy and views; the North has no bond of Union" to rank with the importance of slavery in the South.[10]

Each of these statements contained a kernel of the ideology that the party developed from its ascent to the presidency to the end of the Civil War. Republicans had argued in favor of freedom, and with victory came a duty to protect it. But the North and South defined freedom differently. They saw different purposes for the Union, and the North divided on the issue more easily than the South. Enough Northerners were ambivalent about slavery to place Republicans in a precarious position: if they wanted freedom, as their efforts to end the spread of slavery suggested, they could have it only with or in the Union. Accordingly, Republicans needed the North united behind them, and achieving this goal would take more than mere acceptance of the free labor ideology. Thus, freedom and union became inseparable. "Freeing the slaves and saving the Union were linked as one goal, not two optional goals," wrote Phillip Paludan. "The Union that Lincoln wanted to save was not a union where slavery was safe. He wanted to outlaw slavery in the territories, and thus begin a process that would end it in the states. Slave states understood this; that is why they seceded and why the Union needed saving." While addressing mainly the situation during the secession winter, Paludan described a process and an awareness that culminated in the creation of a different worldview from that with which Republicans had entered and waged the campaign of 1860.[11]

Peaceful Secession?

Power, naturally, came from the Republican presence in high office. With this came the need to convince Northerners and Southerners alike that the party was responsible enough to hold office and hold the Union together. To win the presidency and dissolve the Union would doom the party to a fate like that of the Whigs or Know-Nothings before Lincoln took the oath. Not that this sentiment was universal: if the South seceded, Ohio moderate Rutherford Hayes foresaw a Union "free—all free" and "full of vigor, industry, inventive genius, educated and moral," while Vermont moderate Justin Morrill, the financial wizard of the House, confessed, "If we could legally let all the slaveholders go, I don't know but I would say amen." How much of these sentiments amounted to bluster or wishful thinking is unclear; since Hayes wrote in his diary and Morrill to his wife, neither utterance was public. Yet some Republicans were disgusted enough with slavery and the South's unremitting defense of it to dream. If enough Southerners left Congress, Republicans could pass the legislation they deemed necessary to the nation's economic and social—it might even be called spiritual—development. By then the South would awaken to the inevitable: it could not survive on its own, and would return to a regenerated republic.[12]

Horace Greeley was the Republican who most staunchly advocated this sort of position, or so it appeared. Actually, as with Greeley himself, the appearance and reality of his positions were different from what they seemed—and reflected his and the party's uncertainties. Greeley had long denied a desire for office or power, but thirsted for them; his inability to obtain the former prompted him to dissolve his close relationship with New York bosses Seward and Weed, but he wielded the latter. His national weekly New York readership and lecture tours lent enormous weight to his views, which he expressed in the *Tribune* with an openness and inconsistency that left him ripe for attack and disputation. Believing that the South sought "to bully the Free States into concessions," he became the leading party spokesman for those who preferred to ignore the threats and let the rebels leave the Union if they wished. But as usual, his position was more complex than his critics claimed. If "champions of the Union have a fair opportunity to present and argue the matter to the People, secure against violence and outrage," he told a defender of the South, "and if the South declares for Disunion, I will join you in urging the requisite change in the Constitution to let them out." In case of an unprovoked war, he said, "If the Cotton States . . . become satisfied that they can do better out of the Union than in it, we insist on letting them go in peace." Then, to use force to keep them in the Union would be inconsistent with the Declaration of Independence.[13]

Greeley was familiar with inconsistency, but his qualifications rendered his call for peaceful secession far from adamant: Republicans and Southern unionists never presented their views to the South without impingement, and his writings about slavery and its defenders showed that he expected them to cause a war before he and other anti-slavery men did so. Greeley ultimately equated concessions to tossing aside the party's platform and principles, making its victory meaningless. Thus, peaceful secession was, for him, not to abdicate the party's newfound responsibilities, but to accept and realize them. The Republican ideology of free soil and free labor demanded commitment; Greeley simply tried to make clear that this commitment extended to a love of the Union, and that he was willing to tar Southerners with the brush of treason against the creation of the fathers.[14]

While Greeley's paeans to peaceful secession stamped him as actively inactive, many other Republicans similarly preferred to stand by and let the South react. Not only could they do little anyway, but they knew that many saw them as too radical to be trusted with power. At the same time, their political sensitivity petered out at the Mason-Dixon line; they viewed Southern unionism as a strong but sleeping force, sure to awaken. Despite cynicism about the South, and hindsight that shows the limited scope of Southern unionism, Republicans felt obligated to assure the North and South that they had no desire to turn the constitutional order upside down. As Seward waited for "popular solicitude" to "awaken patriotism in the South," he urged "respect and forbearance." Newly elected Governor John Andrew of Massachusetts, who veered between moderate and radical, told conservative Montgomery Blair that to aid Southerners "who are well disposed and have 'their faces zion-ward' . . . I would not, by irritating or mortifying words, add a feather's weight to the burden . . . imposed on them."[15]

In the days after Lincoln's victory, Republicans were willing to offer an olive branch—within limits. The *Chicago Tribune* repeated that the party would not interfere with slavery in the states, "to avoid . . . additional irritation and to convince the people of the South by our words and acts that we are not half so fierce and ravenous as we have been represented—that we are still their countrymen—bound to them by a thousand ties, which we would not rupture if we could." Philadelphia's *North American and United States Gazette* went further, disowning slavery as a key to Lincoln's victory and citing support for internal improvements, admitting Kansas, homesteads, and building a railroad to the Pacific. It reminded the South of the "vast difference between the . . . candidate for the Presidency and the President of the Union. One represents a party and the other the nation in its unity." That Republicans were adjusting to that difference was clear; what was clearer to the South than to the North was that however much Republicans played down slavery, that issue had united the party. Its policies had been and would remain anti-slavery.[16]

Republicans expected soothing words to help neither the South nor themselves. Even if moderation stalled secession in the upper South, they feared seeming cowardly. Worse, the party's platform and years of propaganda had convinced Southerners that Republicans planned to strike at slavery at the first opportunity. As they began to concede, if grudgingly, that the South might back up its words with action, Republicans were in the anomalous position of trying to be both strong and amenable, resulting in a policy of "masterly inactivity": the more they delayed, the less likely they were to stumble, and the better the chances of the South taking the initiative, thereby uniting the North and absolving Republicans of blame in the crisis. Bridging the gap between ideologue and politician, Senator William Pitt Fessenden of Maine advised that other Republicans should watch, "coolly, the enemy's game—for it is a game—give no occasion to our friends at home to think us either rash or timid."[17]

Yet Republicans debated meeting rashness with rashness. Two party groups, both crucial but neither in control of policy, claimed to be ready to fight. One, from border states, was more exposed to slavery and its defenders. Frank Blair saw two choices for his party: give in or go to war. "I do not hesitate to embrace the last alternative. Their arrogance has become intolerable and requires a rebuke," he said. The other group consisted of ardent radicals. One of them, Senator Zachariah Chandler of Michigan, told his state's governor, "Characterize Secession as

Treason. . . . There is nothing which the South dreads so much as trouble with the Northwest. Let her speak in *thunder tones.*"[18]

To find the Blairs and Chandler agreeing is revealing in several ways. The first is in what they had in common politically: western radical and border state Republicans faced a tougher fight for primacy in their region than party members elsewhere; pugnacity served them well. Proximity to slavery in the border states and the Northwest's proslavery or neutral views exposed them to the issue in more searing ways than it did New England Republicans, whose anti-slavery and party service won more notice from historians and contemporaries. Finally, four years and much party warfare later, Chandler helped engineer Montgomery Blair's departure from the Cabinet when the border state Republican's conservatism became too far out of step for radicals like Chandler to stomach. By 1864, circumstances and issues had changed dramatically, requiring that the party change, too.[19]

That evolution sped up when secession put the party in a delicate new position. When South Carolina seceded on 20 December 1860, the party's reaction revealed its unionism. The rhetoric with which Republicans attacked the South was more appropriate for that of a party taking responsibility for preserving a Union that one of its states would destroy than for an opposition fighting against slavery. Republicans denied that a state could secede and hoped to avoid war. But if firmness meant a fight, they were ready. While Lincoln vowed to regain any federal forts the South might take, other Republicans warned against testing their limited willingness to compromise. More important, anyone who assailed "this Union, which we prize so dearly, will be hung as high as Haman," said a New Yorker.[20]

Although such references to union reflected the refinement in the party's thought, the idea of freedom retained immense vitality. Republicans never doubted the triumph of free labor, but secession reminded them that the battle would be tough. For radicals to feel this way was understandable. Looking for any sign of the doom of slavery, they hoped that secession would turn more Northerners against it. But Frank Blair foresaw before South Carolina seceded that "the collision which they have determined to bring about must end in the destruction of slavery or the overthrow of our free institutions." His brother Montgomery added that the sin of Southern "pride which revolts against submission to supposed inferiors" had one solution: "a decisive defeat on this field. It will show the Southern people that they wholly mistake the . . . men they are taught by demagogues to despise." Seward's "irrepressible conflict" could end only one way, and Republicans sensed that the South was hastening it.[21]

Thus, the secession winter both frustrated and satisfied Republicans. Besides their usual criticism of the South's thirst for power and profit, they could add another complaint: Southerners were so determined to control the government that they would dissolve it if they failed to get their way. The party seemed as steadfast as ever in its refusal to mollify the South, but for different reasons: still hoping to stop the spread of slavery, Republicans argued more strongly for the Union's preservation. In particular, radicals made clear that only total capitulation—a wholesale denial of the platform on which their party had been elected—would satisfy the South. The bond of union that Henry Winter Davis had seen as unifying the South and dividing the North now helped unite Republicans.

The Power-to-Be in Opposition

The government itself also helped unite Republicans, by the way in which Buchanan reacted to secession and by Republicans' belief that they could do better. Adams deemed Buchanan's "zig-zag policy especially fitted to encourage disorder and revolution." Even the defense by John Dix, briefly his Treasury secretary and a War Democrat who later backed Lincoln, damned the old Democrat's judgment: "There is no warmer friend of the Union. I know no instance in history, in which the head of a government was more grossly deceived by those, in whom a generous confidence had been reposed."[22]

As much as they already disliked Buchanan, Republicans found his policy toward secession unspeakable. When his annual message attacked them for causing the crisis and denied both the right of secession and his power to stop it, Republican criticism reached a new crescendo. Seward decoded his words: "No state has the right to secede, unless it wants to. The Executive is bound to coerce a seceding state, unless the Executive be opposed in its efforts to do so." James Russell Lowell wrote that Buchanan considered the presidency "a retaining-fee paid him by the slavery-propagandists, and his Message to the present Congress looks like the last juiceless squeeze of the orange which the South is tossing contemptuously away." While Republicans never abated their criticism, the underlying tone changed: once the tool of the slave power, now Buchanan was to blame for failing to protect the Union. They had always believed that they could do a better job than he; now they would have the chance to prove it.[23]

But Republicans retained oppositionist tendencies. Judging Buchanan against his predecessors and successor, they assailed not just his policy but his patriotism. His failure to stand up to the South had nothing to do with perceptions of executive power; it was that he was putty in Southern hands. The *Chicago Tribune* said, "Honest Old Abe will not be a wooden President. . . . He promises to be a General Jackson"; Buchanan was "jelly to be moulded at will by the first man who seizes upon him." Unlike their Whig ancestors, who accused him of usurpation, Republicans saw Jackson as a guide. They tempered their attacks only when Buchanan shuffled his Cabinet, replacing secessionists with unionists who worked with the party: Attorney General Edwin Stanton gave inside information to Seward, Chase, and Sumner; and Dix sought aid from Seward and Governor Edwin Morgan of New York to push a financial program through Congress and obtain bank loans to keep the government running.[24]

Even as they built bridges, Republicans distrusted their foes. Although hoping to unite everyone in one party devoted to the Union, and aware of divisions among the opposition, they accused Democrats of lacking devotion to the Union—reversing Democratic criticisms and showing a stronger Republican commitment to the Union. Long before the lower South finished seceding, Morrill expected Northern Democrats to "leave the job of sustaining the Union and fighting traitors to the Republican Party." When Illinois Democrats met, the *Chicago Tribune*'s Charles Ray observed their convention and warned that "we have got an enemy right here in Illinois whom we must put down before we can approach the South." Republicans did little to convince Democrats that there was a place for them in the party and the government, but Democrats showed few signs of persuading Republicans that they deserved trust and were not out to divide and conquer the Republicans by inciting the North against them. When Senator Stephen Douglas of Illinois attacked the South for seceding but charged Republicans with making "partisan capital out of a question involving the peace and safety of the country," Representative Elihu Washburne of Illinois called his speech "utterly infamous and damnable" and "the crowning atrocity of his life."[25]

No Concession to Secession

Since they lacked official power and could ill afford, for the sake of their futures, to cave in to Democratic or Southern attacks, Republicans were in no position to compromise. That issue lay at the heart of their evolving ideology that winter. Despite their antipathy for the South, most Whigs and Democrats became conservative or moderate Republicans. They shaped a platform and nominated a candidate with broad appeal. More devoted to the Union as an end than radicals who saw it as a means to freedom, the end they sought, they would sacrifice minor principles to preserve the Union and their victory, enabling them to put larger principles into practice. If forced to choose between a small union of free states and a large union with slavery, radicals preferred the latter. Refugees from abolitionism and the Whig and Democratic anti-slavery fringes, they were used to working outside the political framework that the slave power dominated. Sumner ally Samuel Gridley Howe revealed how they differed from Republicans of more traditional ancestry: "What a Fetish do people make of this Union! How do they worship, and cherish, even the cancerous excrescences which shoot out from its Southern extremities!" Welcoming the power to turn their words into deeds, radicals were torn between guiding the South on the right path and ridding the Union of the obstacle to bigger anti-slavery plans. But if secessionists went South, Republicans would be hard-pressed to find reasons other than their avarice for power to justify why they let their most bitter opponents leave the Union.[26]

The response to this conundrum lay in a view common to most Republicans: it was impossible to satisfy the South without crippling the Union and the freedom they foresaw. Concessions that violated principle would be futile and prostitute their platform. Strong said, "The masses of the North must declare slavery just, beneficent, and expedient, and allow every Mississippian who chooses to visit New York to bring his niggers with him. Not merely his niggers; his rights over them." That was too much to concede. Worse, caving in to a threat might create more danger. The last thing the party needed upon taking power was to deny the right to use it to save the Union; destroying the Union might encourage a Southern republic or European powers to overrun what remained of the Union. Congressman Owen Lovejoy of Illinois summarized the party's concerns: it was "unpatriotic and unstatesmanlike to place all the glories of the past, all the immense and varied interests of the present, and all the glorious hopes of the future, at the mercy and caprice of any one State."[27]

Indeed, many Republicans saw placating the South as treasonous to their platform and supporters. The core of their argument was principle: they articulated a set of beliefs that could not be ignored. Many in the party agreed with Chase: "Inauguration first—adjustment afterwards." New Hampshire's Amos Tuck reflected a popular view: "We have nothing to give up, but principle, and that is sacred." Senator Preston King of New York "would rather die" than compromise. In power, Trumbull "would willingly concede almost anything, not involving principle," but to act beforehand meant "that the principles on which we carried the election are impracticable and wrong." That seemed like an unprecedented and unreasonable condition for taking power, but their words reveal that to Republicans, saving the Union and stopping the spread of slavery were, in fact, their principles. Thus, they had nothing to concede.[28]

Worse, if Republicans supplicated their way into power, what power would they have? They had always accepted the election of Southerners and Democrats. Daniel Gooch of Massachusetts asked the House, "Have the people of the free States fallen so low that they are willing . . . to buy the right . . . to administer the Government?" It would be wrong, and they would admit to being too weak to take power without selling their souls and putting themselves on the defensive even before they took responsibility for the government. To make matters worse, the slave power they had assailed for so long played into their hands by proving as grasping and lawless as they claimed. Consequently, the idea of power played a large role in Republican minds as the party tried to resolve how to preserve the Union and its commitment to freedom.[29]

Underscoring these concerns were the concessions that Republicans did suggest. They wanted to present themselves as firm, yet reasoned and responsible. Wade expressed the radical opposition to concessions when he proposed threatening to hang 200 traitors and compromising on 150. Some moderates backed restoring the Missouri Compromise line, and a few conservatives evinced interest in popular sovereignty. A popular idea was to require a two-thirds vote of Congress for expansion, giving the South a veto over growth into anti-slavery areas. Morgan urged Lincoln to pacify the South with new land by buying Cuba. Others showed inexperience with power by contradicting themselves. Representative Schuyler Colfax, a moderately radical young publisher from Indiana, opposed concessions and supported a restored 1820 line and a two-thirds vote of Congress to add new territory. Kentucky abolitionist Cassius Clay assailed compromises, proposed one of his own, and denied being at odds with the platform or his previous stands. Critics charged that he sought to look moderate in hopes of winning the kind of patronage job unlikely to go to Republicans who occupied the most radical, and seemingly least responsible, ground. Even if true, those comments revealed their concerns about appearances—to seem responsible and responsive might disarm and win over opponents.[30]

In addition to debates over compromise, the party's youth and the fluid political climate combined to create further problems. Before electing a president Republicans had spent only six years in the wilderness, a speedy rise that alarmed their foes. The party saw the need to prove trustworthy. Governor-elect Henry Lane of Indiana did not "feel like apologizing . . . for being found in the majority once in twenty years," but Republicans were concerned about reactions to them. The Whigs proved more ephemeral than expected, joining the Federalist, Know-Nothing, Free-Soil, and Liberty parties in the political graveyard. With three parties buried in a decade, Constitutional Unionists on the brink, and allegiances in flux, Republicans feared a similar fate. Adams and Ohio radical James Ashley fretted that "old Whigs" might talk other conservatives into compromising—the kind of weakness that helped kill the Whig party. Foes of compromise like John Potter of Wisconsin prepared to create "a genuine republican party, should the conservative influence in the present one destroy or demoralize us." To call them torn would overstate the case, but Republicans knew that to give up too much might rend them asunder; to give up too little would make them more susceptible to attack from all sides.[31]

Thus, Republicans looked askance at outsiders proposing compromise. Senator John Crittenden of Kentucky suggested extending the Missouri line and amending the Constitution to protect slavery. To some it was appealing: after all, conservatives reasoned, the 1820 compromise had worked until the Kansas-Nebraska Act. But more Republicans, especially radicals, found the plan appalling, a contradiction of their platform. Nor would they do what the framers had refused to do: put the word *slavery* into the Constitution. When the House and Senate voted down the plan, no Republican voted for it. Old Ohio Whig Thomas Corwin's proposal to amend the Constitution to ban interference with slavery where it existed attracted a few conservative Republicans, who knew that it would never pass. Republicans saw that the desire for compromise was prevalent outside—and to some extent inside—the party and moved carefully.[32]

Nor did it soothe the party's nerves when a Peace Conference met in Washington in February 1861. Not yet in power, Republicans made clear that compromise was unacceptable. While New York legislators urged delegates to stand by the Constitution, Governor William Buckingham of Connecticut backed concessions if there were no "new guarantees for the protection of property in men"—in other words, no concessions. Other Republican governors took the hint, refusing to send delegates or naming only those who would give no ground. By sending delegates who opposed compromise without hostile rhetoric, they showed border states and wavering Southerners that they could acclimate themselves to power and responsibility. Their caution paid off: when others proposed to limit expansion and restore the Missouri Compromise, Republicans held out for "free labor and free institutions," reminding Southerners that secession would leave them at fault in case of war. As moderate John Murray Forbes of Massachusetts wrote, "So our tremendous Peace Congress has adjourned. . . . Yes, we did one thing—talked three weeks & amused the readers of the Tribune. Not such very bad eggs to hatch after all."[33]

Many Republicans supported and engineered these tactics out of a belief that holding the line until Lincoln took power would serve the party and country. Republicans believed in promoting freedom, and saving the Union seemed the best means to that end. Besides, they felt, if the North gave up anything, the South would ask for more. That required Republicans to stand up to the South. Perhaps that would endanger the Union. But ideally it would save the Union and freedom and demonstrate, for themselves and to others, an acceptance of power. To stand firm would not place freedom above union, but would acknowledge their connection in the face of a threat to both. Nor would Republicans accept the Southern view that concessions would serve freedom and union. Adams cut through the rhetoric: "The true grievance . . . is the loss of power and the apprehension that power in other hands than theirs will gravitate us towards a policy of freedom."[34]

The Three Wisest Men

Understanding what the party did and did not do during the secession winter requires insight into the evolving minds of its leaders. Three men stood out as shapers of the party's thought: Seward, who saw himself as the leading Republican regardless of the nominee; his close friend Adams, whose background gave him particular insight; and Lincoln. Since he was outside Washington, Lincoln was the most distant from power at that time; as president-elect, the most powerful of all; and as the least-known of the three, the least accustomed to power. What they said and did while the party lacked the power to settle the fate of freedom and union is crucial to analyzing the party's changing ideology.

That winter was one of change for Republicans, and Seward and Adams knew it better than most of their party. Unlike most Republicans, they not only advocated compromise but led the charge for it, or so it seemed. To offer concessions, they felt, would not deviate from principle since they expected the South to say no—a crucial point. It also would keep the two sides talking and lull the South into taking no action. They knew that Lincoln would be less pliable than Buchanan, yet Lincoln stopped short of what Seward and Adams offered the South. Seward and Adams sought to buy time for the party to cultivate Northern opinion, build union sentiment in the South and the border states, and assure the transfer of power to Lincoln. Their efforts created party fissures that proved hard to heal. Many radicals believed that they succeeded only in selling out the party, but Seward and Adams achieved enough of their goals to smooth the path to taking power and governing effectively. Seward called Adams "the only man who has comprehended the policy for the present emergency," but

Adams found it "useless to look so far forward at this time." While untrue, the comment distinguished him from the more visionary Seward and highlighted how Republicans had to think of the present and future.[35]

Still, Adams's vision was broader than that of most. His father, John Quincy Adams, had opposed the South's "gag rule" against abolitionist literature in the mails; Charles Francis Adams had been the Free-Soil vice-presidential candidate in 1848 and earned a reputation as a leader after only one term in the House. He had a finely tuned sense of history from a heritage that enhanced his symbolic role. Only capitulation would satisfy the South, he reasoned; if the North refused, the South would be at fault and the world would know it—a view that stamped him as seeing that the party must look beyond the issue of freedom to the court of public opinion for the power to govern. Seeking a better way out than Crittenden's, he hoped to avoid a party split, "combine the preservation of our principles with a policy sufficiently conciliatory to bridge over the chasm of a rebellion," and "re-establish confidence . . . to dispel panic, to rouse the loyal."[36]

His reputation and views made Adams a logical choice for the House Committee of Thirty-Three, created that December. Expecting any deal to play into secessionist hands, radicals opposed creating the group, which consisted of a congressman from each state. Neither it nor its Senate counterpart, the Committee of Thirteen, produced a compromise agreeable to either side, but Adams conjured up a ploy: statehood for New Mexico. Despite having opposed the Compromise of 1850, Adams proposed to honor its provision allowing slavery in the sparsely populated area. Since slavery had never gained a foothold and the territory's economy had few links to the South, Adams was offering the South a pyrrhic victory—a slave state with fewer than one hundred slaves. As he expected, Southerners said no. By declining what they claimed to want—the growth of slavery—they appeared unreasonable, thus doing what Adams wanted and expected.[37]

While a few Republicans saw what Adams was up to, his plan unleashed a torrent of criticism. Lincoln agreed on the need to aid the border states, Seward lauded him, and even old Jacksonian Gideon Welles appreciated his motives. But radical reactions ranged from perplexity to apoplexy. John Jay, another founder's grandson, asked, "Is it Charles Francis Adams . . . who consents that New Mexico shall be cursed with slavery? and *[sic]* recommends to the Republican party to deny their principles and appease a state in armed rebellion, and mollify others that are insulting and outraging . . . Northern citizens within their borders?" Others complained that he had revitalized slavery and ruined the party in one fell swoop.[38]

Thus, Adams ended up in the odd position of defending his antislavery credentials. Piqued at his friend for what he saw as a lack of principle, Sumner accused him of apostasy. Adams countered that his party needed to adapt to power, and he doubted that Sumner could because he was not "tolerant of differences of sentiment." Besides, the South had turned him down, so his plan must have been meaningless. He said, "Others may differ . . . but I can scarcely imagine a more impregnable position for the free states." He hoped that it was clear to the border state men he tried to influence that the North was accommodating and the South was intransigent. That was the point of the speech he delivered to the House on 31 January 1861. The South had no need to fear that his party would stop the spread of slavery, because it would stop anyway: "The law of political economy . . . guides this species of labor to the most suitable place, and that place is not the Territory of the United States." He spun the issue from his party's radicalism to Southern obstructionism. He urged that the South accept defeat with the equanimity the North showed in defeat and, with the New Mexico proposal, in victory. If the South refused, it was at fault.[39]

Adams played a dangerous game. Had the South accepted his proposal, he would have been unprincipled if he went along and dishonest if he did not. But he knew better. The South was too far out on the secessionist limb to climb off it for so little. Adams made clear that some in his party saw compromise as a ploy that cost them nothing; to others, even to hint at concession was unconscionable. This was hardly the first division over the means to the ends the party sought, but it typified how, seeking the same ends, Republicans argued over details. This was a holdover from their days in opposition, when they had regularly attacked those who disagreed with them; it was also a sign of the realities and ambitions of pure politics. At times they forgot what Adams remembered: "I think I know the difference between surrendering unimportant points and sacrificing principles."[40]

Many Republicans doubted that was true of Seward. If Adams appeared to be on the wrong path, Seward seemed lost. Differing from

Adams more in style than in substance, Seward shared the goal of delay, but his actions were suspect because he was so many things that Adams was not: fun-loving, personable, amoral, humorous, a politician to his toenails. For a generation he and Weed had run New York's Whig and Republican machine. He said, "Seward is Weed and Weed is Seward. What I do Weed approves. What he says, I endorse. We are one," and Weed's *Albany Evening Journal* was their organ. That proved risky when Weed offered what many saw as a capitulation to the South. Two weeks after Lincoln won, sure that an "overawed Union sentiment" would overtake the South if encouraged, Weed suggested several concessions, most notably restoring the Missouri line. This contradicted the platform and Seward, but Weed was at the forefront of mingling the ideas of freedom, union, and power. "In abhorrence of slavery I am behind no man," he said, but, like Adams, "I want to occupy practical and efficient, instead of absurd and useless ground. Some of the Slave States can be saved." He would neither go far nor give up much: if the South refused to be reasonable, "war with all its miseries must be accepted. Freedom is worth all it ever costs. . . . If war shall be . . . waged against freedom, there can be no question as to how it will terminate."[41]

The reaction to Weed showed that the party's acclimation to the mix of freedom, union, and power was not painless. Radicals and ex-Democrats questioned his proposals, partly because they distrusted him; as Sumner said, "he is a politician—not a statesman." The more critical question of where Seward stood went unanswered. Confessing that Weed "brought perplexities about me, which he, with all his astuteness, did not foresee," Seward found it amusing when Charles Dana—Greeley's aide and, given his employer's view of Seward, a dubious source—accused him of delusions of succeeding Clay as an architect of compromise and claimed that "the voice was the voice of Seward, though the hand was the hand of Weed." Many surmised that Seward floated a trial balloon, with Weed poised to take the fall in case of trouble. For his part, when a Senate caucus demanded that he explain himself, Seward said, "I told them they would know what I think and what I propose when I do myself."[42]

The mystery was as Seward wanted it. He devoted himself to intricate maneuvering and keeping everyone guessing. He met with Crittenden and Douglas to seek common ground and consulted with members of Buchanan's Cabinet. He gave a toast at Douglas's home:

"Away with all parties, all platforms, all previous committals, and whatever else will stand in the way of restoration of the American Union." In December at a New York dinner, Seward announced that all would be well in sixty days, and his optimism was so much more buoyant than that of other Republicans that it made them suspicious. Sumner warned of "Sewardism which sees nothing but peace and fraternity," but Strong found him "talking of conciliation and arrangement as likely to be effected, perhaps—but not worth much effort." Fire-eater Robert Toombs called Seward the least conciliatory member of the Senate committee appointed to seek a compromise. Seward even said, "I want the north to be mad. . . . If they can only be kicked hard enough to make 'em hit out, there's some chance of settling this matter," but what settlement he preferred was a mystery.[43]

Addressing the Senate on 12 January amid criticism and uncertainty, Seward showed the change in party thought from freedom to a Union with freedom. Like partisanship, "Republicanism is subordinate to the Union, as everything else is and ought to be," he told the Senate; the "Union is not more the body than Liberty is the soul of the nation." What his party wanted for the Union was clear: "Free movement everywhere through our own land and throughout the world; free speech, free press, free suffrage." While "legislative compromises which sacrifice honestly cherished principles . . . are less sure to avert imminent evils than they are certain to produce . . . greater dangers," the real danger was disunion and its effect on "the majestic drama of national progress." Thus, to radicals' horror, he backed a constitutional amendment to protect slavery in the states, since the party platform said much the same thing. He proposed to repeal the personal liberty laws that Northern states had instituted to stop the return of fugitive slaves; enforce the fugitive slave law more stringently; build a railroad to the Pacific for each section; hold a national convention to hear all disputes; and split all unorganized land into slave and free territory.[44]

Seward's oration reflected his party's changing ideology amid changing circumstances. He saw two key issues. One was to inaugurate Lincoln with as undivided a union as possible, assuring the ascent of a party ready to wield its new power to protect both freedom and union. The other was himself. Sure of his indispensability to the Republican and Union cause, Seward considered himself the party's shrewdest operator, best suited to keep it pointed the right way until it took over the White House. Thus, in contradicting much of what he had said over the years, he gave up little or nothing substantial. Republicans had no need for what he conceded, and the South had no desire for it. This begs the question: If concessions would fail, why offer them? The answer is that Seward, like Adams, saw the value of appearances. As they entered power, it was crucial for the party to appear and to be reasonable and responsible. In the process, Seward put the onus on the South to accept or reject what his party was willing to offer.[45]

Whether Republicans agreed with or understood Seward's machinations depended on their spot on the ideological spectrum. Radicals were livid, contending that he had abandoned whatever scruples he had. Yet, wittingly or not, they saw his intentions. Attacking his "tone of surrender," Sumner said that he backed no "positive scheme of compromise." Hale wrote from his desk that Seward "has been talking an hour without . . . saying anything, and . . . probably will not." Thaddeus Stevens said, "I have listened to every word, and by the living God, I have heard nothing." When John Ten Eyck, a New Jersey conservative, backed his proposals in a Senate caucus, Seward refused to introduce them as legislation. He saw his suggestions as part of the party's effort to obtain power; the paean to freedom and union, and the irresponsibility he sought to pin on the rebels, mattered more.[46]

What Lincoln thought and did about compromise and the Republican role was potentially still more important. Other Republicans tried to influence him. Party secretary George Fogg warned him that Seward was disloyal. Weed visited Springfield and tried to make Lincoln his puppet; instead, Lincoln used him as a mouthpiece, an intermediary, and an adviser. Seward served as Lincoln's capital correspondent, reporting what was—or what he thought was—going on, never giving himself the worst of it. But Lincoln had a role to play and ideas to express. He did so subtly and well, adding his views to the party's evolving ideology.[47]

Amid uncertainty about where and how firmly he stood, Lincoln proved to be a rock for his party to lean on. Hoping to calm the South, he inserted a paragraph in a Trumbull speech, repeating his promise not to interfere with slavery in the states but attacking the fire-eaters who "persistently bespattered every Northern man by their misrepresentations." He warned Republicans against yielding on slavery in the territories and dismissed popular sovereignty as wrong because it "acknowledges that slavery has equal rights with liberty." If firmness meant war, Lincoln found that acceptable sooner rather than later, and "would use all the constitutional powers of the Government for its preservation," foreshadowing a broad vision of what the president could do, at least in wartime.[48]

Lincoln instilled confidence in Republicans, but he also worried them. He left Springfield for Washington on 11 February and spoke at train stops en route. While he was true to the party's ideology, his words were like his route: circuitous. He was loath to say much before taking office, and many felt that he should have been satisfied with his performance. His vague, seemingly theoretical speeches appeared to contain nothing of use or note. Yet their cumulative reading and effect were significant. He often referred to the responsibility he faced, the evils of partisanship, and the need to preserve the Union—the sometimes contradictory thoughts with which many Republicans wrestled that winter. His comments represented and foreshadowed the ideology of freedom, union, and power that drove Republicans then and especially during the war to come.[49]

In tiptoeing around the issues to avoid giving offense, Lincoln irked those who sought substance, but he conveyed his thinking to his audiences. With Sewardian optimism, he assured the North that all would be well. He denied that slavery was in danger, shifting blame to the South, and deemed the crisis artificial. He joined Seward in seeking to buy time and voicing reverence for the Union, expressed in allusions to the unionism of Henry Clay and Daniel Webster and in reminders to the South that "we are all united in one feeling for the Union." Like Seward, he also linked the Union and freedom: "When the people rise in masses in behalf of the Union and the liberties of their country, truly may it be said, 'The gates of hell shall not prevail against them.'" In calling "working men . . . the basis of all governments," repeating his support for a Homestead Act, and preaching about man's "duty to improve . . . his own condition," he showed that free labor and free laborers remained a key component of Republican thought as the party played for the bigger stakes of power and the Union.[50]

Yet his words vexed many Republicans, even those who agreed with him. His ambiguous comments on the tariff left protectionist Pennsylvanians cold. Echoing those who doubted that he took the crisis seriously, Samuel Bowles of the *Springfield Republican* said, "Lincoln is a simple Susan." An abolitionist dismissed his speeches but added, "I am obliged to own that I do not see how under the circumstances Cicero himself could make wise ones." Others saw his trip as beneficial, introducing him to the public and revealing a mixture of kindness and toughness that gave Northerners more confidence in him than before. The *Chicago Tribune* claimed that he gave "the fishy ones 'fever and ague.' . . . They see fight in the old fellow's eye."[51]

Indeed, Lincoln was less oblique than his detractors claimed. Nothing, he said, "can ever bring me willingly to consent to the destruction of this Union"—as blunt a warning to the South as could be delivered. A tribute to the Constitution dismissed John Calhoun's theory of minority rights as antithetical to the American system of politics and government. Lincoln vowed "no blood shed unless . . . forced upon the Government," meaning an attack would be repelled and the South would cause it. He also qualified his commitment by promising "to preserve the peace of this country so far as it can possibly be done, consistently with the maintenance of the institutions of the country." He meant to maintain them, come what may.[52]

In the days before his inaugural, Lincoln and his party further revealed their ideological shift, their eagerness to grasp power, and their growing sense of responsibility. Warned of an assassination plot in Baltimore, Lincoln skulked into Washington in the early morning, irking Republicans opposed to any sign of weakness, even at the risk of his life. Avoiding a show of fear or mercy, Republicans vowed to act forcefully. Chandler "would have had him go through Baltimore in open day if a thousand had to be killed." But Lincoln told Peace Conference delegates, "My course is as plain as a turnpike road. It is marked out by the Constitution," which must be "respected, obeyed, enforced, and defended, let the grass grow where it may"—a sign of his readiness to take charge. A *Chicago Tribune* reporter said, "Thank God, the country has at last got an honest brave and true MAN for President. . . . All hail to the national regeneration!"[53]

An Inaugural Salvo

Lincoln hoped to promote regeneration in his Inaugural Address, one of the critical documents in the history of Republican ideology. This was the ultimate guide to its author, who knew that everyone would scrutinize it. It offered insight into its editors, who shared its sentiments but softened its rhetoric: Seward, who urged a conclusion that reassured the South and bolstered Southern unionism; the Whiggish Orville Browning, who wanted Lincoln to blame the South; old Democrat Francis Preston Blair, who called the speech "strong and correct"; and Douglas, who agreed with Seward and promised to put the Union above partisanship. It revealed whether Lincoln would appease the South. Above all, it encapsulated how Republicans had changed over a long winter in which they had learned to accept responsibility for their words and deeds, and for the powers of government.[54]

Thus, on 4 March 1861, Lincoln took the oath of office and delivered a conciliatory yet firm address. Citing his speeches and the party platform, he recited the familiar litany, but additional meanings could be read into it. In saying that Southerners had nothing to fear from him, he made clear that power now rested in his hands, not theirs. Assuring that "all the protection which, consistently with the Constitution and the laws, can be given, will be cheerfully given to all the States when lawfully demanded, for whatever cause," he reminded the South that its demands, expressed through secession, were unlawful. Despite misgivings, he vowed to abide by the Fugitive Slave Act, but the rebellion could change that. In calling the Union "much older than the Constitution," he argued for its perpetuity by hearkening to the Declaration of Independence, presaging the "new birth of freedom" at Gettysburg and underscoring the importance that Republicans attached to freedom in creating and preserving the Union. Peaceable or not, secession was "legally void" and "insurrectionary and revolutionary." In promising to execute the laws, Lincoln sought to avoid "bloodshed or violence" unless it was "forced upon the national authority." He signaled that he might use force, but preferred not to do so—at least not yet.[55]

After this mixture of the carrot and the stick, Lincoln merged logic and toughness with double-edged eloquence. The "only substantial dispute," he said, was clear: "One section of our country believes slavery is right, and ought to be extended, while the other believes it is wrong, and ought not to be extended." His stand was clear. Given their proximity and the chances of discord, "Physically speaking, we cannot separate," perhaps admitting that mentally, they had separated. His conclusion, suggested by Seward, assured Southerners of his belief in union; while accommodating, he would take responsibility for the common good; and the North and South once had united for freedom, and the North still believed in it. He said, "The mystic chords of memory, stretching from every battle-field, and patriot grave, to every living heart and hearthstone, all over this broad land, will yet swell the chorus of the Union, when again touched, as surely they will be, by the better angels of our nature," showing that he remained convinced of the power of Southern unionism. But as often happened in Lincoln's speeches, the penultimate paragraph had a slightly different voice from the last: "In your hands, my dissatisfied fellow countrymen, and not in mine, is the momentous issue of civil war. The government will not assail you. You can have no conflict, without being yourselves the aggressors. You have no oath registered in Heaven to destroy the government, while I shall have the most solemn one to 'preserve, protect and defend' it." He would honor that oath and in the process put the onus on the South.[56]

If Lincoln meant his speech to be all things to all people—and he did—he succeeded admirably. Radicals blanched at his support for the fugitive slave law, conservatives at his characterization of slavery as potentially offensive to Southern unionists. From the middle came complaints that declining to use force, if only for the moment, was redolent of Buchanan. Most Republicans, praising what he said and how he said it, were relieved that Lincoln now held the office that empowered him to say it. They saw that he veered from forcefulness to accommodation, offering something for everyone. They could take solace that Douglas muttered agreement as Lincoln spoke, puzzled over just what he meant, and concluded, "I defend the inaugural if it is as I understand it, namely, an emanation from the brain and heart of a patriot, and as I mean . . . to act the part of a patriot, I indorse it." The speech was murky enough to confuse possible foes, but not at the cost of ideological purity: Lincoln would protect freedom and union with the power that grew from them and, as the *New York Times* warned, "If the Union cannot be saved on this basis and consistently with these principles, then it is better that it should not be saved at all."[57]

Lincoln, Seward, and Adams symbolized what their party stood for and would stand for. Radicals complained that Seward thought "Union worth more than Liberty," but the truth was more complex. Republicans had had no desire for war with Buchanan still in office;

Seward and Adams had sought to slow the Southern gallop into secession to a crawl, if not stop it. Despite pressure from seceded states and from within, the border states stayed in the Union. To give Seward and Adams all of the credit would go too far, but they contributed significantly to the party's evolving ideology. After making a speech that reflected the party's shift in emphasis, Seward encapsulated the change. "Twelve years ago, freedom was in danger, and Union was not. I spoke then so singly for freedom that short-sighted men inferred that I was disloyal," he said in February. "Today . . . freedom is not in danger and the Union is. . . . Now, therefore, I speak singly for Union." While slaves and their sympathizers would have disputed his view of freedom, his analysis had merit, but it would have been more correct to say that freedom was in danger because the Union was in danger. Seward, Adams, and other Republicans spoke for both in an effort to assure that their party would have the power to guide freedom as well as union out of danger.[58]

During the secession winter, Republicans had been caught between external and internal forces. From without, they belonged to a large, unionist bloc of Northerners who supported the Union but had to overcome the sense among their foes, and perhaps themselves, that their stand on slavery contributed to disunion. From within, Republicans had to reconcile what they had been with what they were becoming. As outsiders they could oppose the actions of insiders—Buchanan and his allies. On the issue of disunion, though, Republicans acted with a sense of responsibility for the Union; they lacked the power to lead, but their constituents watched closely enough for them not to lapse into the role of constant critics. While used to that role, they changed in approach and view, attacking Democrats not just as tools of slavery and opponents of freedom, but as acquiescent accomplices in the Union's destruction. Unused to power and uncertain about how much of it they would exercise, Republicans saw themselves as what Lincoln later called "the last best hope of earth." Republican leaders had the self-assurance needed in successful politicians and expected in those dedicated to a cause. What they knew, what was sure, was their belief in an ideology devoted to freedom and union. That was more than they could say of Southerners out to destroy that Union, and of Democrats seemingly willing to let them do so. Their distrust of and disrespect for those who allowed or encouraged secession, and their confidence in their own abilities, made Republicans certain that, as Lincoln said, if "the tug has to come," they could handle it. Accordingly, they had little patience with those who threatened the Union or asked them to compromise their principles to save it.[59]

For Lincoln and most of the rest of his party, it was the first time they could significantly affect the policy of the country and its government. The possibility of power had done little to alter the Republican ethos; the 1860 platform had combined all that its authors had said for several years. But the preparation for power that secession winter had been another matter entirely. Whatever Republicans said or did between Lincoln's election and inaugural would affect the Union's survival. They had long campaigned for a form of freedom—free soil and free labor—and finally succeeded on that issue. With success came a potentially devastating price: the dissolution of the Union they had been elected to govern, and the loss of the power to spread freedom throughout that Union. The secession winter revealed to Republicans the inseparable nature of freedom, union, and power, and provided them with a course of thought to follow and to guide them. They could be true to their principles and their goal of extending freedom, securing the Union, and gaining and wielding the power to do both.

NOTES

1. Tuesday, 6 November 1860, in Nevins and Thomas, eds., *The Diary of George Templeton Strong,* vol. 3, 58–59; Stephen B. Oates, *With Malice Toward None: The Life of Abraham Lincoln* (New York: Harper and Row, 1978), 195; George Hochfield, ed., *Henry Adams: The Great Secession Winter of 1860–1861 and Other Essays* (New York: Sagamore Press, 1958), 1–32.

2. Potter, *Lincoln and His Party;* Stampp, *And the War Came;* and Maury Klein, *Days of Defiance: Sumter, Secession, and the Coming of the Civil War* (New York: Alfred A. Knopf, 1997).

3. John G. Nicolay to Therena Bates, Springfield, 11 November 1860, John G. Nicolay Papers (Nicolay ms), LC, in Helen Nicolay, *Lincoln's Secretary: A Biography of John G. Nicolay* (New York: Longmans Green, 1949), 45; Irving Bartlett, *Wendell Phillips, Brahmin Radical* (Boston: Beacon Press, 1962), 223. See *New York Evening Post,* 7 November 1860; Henig, *Henry Winter Davis,* 139.

4. *Weekly Chicago Democrat,* 17 November 1860, in Don E. Fehrenbacher, *Lincoln in Text and Context* (Stanford: Stanford University Press, 1988), 43; Salmon P. Chase to Lincoln, Columbus, 7 November 1860, Robert Todd Lincoln Papers (Lincoln ms), LC; Chase to Edward L. Pierce, Columbus, 7 November 1860, in Albert Bushnell Hart, *Salmon Portland Chase* (Boston: Houghton Mifflin, 1899); Carl Schurz to Lincoln, n.p., 7 November 1860, Lincoln ms, LC; John Greenleaf Whittier to Chase, n.p., 9 November 1860, in William B. Hesseltine, *Lincoln and the War Governors* (New York: Alfred A. Knopf, 1948); Galusha Grow to Israel Washburn, Glenwood, 12 November 1860, Israel Washburn Papers (Israel Washburn ms), Volume 2, LC; Trefousse, *The Radical Republicans,* 138; Quincy, 6 November 1860, Diary of Charles Francis Adams, Adams Family ms, Series I, Reel 75, MHS; John Bigelow to William Hargreaves, New York, 10 November 1860, Bigelow ms, Box 1, NYPL. On religion and abolitionism, see James Brewer Stewart, *Holy Warriors: The Abolitionists and American Society* (New York: Hill and Wang, 1976).

5. *New York Evening Post,* 7 and 9 November 1860; *The Liberator,* 16 November 1860, in Stampp, *And the War Came,* 249; *New York Tribune,* 17 November 1860.

6. *Chicago Tribune,* 8 and 9 November 1860, in Phillip L. Kinsley, *The Chicago Tribune,* 3 vols. (Chicago: *Chicago Tribune,* 1960), vol. 1, 133–34; Trumbull to Chase, Springfield, 8 November 1860, Salmon P. Chase Papers (Chase ms), Box 11, Historical Society of Pennsylvania, Philadelphia (HSP); 22 November 1860, in Howard K. Beale, ed., *The Diary of Edward Bates, 1859–1866,* vol. 4 of the Annual Report of the American Historical Association for the Year 1930 (Washington: Government Printing Office, 1933), 157; Bigelow to Hargreaves, New York, 10 November 1860, Bigelow ms, Box 1, NYPL; Wade to Trumbull, Jefferson, 14 November 1860, Trumbull ms, Reel 7, LC; Bartlett, *Wendell Phillips,* 234; Stampp, *And the War Came,* 14–17; Nevins and Thomas, eds., *The Diary of George Templeton Strong,* 9 November 1860, 61.

7. Oates, *With Malice Toward None,* 196–98; Potter, *Lincoln and His Party,* 295–96, 310; Frank Blair to Chase, St. Louis, 20 December 1860, Chase ms, Box 2, HSP; Horner, *Lincoln and Greeley,* 188; George H. Mayer, *The Republican Party, 1854–1964,* 2d ed. (New York: Oxford University Press, 1967), 77; *New York Tribune,* 8, 12, 15, and 20 November 1860.

8. E. F. Read to John P. Hale, West Swanzey, 10 November 1860, John P. Hale Papers (Hale ms), Box 12, New Hampshire Historical Society (NHHS). See also *New York Evening Post,* 7 November 1860; Stampp, *And the War Came,* 175, 206; *New York Times,* 12 November and 4 December 1860; Potter, *Lincoln and His Party,* 275; R. T. Eldredge Jr. to Weed, Centre White Creek, 7 November 1860, Thurlow Weed Papers (Weed ms), UR; Fish to Weed, New York, 15 December 1860, ibid.; Thomas C. Durant to Weed, 6 January

1861, ibid.; Chase to George G. Fogg, Columbus, 15 December 1860, George G. Fogg Papers (Fogg ms), Box 1, NHHS; James G. Randall, *Lincoln the President: Springfield to Gettysburg,* 2 vols. (New York: Dodd, Mead, 1945), vol. 1, 226.

9. Wade to Trumbull, Jefferson, 14 November 1860, Trumbull ms, Reel 7, LC; Chase to Trumbull, Columbus, 12 November 1860, ibid.; *St. Louis Democrat,* n.d., in Herbert Mitgang, ed., *Lincoln As They Saw Him* (New York: Praeger, 1980), 211–12; James C. Stone to Sumner, Charlestown, 17 December 1860, Reel 21, SP.

10. *Hartford Evening Press,* 3 December 1860, in Perkins, ed., *Northern Editorials on Secession,* vol. 1, 112; *New York Courier and Enquirer,* 1 December 1860, in Stampp, *And the War Came,* 244 and *passim; CG,* 36, 2, 7 February 1861, Appendix, 185.

11. Paludan, *The Presidency of Abraham Lincoln,* xv, 3–68. On differing definitions of freedom, see Morgan, *American Slavery, American Freedom;* Eric Foner, "The Meaning of Freedom in the Age of Emancipation," *Journal of American History* 81, no. 2 (September 1994), especially 441–47; Foner, *The Story of American Freedom.*

12. 24 January 1861, in Charles R. Williams, ed., *The Diary of Rutherford B. Hayes,* 5 vols. (Columbus: Ohio State Archaeological and Historical Society, 1922), vol. 2, 2–3; Justin S. Morrill to Ruth Morrill, Washington, 29 December 1860, and 13 January 1861, Morrill ms, Reel 6, LC.

13. Potter, *Lincoln and His Party,* 52–53; *New York Tribune,* 8, 12, 15, 20, 26, and 30 November 1860; 14 January 1861; 23 February 1861; Robert S. Harper, *Lincoln and the Press* (New York: McGraw-Hill, 1951), 102; Horner, *Lincoln and Greeley,* 189–91; Alexander, *A Political History of the State of New York,* vol. 2, 335.

14. On Greeley's twists and turns in the secession winter and throughout his life, see Van Deusen, *Horace Greeley,* and Isely, *Horace Greeley and the Republican Party.*

15. William Seward to Israel Washburn, Albany, 16 December 1860, Washburn ms, Volume 2, LC; John Andrew to Montgomery Blair, 24 November 1860, Blair-Lee Family Papers (Blair-Lee Family ms), Box 7, Princeton University; *New York Tribune,* 1–14 February 1861; Potter, *Lincoln and His Party,* 238–39, 331.

16. *Chicago Tribune,* 9 and 24 November 1860, in Kinsley, *The Chicago Tribune,* vol. 1, 134–36; *New York Times,* 6–8 November 1860; Stampp, *And the War Came,* 64; *North American and United States Gazette,* 7 November 1860, in Perkins, *Northern Editorials on Secession,* 80–82.

17. James Dixon to Jeremiah Black, 14 November 1860, Jeremiah S. Black Papers (Black ms), LC; Joseph Schafer, ed., *Intimate Letters of Carl Schurz,*

1841–1869 (Madison: State Historical Society of Wisconsin, 1928), 232; *Springfield Republican,* 19 December 1860, in Stampp, *And the War Came,* 45; William Pitt Fessenden to Fish, Washington, 15 December 1860, Fish ms, Volume 47, LC; Duane E. Tucker, "Schurz's Jubilation Speech," in J. Jeffrey Auer, ed., *Antislavery and Disunion, 1858–1861: Studies in the Rhetoric of Compromise and Conflict* (New York: Harper and Row, 1963), 287–88; John W. North to George Loomis, Springfield, 21 November 1860, John W. North Papers (North ms), Box 8, Henry E. Huntington Library, San Marino, California (HL); David Davis to Trumbull, Bloomington, 18 December 1860, Trumbull ms, Reel 7, LC; Joshua Giddings to George Julian, 14 December 1860, Joshua R. Giddings–George W. Julian Papers (Giddings-Julian ms), LC.

18. Frank Blair to Montgomery Blair, St. Louis, 23 November 1860, Blair-Lee Family ms, Box 7, Princeton; Mary K. George, *Zachariah Chandler: A Political Biography* (East Lansing: Michigan State University Press, 1969), 33–34.

19. Sumner to Samuel Gridley Howe, Washington, December 1860, in Reel 64, SP; Sumner to the Duchess of Argyll, Washington, 14 December 1860, Reel 74, ibid.; Diary of Charles Francis Adams, 12 November 1860, Adams Family ms, Reel 550, MHS; Younger, *John A. Kasson,* 117.

20. *Indianapolis Daily Journal,* 22 December 1860, and 17 January 1861, and *Illinois State Journal,* 20 December 1860, in Perkins, *Northern Editorials on Secession,* 331, 344, 121; Nevins and Thomas, eds., *The Diary of George Templeton Strong,* vol. 3, 21 December 1860, 79–80; Stampp, *And the War Came,* 68–69.

21. *Indianapolis Daily Journal,* 14 December 1860, in Perkins, ed., *Northern Editorials on Secession,* 117; Howe to Sumner, Boston, 11 December 1860, in Series II, Reel 74, SP; Sumner to Samuel Cabot Jr., Washington, 6 January 1861, ibid.; Sumner to Edward L. Pierce, Washington, 10 December 1860, Series I, Reel 64, ibid.; Chase to the Citizens of New Orleans, Columbus, 30 November 1860, draft, "Chase, Letters and Drafts, 1825–1863," Chase ms, HSP; Frank Blair to Francis P. Blair, St. Louis, 29 November 1860, Blair-Lee Family ms, Box 6, Princeton; Montgomery Blair to Gustavus V. Fox, Washington, 31 January 1861, Fox ms, Box 1, NYHS.

22. Nevins and Thomas, eds., *The Diary of George Templeton Strong,* vol 3, 15 January 1861, 89; Fessenden to Fish, Washington, 15 December 1860, Fish ms, Volume 47, LC; Charles Francis Adams to John Gorham Palfrey, Washington, 5 January 1861, Adams Family ms, II, Reel 164, MHS; John A. Dix to James Watson Webb, Washington, 1 February 1861, James Watson Webb Papers (Webb ms), Box 6, Sterling Library, Yale University; Niven, *Gideon Welles,* 308; Stampp, *And the War Came,* 46–62; Brooks D. Simpson, *Let Us Have Peace: Ulysses S. Grant and the Politics of Reconstruction, 1861–1868*

(Chapel Hill: University of North Carolina, 1991), 8–9; William Kelley to Daniel Ullmann, Philadelphia, 17 January 1861, Daniel Ullmann Papers (Ullmann ms), Box 4, NYHS.

23. *CG*, 36, 2, 9 February 1861, Appendix, 199; *Quincy Daily Whig and Republican*, 10 December 1860, in Perkins, ed., *Northern Editorials on Secession*, 152; Stampp, *And the War Came*, 56; Nevins and Thomas, eds., *The Diary of George Templeton Strong*, vol. 3, 7 December 1860, 71; Henig, *Henry Winter Davis*, 142–43; Martin B. Duberman, *Charles Francis Adams, 1807–1886* (Boston: Houghton Mifflin, 1961), 227.

24. *Chicago Tribune*, 21 January 1861, in Kinsley, *The Chicago Tribune*, vol. 1, 161–62; Merriam, *The Life and Times of Samuel Bowles*, vol. 1, 278. Van Deusen, *Thurlow Weed*, 261; Monaghan, *The Man Who Elected Lincoln*, 217–19; *Harper's Weekly*, 12 January 1861, 32; Seward to Lincoln, Washington, 29 December 1860, Lincoln ms, LC; Henry Adams to Charles Francis Adams Jr., Washington, 18 December 1860, Adams Family ms, IV, Reel 550, MHS; *New York Times*, 12 January 1861; Benjamin P. Thomas and Harold M. Hyman, *Stanton: The Life and Times of Lincoln's Secretary of War* (New York: Alfred A. Knopf, 1962), 89–118; Potter, *Lincoln and His Party*, 259–60; Stanton to Chase, Washington, 23 January 1861, Chase ms, Box 10, HSP; Stanton to Jacob Brinkerhoff, Washington, 20 January 1861, Stanton ms, LC; Sumner to Andrew, Washington, 17 and 26 January 1861, in Reel 74, SP; Seward to Weed, Washington, 30 and 31 January 1861, Weed ms, UR; Edwin D. Morgan to Weed, Albany, 7 February 1861, ibid.; Dix to Seward, Washington, 30 January 1861, ibid.; Morgan to Dix, Albany, 9 March 1861, Dix ms, Box 7, Department of Rare Books and Manuscripts, Butler Library, Columbia University (CU).

25. Morrill to Ruth Morrill, 18 January 1861, Morrill ms, Reel 6, LC; Charles H. Ray to Elihu B. Washburne, n.p., ca. January 1861, Washburne ms, Volume 13, LC; Stampp, *And the War Came*, 91–92; Washburne to Lincoln, Washington, 4 January 1861, Lincoln ms, LC; Robert W. Johannsen, *Stephen A. Douglas* (New York: Oxford University Press, 1973), 806–24; Douglas to *Memphis Appeal*, 2 February 1861, Scrapbook, 1863–65, Joseph McDonald Papers (Joseph McDonald ms), IU; Douglas to August Belmont, Washington, 25 December 1860, Stephen A. Douglas Papers (Douglas ms), Chicago Historical Society; Nichols, *The Disruption of American Democracy*, 472–73; Henry L. Dawes to Ella Dawes, Washington, 15 December 1860, Henry L. Dawes Papers (Henry L. Dawes ms), Box 12, LC; Norman B. Judd to Trumbull, Springfield, 17 January 1861, Trumbull ms, Reel 8, LC.

26. Howe to Sumner, Boston, 20 January 1861, in Reel 74, SP; Trefousse, *The Radical Republicans*, 164. Foner, *Free Soil*, offers the best analysis of how Republicans viewed the South.

27. Nevins and Thomas, eds., *The Diary of George Templeton Strong,* vol. 3, 22 January 1861, 91; *CG,* 36, 2, Appendix, 29 February 1861, 229, 231; 1 February 1861, 132; and 23 January 1861, 87; Morrill to Ruth Morrill, Washington, 7 December 1860, Morrill ms, Reel 6, LC; *Chicago Tribune,* 19 December 1860, in Kinsley, *The Chicago Tribune,* vol. 1, 137.

28. Chase to James W. Grimes, Columbus, 14 January 1861, draft, "Chase, Letters and Drafts, 1825–1863," Chase ms, HSP; Chase to Stephen S. Harding, Columbus, 27 January 1861, Stephen S. Harding Papers (Harding ms), IU; Amos Tuck to Washburne, Exeter, 14 December 1860, Washburne ms, Volume 11, LC; Potter, *Lincoln and His Party,* 177; Trumbull to E. C. Larned, Washington, 16 January 1861, in Horace White, *The Life of Lyman Trumbull* (Boston: Houghton Mifflin, 1913), 113–14; Trefousse, *Benjamin Franklin Wade,* 131–32; *Chicago Tribune,* 5 December 1860, in Kinsley, *The Chicago Tribune,* vol. 1, 136–37; Edward Magdol, *Owen Lovejoy: Abolitionist in Congress* (New Brunswick: Rutgers University Press, 1967), 273.

29. *CG,* 36, 2, Appendix, 23 February 1861, 263; 31 January 1861, 121; 9 February 1861, 201; Jacob D. Cox to Wade, Warren, 21 December 1860, Wade ms, LC; Robert G. Gunderson, *Old Gentlemen's Convention: The Washington Peace Conference of 1861* (Madison: University of Wisconsin Press, 1961), 36; Monaghan, *The Man Who Elected Lincoln,* 199; Edgar Ketchum to Hiram Barney, New York, 8 January 1861, Hiram Barney Papers (Barney ms), Box 20, HL; William Pennington to Unknown, Washington, 25 December 1860, William Pennington Papers (Pennington ms), NJHS.

30. Trefousse, *Benjamin Franklin Wade,* 141; Henry W. Lathrop, *The Life and Times of Samuel J. Kirkwood, Iowa's War Governor, and afterwards a Senator of the United States, and a Member of Garfield's Cabinet* (Chicago: Press of Regan Printing House, 1893), 108–9; William B. Hesseltine, *Lincoln's Plan of Reconstruction* (Tuscaloosa: Confederate Publishing, 1960), 13; Samuel Sewall to Adams, Boston, 13 December 1860, Adams ms, IV, Reel 550, MHS; John Greenleaf Whittier to Sumner, Newbury, 6 February 1861, Reel 21, SP; Sumner to Chase, Washington, 24 January 1861, LC, Reel 74, ibid.; *New York Tribune,* 19 January 1861; Morgan to Lincoln, 16 December 1860, Lincoln ms, LC; Schuyler Colfax to Lincoln, 1 February 1861, ibid.; Colfax to Orville Browning, Washington, 13 January 1861, Orville H. Browning Papers (Browning ms), Box 1, Illinois State Historical Library; Cassius Clay to Greeley, n.p., 1 March 1861, Greeley ms, Box 6, LC; Potter, *Lincoln and His Party,* 179–80; David L. Smiley, *Lion of White Hall: The Life of Cassius M. Clay* (Madison: University of Wisconsin Press, 1962), 173–74.

31. Robert G. Barrows and Shirley S. McCord, eds., *Their Infinite Variety: Essays on Indiana Politicians* (Indianapolis, Ind.: Indiana Historical Bureau,

1981), 68–69; Adams to Richard Henry Dana Jr., Washington, 23 December 1860, Adams ms, II, Reel 164, MHS; Stampp, *And the War Came,* 156–57; *CG,* 36, 2, 17 January 1861, Appendix, 62 (Representative John Potter of Wisconsin). See also Holt, *The Rise and Fall of the American Whig Party.*

32. Potter, *The Impending Crisis,* 514–54; Potter, *Lincoln and His Party,* 119–20, 182, 196; George Brown, et al., to Sumner, Haverhill, 15 February 1861, in Reel 74, SP; Whittier to Sumner, Newbury, 26 January 1861, Reel 21, ibid.; Frederic Bancroft, *The Life of William H. Seward,* 2 vols. (New York: Harper and Brothers, 1900), vol. 2, 532–33; Henry S. Lane to A. H. Donihue, et al., Indianapolis, 17 January 1861, typescript, Lane ms, IU; R. P. Spaulding to John Sherman, Cleveland, 7 February 1861, John Sherman Papers, Manuscript Division (Sherman ms), LC; Charles A. Dana to Colfax, New York, 8 February 1861, Colfax ms, Indiana State Library; Randall, *Lincoln the President: Springfield to Gettysburg,* vol. 1, 225; *New York Tribune,* 2 and 31 December 31 1860, and 7 January 1861.

33. Buckingham, *The Life of William A. Buckingham,* 79; Lucius E. Chittenden, *Recollections of President Lincoln and His Administration* (New York: Harper and Brothers, 1891), 20–21; Gunderson, *Old Gentleman's Convention,* 92 and *passim;* Morrill to Ruth Morrill, Washington, 1 March 1861, Morrill ms, Reel 6, LC; Godlove Orth to Lane, Washington, 8 February 1861, typescript, Lane ms, IU.

34. Adams to Dana, Washington, 23 December 1860, Adams ms, II, Reel 164, MHS. See also Hesseltine, *Lincoln and the War Governors,* 116; James G. Blaine to Israel Washburn, Augusta, 1 December 1860, in Gaillard Hunt, *Israel, Elihu, and Cadwallader Washburn: A Chapter in American Biography* (New York: Macmillan, 1925), 75–76; Smith, *Colfax,* 145; Stampp, *Indiana Politics during the Civil War* (Indianapolis, Ind.: Indiana Historical Bureau, 1949), 52; "Resolutions," in Thomas Dudley to "Dear Sir," Camden, 26 December 1860, Washburne ms, Volume 12, LC.

35. Thursday, 28 February 1861, and Tuesday, 15 January 1861, Washington, Diary of Charles Francis Adams, Adams Family ms, I, Reel 76, MHS; Adams to Erastus Hopkins, Washington, 15 December 1860, II, Reel 164., ibid.

36. *CG,* 36, 2, 31 January 1861, Appendix, 127; Monday, 21 January 1861, Washington, Diary of Adams, Adams ms, I, Reel 76, MHS; Adams to Charles Francis Adams Jr., Washington, 7 December 1860, IV, Reel 550, ibid.; Adams to W. S. Robinson, Washington, 5 January 1861, II, Reel 164, ibid.; Adams to Dana, Washington, 9 February 1861, ibid.; Adams to E. C. Banfield, Washington, 16 February 1861, ibid.; Adams to George Morey, Washington, 26 December 1860, ibid., Reel 164; Adams to Horace Gray, Washington, 30 December 1860, ibid.; Adams to Robert Winthrop, London, 10 October 1861, II, Reel 166, ibid.

37. Robert Horowitz, *The Great Impeacher: A Political Biography of James Ashley* (Brooklyn: Brooklyn College Press, 1979), 58; Magdol, *Owen Lovejoy,* 263; Duberman, *Charles Francis Adams,* 227–28, 235–41; Johannsen, *Douglas,* 812; Henig, *Henry Winter Davis,* 285, n. 28; Adams to Banfield, Washington, 13 January 1861, Adams ms, II, Reel 164, MHS; Adams to B. Wood, Washington, 8 January 1861, ibid.; Adams to Robinson, Washington, 5 January 1861, ibid.; Friday, 1 March 1861, Washington, Adams Diary, I, Reel 76, ibid.; Adams to Dix, Washington, 6 January 1861, Dix ms, Box 1, CU; Potter, *Lincoln and His Party,* 294–303.

38. Jay to Sumner, Katonah, 31 December 1860, Reel 21, SP; Potter, *Lincoln and His Party,* 300; Niven, *Gideon Welles,* 318; Welles to Pierce, Hartford, 11 January 1861, Edward L. Pierce Papers, Houghton Library (Pierce ms), Harvard University (HU); Chase to Harding, Columbus, 27 January 1861, Harding ms, IU; Washburn to Hannibal Hamlin, Hallowell, 2 January 1861, Hannibal Hamlin Papers (Hamlin ms), Reel 1; University of Maine, Orono; Trefousse, *Benjamin Franklin Wade,* 41.

39. Adams's diary for January and February 1861, Reel 76 of the Adams papers, often refers to his dealings with Sumner. For his speech, see *CG,* 36, 2, 31 January 1861, Appendix, 124–27. See also Adams to Pierce, Washington, 1 January 1861, Adams ms, II, Reel 164, MHS; Adams to Francis Bird, Washington, 6 January, 11 February, and 16 February 1861, ibid.; Adams to Palfrey, Washington, 5 January 1861; Pierce to Adams, Boston, 29 and 31 December 1860, IV, Reel 550, ibid.; Duberman, *Charles Francis Adams,* 241–42. On Sumner and Adams, see Sumner to John A. Andrew, Washington, 8 and 10 February 1861, Reel 74, SP; William Claflin to Sumner, Newton, 4 January 1861, Reel 21, ibid.; George L. Stearns to Sumner, Boston, 3 January 1861, ibid.; Pierce to Sumner, Boston, 31 December 1860, and 8 January and 10 February 1861, ibid.; Pierce to Chase, Boston, 24 February 1861, Chase ms, Box 9, HSP.

40. Adams to Ira Steward, Washington, 7 January 1861, Adams ms, II, Reel 164, MHS; Adams to Samuel Sewall, Washington, 30 December 1860, ibid.; Adams to Gray, ibid.; 26 January to 8 February 1861, Washington, Adams Diary, Reel 76, ibid.; Adams to Pierce, Washington, 1 January 1861, ibid.; Adams to Andrew, Washington, 8 February 1861, ibid.; Adams to J. D. Baldwin, Washington, 11 January 1861, ibid.; Adams to William H. Price, Washington, 31 December 1860, ibid.

41. *Albany Evening Journal,* 22, 24, 26, and 30 November 1860; *New York Times,* 14 November 1860; Weed to King, Albany, 10 December 1860, Weed ms, University of Rochester; Barnes and Weed, *Life of Thurlow Weed,* 305–06, 316, 320; Van Deusen, *Thurlow Weed,* 265–69 and *passim;* Potter, *Lincoln and His Party,* 70, n. 53; Burton J. Hendrick, *Lincoln's War Cabinet* (Boston: Little, Brown, 1946), 159–60.

42. Sumner to Andrew, Washington, 8 January 1861, Reel 74, SP; Seward to Weed, Washington, 3 December 1860, and 5 February 1861, Weed ms, University of Rochester; Barnes and Weed, *Life of Thurlow Weed,* 308; Samuel Flagg Bemis, ed., *The American Secretaries of State and Their Diplomacy,* 12 vols. (New York: Pageant Books, 1958), 15; Hendrick, *Lincoln's War Cabinet,* 159–60; Barney to Fogg, New York, 10 December 1860, Fogg ms, Box 1, NHHS.

43. Potter, *Lincoln and His Party,* 26–27, 182–83, 305–6; Adams to Charles Francis Adams Jr., Washington, 7 December 1860, Adams ms, IV, Reel 550, MHS; Henry Adams to Charles Francis Adams Jr., Washington, 29 December 1860, ibid.; Fogg to Lincoln, 19 December 1860, Lincoln ms, LC; Hendrick, *Lincoln's War Cabinet,* 165–66; Johannsen, *Douglas,* 815, 827–28; George E. Baker, ed., *The Works of William H. Seward,* 5 vols. (Boston: Houghton Mifflin, 1853–89), vol. 4, 644–50; Sumner to Andrew, Washington, 6 December 1861, in Reel 74, SP; Sumner to Dana, ibid.; Nevins and Thomas, eds., *The Diary of George Templeton Strong,* vol. 3, 5 February 1861, 97, and 5 January 1861, 86–87.

44. Baker, ed., *The Works of William H. Seward,* vol. 4, 650–69.

45. Seward to Washburn, Washington, 16 December 1860, Washburn ms, LC; Potter, *Lincoln and His Party,* 82, 183–84, 287; Nichols, *The Disruption of American Democracy,* 445–46; Stampp, *And the War Came,* 170–71; Arnold, "The Senate Committee of Thirteen, December 6–31, 1860," in Auer, ed., *Antislavery and Disunion,* 310, n. 4.

46. Sumner to Dorothea Dix, Washington, 14 January 1861, in Reel 74, SP; Sumner to Longfellow, Washington, 23 January 1861, ibid.; Sumner to Chase, Washington, 19 January 1861, ibid.; Sumner to Andrew, Washington, 18 January 1861, ibid.; Trefousse, *The Radical Republicans,* 152–53; *New York Tribune,* 4 February 1861; Schurz to Margarethe Schurz, Hillsdale, 4 February 1861, in Schafer, ed., *Schurz Letters,* 242–44; Hale to Lucy Hale, Washington, 12 January 1861, Hale ms, Box 2, NHHS; Horowitz, *The Great Impeacher,* 60; Van Deusen, *William Henry Seward,* 241–46; Thomas Eliot to Washburn, Washington, 14 January 1861, Washburn ms, Volume 2, LC; Nevins and Thomas, eds., *The Diary of George Templeton Strong,* vol. 3, 14 January 1861, 89; Tuesday, 15 January 1861, Washington, Adams Diary, Adams ms, I, Reel 76, MHS; Hendrick, *Lincoln's War Cabinet,* 175.

47. Nevins and Thomas, eds., *The Diary of George Templeton Strong,* vol. 3, 23 February 1861, 102; Fogg to Lincoln, Washington, 2 February 1861, Fogg ms, Box 1, NHHS; Potter, *Lincoln and His Party,* 165–69, and 173, n. 53 and 54; Barnes and Weed, *Life of Thurlow Weed,* 604–05, 614; Seward to Lincoln, Auburn, 16, 26, and 27 December 1860, Lincoln ms, LC; Francis Preston Blair to Lincoln, Silver Springs, 14 January 1861, ibid.

48. *CW,* vol. 4, 141–53. See Henry Villard, *Lincoln on the Eve of '61: A Journalist's Story,* Harold G. Villard and Oswald Garrison Villard, eds. (New York: Alfred A. Knopf, 1941), 34; *New York Times,* 21 November 1860; Trumbull to Lincoln, 17 December 1860, Lincoln ms, LC; Ralph J. Roske, "Lincoln's Peace Puff," *The Abraham Lincoln Quarterly* 6, no. 4 (December 1950): 244; David Herbert Donald, *Lincoln's Herndon* (New York: Alfred A. Knopf, 1948), 145; William H. Herndon to Trumbull, Springfield, 21 December 1860, Trumbull ms, Reel 7, LC; Herndon to Sumner, Springfield, 10 December 1860, Reel 21, SP; Stampp, *And the War Came,* 147; Lathrop, *The Life and Times of Samuel J. Kirkwood,* 107.

49. Chase to Stevens, Columbus, 9 January 1861, Stevens ms, Box 1, LC; Basler, ed., *The Collected Works of Abraham Lincoln.* vol. 4, 195, 230–31; Randall, *Lincoln the President: Springfield to Gettysburg,* vol. 1, 247, 279–83; Harry Carman and Reinhard Luthin, *Lincoln and the Patronage* (New York: Columbia University Press, 1943), 45; Bradford Wood to Barney, Albany, 20 February 1861, Barney ms, Box 30, HL; Hesseltine, *Lincoln's Plan of Reconstruction,* 17–19; David Davis to Simon Cameron, Bloomington, 8 February 1861, Cameron ms, Reel 6, LC; Springfield, Monday, 11 February 1861, in Theodore C. Pease and James G. Randall, eds., *The Diary of Orville Hickman Browning,* 2 vols. (Springfield: Illinois State Historical Library, 1925–33), vol. 1, 453–54; William Dudley Foulke, *Life of Oliver P. Morton: Including His Important Speeches,* 2 vols. (Indianapolis: Bobbs-Merrill, 1899), vol. 1, 107.

50. *CW,* vol. 4, 191–94, 199, 202, 204, 210–11, 215, 230, 240, 242.

51. *Pittsburgh Gazette,* 16 February 1861, in Arthur M. Lee, "Henry C. Carey and the Republican Tariff," *The Pennsylvania Magazine of History and Biography* 81, no. 3 (July 1957): 292; Stampp, *And the War Came,* 111, 196–97; Bigelow to Hargreaves, New York, 21 February 1861, Bigelow ms, Box 1, NYPL; Samuel Bowles to Henry L. Dawes, Springfield, 26 February 1861, in Merriam, *The Life and Times of Samuel Bowles,* vol. 1, 318; Charles Congdon to Sydney Howard Gay, n.p., 16 February 1861, Sydney Howard Gay Papers (Gay ms), Reel 1, CU; Blaine, *Twenty Years of Congress,* vol. 1, 279–80; James A. Garfield to Crete Garfield, Columbus, 17 February 1861, James A. Garfield Papers (James A. Garfield ms), Series 3, Reel 4, LC; *Chicago Tribune,* 16 February 1861, in Stampp, *And the War Came,* 193.

52. *CW,* vol. 4, 195–244.

53. George, *Zachariah Chandler,* 44; Chittenden, *Recollections of President Lincoln and His Administration,* 74–75; Michael Davis, *The Image of Lincoln in the South* (Knoxville: University of Tennessee Press, 1971), 48; Monaghan, *The Man Who Elected Lincoln,* 219; *Illinois State Journal,* 11 February 1861, in Harper, *Lincoln and the Press,* 79; *New York Tribune,* 4 March 1861; Greeley

to Brockway, n.p., 28 February 1861, Greeley ms, LC; Congdon to Gay, Quincy, February 1861, Gay ms, Reel 1, CU; Hale to Lucy Hale, Washington, 24 February 1861, Hale ms, Box 2, NHHS.

54. *CW,* vol. 4, 249–71; Nevins and Thomas, eds., *The Diary of George Templeton Strong,* vol. 3, 4 March 1861, 105–6; Sumner to Fish, Washington, 3 March 1861, in Reel 74, SP; Springfield, Friday, 15 February 1861, in Pease and Randall, eds., *The Diary of Orville Hickman Browning,* vol. 1, 455–56; Browning to Lincoln, Springfield, 17 February 1861, Lincoln ms, LC, in Baxter, *Orville H. Browning,* 110; John G. Nicolay and John Hay, *The Life of Abraham Lincoln,* 10 vols. (New York: Century Company, 1890), vol. 3, 322, 333–34; Rice, ed., *Reminiscences of Abraham Lincoln,* 225; Johannsen, *Douglas,* 842.

55. *CW,* vol. 4, 262–66.

56. Ibid., 268–71; *New York Tribune,* 6 March 1861.

57. Nevins and Thomas, eds., *The Diary of George Templeton Strong,* vol. 3, 5 and 6 March 1861, 106–7; Johannsen, *Douglas,* 844; *New York Times,* 5 and 7 March 1861. See *The Liberator,* 8 March 1861, in Theodore D. Lockwood, "Garrison and Lincoln the Abolitionist," *The Abraham Lincoln Quarterly* 6, no. 4 (December 1950): 210; Banks to Bowles, Chicago, 5 March 1861, Bowles ms, Box 1, Sterling Library, Yale University; *Chicago Tribune,* 5 March 1861, in Marie Hochmuth Nichols, "Lincoln's First Inaugural Address," in Auer, ed., *Antislavery and Disunion,* 409; Trefousse, *The Radical Republicans,* 158; Rice, ed., *Reminiscences of Abraham Lincoln,* 82–83; Morrill to Louise Swan, Washington, 5 March 1861, Morrill ms, Reel 6, LC; Younger, *John A. Kasson,* 119; *New York Tribune,* 6 March 1861; Stampp, *And the War Came,* 201–3.

58. Magdol, *Owen Lovejoy,* 269; Samuel Hooper to Banks, Boston, 1 February 1861, Banks ms, Box 13, LC; Seward to Joseph Thompson, 23 February 1861, in Baker, ed., *The Works of William H. Seward,* vol. 4, 613–14; Henry Adams to Charles Francis Adams Jr., Washington, 9 December 1860, Adams ms, IV, Reel 550, MHS; *Boston Daily Advertiser,* 7 March 1861, in Stampp, *And the War Came,* 20; Mayer, *The Republican Party,* 82–83; Frederick W. Seward, *Seward at Washington,* 2 vols. (New York: Derby and Miller, 1891), vol. 2, 505; Alexander, *A Political History of the State of New York,* vol. 2, 380, n. 40; Major L. Wilson, *Space, Time, and Freedom: The Quest for Nationality and the Irrepressible Conflict, 1815–1861* (Westport, Conn.: Greenwood Press, 1974), 20–21.

59. "Annual Message to Congress," 1 December 1862, in *CW,* vol. 5, 537.

4

Lincoln's Warring Cabinet: Many Secretaries, One Ideology

BY THE MORNING after his victory, Abraham Lincoln had made a wish list of Cabinet members based on two key considerations: political ancestry and geography. Senator William Henry Seward of New York, once a Whig, was first. Former Democrat Salmon Chase of Ohio represented radicals; Edward Bates of Missouri, in many ways still a Whig, came from a border state. The next tier of choices was a pastiche: William Dayton of New Jersey, Montgomery Blair of Maryland, Simon Cameron of Pennsylvania, Caleb Smith of Indiana or Norman Judd of Illinois, and Nathaniel Banks of Massachusetts or Gideon Welles of Connecticut—all balanced by previous affiliation and region, all moderate or conservative. This Cabinet was unique in including Lincoln's opponents for the nomination and in its inexperience: except Seward, none had been a national leader as a Whig or Democrat, or had served in a Cabinet. In the end Lincoln appointed many of his choices, but his political manager, Leonard Swett, doubted that he would succeed. Given "the fiery crucible of treason in which we are being tried," he said, "It is . . . unanimity of sentiment and action he wants."[1]

These concerns proved prescient in some ways, unfounded in others. The Cabinet members divided as much as they united, or so it seemed. Still the classic study, Burton Hendrick's *Lincoln's War Cabinet* depicts a petty, intelligent, able, and ambitious group, subtly managed by a shrewd president to whom each, at least at some point, considered himself superior. Students of the Cabinet and Civil War politics have been kinder to Lincoln and certain ministers than have others, but have generally followed Hendrick's lead. And, to be sure, any assessment of the Cabinet, and of Lincoln's relations with them, must examine party politics. Each minister was involved in the affairs of his state and with those who shared his radical, moderate, or conservative place on the Republican spectrum; what each did in his capacity as a Cabinet minister and on related issues cannot be understood without grasping what it meant to him politically.[2]

Missing from these interpretations is a comprehension of their ideology: freedom, union, and power. Such an understanding can be hard to achieve. An examination of the words of wartime Republicans, especially those in the Cabinet, seems to reveal them to have been less interested in analyzing and refining their party's thought than they had been before the war. A logical explanation is that they were now leaders rather than opponents. More responsible for government action, they had less time to muse as they dealt with constantly changing circumstances. More important, as party leaders, Cabinet members were sure of themselves and their party's views; they were more interested in pursuing their and the government's agenda than in reminding one another of what their belief system entailed. This belief system managed to unite and divide the Cabinet, but the divisions fell within that ideology. This disparate group saw that the war imposed new, unexpected requirements on Republicans to reunite and preserve the Union, protect and propagate freedom, and wield the power to do both wisely and responsibly. On this they agreed. But they disagreed on several questions with the potential to destroy their party. In a real or perceived collision between the existence of the Union and the spread of freedom, which should come first? For the sake of either or both, how much power should they be prepared to use? Which wing of the party and which branch of the government should use it? And if they failed, who should be blamed?

Another issue was who held more power: Lincoln, with the Cabinet functioning as his virtual equals, or the legislative branch. Central to this matter was the leadership technique that each preferred—in a sense, the ways in which personality shapes a response to an ideology. David Donald has been the most prominent member of the school of thought placing Lincoln in the "Whig" concept of the president as administering a Cabinet and deferring to Congress. Stephen Oates has countered that Lincoln was a Republican, not a Whig, and sought to strengthen executive power. When Republicans discussed presidential power and its use, the role of ideology must be drawn and inferred. Whatever the merit of contemporary assessments and historiographic arguments, Republicans at the time were sure of their intellectual and political superiority to Lincoln. These attitudes colored the judgment of Republicans; how much they believed in congressional or Cabinet supremacy varied according to whether Lincoln and his choices in the Cabinet and on the battlefield performed as they and other Republicans wished. Thus, in examining the interplay within and toward the Cabinet, the differences over policy lay with degree and ambition; the power to affect the future of freedom and union was crucial.[3]

The Making of the Cabinet

The debate over these issues began in the secession winter with the making of the Cabinet, which turned into an intramural battle for the soul of Lincoln and the party. To many Republicans, Lincoln's biggest hurdle was the New York machine run by Seward and Thurlow Weed. Not only did Seward seem increasingly conservative, but neither he nor Weed enjoyed a reputation for probity. If Seward became secretary of state, Thaddeus Stevens asked, "Can [Lincoln] stand up against such a prime minister?" Fearing that ex-Whigs Weed and Seward would conspire to keep them out of office, former Democrats ascribed sinister motives to them. These fears were understandable. For one thing, Republicans had attacked Democratic corruption and were loath to think that they could be accused of the same. For another, Seward and Weed angled for a Cabinet Whiggish in outlook, with Lincoln functioning much like a chairman of the board and a "prime minister" really in charge. Hearkening to the Whig concept of the presidency, Seward would approve or disapprove his colleagues, control policy making, and perhaps broker a compromise to avert civil war.[4]

Weed met with Lincoln, and the result should have signaled Lincoln's intent to wield executive power more directly than had his Whig predecessors. Lincoln gently made clear that he was in charge, telling Weed the party included not just Whigs, but Democrats entitled to fair treatment. To Weed's complaint that the list contemplated a Democratic majority in the Cabinet, Lincoln replied, "You seem to forget that *I* expect to be there; and counting me as one, you see how nicely the Cabinet would be balanced"—possibly a sign that he would run his administration democratically and thus Whiggishly, possibly a sign of his independence. Nor was Weed happy when he failed to obtain more influence for Southern unionists. Lincoln and Weed hoped that North Carolina's John Gilmer would join the Cabinet, but he seceded with his state. Weed suggested Maryland's Henry Winter Davis, a fellow ex-Whig and cousin of Lincoln's friend and manager David Davis. Instead Lincoln chose Montgomery Blair, their Democratic rival. Unhappily growing used to conceding defeat, Seward told Weed, "Mr. L has undertaken his Cabinet without consulting me. For the present I shall be content to leave the responsibility on his own broad shoulders." Clearly expecting more responsibility later, Seward admitted that at least for the moment, the Whig concept of the presidency held no charm for Lincoln.[5]

Lincoln's handling of Seward's Cabinet appointment revealed their—and the party's—differing views of presidential power. In late 1860 and early 1861, Lincoln claimed to prefer Seward for the State Department, the preeminent Cabinet position and in Whig theory the premiership. Unsure that Lincoln meant it, and debating whether he belonged in the Cabinet, the London mission, the Senate, or retirement, Seward seemed uninterested. After Lincoln reassured him, Seward said yes, due partly to his ego: citing their "common responsibility and interest," he wrote, "I will not decline. . . . I will try to save freedom and my country." Even amid a potential clash of machismos, Lincoln and Seward thought alike: the issue was Republican responsibility for the country's unity and well-being.[6]

Lincoln's handling of Seward mirrored his dealings with Chase. As had Seward, Chase talked about preferring the Senate or retirement, but heard the call of duty, ego, and a genuine commitment to service, his party, and his cause. Similarly, Chase wished to be massaged, and Lincoln met his requirements while maintaining his independence. He invited Chase to Springfield and discussed his desire to name him to the Treasury, his fear that protectionist Pennsylvania would object to the radical free-trader, and his inability to make a firm offer just yet. Impressed with Lincoln's devotion to the party platform yet perturbed by the uncertainty, Chase vowed to do all he could to help Lincoln, admitted his preference for the Senate, and showed signs of the jealousies and in-fighting to follow. Assured that he would be secretary of state if Seward declined, Chase wrote, "Had it been made earlier and with the same promptitude and definiteness as that to Mr. Seward, I should have been inclined to make some sacrifices." Lincoln had been independent and politically cautious, putting Chase in the position of having to wait for him to act.[7]

The response of Chase's—and Seward's—supporters to his appointment also offers insight into the party's evolving ideology and leader. Radicals deemed Chase the most honest man to handle federal funds, demonstrating their concerns about comparison to the corrupt Democrats of the 1850s and their chances of retaining the presidency if the party exercised its new power unwisely. Radicals and former Democrats expected him to balance Seward's Whiggery and slipperiness. In Chase's mind, to avoid the Cabinet would be "to shrink from cares and labors for the common good which cannot be honorably shunned." Yet he and his backers tried to enhance his standing and responsibility by elevating him to the more prestigious State Department and ousting Seward. The feeling was mutual. When the Seward wing tried to dislodge Chase, Lincoln cut off the discussion by offering to retool the Cabinet without the New Yorker; when Horace Greeley and the Blairs egged on a New York clique that tried to push out Seward, Lincoln quickly dismissed his callers. Telling his secretary, John Nicolay, that he could not "let Seward take the first trick," Lincoln saw that the Cabinet's two leading members were powerful men of ambition, ego, ability, and acumen. That he managed them, their appointments, and their supporters so well even before taking office signified (to later observers if not at the time) that he planned to control them. If Lincoln had his way, power in his administration would rest with him, and the issue of power within the party would be resolved before it was ever open to debate. Yet the question lingered throughout Lincoln's tenure, often creating more personal battles for him and his Cabinet than the important ideological issues of freedom and union.[8]

Indeed, the underpinnings for the Cabinet rested mainly on one of the three prongs of the party's ideology: Lincoln assumed a belief in freedom and union, but foremost in his mind was how an appointee aided the party in wielding power. Cameron's selection as War secretary, despite his poor reputation, was a case in point. Because Pennsylvania had been crucial to his election, his managers may have promised Cameron a Cabinet post at the convention, and Seward and Weed saw him as an ally, Lincoln decided to offer him the War or Treasury portfolio. This rang Republican alarm bells. "We got Lincoln nominated on the *idea* of his honesty and elected him by endorsing him as *Honest Abe,*" Joseph Medill of the *Chicago Tribune* said. "His first act is to select . . . the one having the *worst* reputation for honesty."

Pressured by Cameron's friends and foes to offer and then withdraw the Cabinet seat, Lincoln slid him into the War Department because no one else from Pennsylvania was acceptable to all wings of the party. Whatever his past, Cameron was a Republican and shared the beliefs that mattered; otherwise, location and what it meant to the party's unity, and thus its power, mattered above all.[9]

Similar reasoning motivated the selection of Cabinet members from the border states. Lincoln told a border state ally that he faced pressure to appease the South by naming a secretary or two from there, "but that he could scarcely maintain his self respect and listen to such propositions." In an editorial that Lincoln wrote or suggested, the *Illinois State Journal* asked, "*First.* Is it known that any such gentlemen of character would accept a place in the cabinet? *Second.* If yea, on what terms does he surrender to Mr. Lincoln, or Mr. Lincoln to him, on the political differences between them; or do they enter upon the administration in open opposition to each other?" Thus, the only route to unearthing Southern unionism went through the border states. Naming Blair postmaster general, Lincoln angered Winter Davis. But he pacified the party's most powerful family and old Democrats in the Blair strongholds of Maryland and Missouri, and put perhaps the most important job for dispensing patronage in the hands of someone with links to the South. Balancing his border ticket with an ex-Whig, Lincoln named Bates attorney general. Bates's conservatism was agreeable to Greeley, who had backed him for the Republican nomination in 1860 as an old-line Whig who could win border state support, and to Weed, who seems to have seen in him a steady hand, more likely to follow than lead. More important, by naming Blair and Bates, Lincoln pleased enough of their supporters to make them overlook their displeasure with other selections and keep them working together—a tribute to his acumen and a necessary component in the party's ability to use its power.[10]

For the sake of retaining and extending that power, region and political ancestry determined who would hold the northeastern and western Cabinet seats. Lincoln hoped to balance democracy and Whiggery; thanks to shrewd maneuvering, he succeeded. He sought an ex-Democrat from New England, incurring the displeasure of Seward and Weed and thereby elating radicals; nor did it hurt Lincoln politically to entrust the choice to Hannibal Hamlin, his running mate, a radical ex-Democrat from Maine. Lincoln expected Gideon

Welles of Connecticut, a conservative Jacksonian, to be the result, and he won the Navy portfolio. The Interior seat went to Caleb Smith, an Indiana Whig repaid for supporting Lincoln at the 1860 convention. That selection irked radicals and former Democrats backing Illinoisan Norman Judd, because he was one of their own and would give Lincoln a friend in the Cabinet. Granting the political back-stabbing involved, Lincoln showed independence. He gave Hamlin a role because he was sure of the outcome. He acceded to Smith to please his advisers and because he believed that he could manage the Cabinet without a close friend. It should have signified where Lincoln expected Republican power in this government to rest.[11]

At the time, though, Republicans cared less about individual power than that the Cabinet was in place for them to wield power. As the controversy over each choice showed, ambition, personality, and the speed at which to turn the party's ideology into policy mattered more than an ideology on which all agreed. The Cabinet reflected the party's nature: a coalition of common belief newly entrusted with power, but not yet seen as entirely trustworthy and including leaders once considered too radical in their old parties. The result, Charles Francis Adams cynically said, was a "motley mixture, containing one statesman, one politician, two jobbers, one intriguer, and two respectable old gentlemen." But it united the party's disparate elements on the basis of region and background. That Chase was the only obvious radical showed that Lincoln hoped to avoid the appearance of extremism, since Southerners and many Democrats considered even conservative Republicans too radical. Yet Lincoln refused to name anyone from outside the party, revealing an assumed ideological commitment: whatever his leanings, each Cabinet member was a Republican, committed to the same beliefs. In one way or another, all of them supported freedom, made clear their support for the Union, and showed a desire to use power to preserve, protect, and strengthen freedom and union.[12]

The Making of a Cabinet Leader

The first problem to confront the administration brought these issues into sharp relief: whether to provision Fort Sumter, abandon it, or fight. An inexperienced president and Cabinet faced the ultimate test of their and the nation's power and unity. When Lincoln asked his advisers for their views, one stood resolutely for force: Blair, the Cabinet's lone West Pointer, a conservative Marylander who claimed to understand Southerners and the need to fight fire with fire. He was unimpressed when General Winfield Scott, an old Virginia Whig, advocated giving up Sumter; he accused the general of crossing the line into politics. It was no coincidence that Blair, whose family had been close to Andrew Jackson and left the Democrats in part over Franklin Pierce's quavering, urged action and was prepared to resign if ignored.[13]

Next to Blair, Chase was most inclined to reinforce Sumter, and he was unsure. He saw two options: enforcing federal law or accepting the rebellion "*as an accomplished revolution* . . . but maintaining the authority of the Union, and treating secession as treason everywhere else." As the most radical secretary, he went so far as to say, a Southern friend said, that "we could come back or not *as we pleased after they had accomplished their object, which was to free the negro, who was the cause of the war.*" Yet he was susceptible to the pressures the party faced as it took power. The night before the inauguration, aware that precipitous action might drive out the border states and of debate over whether to give up Sumter or fight, he could think of one way to avoid war: adopt Greeley's posture of peaceful secession. Otherwise, the result would be "compulsion, and a compulsory Union would be no Union," but "an utter subversion of our system and of republican government." While they agreed on the result, Chase differed with Blair, whose different background and experience with the problems of power inclined him to place union above all else. Chase faced a paradox of power that often plagued Republicans: how to be true to freedom and a Union with slavery. The answer was that the Union must be saved for the sake of freedom; the party's devotion to each would avert the despotism feared by Republicans, radical or conservative.[14]

The other ministers revealed similar uncertainty, born of inexperience with their party's new role, over how to respond to the threat to the Union. Smith, a deservedly unassuming ex-Whig, would surrender all to avoid war. Although awaiting a rise in Southern unionism, Bates felt that "the property of the government should be protected." Cameron took the coldly logical stand that reinforcing Sumter would cause more trouble than it was worth because it was impossible to hold anyway. Waffling more than he later admitted, Welles supported and then opposed sending supplies to Sumter as he grew to share Lincoln's concerns that moving too boldly would frighten off the border states. The Cabinet was indeed divided, and the division was due to the evolving beliefs of its members: how much power would save the Union and how much would destroy it.[15]

Seward was pivotal, partly due to his influence, mainly because he was as slippery as ever. He told Lincoln that a Northern offensive would make a restored Union "hopeless, at least under this administration." In mid-March the *New York Times,* published by his ally Henry J. Raymond, opined, "The true policy of the Government is unquestionably that of *masterly inactivity.* The object to be aimed at is, the conversion of the Southern people from their Secessionism"—it even read like Seward. He dickered with rebel emissaries, urged a foreign war as a means of reunification, and may have promised that Northern troops would be withdrawn, none of which he had authority to do. Given his low opinion of the inexperienced Lincoln and high opinion of himself, Seward's efforts reflected his perception of a power vacuum that only he could fill. Clearly he continued to try to buy time for Southern unionists, avoid war, aid Northern preparedness, and flex his muscle. He succeeded at least in part in helping to promote delay, which gave the administration time to acclimate itself to power and nettled the South into shooting first.[16]

But the party who suffered the most damage in the first month of Lincoln's term proved to be Seward himself. Once the firebrand who spoke of revolutions never going backward and irrepressible conflicts, he seemed sure of the Union's speedy restoration, creating doubts about him in Republican minds. Sumner maintained a steady flow of criticism, and even Weed thought his partner went too far. But Seward had been applying the brake all winter and kept doing so as Lincoln's term began, trying to deceive the South and possibly deceiving himself, all to preserve the Union and his party's—and his own—power.

Two related problems plagued Lincoln and his new administration: the appearance of weakness and reality of inexperience. In the confines of his diary, showing that even the most elegant conservative could advocate a forceful response to Southern intransigence, George Templeton Strong fumed, "The bird of our country is a debilitated chicken, disguised in eagle feathers." But his next comment encapsulated a fear and dilemma for his party: "We have never been a nation; we are only an aggregate of communities, ready to fall apart at the first serious shock and without a centre of vigorous national life to keep us together." If Republicans were wrong and freedom and union lacked resonance with the Northern populace, all would be lost and the new administration would be at fault. This only added to the caution caused in part by a factor that Sumner captured in an optimistic appraisal for his European friends: "Our new Administration . . . has an awkwardness . . . partly attributable to its inexperience. I trust, however, that it will shew itself able to deal with events as they occur."[17]

As the administration's first month ended, the need to do something outweighed the issue of what to do. Republicans complained that Lincoln shirked responsibility and Seward shirked reality. Fearing a Democratic revival at their expense and any sign of weakness, Republicans displayed an impatience born of inexperience, uncertainty, and concerns that they would have to take responsibility for the Union's collapse. On 3 April the *Times* issued an editorial wake-up call, "Wanted—A Policy." It attacked "a blindness and a stolidity without parallel in the history of intelligent statesmanship." Leaving Washington late in March, Weed foresaw "all sorts of evils," and followed up with editorials asking, "The President and Cabinet—What is their Policy?" He had no answer, and was disappointed by that very fact, for the sake of the country and his own power.[18]

Seward's answer ended his premiership before it began and established Lincoln, if only in Seward's mind, as the real leader. On 1 April he sent Lincoln a note bemoaning the lack of a domestic or foreign policy. He said, "*Change the question before the Public from one upon Slavery, or about Slavery,* for a question upon *Union or Disunion.* In other words, from what would be regarded as a Party question to one of *Patriotism* or *Union.* The occupation or evacuation of Fort Sumter, although not in fact a slavery, or a party question is so *regarded.*" Urging a foreign war to unite the Union, he was willing to institute any proposals that Lincoln chose to heed. In a private meeting, Lincoln replied that he would make any decisions, that a policy existed, and that Seward was wrong. Seward came away aware that Lincoln was in charge of his administration, but many Republicans clung to the perception of him as the puppeteer, with Lincoln on his string. Both knew better. Yet in referring to shifting the issue from slavery to union, Seward reflected his party's ideological evolution. He emphasized the

Union over freedom and slavery, but realized that the issues ran deeper. Understanding the need for unity and for his party to exert power, he sought to protect all three pillars of the party's belief system.[19]

Indeed, Lincoln and his Cabinet formed a policy that suited the Union's needs and their evolving ideology. On 4 April, Lincoln decided to reinforce Sumter and retain control of another threatened fort, Pickens in Florida. Among the secretaries, only Seward and Smith dissented. While Smith's Whiggery and conservatism explained his stand, Seward advocated holding Pickens to show that the Union refused to back down completely. "I do not think it wise to provoke a civil war beginning at Charleston, and in rescue of an untenable position," he said, revealing his adaptation to the party's new way of thinking. His choice of words was important: he had no desire to cause a war, or to do so in that location, or to fight a battle the Union was sure to lose. While Seward wanted to avoid weakening the Union's power, Lincoln's judgment proved surer. His old Whig ally from Illinois, Orville Browning, told him the key was to force the South to be the aggressor. Weed saw that "responsibility will rest, where it belongs, upon the heads of secession leaders." Republicans closed ranks with the argument that the Union's existence transcended partisanship and begged the question of whether the survival of republican government was at stake. Although convinced that Lincoln had been unrealistic about averting war, Greeley wrote that no administration "in 30 years, had so quietly and efficiently matured and directed its policy as that now in power."[20]

A sense of unity survived the firing on Sumter on 12 April, but the party indulged in revealing recriminations. Criticisms of the performance of Lincoln and his Cabinet came from all sides of the party spectrum, yet they shared a common opinion: the result may have been satisfactory, but the executive branch had failed to manage the crisis properly. Adams said that the war's opening act proved Seward right: Lincoln "would hesitate and delay and thus end by doing the thing from necessity," suggesting that "the thing" would have been Seward's goal. Radical Senator Benjamin Wade of Ohio said that "the South has got to be punished and traitors hung, if it can be by assent of the President and in a Constitutional way, but the stern demand for justice of a united people cannot and must not be baffled by the perverseness of one man though he be the President," a frighteningly strong demand for federal power. The general consensus, a Chase loyalist wrote, seemed to be not to fault "the Administration for any thing it *has* done," but "for what it has *not* done." What Lincoln did, though, worked because he used his power wisely, as befit the party's ideological response to changing circumstances. As Seward said, he defended freedom when it was in danger and the Union when it was in danger. To defend both, Lincoln and his administration had to use their power carefully. If they blundered, they did so because they were adapting, and that process would continue.[21]

Lincoln's response to the first shot similarly reflected the party's adaptation to its new power. He acted decisively and, to those expecting a "Whig" president controlled by Seward, so overpoweringly that it should have been troubling. The events of 12 April awakened Lincoln to the problems befalling him and his party. Most military officers were Southern and seceded with their states, and many who remained were aged. With a Cabinet he barely knew, in unprecedented times, Lincoln took responsibility in every sense. When a Baltimore group asked for concessions, he said, "There is no Washington in that—no Jackson in that—no manhood nor honor in that." He proclaimed a blockade and called up the militia, acts within his purview as president. He requested a congressional session on 4 July, giving him time to deal with the rebellion on his own, and he ordered funds for the military. He went well beyond the executive's traditional powers, even in war. Lincoln took control of the war for the executive and kept it for four years, amid challenges and criticism. But the legislative branch had few objections, at least at the time.[22]

Still, Lincoln and his Cabinet remained at odds in some ways. Seward became "the fiercest of the lot," as Cameron wrote, and Chase assured supporters that the executive branch would wage war together, with vigor and unity. Chase rejected charges of "dictatorship," calling it "nothing more nor less than *prudence,* and that of a very necessary kind." But as Pennsylvania editor and politician Alexander McClure recalled, "Lincoln found . . . the strangest confusion and bitterest antagonisms pervading those who should have been in accord." Several of his appointees remained at loggerheads, differing over how to perpetuate freedom, restore the Union, and wield the power to do both. That was the point: as with other Republicans, Cabinet members differed over how to reach the goal, not the goal itself. They shared hatreds, ambitions, shrewdness, and, above all, an ideology. They knew that they could have let the slave power slip out of the Union, but that would have been a different Union from the one they had been elected to govern. They had learned that much, and had still more to learn.[23]

THE POLITICS AND IDEOLOGY OF IMPATIENCE

Two related aspects of power that Republicans had trouble learning and reconciling themselves to were the importance of the presidency and the need for patience. In 1861 and 1862, Union armies won key victories—Belmont, Forts Henry and Donelson, and Shiloh in the West and Antietam in the East, for example—and avoided potential disasters even more often. But the North lost more than it won and failed to deliver a knockout punch to the South for several reasons: problems with waging an offensive war, inferior generalship, and a president and Cabinet still searching for how best to use their power. Republicans in Congress and across the North were quick to criticize and to demand a response, preferably some kind of firing, for every failure; if no general was cashiered, cries went up for the departure of Cameron from the War Department and Welles from the navy out of the belief that their alleged incompetence trickled down through the ranks. Radicals in Congress created the Joint Committee on the Conduct of the War, chaired by Wade, to make sure that generals paid heed to the anti-slavery faith. Senator John P. Hale investigated the Navy Department until his hounding of Welles brought sympathy that the flinty secretary otherwise might never have won and cost Hale his chairmanship of the Naval Affairs Committee. Greeley said, "No President could afford to have it said that a newspaper had forced him to give battle, and then turned out his Cabinet because he lost that battle." Standing his ground, Lincoln enhanced the powers of his office. That he had any need to stand his ground showed that Republicans were gradually working out which individuals, wings of the party, and branches of government would wield power, and how quickly they would turn their ideology into practice.[24]

The first Cabinet change signaled that Lincoln intended to hold the reins of power. As the army foundered, Cameron was vulnerable but wily. He allied with Seward before switching his allegiance to Chase, aiding his standing with the radicals. Cameron stood pat when John

Frémont ordered abolition in his command and declined Lincoln's request to rescind his order. That angered the Blairs, whose feud with Frémont hurt his standing with Lincoln, who had to overrule Frémont. Worse, and typically, Cameron had been free and loose with deals for friends. But he guaranteed his departure when he ignored Lincoln's wishes and called in his 1861 annual report for arming black soldiers. Radicals were thrilled, no matter their doubts about his motives, but Lincoln saw that he outran public opinion—a risk that, as president, he could ill afford. Despite radical pressure, Lincoln literally and figuratively sent Cameron to Siberia as minister to Russia. Cameron remained loyal, aiding in Lincoln's reelection, and he retained political power in Pennsylvania.[25]

Ultimately, the situation was more political than ideological. Besides Cameron's honesty and competence, the speed with which freedom should be expanded was at issue, not whether it ever should. The party demonstrated solidarity on its beliefs, and Lincoln demonstrated that he could and would remove a secretary who was popular with at least part of the party if he deemed his appointee expendable. It was another sign of Lincoln's independence, and thus his power.

The same could be said of Edwin Stanton, Lincoln's choice as Cameron's successor. Unlike his colleagues, he enjoyed bipartisan support as a War Democrat and entered the Cabinet with administrative experience, which was the rub: he had been Buchanan's attorney general and had spent the past year belittling Lincoln's "painful imbecility" to Democrats. In office Stanton seemed determinedly unpopular. While other ministers welcomed his commitment to getting the army moving, he appeared to trust no one and like few; even Chase, who cultivated him and welcomed his approach, admitted that "no one has much *influence*" with him. Yet Lincoln and Stanton worked well together. Stanton provided the department with the honesty and administrative ability it and Lincoln needed. Stanton sought and won radical backing, especially from the Joint Committee on the Conduct of the War, and treated the president as brusquely as he treated everyone else. But he had no political constituency and owed Lincoln his job. Lincoln's appointment of a non-Republican showed his independence: he pleased Pennsylvania, but acted largely on his own.[26]

As with Stanton's appointment, how Lincoln handled the related issues of the army and emancipation should have shown the Cabinet that in the debate over power, Lincoln saw himself as the key figure. The Army of the Potomac struggled against Robert E. Lee's Army of Northern Virginia and moved slowly under George McClellan's dilatory leadership. Even Lincoln agreed that McClellan, having built a magnificent army, feared destroying it in battle. McClellan's severest Cabinet critics, Chase and Stanton, hoped that an ultimatum would force Lincoln to make a change and wrote a petition demanding the general's ouster. Fearing an invasion of his home state of Missouri and wanting a stronger army, Bates agreed to sign if he could reduce it to a simple request to relieve McClellan. Smith followed suit. Welles refused to go along. Not bothering to ask Seward and Blair, the closest McClellan had to defenders, the quartet went to Lincoln. He made clear that he was commander-in-chief, their leader and McClellan's, and the decision was his. As president or as commander-in-chief, Lincoln left no doubt who was in charge.[27]

Lincoln conceived of his power similarly on emancipation. The Cabinet agreed that slavery endangered the Union and that the government had to act. What to do was another matter. Smith wanted the army to use or colonize slaves as it moved through the South. Blair agreed but would compensate slave-owning unionists with profits from the sale of land confiscated from rebels. Stanton, Welles, and Bates were for it because they expected emancipation to aid the war effort. Chase lobbied Lincoln to free the slaves and recruit black troops. Seward was elliptical, but even Chase admitted that he questioned only whether it was the right time. Yet all saw freedom and union as inseparable, and raised no doubts about federal power to take action.[28]

Late in July 1862, Lincoln talked with his Cabinet about taking action, with an emancipation proclamation to apply to the rebellious areas. Their responses revealed political calculations and concerns about whether his proposal would work. Seward, Chase, and Welles doubted that it could be enforced; as secretary of state, Seward feared its effect on foreign nations more interested in cotton than in freedom. Chase would let army commanders emancipate in their districts. Dissenting, Blair saw no public support for it and expected it to cost the party control of Congress in the fall elections. Smith was silent, but known to be cautious to the point of paralysis on the issue of slavery. Stanton and Bates shared Lincoln's goals but felt that he might be going too far. Finally, Seward's logic prevailed: better to wait for a victory and issue any proclamation from a position of strength, not with the appearance of desperation. But the debate showed how far they had come. Privately they leaned toward emancipation, but when called to account as government leaders, they weighed the effect of freedom on the Union and their power to act in the interest of both.[29]

In the end, though, the Cabinet lacked the power to act on this question because Lincoln assumed the responsibility. After McClellan won a narrow victory at Antietam on 22 September 1862, Lincoln told his secretaries that he was issuing the proclamation, to take effect on 1 January 1863; he did not ask. All of them fell into line. Blair, Bates, and Smith backed colonization and murmured misgivings, Welles admitted that Lincoln might be overreaching his war powers, and Chase wished that he had gone further and given the soon-to-be-freed slaves the vote. But, whatever their concerns, they deferred. Ironically, a group of governors met that day at Altoona, Pennsylvania, to urge stronger war measures. Their main goals were emancipation and the radical Frémont's return to command. When they saw Lincoln five days later, with their first hope fulfilled, they could do no more than assail the conservatism of Seward and Blair. Accusing them of just wanting to get Seward, Lincoln sent them away. The combination of the proclamation and Lincoln's courteous yet curt treatment of the governors should have made clear who was in charge of the executive branch, and, indeed, of the Republican party's policies.[30]

The Putsch That Failed

As the proclamation's deadline approached, the administration was in a highly combustible situation—partly because Lincoln was in control, partly due to those policies, and partly due to external forces. Despite Stanton's best efforts, the army was, if anything, more bogged down than ever: Ulysses Grant seemed mired in the mud near Vicksburg, which he besieged to capture, and in December the Army of the Potomac collapsed like a column of sand at Fredericksburg. The party lost governorships and congressional seats in the midterm elections, a normal pattern for the party in power, but during an insurrection it was another matter entirely. Republicans wanted and needed an explanation for these failures. If the guilty party was not the policies they pursued, then it had to be those who were failing to execute the policies. The Republican response to what to do about it affected and reflected the continuing debate over who in their party and in the government had the responsibility for wielding power.[31]

Between congressional Republicans who were legislative supremacists and Cabinet members with their ambitions and jealousies, blame fell on Seward. At issue was who held power in the administration and the party. Wade called Lincoln a "fool" controlled by Seward, who was "by nature a coward & a sneak," and, Medill claimed, "kept a sponge saturated with chloroform to Uncle Abe's nose." Chase envied what he saw as Seward's close relationship with Lincoln, although that appears to have had more to do with enjoying one another than with political power, as Chase thought; also, Seward's diplomatic domain interested Lincoln more than Chase's fiscal problems. Chase felt that Lincoln met too rarely with the Cabinet as a unit, leaving each secretary to run his department; that may have produced more cohesion, but it may also have increased in-fighting, and Chase seems not to have considered that this was Lincoln's subtle way of wielding power. Clearly, the issue was more personal and political than ideological, related to the means to the ends, not the ends themselves. For one thing, criticism of Lincoln's management style came from all sides. And, as Chase admitted after dining with Seward, "He . . . sometimes does things he ought not to do; but he does talk and act very much like a man desirous above all things to serve his country."[32]

But late in 1862, congressional Republicans were so concerned about the state of the Union and their party, and whether power was in the right set of hands, that they took an action whose implications were so crucial to Republican ideology and the functions of the government that it must be examined in detail. After the Fredericksburg debacle, Senate Republicans met in caucus on 16 December. They claimed that Seward lacked devotion to the cause and that Lincoln consulted his Cabinet too rarely. When moderate William Pitt Fessenden of Maine complained of "a back stairs and malign influence which controlled the President, and overruled all the decisions of the cabinet, and he understood Mr. Seward to be meant," his colleagues surmised that Chase was his source. Iowa moderate James Grimes, who was close to Fessenden, offered a resolution of no confidence in Seward, the kind of vote with which parliaments try to remove prime ministers and a dubious move for Congress to consider. More cautious Republicans—conservatives Browning and Edgar Cowan of Pennsylvania and New York's Preston King, who was close to Seward—preferred an investigation. That day, learning from King of the Senate discussion and wanting to protect Lincoln, Seward and his son, who served as his deputy, resigned.[33]

While the senators debated how best to approach the president, Lincoln faced the question of how to assert his power without costing himself needed congressional support, the very kind of issue that Republicans had never had to confront when they had been in the opposition. The caucus toned down its resolution to urge "a change and partial reconstruction of the Cabinet" to avoid the chance that Lincoln would fire everyone, including Chase, whom they sought to protect. To meet with Lincoln they chose a mostly radical committee, but its chairman was Jacob Collamer, a Vermont conservative and former Whig. Meanwhile, Lincoln was angry and depressed at this challenge to his authority. As Bates described his reaction, "they seemed to think that when he had in him any good purposes, Mr. Seward contrived *to suck them out of him unperceived.*" Lincoln told Browning, "They wish to get rid of me, and I am sometimes half disposed to gratify them." But when the senators arrived, Fessenden assured Lincoln that he had the Senate's confidence; the Constitution gave the senators the power to advise and consent, and they advised a change wholly in the spirit of helpfulness. Lincoln felt differently. A *New York Tribune* reporter wrote privately that he was saying "that if there was any worse Hell than he had been in for two days, he would like to know it. He is awfully shaken."[34]

Actually, Lincoln was less shaken than he appeared. At his request, the senators returned the next night and found a disagreeable surprise: all of the Cabinet except Seward, and a president who asserted his power and discounted theirs. For several hours, the secretaries defended themselves and claimed to work well together. While claiming to consult his Cabinet as much as necessary, Lincoln confessed to making key decisions, mostly about McClellan, on his own. But he warned that he expected "a general smash-up" if Seward left under these circumstances. Blair admitted to differing with his conservative rival, but praised his loyalty and attacked the senators for taking this step. Chase praised Lincoln and the Cabinet, defended Seward's position on emancipation, and voiced displeasure at being set up. When Browning reported that Chase had been the instigator, Lincoln replied "with a good deal of emphasis that he was master."[35]

As the repercussions proved, Lincoln was right: he was the master. The embarrassed Chase offered his letter of resignation. Lincoln eagerly replied, "Let me have it. Now I can ride; I have a pumpkin in each end of my bag." Seward and Chase claimed not to want to return to their posts; naturally, their friends urged them to reconsider and their enemies rejoiced. However, Lincoln asked them to resume their jobs, and they did so, declaring their commitment to serving the public. In the end they served Lincoln in a variety of ways, not just as able secretaries. With the Senate having made clear how precarious his position was, and aware that his old power base had eroded considerably, Seward devoted himself to supporting Lincoln and to his diplomatic duties; any knavery in his future would be in Lincoln's behalf. Chase remained as ambitious as ever to succeed Lincoln, and superb as ever at running the Treasury, but stopped trying to force the president into remaking the Cabinet to suit his tastes.[36]

Thus, if "the muss over the Cabinet" seemed over, the results were far-reaching. Some observers detected more respect for Lincoln among his party's senators; while still doubtful about Seward, they somehow seemed to sense that they had met their match. Indeed they had. Chase's actions and the Senate's failure to jettison Seward served the purposes they were meant to thwart: they enhanced Lincoln's power and diminished the influence of the Cabinet and Congress by showing that changes could not be forced and would be made by Lincoln. Many Republicans found the Senate's efforts troubling. Governor William Dennison of Ohio asked, "Is it not a dangerous innovation for Senators to interfere with Cabinet matters in caucus form? Will it not be a precedent that may in the future completely subordinate the Executive to the Legislative branch of the Govt and thus virtually destroy the whole theory of our political system." Although he abhorred Seward, Welles wrote, "A Senatorial combination to dictate to the President in regard to his political family . . . cannot be permitted to succeed, even if the person to whom they object were as obnoxious as they represent." Even Edward Everett, an old Massachusetts Whig friendly to Lincoln and the Republicans out of unionism, told Seward that Congress could pass the equivalent of a parliamentary vote of no confidence, but not a party caucus.[37]

While Lincoln outfoxed two feuding secretaries and a captious Senate, he made a powerful statement in behalf of presidential power and authority over his Cabinet at a point in history when he could have set a precedent that might circumscribe future presidents and Congresses—and himself. This was a fight over power: who could wield it best to help the party reach its goals. No one questioned or debated the goals themselves. Whatever Republicans did at that time, what they did not say was important. They could leave unspoken their commitment to freedom, union, and power; that was agreed upon.

Family Feuds

Similar motives characterized the fights over the Cabinet that would continue for the rest of the war. Whatever feuding existed, and its many layers, was separate from the party's ideology. Conservatives like Blair and radicals like Chase agreed on preserving freedom and union, and on the need for the government to wield the power to accomplish that. Beyond that it was less simple. As Republicans they opposed the extension of slavery. As conservatives, the Blairs grudgingly reconciled themselves to emancipation. But they feared how freedom would affect the South and the North's ability to reunite with it, and were queasy about how much power the government could claim to impose on it. As a radical—or, in modern parlance, a liberal—Chase verged on abolitionism and supported broad federal powers. That they worked together at all, albeit often in disharmony, in the same administration reflected the depth of their party's beliefs and their commitment to them; that they became such bitter enemies, mostly over politics, said much the same thing. If the party's unity proved tenuous when the war ended, it was demonstrably strong while the nation seemed at risk.

Rumors swirled throughout 1863 and 1864 about wholesale changes in the Cabinet. When radical *New York Evening Post* editor William Cullen Bryant asked about driving conservatives, especially Seward, from the Cabinet, Fessenden replied that if the effort failed, the opposition would detect a dispute that might harm the government. But without victories, Lincoln would be "compelled by public opinion to reorganise his Cabinet." This response was multilayered: it was an admission of the importance of unity and power, and of general agreement on principles; it was also a confession that even a caucus of powerful senators lacked the wherewithal to budge Lincoln. Yet the complaints against various Cabinet members continued unabated: the increasingly radical Winter Davis publicly and privately skewered Blair over Maryland politics and Welles for his treatment of an admiral friend Davis believed to have been wronged. Conservatives and political opponents refused to trust Chase; radicals and political opponents refused to trust Seward. For any party to engage in intramural squabbling was normal, but politics and ambition remained at the heart of it.[38]

The only Cabinet change between the failed putsch against Seward and the 1864 party convention revealed the assumption that Republicans shared similar views and the role of pure politics. When Smith left the Interior Department for a federal judgeship, radicals welcomed his departure. But Lincoln chose the Indianan's successor on the basis of geography, not his place on the party spectrum. He reportedly preferred Browning, who could be fairly described as ultra-conservative, but offered the seat to Schuyler Colfax, a young representative from Indiana with close ties to Horace Greeley, and far afield from Smith or Browning. When Colfax declined—he was a rising star in the House, soon to be Speaker—Lincoln chose Smith's deputy, John Usher, mainly to please Indiana Republicans. Usher drew little attention, although he joined Chase, Stanton, and Welles to argue in favor of ending slavery immediately, if possible. Whatever the discussions that preceded Usher's appointment, Lincoln thought geographically and politically. Ideology was no problem, because however much they disagreed, Republicans ultimately agreed on that score.[39]

But Lincoln's reelection campaign and the Union's inability to end the war prompted dramatic changes in the Cabinet in the summer and fall of 1864. The most bombastic conservative, Blair, and the most ambitious radical, Chase, left—one involuntarily, hoisted on his own petard; one voluntarily, under pressure from his enemies and at Lincoln's request. To recount how they departed, how they reacted, and how Lincoln replaced them is to demonstrate that party differences had far more to do with personalities and partisanship than with ideology. Clearly, Chase believed more strongly than did Blair in emancipation, enfranchisement, and black civil rights. Equally clearly, Chase was more willing than Blair to back federal action in behalf of those policies. However, as the *New York Tribune*—a pro-Chase paper whose editor, Greeley, had a respectful relationship with Francis Preston Blair, the postmaster general's father—said of the Cabinet in 1863, "No member harbors for a moment the idea of reconstructing the Union on a basis of slavery." They had similar ideas, differently expressed; similar ends, differently achieved. The similarities were great enough for the Cabinet to function as a unit, if a carping and captious one, at odds with Lincoln or one another over patronage or how best to approach the issues more often than over the issues themselves; the differences were personal, but they ran deep enough and eventually grew wide enough to tear the secretaries' relationships, and certainly that of Chase and Blair, asunder.[40]

One point of dispute in the Cabinet, especially between Chase and Blair, concerned the future: with the Union restored, how much should freedom spread, and who had power to spread it? Speaking in Rockville, Maryland, late in 1863, Blair argued the more conservative view. But by attacking the radicals, he only caused more divisions. "The Abolition party, whilst pronouncing philippics against slavery, seek to make a caste of another color by amalgamating the black element with the free labor of our land," he warned. He told Sumner that they agreed on ending the war and slavery and on protecting Southern unionists and freedmen "*effectively* and *constitutionally,*" but Blair's conservatism and racism rankled radicals. Thaddeus Stevens wanted a delegation to go to Lincoln to demand Blair's ouster—the same approach that had failed with Seward. Informed that his words could hurt the party, Blair countered that he spoke only for himself, prompting Lincoln's editor friend John Forney to urge him to leave the Cabinet and "not load down" Lincoln with his views. Ironically, two of Lincoln's closest allies disagreed on how best to serve him, symbolizing that Blair was becoming a personal liability to his president. Always a loyal soldier, Blair put himself in the position of diluting Lincoln's power by creating controversy for him, and isolated himself from the rest of the Cabinet. He was especially distant from Chase, who sincerely believed in the need to enfranchise blacks and for the federal government to take the lead in determining the future of the freedmen and the South.[41]

Among those doubting Chase's honesty were the Blairs; their feud shows what divided Republicans during the Civil War. While they differed violently, and sought ways to draw what each saw as genuine

Democrats into the Republican tent, they agreed on the issues far more than they disagreed: slavery was a blot on the national escutcheon that eventually would have to die; the Union must be restored in such a way as to assure no recurrence of insurrection; and some form of government power—Chase preferred the federal level, the Blairs the states—would have to impose its will. What drove apart Chase and the Blairs were personal differences, loyalties, and ambitions. Chase wanted to be president and worked to achieve that goal even as he served in Lincoln's Cabinet; with Montgomery as postmaster general and Frank as a general and congressman, the Blairs considered themselves soldiers of the Union and of Lincoln's reelection, and they would allow no one to stand in the way.[42]

But what triggered major changes in the Cabinet was not ideaology, it was politics: the 1864 election, and Chase's role in it. Greeley privately called him Lincoln's ablest secretary and publicly said that "since Henry Clay, we have known no man better fitted for President, by natural ability, by study and reflection, by training and experience, by integrity and patriotism, by soundness of principle and greatness of soul than is Salmon P. Chase." The only person who felt even more strongly than Greeley was Chase himself, who desperately wanted to be president and so furiously dedicated himself to that goal that the waspish Welles, who was no fan of his, concluded that it "warped" him. Chase became immersed in politics in his home state of Ohio, whose endorsement would be crucial to his chances. He interfered in Maryland in behalf of Winter Davis, which made the Blairs apoplectic. And he reputedly used Treasury clerks to campaign for him, which did nothing for his relations with Lincoln.[43]

For Lincoln, the key was to dispose of Chase as a presidential contender without destroying his usefulness or already doubtful loyalty as a Cabinet member. The only ideological issue was that Chase appealed to radicals and Lincoln to moderates and conservatives, but even that was political, granting the question of who best stood for what the party believed and how quickly those beliefs should be turned into action. New Hampshire, where Chase had been raised, offered Lincoln an early endorsement, thanks to the efforts of Blair and Welles. They reminded state party leader William Chandler that radical Senator John Hale's support for Chase and reelection would keep rising moderates like himself from enjoying patronage and higher office. At the party conclave in Ohio, where Chase spent the bulk of his career, he proved unable to win even an endorsement of his work as a Cabinet member; Lincoln's backers carried the day. And if Ohio and New Hampshire drove nails into Chase's coffin, the "Pomeroy Circular" shut the lid. When radical Senator Samuel Pomeroy of Kansas issued a letter endorsing Chase's nomination and attacking Lincoln's, Chase offered to quit, but Lincoln declined the resignation and claimed not even to have read the circular. "Corruption intrigue and malice are doing their worst, but I do not think it is in the cards to beat the Tycoon," John Nicolay told John Hay, his fellow presidential secretary. Chase agreed and announced that he would not seek the office, but less radical Republicans were dubious: Senator Edwin Morgan of New York predicted that Chase would keep scheming until Lincoln had officially been chosen, and David Davis called the move "a mere sham, and very *ungracefully* done."[44]

To say that the Blairs hoped to move in for the kill is no overstatement: Montgomery said, "When the Blairs go in for a fight, they go in for a funeral." Welles's aide and Blair's brother-in-law Gustavus Fox charged Chase with trying to shift a congressional inquiry from the Treasury to the Navy, taking the heat off himself at the expense of the Blairs. The intrigue culminated when Frank Blair, representing Missouri in the House, rose to accuse Chase of "profligate administration . . . rank and fetid with . . . fraud and corruption." Then he left the chamber and strode to the White House, where Lincoln named him a general and he left for the army. At issue was whether Lincoln condoned one of the blunter public attacks a Cabinet member received within his party. Montgomery Blair felt that his brother had painted "the truthful portraiture of a cold blooded corrupt intriguer. . . . It is the verdict of the nation too." Other conservatives smelled blood: Thurlow Weed stepped up his assaults on Chase as guilty of "official rapacity which will bankrupt the Treasury, disgrace the Administration and destroy the Government."[45]

The understandably wounded response of Chase and his friends had more to do with politics than with any particular issue. When Chase urged Wade to seek Montgomery Blair's removal, Wade said, "No, you don't—I remember you near blocked the wheels of the Republican Party when I represented them as one of a committee in the case of Brother Seward." Livid at the speech, Chase fumed at "the villainous, malignant, and lying assault of the Blairs—for the congressional general was only the mouth-piece of the trio." Worse, unwilling to concede any cause for criticism, his reward for his service was Lincoln's "apparent—but as I hope and believe merely apparent—endorsement only in outrageous calumny." Fearing that he would quit, Chase's emissaries went to Lincoln, who assured them that he had had no role in Blair's assault, but neither did he offer the public disavowal that Chase wanted. Chase thought of resigning but claimed to put public service above personal matters, which relieved his supporters. But Medill asked, "Is it possible that Lincoln will let Chase go to retain the d——d infernal Blair family, who are a perfect incubus and curse to him?"[46]

The answer was that Lincoln kept Blair longer—but not much, and only due to partisan politics, not to their feud or any ideological disputes. After Lincoln's renomination, Chase's aide in New York, John Cisco, quit. Chase chose radical Maunsell Field to succeed him. Lincoln reported that two New York leaders, Weed and Morgan, found Field unacceptable. Chase induced Cisco to stay, then offered to resign. Since previous offers had gone unaccepted, Chase apparently expected Lincoln to massage his ego. Instead, he replied, "Of all I have said in commendation of your ability and fidelity, I have nothing to unsay, and yet you and I have reached a point of mutual embarrassment in our official relation which it seems can not be overcome, or longer sustained, consistently with the public service."[47]

The contrasting responses of Lincoln and Chase, and those of their defenders, were telling. Jay Cooke, the investor with whom Chase worked closely, feared economic and political disaster. A slew of Ohio politicians asked Chase to reconsider. But while he complained about how Lincoln's allies treated him, he refused to see in himself what he saw in others. He declared that since "local politics" now outweighed "simple fidelity to the general cause and fitness," he could serve no longer. That his political empire-building had contributed mightily to his problems was beyond his ability to admit or see. While Chase could claim ideological reasons for departing, the reality was that politics was the cause. Ideology mattered only to the extent that as he ran for reelection, Lincoln needed subordinates who were loyal to him and his administration. Chase had failed that test.[48]

Lincoln demonstrated the importance of that test in his response to the resignation and in choosing a replacement. When Governor John

Brough of Ohio urged him to keep Chase, Lincoln said that "this is the third time he has thrown this resignation at me, and I do not think I am called on to continue to beg him to take it back, especially when the country would not go to destruction in consequence." Indeed, when a Treasury official called Chase indispensable, Lincoln replied, "How mistaken you are! Yet it is not strange; I used to have similar notions. No! If we should all be turned out to-morrow, and could come back here in a week, we should find our places filled by a lot of fellows doing just as well as we did, and in many instances better." No man, he felt, was bigger than the cause or what it stood for—especially when the friction to which he contributed might endanger the power of the party, the administration, and the Union more than he could help preserve them.[49]

Thus, when Lincoln sought a successor he looked first to an Ohioan, former governor David Tod, whose fiscal views were the opposite of Chase's. This was a sign that Lincoln thought more about politics as being the problem than ideology, and it may also have been evidence that Lincoln was consolidating or centralizing power with himself and out of the hands of his secretaries. When Tod declined, Lincoln effected a political master stroke by appointing Fessenden, a Chase ally on financial issues, a moderate in all matters, and the party's leader in the Senate. No one could, or for that matter did, question Fessenden's fitness for the job, even if they found him disagreeable on some issues or in person.

Ideologically and politically, Fessenden was a superlative choice. As he said, he kept the government from "directly operating upon the market," perhaps a harbinger of the hands-off attitude the party later adopted, certainly a sign that he accepted Chase's policies to fund the Union war machine. Unlike Chase, Fessenden easily acceded to patronage requests, never discomfiting Lincoln, who otherwise left him alone to do his job. Unlike Chase, he had no higher ambitions; like Stanton, he owed his allegiance to Lincoln, who had appointed him. While the effects can only be speculated on, Fessenden's exposure to Lincoln could have affected the relationship between Congress and the president if Lincoln had lived. Once a leader in the Senate revolt due to Seward's presumed power over Lincoln, Fessenden concluded that Lincoln was "a man of decided intellect, and a good fellow, able to do well any one thing, if he was able, or content, to confine his attention to that thing until it was done. In attempting to do too much, he botches them all." This was a reasoned criticism, with no trace of the belief that Lincoln was Seward's patsy. Indeed, Fessenden decided, in a less egotistical, more analytical statement than Chase could or would have made, "Lincoln is not now so strong as he has been, but he is an astute politician, and, at any rate, much more than a match for any of his Cabinet."[50]

Lincoln was a politician seeking reelection; thus, politics more than ideology prompted a Cabinet change. The convention that renominated him agreed that "the necessities of the hour require the reconstruction of the cabinet," a recommendation from a party instead of a Senate caucus creating or crossing constitutional lines, and just vague enough to give Lincoln room to maneuver. Speculation focused on Welles, whom party chair Raymond wanted replaced for refusing to lean on naval workers to give time and money to the campaign. Welles won praise for increasing the pay of Boston Navy Yard workers and, Representative Samuel Hooper said, showing "that the Government wished always to do justice to the mechanics and laborers." The combination of events showed that the party recalled the antebellum ideology it had refined on assuming power—and that Lincoln intended to keep the powers of the executive branch for himself.[51]

When Lincoln finally changed his Cabinet, politics far outweighed the few ideological factors. Blair's Rockville speech infuriated radicals, but old Whigs such as Weed were equally unhappy with him. For an ex-Whig like Seward and a Jacksonian like Blair to set aside old disputes may have been too much to ask. They shared an ideological commitment but approached it from different directions: Blair recalled Jefferson in telling Maryland legislators, "We are all Republicans—all Democrats," while Seward told Massachusetts conservative Richard Henry Dana that "the government is back on the platform of Hamilton & the Federalists & . . . nothing less is capable of carrying it through the crisis." Worse, Blair caused a more personal dispute. In 1864, when rebel raiders burned his family home at Silver Spring, Maryland, he responded by charging Stanton and the army's chief clerk, General Henry Halleck, with incompetence for letting it happen. Stanton had never liked Blair, who could be as flinty as he; speaking to a Winter Davis ally about Blair and Maryland politics, the War secretary told him to "skin him, turn his hide, pickle it—and stretch it on a barn door to dry!" For his part, learning of Blair's criticism, Halleck went to Lincoln and demanded the postmaster general's dismissal. The president replied that he alone would decide when and why to fire a Cabinet member, another reminder of who really was in charge.[52]

But Lincoln faced pressure from other sources, again less ideological than political. The Blairs were in a deeply personal battle with Davis for control of Maryland's Republican apparatus. They differed on the means to the ends the party sought: the Blairs, Jacksonians who still hated their old Whig foes, preferred compensated emancipation and limited federal interference; Davis, an ex-Whig who despised Democrats, saw the former as a chance to steal state money and the latter as a sop to the Southern aristocracy and its Democratic allies. The real issue was power, and Lincoln's tendency to delegate authority and defer on patronage gave the Blairs a clear advantage. Thus, when Frank Blair defended Welles against Davis's charges of corruption, which were rooted in how Welles had treated an admiral friend of his, it was Democrat versus Whig, conservative versus radical, family (Welles's deputy was Montgomery Blair's brother-in-law) versus friend, and civil war in Maryland. When Davis lost his bid for reelection to the House, he blamed Lincoln for his support of the Blairs.[53]

Ironically, Davis exacted revenge by hurting himself politically, which helped force Blair's departure from the Cabinet and enabled Lincoln both to increase the party's unity and to show subtly that he held power. The growing unhappiness and dubious political acumen of the radicals caused the change. In the summer of 1864, when Lincoln used a pocket veto and a presidential proclamation to undermine the more stringent reconstruction plans in a bill by Davis and Wade, the two radicals accused him of "grave Executive usurpation" and "a blow at the friends of his Administration, at the rights of humanity, and at the principles of Republican Government." The manifesto was so nasty and impolitic that many radicals disowned it, but it symbolized radical concerns about Lincoln's seeming conservatism, or at least support for those who embodied that point of view. Nor did it help Lincoln's cause that War Democrats and some extreme radicals bolted to support the quixotic presidential bid of John C. Frémont, the radical general he had fired twice for incompetence and an enemy of the Blairs. These developments were unlikely to derail Lincoln's reelection, as subsequent events revealed. But McClellan's nomination and Sherman's success were in the future, and in the meantime the party was in danger of splitting over how best to put its ideology into practice and who should be responsible for it. Lincoln and the radicals needed grounds for unification, and Zachariah Chandler came up with a deal that both sides promptly denied making: Frémont's withdrawal for Blair's removal.[54]

The responses to Blair's departure revealed how nonideological and how political the fight had been. Wade thought that the senator from Michigan played "on Old Abe's fears, for . . . he would not have done it because all his political friends desired it"; this may suggest that Wade saw himself as Lincoln's political friend, and that their differences may have been less than even they thought. Davis derided Lincoln for abandoning his friends but welcomed Blair's departure; his reaction was more personal and political than ideological. More important, Lincoln and the Blairs thought in political terms. Lincoln wrote to Blair, "You have generously said to me more than once, that whenever your resignation could be a relief to me, it was at my disposal. The time has come," and "this proceeds from no dissatisfaction of mine with you personally or officially." Indeed, Frank Blair commented that his brother's departure was a small price to pay if it reelected Lincoln, and Montgomery Blair campaigned ardently, telling Welles that his removal would assure Lincoln of radical support and informing crowds that he had quit not because he opposed Lincoln's policies but "to allay animosities among the friends of these principles" and "secure their triumph." While the Blairs seethed at the radicals, they avoided reopening or widening old wounds; they were out to reelect their party's standard-bearer and did their best for him. So did some radicals, despite misgivings, and he easily won a second term.[55]

The remaining Cabinet changes further underscored the role of politics and the assumed ideological agreement that had characterized other arrivals and departures. Lincoln chose William Dennison of Ohio, a state that had been unrepresented in the Cabinet since Chase's exit, to succeed Blair. When Bates retired, Lincoln said, "I suppose if the twelve Apostles were to be chosen nowadays the shrieks of locality would have to be heeded," and chose Kentuckian James Speed, the brother of his oldest friend. Usher was expendable if Lincoln wanted to offer a radical a seat from which he could do little for his cause. He did, but his choice, Senator James Harlan of Iowa, was a friend whose daughter was engaged to Lincoln's oldest son. When Fessenden returned to the Senate, Lincoln turned to the comptroller of the currency, Hugh McCulloch, who was no politician; but he was from Indiana, which lacked a Cabinet representative, and he had a reputation as the kind of financial expert the reunited Union would need to get its fiscal house in order. With all of these appointees, only their political utility or obvious competence were at issue; four years of war and loyalty had made their dedication to the party's cause safe to presume.[56]

Indeed, the speculation and rumor-mongering over who might join the Cabinet demonstrated how political effects concerned Republicans more than ideological purity. When Bates left, one rumored replacement was Andrew, whose tenure as governor of Massachusetts was done; Sumner cared less about ideology than about diverting any of Andrew's ambitions for his Senate seat. Fessenden's departure from the Treasury prompted similar jockeying. Weed proposed Adams, who hoped to retire; instead, he stayed at his post in England. Others urged Morgan, who was well qualified but came from the same state as Seward—which was why some radicals liked the idea. After Seward and his allies induced Morgan to withdraw from consideration, Lincoln told Weed to choose between McCulloch and Samuel Hooper, a Boston businessman who served on the House Ways and Means Committee and happened to be close to Sumner. That Weed chose McCulloch over a Sumner ally, after radicals used Morgan to try again to dislodge Seward, was an obvious sign of the dispute between radicals and conservatives. But it was political, as the other appointments and rumored appointments had been. Andrew, Hooper, and Morgan were moderates who worked well with all sides; their names were useful to one or the other and mattered far more than the side toward which they might tilt.[57]

The Cabinet's composition and the rumors surrounding it reflected political reality. For most of Lincoln's tenure, he needed the kind of unity that only choosing Republicans from all of the party's antecedents and branches could provide. This required him to sacrifice another form of unity: loyalty to him. None of his original appointees won his office on the grounds of fealty to Lincoln. Their common characteristic was their usefulness—their geography, Democratic or Whig background, radical or conservative leanings, or power in their home state's party. As the war went on and Lincoln faced new problems, he retained his old yardstick for determining who served in his Cabinet. As the political fortunes of such secretaries as Seward, Blair, Welles, and Bates ebbed far more than they flowed, Lincoln defended and kept them; one left voluntarily, one quit involuntarily but agreeably, and the other two were still there at the end of the second term that Lincoln did not live to complete. When Cameron became too much of a liability, his ethics and ability too questionable, Lincoln jettisoned him but found a replacement, Stanton, of demonstrable ability. Chase was, politically, as disloyal to Lincoln as a Cabinet member could be, if trying to unseat the incumbent and use others to force him to remove other secretaries are examples of disloyalty. But Lincoln kept him until he no longer found him necessary; Chase's earlier behavior contributed to the president's final decision, but that decision came long after the earlier behavior had created problems for Lincoln.

This description and analysis may seem nonideological, and that is the point. Republican discussions of the Cabinet rarely referred to the party's ideology, which suggests two crucial factors in any analysis: the party was so preoccupied with trying to win a war that no great need existed for forays into political theory; Republicans understood where they stood and had no reason for repetition. Thus, the disputes involving Cabinet members had more to do with political ambition than with political ideology. Republicans differed over degree or speed: Chase wanted emancipation and civil rights to come sooner, while Seward would move more slowly; Chase backed centralized federal power but doubted that Lincoln was the one to exercise it, while Blair opposed expanding federal influence but had faith that Lincoln would use it wisely. But these were disputes over the means to be used to reach the party's ends. The members of Lincoln's Cabinet agreed on those ends, but fought over how to achieve them and who would have the most power to achieve them: themselves, Congress, or the president. They varied between their desire and commitment to serve, their professed preference for repose, their ambitions for themselves and their supporters, and their residue hatreds for those who had opposed them and, in some cases, still opposed them.

Thus, the battles within and over the Cabinet involved power, one of the three components of the party's ideology. To that extent, the story of Lincoln's Cabinet may be seen as one of ideological warfare.

But party disputes over power were less ideological than personal and political. After the 1864 election, Andrew suggested that Lincoln employ "advisers all heartily, unselfishly devoted to a common purpose," not "'a happy family' of presidential candidates, nor of merely able representatives of different sections or different wings of the party." What common purpose Andrew had in mind for the composition of the Cabinet was clear. He wrote these words as the war ended, as the party's belief in freedom, union, and power came to fruition. Restoring the Union would demand another form of unity. Whether Andrew hoped for singular devotion to the means he sought or the means Lincoln sought was less clear. That is partly because new circumstances and issues awaited Republicans and the nation they had been empowered to govern. The reelection of Lincoln and a Republican majority showed that whatever they had done had satisfied the voters. Lincoln's leadership and how he used it had been sustained. In the end, in the race to decide how to protect and perpetuate freedom and union, democratic power approved of Lincoln's power.[58]

Part of the problem with understanding this interplay—and the lack of it—between politics and ideology is the circumstances in which they occurred. However trite it seems to say it, the Civil War was a time like no other. A Maine daily hazarded a perceptive comment about Lincoln's second term: "His Cabinet during the first term were subject to the most unsparing criticism, and frequently to exceedingly unjust censure. There are reasons for the belief that the present Cabinet of his choice will be the recipients of fairer treatment and more generous confidence than its predecessor." Unaccustomed to power, then even more covetous of it, Republicans had engaged in a lot of extracurricular pouting and complaining. Now that they were more experienced, their leaders might have been expected to settle down, or, with victory in the war at hand, step aside or at least back and begin to heal themselves and the country.[59]

By 1865 a change was evident, but perhaps not the change the party had in mind. Hearkening to old differences, Chandler complained, "We want Seward out, but Old Abe dont & so I am of the opinion that he will stay." Therein lay the difference: a radical who joined other senators in trying to drive out Seward in 1862 saw after Lincoln's reelection who firmly held the levers of power. One reason, besides victory, was the nature of the American political system itself. Wendell Phillips surmised, "The trouble is neither the Senate or the House has a Head—as Clay or Webster was. Sumner leads ten; Trumbull twenty. Fessenden some. *But the three quarrel.*" In fact, he concluded, "Congress is a mob—the Administration a *unit.* Hence its success."

Even if the Lincoln administration was never entirely a unit, Phillips came close to the truth, and thus the irony: the radicals with whom the abolitionist felt more comfortable helped unite some of the feuding members of Lincoln's Cabinet by trying to oust them, creating for men like Seward and Blair a common enemy. Yet the radicals seemed to have won the battle for Lincoln's soul that had begun inauspiciously for them with the making of the Cabinet. At a Cabinet meeting on 14 April 1865, Lincoln "never seemed so near our views," Speed told Chase, who continued to advocate radical policies such as black enfranchisement. The next day Chase mourned, "All Mr. Speed said deepened my sorrow for the country's great loss." By year's end, radicals like Wade, who had been optimistic that Andrew Johnson could rise above "the timorous, halting, hesitating, negative instrumentalities, which served well enough the late Administration," had begun to understand that their problem with Johnson's policies, as with Lincoln's, lay not around the Cabinet table but with the man at the head of it.[60]

The lesson was valuable, but it was learned too late. Lincoln's "ministry of all the talents" often revealed more talent for invective and political scrimmaging than for anything else. Nor, given his administrative methods, did his Cabinet function as one conventionally did or does. All too often the members divided over their ambitions for the party and themselves. Chase was radical, Blair noisily conservative, Bates quietly conservative, Cameron and Stanton all things to all people, Seward fluctuating, Smith and Usher nothing in particular. While this is important in figuring out why the ministers were so divided, it is more crucial to understand that despite this litany of dispute, they succeeded: the government for which they shared responsibility under Lincoln won its war. Yet it was no wartime "coalition" like that which governed Churchill's England. Whatever their divisions, the ultimate end of winning the war never changed; only how to achieve it. Thus their ideology, their shared beliefs, and shared goal proved to be the adhesive that unified them.

NOTES

1. Leonard Swett to David Davis, Washington, 1 January 1861, David Davis Papers (Davis ms), Illinois State Historical Library; Carman and Luthin, *Lincoln and the Patronage;* Oates, *With Malice Toward None,* 195; Blaine, *Twenty Years of Congress,* vol. 1, 283; B. Gratz Brown to Francis P. Blair Sr., St. Louis, 8 November 1860, Blair-Lee Family ms, Box 7, Princeton University. The classic study is Hendrick, *Lincoln's War Cabinet.* See also Paludan, *The Presidency of Abraham Lincoln.*

2. Hendrick, *Lincoln's War Cabinet, passim.* The standard biographies include Donald, *Lincoln;* Van Deusen, *William Henry Seward;* Niven, *Salmon P. Chase;* Niven, *Gideon Welles;* Marvin R. Cain, *Lincoln's Attorney General: Edward Bates of Missouri* (Columbia: University of Missouri Press, 1965); Thomas and Hyman, *Stanton;* Erwin S. Bradley, *Simon Cameron, Lincoln's Secretary of War: A Political Biography* (Philadelphia: University of Pennsylvania Press, 1966).

3. David Donald, "Abraham Lincoln: Whig in the White House," in Norman A. Graebner, ed., *The Enduring Lincoln* (Urbana: University of Illinois Press, 1959), 55–66; Stephen B. Oates, "Abraham Lincoln: *Republican* in the White House," in Thomas, ed., *Abraham Lincoln and the American Political Tradition,* 90–110. Donald further extended his argument in his biography *Lincoln.* The historiographic problem seems to me that Donald is making his argument based on the premise that Lincoln had little to do with anything other than the war effort. But that effort was so all-consuming that it is hardly possible to assume that Lincoln had much of an opportunity to involve himself in other activities. As I will argue throughout, when Lincoln had the time and inclination to involve himself in other matters, he did so.

4. Stevens to Chase, Washington, 3 February 1861, Chase ms, Box 10, HSP; Norman B. Judd to Trumbull, Chicago, 21 December 1860, Trumbull ms, Reel 7, LC; Fogg to Lincoln, Washington, 2 February 1861, Fogg ms, Box 1, NHHS; Manuscript, n.d., Welles ms, Box 7, NYPL; Hendrick, *Lincoln's War Cabinet,* 97–149; Barnes and Weed, *Life of Thurlow Weed,* 301–2.

5. Weed to Davis, Albany, 26 December 1860, and 20 January 1861, Davis ms, Illinois State Historical Library; Seward to Weed, Washington, 21 January 1861, Weed ms, UR; Barnes and Weed, *Life of Thurlow Weed,* 293–95, 606–11; Oates, *With Malice Toward None,* 199–200; Van Deusen, *Thurlow Weed,* 259–61; Randall, *Lincoln the President: Springfield to Gettysburg,* vol. 1, 261–62.

6. Lincoln to Seward, Springfield, 8 December 1860, Lincoln ms, LC, in *CW,* vol. 4, 148–49; Seward to Lincoln, Auburn, 13 and 28 December 1860, ibid.; Van Deusen, *Thurlow Weed,* 259–60; Barney to William Cullen Bryant, n.p., 9 January 1861, Bryant-Godwin Papers (Bryant-Godwin ms), Box 3,

NYPL; Hamlin to Trumbull, Hampden, 27 December 1860, Trumbull ms, Reel 7, LC; Cameron to Weed, Senate, 13 November and 20 December 1860, Simon Cameron Papers (Cameron ms), Reel 5, LC; Weed to Cameron, Albany, 17 November 1860, ibid.; Hendrick, *Lincoln's War Cabinet,* 125–56.

7. Chase to Charles A. Dana, Columbus, 10 November 1860, Dana ms, LC; Chase to Julian, Columbus, 15 December 1860, Giddings-Julian ms, Volume 3, LC; Chase to Trumbull, Columbus, 12 December 1860, Trumbull ms, Reel 7, LC; Chase to George Opdyke, Columbus, 9 January 1861, "Chase, Letters and Drafts, 1825–1863," Chase ms, HSP; David Donald, ed., *Inside Lincoln's Cabinet: The Civil War Diaries of Salmon P. Chase* (New York: Longmans Green, 1954), 8; Hart, *Salmon Portland Chase,* 203.

8. Chase to William Dennison, Washington, 6 March 1861, "Chase, Letters and Drafts, 1825–1863," HSP; ibid.; Hendrick, *Lincoln's War Cabinet,* 138–49; Oates, *With Malice Toward None,* 215; Carman and Luthin, *Lincoln and the Patronage,* 42–43; Francis P. Blair to Hamlin, Washington, 4 February 1861, Hamlin ms, Reel 1, University of Maine, Orono; William Salter, *The Life of James W. Grimes, Governor of Iowa, 1854–1858; A Senator of the United States, 1859–1869* (New York: D. Appleton and Company, 1876), 133; Ray to Washburne, Springfield, 16 January 1861, Washburne ms, Volume 13, LC; Randall, *Lincoln the President: Springfield to Gettysburg,* vol. 1, 312–13; *New York Times,* 22 February 1861; *New York Evening Post,* 22 February 1861; Johnson Brigham, *James Harlan* (Iowa City: State Historical Society of Iowa, 1913), 158–59; Pennington to A. P. Burdit, Washington, 17 January 1861, Pennington ms, NJHS; Clapp, *Forgotten First Citizen,* 142–43; Diary of John Bigelow, 1 and 27 March 1861, Bigelow ms, NYPL; John Bigelow, *Retrospections of an Active Life,* 5 vols. (New York: Baker and Taylor Co., 1913), vol. 1, 366.

9. Joseph Medill to Charles H. Ray and John Scripps, 6 January 1861, Trumbull ms, Reel 8, LC; Medill to White, 4 January 1861, ibid.; Horace White to Trumbull, Chicago, 10 January 1861, ibid. Reel 6 of the Cameron papers in the Library of Congress is a stream of letters on the Cabinet appointment. See also Swett to Cameron, Harrisburg, 8 December 1860, Cameron ms, Reel 5, LC; Seward to Cameron, Auburn, 15 November 1860, ibid.; Weed to Cameron, Albany, 17 November 1860, ibid.; Lincoln to Hamlin, Springfield, 27 November 1860, in *CW* vol. 4, 145; Lincoln to Cameron, Springfield, 3 and 13 January 1861, ibid., 174; Bradley, *Simon Cameron, passim;* Hendrick, *Lincoln's War Cabinet,* 51–52, 126–33; Randall, *Lincoln the President: Springfield to Gettysburg,* vol. 1, 264–66; Carman and Luthin, *Lincoln and the Patronage,* 27–29, 39–52; Alexander K. McClure, *Abraham Lincoln and Men of War-Times* (Philadelphia: Times Publishing Company, 1892), 159.

10. Frank Blair to Montgomery Blair, n.p., ca. November or December 1860, Blair-Lee Family ms, Box 15, Princeton; *Illinois State Journal,* 12 December 1860, in Harper, *Lincoln and the Press,* 75–76. See also Henry Winter Davis to Justin Morrill, ca. March 1861, Morrill ms, Reel 6, LC; Swett to Davis, Washington, 1 January 1861, Davis ms, Illinois State Historical Library; Preston King to Francis P. Blair Sr., Ogdensburgh, 15 November 1860, Blair-Lee Family ms, Box 15, Princeton; Elbridge G. Spaulding to Weed, Washington, 22 December 1860, Weed ms, UR; Nicolay, *Lincoln's Secretary,* 51–54; Naperville, Sunday, 9 December 1860, in Pease and Randall, eds., *The Diary of Orville Hickman Browning,* vol. 1, 440, and Chicago, Saturday, 19 January 1861, vol. 1, 449; Hendrick, *Lincoln's War Cabinet,* 60, 87–88; Barnes and Weed, *Life of Thurlow Weed,* 607–11; Smith, *The Francis Preston Blair Family,* vol. 1, 51, 514–16; Smith, *Francis Preston Blair,* 270–71; Henig, *Henry Winter Davis, passim.*

11. On Welles, see Lincoln to Hamlin, Springfield, 8 November and 8 December 1860, and Hamlin to Lincoln, Washington, 14 December 1860, Lincoln ms, LC, in *CW,* vol. 4, 136, 147–8; Thursday, 21 February and Monday, 25 February 1861, Washington, Diary of Adams, Adams ms, I, Reel 76, MHS; Barnes and Weed, *Life of Thurlow Weed,* 606–14; Niven, *Gideon Welles,* 304–20; Hendrick, *Lincoln's War Cabinet,* 88–97; Randall, *Lincoln the President: Springfield to Gettysburg,* vol. 1, 261–62; Carman and Luthin, *Lincoln and the Patronage,* 16–17. On Smith, see Trumbull to Lincoln, Washington, 7 January 1861, Lincoln ms, LC; Ray to Trumbull, Springfield, 16 January 1861, Trumbull ms, Reel 8, LC; Judd to Trumbull, Chicago, 3 January 1861, Reel 7, ibid.; Chicago, Sunday, 13 January and Wednesday, 16 January 1861, in Pease and Randall, eds., *The Diary of Orville Hickman Browning,* vol. 1, 448; *New York Tribune,* 6 February 1861; Caleb B. Smith to Julian, Indianapolis, 2 January 1861, Giddings-Julian ms, Volume 4, LC; Smith, *Colfax,* 140–42; Horner, *Lincoln and Greeley,* 193; Carman and Luthin, *Lincoln and the Patronage,* 23–37.

12. Washington, Tuesday, 5 March 1861, Adams Diary, Adams ms, II, Reel 76, MHS; Morrill to Ruth Morrill, Washington, 1 March 1861, Morrill ms, Reel 6, LC; Kinsley, *The Chicago Tribune,* vol. 1, 177; Barnes and Weed, *Life of Thurlow Weed,* 605–6; Randall, *Lincoln the President: Springfield to Gettysburg,* vol. 1, 270–71, 312–13; Hendrick, *Lincoln's War Cabinet, passim.*

13. Gustavus V. Fox to Montgomery Blair, New York, 31 March 1861, Fox ms, Box 1, NYHS; Washington, Wednesday, 3 July 1861, in Pease and Randall, eds., *The Diary of Orville Hickman Browning,* vol. 1, 475–76; Nevins and Thomas, eds., *The Diary of George Templeton Strong,* vol. 3, 30 March 1861, 114; Oates, *With Malice Toward None,* 215, 221; Hendrick, *Lincoln's War Cabinet,* 204–6; Randall, *Lincoln the President: Springfield to Gettysburg,* vol. 1, 313–14.

14. Chase to Alphonso Taft, Washington, 28 April 1861, "Chase, Letters and Drafts, 1825–1863," Chase ms, HSP; William Mellen to Chase, Cincinnati, 6 April 1861, Box 7, ibid.; Chase to John A. Stevens Jr., Washington, 11 April 1861, John A. Stevens ms, 1853–1861, NYHS; Donald, ed., *Inside Lincoln's Cabinet,* 8; William Wirt to John Critcher, Baltimore, 16 February 1861, copy, in Critcher to Blair Sr., Richmond, 20 February 1861, Blair-Lee ms, Box 9, Princeton; Oates, *With Malice Toward None,* 21; Chittenden, *Recollections,* 105; Randall, *Lincoln the President: Springfield to Gettysburg,* vol. 1, 320–21; Foner, *Business and Slavery,* 300–301; Stampp, *And the War Came,* 266–67.

15. Welles, "Lincoln's Nomination and Election, II," in Albert Mordell, ed., *Lincoln's Administration: Selected Essays of Gideon Welles* (New York: Twayne, 1959), 36–38; St. Louis, Sunday, 24 February 1861, in Pease and Randall, eds., *The Diary of Orville Hickman Browning,* vol. 1, 457; Cameron to Lincoln, Washington, 15 March 1861, in *Official Records of the War of the Rebellion,* 130 vols. (Washington, D.C.: Government Printing Office, 1880–1901), Series I, vol. 1, 196–98; Randall, *Lincoln the President: Springfield to Gettysburg,* vol. 1, 343; Niven, *Gideon Welles,* 324–27.

16. Seward to Lincoln, Washington, 15 March 1861, Lincoln ms, LC; Mark E. Neely Jr., "The Lincoln Administration and Arbitrary Arrests: A Reconsideration," *Papers of the Abraham Lincoln Association* 5 (1983): 7–24; Potter, *Lincoln and His Party,* 240, 273, 370; *New York Times,* 21 March 1861; Sumner to Jay, Washington, 27 March 1861, Jay Family Papers (Jay Family ms), CU; Washington, Thursday, 28 March 1861, Diary of Adams, Adams ms, II, Reel 76, MHS; New York, 7 March 1861, Nevins and Thomas, eds., *The Diary of George Templeton Strong,* vol. 3, 107; Randall, *Lincoln the President: Springfield to Gettysburg,* vol. 1, 311–50; Henry Villard, *Memoirs of Henry Villard, Journalist and Financier, 1835–1900,* 2 vols. (Boston: Houghton Mifflin, 1904), vol. 1, 160; Oates, *With Malice Toward None,* 223–24; Van Deusen, *Thurlow Weed,* 270–71; Stampp, *And the War Came,* 272; Blaine, *Twenty Years of Congress,* vol. 1, 293; "The Election of Lincoln as a Crucial Event," in Fehrenbacher, *Lincoln in Text and Context,* 63; Hendrick, *Lincoln's War Cabinet,* 189–200; Rice, ed., *Reminiscences of Abraham Lincoln,* 85–86; Richard N. Current, "The Confederates and the First Shot," *Civil War History* 7, no. 4 (December 1961): 357–69.

17. New York, 11 March 1861, Nevins and Thomas, eds., *The Diary of George Templeton Strong,* vol. 3, 108–9; Sumner to Elizabeth, Duchess of Argyll, Washington, 19 March 1861, in Series II, Reel 74, SP; Mark Howard to Welles, Hartford, 11 March 1861, Welles ms, Box 3, NYPL; *Springfield Republican,* 12 March 1861, in Merriam, *The Life and Times of Samuel Bowles,* vol. 1, 287; Magdol, *Owen Lovejoy,* 274.

18. *New York Times,* 21 March and 3 April 1861; Weed to Webb, New York, 27 March 1861, Webb ms, Box 6, Sterling Library, Yale; Van Deusen, *Weed,* 271; Jay to Sumner, New York, 26 and 28 March 1861, in Reel 22, SP; Baxter, *Orville H. Browning,* 116; Potter, *Lincoln and His Party,* 329–30; Stampp, *And the War Came,* 245; Hendrick, *Lincoln's War Cabinet,* 202; Oates, *With Malice Toward None,* 222–23; Gunderson, *Old Gentlemen's Convention,* 102; Nichols, *The Disruption of American Democracy,* 499–500.

19. Seward to Lincoln, and Lincoln to Seward, Washington, 1 April 1861, Lincoln ms, LC, in *CW,* vol. 4, 316–18. The meaning of this memorandum has been much discussed; a rare defense of Seward is Norman Ferris, "Lincoln and Seward in Civil War Diplomacy: Their Relationship at the Outset Reexamined," *Journal of the Abraham Lincoln Association* 12 (1991): 21–42. I share Ferris's admiration for Seward and his sense that Lincoln biographers have created straw men to knock down in the process of building up their subject, but the evidence suggests that he protests a little too much.

20. Hendrick, *Lincoln's War Cabinet,* 205–6; Oates, *With Malice Toward None,* 29–20; Baxter, *Orville H. Browning,* 128; Barnes and Weed, *Life of Thurlow Weed,* 326–27; *The Independent,* 21 March and 4 April 1861, in Van Deusen, *Horace Greeley,* 270; *New York Tribune,* 2–13 April 1861; "General Scott's memorandum for the Secretary of War," *Official Records of the War of the Rebellion* (henceforth *OR*), Series I, vol. I, 200–01; Scott to Seward, Washington, 3 March 1861, Winfield Scott Papers (Scott ms), Personal Miscellaneous, NYPL; Scott, "Suggestions &c.," 2 April 1861, Montague Papers (Montague ms), Box 9, ibid.; Welles, "Lincoln's Administration, I," in Mordell, ed., *Lincoln's Administration,* 57–58.

21. Boston, Saturday, 13 April 1861, Adams Diary, Adams ms, II, Reel 76, MHS; Trefousse, *Benjamin Franklin Wade,* 148; Mellen to Chase, Cincinnati, 4 May 1861, Chase ms, Box 7, HSP; *New York Times,* 23 April 1861; *New York Tribune,* 22 April 1861.

22. Stampp, *And the War Came,* 264–65; Oates, *With Malice Toward None,* 231–33; Sumner to Fessenden, Washington, 16 April 1861, in Series II, Reel 74, SP; Jay to William M. Evarts, Katonah, 16 April 1861, Jay Family ms, CU; New York, 30 April 1861, Nevins and Thomas, eds., *The Diary of George Templeton Strong,* vol. 3, 138; Hesseltine, *Lincoln and the War Governors,* 130. See also Fehrenbacher, "Lincoln and the Weight of Responsibility," *Journal of the Illinois State Historical Society* 68, no. 1 (Spring 1975): 45–56.

23. Sumner to Richard Henry Dana Jr., Washington, 14 April 1861, in Series II, Reel 74, SP; Sumner to Fessenden, 16 April 1861, ibid.; Seward to Weed, Washington, 17 May 1861, Weed ms, UR; Chase to N. S. Townshend, Washington, 6 May 1861, "Chase, Letters and Drafts, 1825–1863," Chase ms, HSP; McClure, *Lincoln and Men of War-Times,* 60; Moorfield Storey and

Edward W. Emerson, *Ebenezer Rockwood Hoar* (Boston: Houghton Mifflin, 1911), 130–31; Oberholtzer, *Jay Cooke,* 135–38; Welles to Sumner, n.p., 15 April 1861, Welles ms, LC; Niven, *Gideon Welles,* 356–57; Blair to Fox, Washington, 26 April 1861, Fox ms, Box 1, NYHS; P. R. Frothingham, *Edward Everett, Orator and Statesman* (Boston: Houghton Mifflin, 1925), 415; Stampp, *And the War Came,* 205–6.

24. Greeley to Moncure D. Conway, New York, 17 August 1861, Conway ms, Box 9, CU. On the key players, see Bradley, *Simon Cameron;* Trefousse, *Benjamin Franklin Wade;* Niven, *Gideon Welles;* and Sewell, *John P. Hale.* See also Randall, *Lincoln the President: Springfield to Gettysburg,* vol. 1, 389; *Chicago Tribune,* 31 July 1861, in Kinsley, *The Chicago Tribune,* vol. 1, 203; Thomas J. McCormick, ed., *Memoirs of Gustave Koerner, 1809–1896,* 2 vols. (Cedar Rapids, Iowa: Torch Press, 1909), vol. 2, 162–63; Cameron to Chase, Washington, 21 July 1861, Chase ms, HSP; Philo Shelton to Weed, Boston, 17 August 1861, Weed ms, UR; Jay to Sumner, Katonah, 28 July 1861, Reel 23, SP; Montgomery Blair to Sumner, Washington, 14 January 1862, Reel 24, ibid.; George D. Morgan to Fox, New York, 29 July 1861, Fox ms, Box 1, NYHS; Adams Hill to Gay, Washington, 24 July 1862, Gay ms, Reel 2, CU; Welles to Abram S. Hewitt, Washington, 9 May 1861, and 1 September 1862, Allan Nevins Papers (Allan Nevins ms), CU; Welles to Hewitt and Peter Cooper, Navy Department, 23 May 1862, ibid.

25. Hendrick, *Lincoln's War Cabinet,* 261–80; Bradley, *Simon Cameron,* 174–84, 208–34; Niven, *Gideon Welles,* 392–93; Donald, ed., *Inside Lincoln's Cabinet,* 60–61; Lincoln to Cameron, Washington, 11 January 1862, in *CW,* vol. 5, 96–97; Montgomery Blair to Cameron, Washington, 22 June 1861, in Marshall, ed., *Private and Official Correspondence of General Benjamin F. Butler,* vol. 1, 155; Cameron to Greeley, Washington, 16 June 1861, Greeley ms, Box 7, LC; Stevens to Simon Stevens, Lancaster, 5 November 1861, Thaddeus Stevens ms, Box 1, LC; Cameron to Chase, Lochiel, 2 May 1862, and St. Petersburg, 18 August 1862, Chase ms, Box 3, HSP.

26. Thomas and Hyman, *Stanton,* 127–37, 141, 147–51, 176–77; Edwin M. Stanton to Dix, Washington, 16 and 19 March, 18 April, 13 and 25 July, 14 August, 26 October, and 1 November 1861, John A. Dix Papers (Dix ms), Box 10, CU; Chase to George W. Neff, Washington, 10 November 1862, Chase ms, microfilm edition, Series I, Reel 23; Chase to Stanton, Washington, 30 May 1862, "Chase, Letters and Drafts, 1825–1863," Chase ms, HSP; Stanton to Dana, Washington, 24 January and 2 February 1862, Dana ms, LC; Horace White to Charles H. Ray, Washington, 26 March 1862, Ray ms, HL.

27. Cain, *Lincoln's Attorney General,* 178–79; Thomas and Hyman, *Stanton,* 219–22; Hendrick, *Lincoln's War Cabinet,* 363–78.

28. Smith to Chase, Bedford Springs, 30 July 1862, Chase ms, Box 10, HSP; Donald, ed., *Inside Lincoln's Cabinet,* 24 September 1862, 156–57; Chase to George Denison, Washington, 8 September 1862, Denison ms, Volume 2, LC; Paul J. Scheips, "Lincoln and the Chiriqui Colonization Project," *Journal of Negro History* 37, no. 3 (October 1952): 426, 433–34; Michael A. Vorenberg, "Abraham Lincoln and the Politics of Black Colonization," *Journal of the Abraham Lincoln Association,* 14, no. 2 (Summer 1993), 38; Francis Preston Blair to Lincoln, n.p., 16 November 1861, Lincoln ms, LC; Montgomery Blair to "Col," probably Thomas Gantt, Washington, 23 August 1861, Blair ms, IU; Smith, *The Francis Preston Blair Family,* vol. 2, 195–96; Charles L. Wagandt, *The Mighty Revolution: Negro Emancipation in Maryland, 1862–1864* (Baltimore: Johns Hopkins University Press, 1964), 62; Bates to A. L. McDowell, Washington, 23 July 1861, National Archives, typescript, Nevins ms, Box 5, HL; Hendrick, *Lincoln's War Cabinet,* 419; Cain, *Lincoln's Attorney General,* 197–200; Oberholtzer, *Jay Cooke,* vol. 1, 196–97; George W. Julian, *Political Recollections, 1840–1872* (Chicago: A. C. McClurg, 1872), 220; George S. Boutwell, *Reminiscences of Sixty Years in Public Affairs,* 2 vols. (New York: McClure, Phillips, and Company, 1902), vol. 1, 308; Leonard P. Curry, *Blueprint for Modern America: Non-Military Legislation of the First Civil War Congress* (Nashville: Vanderbilt University Press, 1968), 209.

29. Hendrick, *Lincoln's War Cabinet,* 423–24; Oates, *With Malice Toward None,* 308–9; Niven, *Gideon Welles,* 389–90; Smith, *The Francis Preston Blair Family,* vol. 2, 186; *CW,* vol. 5, 337, n. 1; John Hope Franklin, *The Emancipation Proclamation* (Garden City: Doubleday, 1963), 43–44; Sumner to Elizabeth, Duchess of Argyll, Boston, 11 August 1862, in Series II, Reel 76, SP; Sumner to John Bright, Boston, 5 August 1862, ibid.

30. Hendrick, *Lincoln's War Cabinet, passim;* Chase to Lincoln, Washington, 28 November 1862, Lincoln ms, LC; Hill to Gay, ca. October 1862, Gay ms, Reel 2, CU; Welles, "Lincoln's Administration III," in Mordell, ed., *Lincoln's Administration,* 106–7; Oates, *With Malice Toward None,* 319; William E. Parrish, *Turbulent Partnership: Missouri and the Union, 1861–1865* (Columbia: University of Missouri Press, 1965), 135; Franklin, *The Emancipation Proclamation,* 59–60; Hesseltine, *Lincoln and the War Governors,* 252–53.

31. On this period, see especially Paludan, *The Presidency of Abraham Lincoln,* 137–84.

32. Wade to Caroline Wade, Washington, 25 October 1861, Wade ms, LC, in Mary Land, "Ben Wade," in Wheeler, ed., *For the Union,* 171; Kinsley, *The Chicago Tribune,* vol. 1, 249; Donald, ed., *Inside Lincoln's Cabinet,* 137; Chase to Kate Chase, Washington, 12 July 1861, "Chase Letters to Daughter

Kate," Chase ms, Box 1, HSP; Chase to Cameron, Washington, 16 November 1862, in Chase ms, Microfilm Edition, Series I, Reel 23.

33. Lafayette Foster to Fish, Washington, 16 December 1862, Fish ms, Volume 49, LC; Curry, *Blueprint for Modern America,* 217–19; Hendrick, *Lincoln's War Cabinet,* 390–93; Tuesday, 16 December 1862, Pease and Randall, eds., *The Diary of Orville Hickman Browning,* vol. 2, 597; George, *Zachariah Chandler,* 73; Seward to Lincoln, Washington, 16 December 1862, Seward ms, Reel 74, UR; Frederick Seward to Lincoln, ibid.; Friday, 19 December 1862, in Beale, ed., *The Diary of Edward Bates,* 268–69; Francis Fessenden, *Life and Public Services of William Pitt Fessenden,* 2 vols. (Boston: Houghton Mifflin, 1907), vol. 1, 231–36, 251–52; Neely, *The Union Divided,* 121–23.

34. Fessenden, *Life and Public Services of William Pitt Fessenden,* vol. 1, 238–43; Friday, 19 December 1862, Beale, ed., *The Diary of Edward Bates,* 269; Thursday, 18 December 1862, Pease and Randall, eds., *The Diary of Orville Hickman Browning,* vol. 2, 600–601; Samuel Wilkeson to Gay, Washington, 19 December 1862, Gay ms, Reel 6, CU.

35. Monday, 22 December 1862, Pease and Randall, eds., *The Diary of Orville Hickman Browning,* vol. 2, 602–4; Friday, 19 December 1862, Beale, ed., *The Diary of Edward Bates,* 270; Fessenden, *Life and Public Services of William Pitt Fessenden,* vol. 1, 248–49.

36. Allan Nevins, *The War for the Union: War Becomes Revolution, 1862–1863* (New York: Charles Scribner's Sons, 1960), 350–65; Randall, *Lincoln the President: Springfield to Gettysburg,* vol. 2, 241–49; Roske, *His Own Counsel,* 96–97; Curry, *Blueprint for Modern America,* 223. For the flavor of the flurry of correspondence on these matters, see Chase to Flamen Ball, Washington, 20 December 1862, Chase ms, Microfilm Edition, Series I, Reel 24, HSP; Chase to Jay Cooke, ibid.; Chase to Lincoln, Washington, 20 December 1862, Lincoln ms, LC; Cameron to Chase, Lochiel, 24 December 1862, Chase ms, Box 3, HSP; Thaddeus Stevens to Simon Stevens, Washington, 21 December 1862, Thaddeus Stevens ms, Box 1, LC; Simon Stevens to Fessenden, New York, 20 December 1862, Fessenden ms, Box 1, Western Reserve Historical Society; Hamlin to Ellen Hamlin, Washington, 23 December 1862, Hamlin ms, Reel 1, University of Maine, Orono; Davis to Swett, Washington, 22 December 1862, Davis Family ms, Illinois State Historical Library; Moses Grinnell to Seward, New York, 21 December 1862, Seward ms, Reel 74, UR; Chase to Seward, Washington, December 1862, ibid.; Seward to Lincoln, Washington, 21 December 1862, ibid.; Chase to Lincoln, Washington, 22 December 1862, Lincoln ms, LC.

37. William Dennison to Francis Preston Blair, Columbus, 22 December 1862, Blair-Lee Family ms, Box 9, Princeton; Welles, "Lincoln's

Administration II," in Mordell, ed., *Lincoln's Administration,* 85; 20 December 1862, in Howard K. Beale, ed., *Diary of Gideon Welles, Secretary of the Navy under Lincoln and Johnson,* 3 vols. (New York: W. W. Norton, 1960), vol. 1, 198–99; Edward Everett to Seward, Boston, 2 January 1863, Seward ms, Reel 75, UR; Cain, *Lincoln's Attorney General,* 206–10; *Chicago Tribune,* 24 December 1862, in Joseph Logsdon, *Horace White: Nineteenth-Century Liberal* (Westport, Conn.: Greenwood Press, 1971), 92–93.

38. Bryant to Fessenden, New York, 12 January 1863, Bryant ms, NYHS; Fessenden to Bryant, Washington, 17 January and 17 July 1863, Bryant-Godwin ms, NYPL; Hart, *Chase,* 304; Curry, *Blueprint for Modern America,* 227–28; Silas Merchant to Horace Congar, Newark, 26 August 1863, Congar ms, Box 1, NJHS; Nicolay and Hay, *The Life of Abraham Lincoln,* vol. 7, 388. On Davis, see especially Henig, *Henry Winter Davis, passim;* Niven, *Gideon Welles,* 472–75; Welles to DuPont, Washington, 15 May 1863, *OR,* I, 14, 63–64.

39. Smith, *Colfax,* 177–78; Caleb Smith to T. J. Barnett, Indianapolis, 17 August 1863, Barlow ms, Box 48, HL; Barnett to Barlow, Washington, 24 September 1863, Box 45, ibid.; Smith to Henry Valette, Indianapolis, 19 April and 2 June 1862, and 19 July 1863, Smith ms, Cincinnati Historical Society; Baxter, *Orville H. Browning,* 111; George Smalley to Gay, Washington, 3 December 1862, Gay ms, Reel 5, CU; David Davis to Swett, Washington, 22 December 1862, Davis ms, Illinois State Historical Library; Richardson and Farley, *John Palmer Usher,* 19–30, 70–71; *New York Tribune,* 27 July 1863.

40. *New York Tribune,* 27 July 1863; Hendrick, *Lincoln's War Cabinet,* 433 and *passim.*

41. Hendrick, *Lincoln's War Cabinet,* 466–68; Montgomery Blair to Sumner, Washington, 24 October and 28 November 1863, Reel 29, SP; Stevens to Sumner, Lancaster, 9 October 1863, ibid.; Stevens to Chase, Lancaster, 8 October 1863, Chase ms, Box 10, HSP; *Sacramento Union,* 26 November 1863; Oates, *With Malice Toward None,* 370; *New York Tribune,* 14 December 1863. Donald, ed., *Inside Lincoln's Cabinet,* and Chase's voluminous correspondence offer ample evidence of his beliefs on these issues.

42. The two finest recent biographies of Chase are Niven, *Salmon P. Chase,* and Frederick J. Blue, *Salmon P. Chase: A Life in Politics* (Kent, Ohio: Kent State University Press, 1987). The Blairs have received far too little attention. See Smith, *Francis Preston Blair,* and Smith, *The Francis Preston Blair Family.*

43. Greeley to M. H. Booll, New York, 11 October 1863, J. W. Hill Papers (J. W. Hill ms), CU; *New York Tribune,* 11 March 1864; Niven, *Gideon Welles,* 470–71; Horner, *Lincoln and Greeley,* 338–39; Chase to Greeley, Washington, 14 January 1864, Greeley ms, Box 7, LC; Hendrick, *Lincoln's War Cabinet,* 433. On Ohio, see Chase to Stanley Matthews, Washington, 16 April 1863,

in Chase ms, Microfilm Edition, Reel 26, LC; Chase to John Bingham, Washington, 4 June 1863, Reel 27, ibid.; Chase to David Tod, ibid.; Chase to John Brough, Washington, 20 June 1863, ibid. On Maryland, see W. G. Snethen to Chase, Baltimore, 5 June 1863, ibid.; Chase to Thomas Swann, Washington, 6 June 1863, ibid.

44. Nicolay to Hay, Washington, 17 February 1864, typescript, Nicolay ms, Box 7, LC; Edwin Morgan to Weed, Washington, 17 March and 29 May 1864, Weed ms, UR; David Davis to Weed, Washington, 14 March 1864, ibid.; Carman and Luthin, *Lincoln and the Patronage,* 236–39, 249–51; Niven, *Gideon Welles,* 479–81; Richardson and Farley, *John Palmer Usher,* 72–74; Chase to Lincoln, Washington, 22 February 1864, Lincoln ms, LC, in *CW,* vol. 7, 200–201; Lincoln to Chase, Washington, 23 and 29 February 1864, ibid., 200–13; Chase to Greeley, Washington, 4 March 1864, Greeley ms, Box 3, NYPL.

45. Hendrick, *Lincoln's War Cabinet,* 455, 494–509; John A. Kasson to Greeley, Washington, 24 January 1864, Greeley ms, Box 3, NYPL; Fox to David D. Porter, n.p., 26 May 1864, Fox ms, Box 8, NYHS; *CG,* 38, 1, Part 4, Appendix; Montgomery Blair to Barlow, n.p., 28 April 1864, Barlow ms, Box 50, HL; *Sacramento Union,* 9 February 1864, and 3 March 1864; Weed to Hanson A. Risley, New York, 23 June 1864, Weed ms, UR; Weed to Frederick Seward, Albany, 2 June 1864, William H. Seward ms, Reel 74, UR; Smith, *Francis Preston Blair,* 340; Smith, *The Francis Preston Blair Family,* vol. 2, 256–58.

46. J. K. Herbert to Butler, Washington, 31 May 1864, in Marshall, ed., *Private and Official Correspondence of General Benjamin F. Butler,* vol. 4, 292; Smith, *The Francis Preston Blair Family,* vol. 2, 90–111; Chase to Greeley, Washington, 29 February 1864, Greeley ms, Box 3, NYPL; Medill to Washburne, Chicago, 29 April 1864, Washburne ms, Volume 37, LC.

47. Chase to Lincoln, Washington, 27 June 1864, "Copies of Special Letters, 1861–1864, Bound," Chase ms, HSP; M. B. Field to Moses Taylor, Washington, 8 June 1864, Taylor ms, Box 209, NYPL; James A. Rawley, *Edwin D. Morgan, 1811–1883: Merchant in Politics* (New York: Columbia University Press, 1955), 196; Cox and Cox, *Politics, Principle, and Prejudice,* 34–35; Carman and Luthin, *Lincoln and the Patronage,* 267–68; Lincoln to Chase, Washington, 28 and 30 June 1864, and Chase to Lincoln, Washington, 28 and 29 June 1864, Lincoln ms, LC, in *CW,* vol. 7, 412–19; Francis Preston Blair to Frank Blair, Silver Spring, 4 July 1864, Blair ms, NYPL.

48. Hart, *Salmon Portland Chase,* 317; Oberholtzer, *Jay Cooke,* vol. 1, 419–22; *Cincinnati Gazette,* 1 July 1864, in Garfield ms, Reel 143, LC; Theodore Tilton to Judge Bond, New York, 1 July [1864], Tilton ms, NYHS; Chase to Denison, Washington, 11 July 1864, and Litchfield, 15 August

1864, Denison ms, Volume 3, LC; Chase to Robert Parsons, Washington, 8 July and 14 September 1864, "Chase, Letters and Drafts, 1864–1873," Chase ms, HSP.

49. "Private Memoranda—War Times," William Henry Smith Papers (Smith ms), Ohio Historical Society; Thomas and Hyman, *Stanton,* 312–16; Chittenden, *Recollections,* 377–80; Lincoln to David Tod, Washington, 30 June 1864, in *CW,* vol. 7, 420; Philo Shelton to Weed, Boston, 30 June 1864, Weed ms, UR; Dawes to Ella Dawes, Washington, 2 July 1864, Dawes ms, Box 13, LC; William Leighton to Barney, Northampton, 4 July 1864, Barney ms, Box 22, HL; Fox to Virginia Fox, Washington, 1 July 1864, Fox ms, Box 2, NYHS; Donald, ed., *Inside Lincoln's Cabinet,* 223–24; Hugh McCulloch to John A. Stevens, Washington, 2 July 1864, John A. Stevens ms, 1864–1868, NYHS.

50. Fessenden to John A. Stewart, Washington, 6 September 1864, Hugh McCulloch Papers (McCulloch ms), IU; Fessenden to Elizabeth Warriner, Washington, 24 July 1864, Fessenden Family ms, Box 11, Special Collections, Bowdoin College; 27 August and 4 September 1864, Box 15, ibid.; Fessenden to Samuel Fessenden, Washington, 16 September 1864, ibid.; John A. Stevens Jr., to Chase, New York, 11 January 1864, John A. Stevens ms, 1864–1868, NYHS; Greeley to Chase, New York, 10 February 1864, Chase ms, Box 5, HSP; Fessenden to Chase, Washington, 6 September 1864, Box 4, ibid.

51. Raymond to Seward, New York, 5 August 1864, Welles ms, Box 3, NYPL; Samuel Hooper to Welles, Boston, 10 November 1864, ibid.; Charles Jones to Raymond, New York, 2 August 1864, ibid.; Raymond to Lincoln, New York, 22 July 1864, typescript, Kenneth P. Williams ms, Box 1, IU; Raymond to Cameron, New York, 17 July 1864, Cameron ms, Reel 10, LC; Niven, *Gideon Welles,* 484–87; Carman and Luthin, *Lincoln and the Patronage,* 288–89; *Sacramento Union,* 4 July 1864.

52. Sumner to James A. Hamilton, Washington, 4 July 1863, Series II, Reel 77, SP; Manton Marble to Barlow, New York, 11 July 1863, Barlow ms, Box 47, HL; T. J. Barnett to Barlow, Washington, 29 June 1863, Box 45, ibid.; Washington, Saturday, 16 July 1864, Pease and Randall, eds., *The Diary of Orville Hickman Browning,* vol. 1, 677; Blair to Butler, n.p., 10 August 1864, Blair Family ms, LC, typescript, Nevins ms, Box 19, HL; Hendrick, *Lincoln's War Cabinet,* 457–58; Smith, *The Francis Preston Blair Family,* vol. 2, 225–26, 274–81; Thomas and Hyman, *Stanton,* 320. See especially Richard Henry Dana Jr. to Mrs. Dana, Washington, 21 April 1864, Dana ms, MHS, typescript, Nevins ms, Box 17, HL; Smith, *Francis Preston Blair,* 333, 345–46.

53. Baker, *The Politics of Continuity,* 66–101; Henig, *Henry Winter Davis,* 196–97; *Sacramento Union,* 26 July 1864; *CG,* 38, 1, 25 February 1864, 834; Oates, *With Malice Toward None,* 391; Davis to James G. Blaine, n.p., 9

November 1864, Blaine ms, Reel 7, LC; Davis to John A. Stevens Jr., Baltimore, 19 October 1864, John A. Stevens ms, 1864–1868, NYHS.

54. Harold M. Hyman, ed., *The Radical Republicans and Reconstruction, 1861–1870* (Indianapolis, Ind.: Bobbs-Merrill, 1967), 125–47; Oates, *With Malice Toward None,* 391–93; Carman and Luthin, *Lincoln and the Patronage,* 273–76; Chandler to Letitia Chandler, Washington, 27 August and 2, 6, 8, 18, and 24 September 1864, Chandler ms, Box 3, LC.

55. Wade to Chandler, Jefferson, 2 October 1864, Chandler ms, Box 3, LC; Henig, *Henry Winter Davis, passim;* Lincoln to Montgomery Blair, Washington, 23 September 1864, Lincoln ms, LC, in *CW,* vol. 8, 18; Welles, "Lincoln's Triumph," in Mordell, ed., *Lincoln's Administration,* 219; Carman and Luthin, *Lincoln and the Patronage,* 278; Smith, *The Francis Preston Blair Family,* vol. 2, 288–91; Horner, *Lincoln and Greeley,* 356; Smith, *Francis Preston Blair,* 347; Blair to Barlow, n.p., 27 May 1864, Barlow ms, Box 50, HL; Clipping, n.d., in George Cass to Barlow, Philadelphia, 30 September 1864, ibid.

56. Lincoln to William Dennison, Washington, 24 September 1864, in *CW,* vol. 8, 20; *New York Tribune,* 26 November 1864; Cain, *Lincoln's Attorney General,* 313, 321–25; Rice, ed., *Reminiscences of Abraham Lincoln,* 240–41; Richardson and Farley, *John Palmer Usher,* 62–63, 75–79; James Harlan to Sumner, Washington, 21 August and 11 September 1865, Series I, Reel 34, SP; Brigham, *James Harlan,* 192–96, 214; McCulloch to Susan McCulloch, Washington, 2 October 1864, McCulloch ms, IU; McCulloch to Jay Cooke, Washington, 24 and 29 March 1865, ibid.; Rawley, *Edwin D. Morgan,* 201–2; Barnes and Weed, *Life of Thurlow Weed,* 620–23.

57. Whitelaw Reid to William Smith, Washington, 18 February 1865, Smith ms, Box 2, Ohio Historical Society, discusses the attorney generalship. On the Treasury, see Hooper to Blaine, Boston, 9 November 1864, Blaine ms, Reel 7, LC; Fessenden to Washburn, Washington, 18 November 1864, Fessenden ms, Reel 3, LC; Blaine to William Chandler, Augusta, 12 March 1865, Chandler ms, Volume 1, LC; Tappan Wentworth to Butler, Washington, 21 February 1865, Butler ms, Box 36, LC; Nicolay to Bates, Washington, 6 January 1865, typescript, Nicolay ms, Box 7, LC; William D. Kelley, et al., to Thaddeus Stevens, Washington, 9 January 1865, Stevens ms, Box 2, LC; Henry C. Carey to Greeley, Philadelphia, 18 November 1864, Greeley ms, Box 3, NYPL; Adams to Charles Francis Adams, Jr., London, 2 and 9 December 1864, Adams ms, IV, Reel 572, MHS; Weed to Andrew, New York, 20 February 1865, copy in Weed ms, UR; Shelton to Weed, Boston, 28 November 1864, ibid.; Sumner to Fish, Washington, 25 January 1865, Fish ms, LC, in Series II, Reel 78, SP; Judd to Trumbull, Berlin, 5 March 1865, Trumbull ms, Reel 16, LC; George Gibbs to John A. Stevens Jr.,

Washington, 15 February 1865, John A. Stevens ms, 1864–1868, NYHS; Rawley, *Edwin D. Morgan,* 201–2; Oberholtzer, *Jay Cooke,* vol. 1, 466–68, 496; Barnes and Weed, *Life of Thurlow Weed,* 622–23.

58. Andrew to Francis Blair Sr., Boston, 13 November 1864, Blair-Lee ms, Box 4, Princeton; Andrew to George Blake, Boston, 16 January 1865, *MHS Proceedings* 57 (October 1924–June 1925): 393–94; Andrew to Weed, Boston, 6 February 1865, Weed ms, UR.

59. *Kennebec Journal,* 24 March 1865, Scrapbook, "Personal," Volume 1, McCulloch ms, IU; Oates, *With Malice Toward None,* 423; Charles L. Wilson to Thomas H. Dudley, Chicago, 12 March 1865, Thomas H. Dudley Papers (Dudley ms), Box 24, HL.

60. 15 April 1865, in Donald, ed., *Inside Lincoln's Cabinet,* 265–69; Wade to Lewis Campbell, Washington, 6 May 1865, Campbell ms, Box 1, Ohio Historical Society. On Johnson, see McKitrick, *Andrew Johnson;* Foner, *Reconstruction,* 176–345; Trefousse, *Andrew Johnson;* Cox and Cox, *Politics, Principle, and Prejudice, passim.* Among the many primary materials, Sumner's correspondence is a feast of exchanges on Johnson.

5

The Republicans and Slavery

ON 4 March 1861, Abraham Lincoln stood on the Capitol portico and sought to reassure the South of his peaceful intentions. "One section of our country believes slavery is right, and ought to be extended, while the other believes it is wrong, and ought not to be extended. This is the only substantial dispute," he said. The dispute was more substantial than that, not only between North and South, but within his party. Republicans agreed on the need to confine slavery within its boundaries, but differed on the depths of their opposition to slavery and what their party should do about it. Even some radicals doubted that if freed, slaves could be equal to whites; many conservatives looked askance at granting rights such as suffrage that might help blacks become equal, in law or in fact.[1]

The passage of four years confirmed some of the wisdom in what was otherwise hyperbole. In the summer of 1863, Horace Greeley called the change of opinion on slavery "comparable with the early progress of Christianity." At Lincoln's request, the 1864 Union platform included a call to amend the Constitution—not to limit slavery, as the 1860 platform sought to do, but to ban it entirely by changing what many Republicans considered a sacred document. By 4 March 1865, when Lincoln stood again on that portico, the amendment had passed Congress. So had a variety of other measures, some of which he supported, some of which he accepted reluctantly. Republicans had been responsible for the prohibition of the domestic slave trade, abolition in the District of Columbia, the confiscation of slaves as rebel property, and the Emancipation Proclamation. At his second inauguration, Lincoln said, "These slaves constituted a peculiar and powerful interest. All knew that this interest was, somehow, the cause of the war." On 11 April he told a White House crowd, "It is . . . unsatisfactory to some that the elective franchise is not given to the colored man. I would myself prefer that it were now conferred on the very intelligent, and on those who serve our cause as soldiers." He was more cautious than radicals like Charles Sumner and Salmon Chase preferred, but more racially advanced than any other president had publicly voiced or, no doubt, privately thought. Three nights later John Wilkes Booth, who was in the crowd on both occasions in 1865 and angry at what he heard, killed Lincoln.[2]

If Lincoln was the classic moderate, wedded to an ideology that he took pains to keep from imprisoning him, his evolution speaks volumes about his party. His hatred for slavery was sure; what he would do about it was less clear. As president he shifted, or the country did, or both. And he encapsulated Republican views with one word shaded with many meanings. When he described slavery as "somehow" the war's cause, he referred not to uncertainty but to the lack of a single motivation. To Sumner the issue was simple: slavery was wrong, blacks should be free and equal, and the consequences were immaterial. The same could be said of Thaddeus Stevens, but he also thought of political economy: unhorsing plantation owners from power and elevating slaves through land ownership was good policy. Nor did conservatives such as Orville Browning and War Democrats such as Andrew Johnson, who joined the Union party, diverge greatly in their views. To them the problem was not the slave's welfare or free labor, but the lengths to which the South went to preserve slavery and the slave power. Complicating matters more, prominent figures such as William Henry Seward devolved from radical to conservative yet never really fit either description. Except for the War Democrats, these Republicans belonged to the antebellum party, which stood for free labor. The wartime party's ideology absorbed free labor into the broader idea of freedom, but free labor remained part of its thought during the war and survived the war largely intact. Republicans retained their belief in individualism, the seed from which the laissez-faire political economy of the Gilded Age would spring. Free labor triumphed, but what that meant was unclear beyond a Republican certainty: free labor meant the freedom to labor. The next issue was how far beyond that syllogism they would go.[3]

What Republicans thought about slavery during the Civil War is best explained by their ideology of freedom, union, and power. Long before the war ended, they agreed that the Union's survival required black freedom. How the party reached that point requires a study of an almost continuous dialogue between ideas, policy, and politics. At issue were how to define freedom—total or gradual emancipation, or none at all—and whether the Union had a better chance of surviving with or without slavery. At least two questions complicated matters. One was the impact of emancipation on the war effort then and on the nation later. What Republicans believed and whether others would sustain them were crucial to that eventual outcome. If emancipation came too soon, soldiers might refuse to fight for a union that Republicans seemed to see as a means to the end of pursuing an anti-slavery policy. But soldiers might see the Union as secondary to a primary goal of freedom. If it came too late, though, there might be no union left to save, because those who placed freedom above union would happily let the South go to create a smaller but slave-free republic.

The other questions concerned the extent of the government's power to act against slavery, and who within the government could or should wield that power. Solving this puzzle involved not only the three branches of government but also the army, whose actions might bear the scrutiny of any or all three. What Republicans believed during the war mattered immensely; what they had believed before the war would affect them. In 1858, Lincoln, a moderate who leaned left and right, had warned that a house divided against itself could not stand, and that he expected slavery to grow or die. Seward, either a radically inclined conservative or a conservatively inclined radical, declared that revolutions only go forward and thus suggested the sure growth of anti-slavery sentiment. What had been clear to two of the party's leading lights two years before Republicans won the White House became in wartime not answers to be declared from the opposition, but questions to be resolved in power. If the answers changed, so did the questions.[4]

Simple Issues Turn Complex

In the war's first year, Republicans had to decipher the subtleties of power. Control of the White House and Congress would presumably enable them to achieve their goals. Setting aside regional and intellectual divisions over various issues, a problem persisted: the seemingly simple—stopping the spread of slavery into the territories—grew more complex. Slavery inspired a rebellion. That could be seen as a warning not to legislate: choosing Republicans to administer the territories might prove as effective as any enactment, and silence might do more than words or deeds to build support for their efforts to save the Union. But it could offer a chance to take action, for the war to change Northern attitudes, or for slaves to rebel or run away into Union lines. If they attacked slavery the consequences might dash their hopes, or turn them into reality more quickly. A mix of political, economic, social, and constitutional issues massed around the deceptively simple question of what to do about slavery.[5]

For some the answer was easy. In 1861, radicals, and moderates who leaned toward their views, wanted to move as fast as possible toward emancipation. William Lloyd Garrison, a critic who warmed to Lincoln, and Greeley argued that the Constitution's war powers gave the president all the power he needed to end slavery. The *Chicago Tribune*'s editors hid their disapproval of Lincoln's failure to urge abolition in his first annual message in December. "The cautious language which Mr. Lincoln employs, does not hide from us, who know the deep moral convictions of the man, the purpose that he has in view, nor the holy hate, which he must feel, of that giant iniquity," they said. "He has come, if not fully up to our advanced position at least within easy hail of those who have been looking anxiously back to see what progress he would make."[6]

Taking power and confronting insurrection forced Republicans to grasp not only governance, but the need to resolve divisions over slavery, across the country and in the party. As the war began, still fearful that the two were mutually exclusive, they felt caught between commitments to freedom and union and discovered the limits to their ability to act on their hopes. In July 1861, Congress approved a resolution by border state unionists John Crittenden of Kentucky and Andrew Johnson of Tennessee that the war was fought only to restore the union—not against slavery. The House tally was telling: of 119 voting, only radicals John Potter of Wisconsin and Albert Riddle of Ohio opposed it. Other members regretted not joining them. Ohio's James Ashley, a vociferous radical, called his vote "the most cowardly act of my life." But, said James Blaine of Maine, the resolution was "a fair reflection of the popular sentiment throughout the North," because the public had yet to see that saving the Union might require the destruction of slavery. Thus, many Republicans deemed it wise to vote for the resolution or abstain, as radicals Stevens and Owen Lovejoy did. They already believed what others would see, some more quickly than others: saving the Union required ending slavery.[7]

Probably the first Republican to test the limits of anti-slavery was John C. Frémont. His brief tenure as Union commander in Missouri revealed his ineptitude and conflicting Republican impulses on the issue. A hero for his western explorations, the party's first presidential candidate in 1856, and one of the few army officers to merge military experience with opposition to slavery, Frémont seemed a logical choice to command in the border state where his late father-in-law, Senator Thomas Hart Benton, had long fought slavery. But corruption flourished under and endangered Frémont's command. Hoping to make a morally correct decision as well as a political splash, he ordered emancipation in his command in August 1861. Asked to reconsider, Frémont refused to budge, and Lincoln rescinded his order, declaring that the power for such an act rested with him alone—another statement in behalf of presidential power.[8]

At first Republicans cared more about action than the circumstances surrounding it. Radicals felt that since slavery was wrong and Frémont had acted against it, Lincoln was wrong to overrule him. Sumner said, "Our President is now dictator, Imperator—what you will; but how vain to have the power of a God if not to use it God-like." He blamed Lincoln's advisers, especially Seward. Senator Ben Wade of Ohio derided Lincoln for believing that "the right of a man to his slaves, is more sacred, than the right to his own life. Such ethics, could only come of one, born of 'poor white trash' and educated in a slave State." He facetiously suggested that Lincoln might recommend giving land to the rebels to reward their disloyalty. Even those who tried to be more restrained—the ambitious and cautious Representative Schuyler Colfax of Indiana and the *Chicago Tribune*'s editors, who saw theirs as Lincoln's organ—voiced displeasure.[9]

Ultimately, though, Lincoln's logic triumphed. For Republicans to back an anti-slavery act made sense, but their newfound power required that act to be wise and constitutional. Frémont failed on several counts. When his conservative friend Browning joined the chorus of critics, Lincoln wrote privately to him, stating his case with clarity, muted criticism, a commitment to principle, and a bow to the realities of power. Calling the order "purely political, and not within the range of military law, or necessity," he agreed that a general could seize property, even slaves, for military use, "but when the need is past, it is not for him to fix their permanent future condition. That must be settled according to laws made by law-makers." As a congressman, he said, he might vote for emancipation, but, "What I object to is, that I as President, shall expressly or impliedly seize and exercise the permanent legislative functions of the government." Then came a revealing transition: "So much as to principle. Now as to policy." He contradicted Browning's concern that he had acted only because border slave states, especially Kentucky, might respond to Frémont by joining the rebels. That had to be a factor in his thinking, but Lincoln assured Browning that it had no effect on his views.[10]

Eventually the tide turned against Frémont. Logic was one explanation: Republican fears of military power made them more likely to side with a popularly elected president than a general, even an antislavery one. News of Frémont's corruption and incompetence also reduced Republican ardor: as Lincoln's secretary, John Nicolay, said, "The d——d fool has completely frittered away the finest opportunity a man of small eminence ever had to make his name immortal." Republican editors argued that the president had authority over the military, and that the federal government was supposed to avoid interfering with state government, as Frémont undeniably had. Radicals felt pained that Lincoln had revoked an order of emancipation, as they would when he would revoke General David Hunter's order in 1862. But that controversy was less captious—they learned a lesson with Frémont, and Hunter was less important politically. In both cases Lincoln made clear that he opposed emancipation by an army commander, but left open the possibility that a politician could act. Conceding that Hunter was unwise and untimely, radical Carl Schurz said that Lincoln avoided saying anything that "would cripple him for future action. It is perfectly certain that measures similar to that proposed by Hunter will before long have to be adopted, and . . . be revived as the most natural thing in the world." He was almost right, but it would happen when Lincoln felt that he had to aid the Union by using his power to strike a blow for freedom.[11]

In the war's first two years, though, Republicans were in flux, adapting to new circumstances. Thus, visiting England early in 1862, the normally conservative Thurlow Weed used the kind of radical tones he condemned in his foes. Generals would have authority to free slaves in their commands, he said, but Frémont had been "premature." Once emancipated, slaves would remain where they were, but plantations would be confiscated, loyal Northerners would take over, and "a kind of apprenticeship" would ease the transition from slavery to freedom. While this fell short of later proposals to confiscate rebel land and give it to ex-slaves, Weed came close to what radicals advocated. When the *New York Times* suggested compensation, colonization, and "a proper period of tutelage" for freedpeople, it was less radical than Weed at the time. The *Philadelphia Press* criticized Lincoln for failing to encourage slave insurrections, which most conservatives opposed. Between the spring and fall of 1861, the conservative *Hartford Courant* went from opposing emancipation to demanding it.[12]

While conservatives showed signs of change, radicals held fast to their view of the war as an apocalyptic event that would end slavery. William Herndon, Lincoln's law partner, told Trumbull, "The question is—Shall the Union go under or shall slavery go out of sight. If this be correct whatever is necessary to save the Union let him do—1st by abolishing slavery, and 2d by arming them if necessary." Francis Lieber, a radical who had lived in South Carolina, agreed. He sent a wish list to Sumner: limit the spread of slavery, end it in the District of Columbia, emancipate the slaves of the disloyal, offer loyal slave owners compensation, free slaves entering Union lines, "and what with increased cotton culture elsewhere and the blow which the institution must receive from our victory after having proclaimed itself a divine institution, it will dwindle and die out." One radical, lacking a vote but not a voice, captured the situation. As the war began, former slave and abolitionist Frederick Douglass said, "So much for the moral movement against slavery. Hereafter, opposition to slavery will naturally take a new form." A year later Lincoln, once a critic of abolitionism, reminded Greeley that he had always hated slavery. War made for strange political bedfellows and changing views. But the moral movement that Douglass cited was limited, the opposition strong, and the difference helped explain the party's wartime and political success: with its ideology refined amid the traps and trappings of power, Republicans could and would attack slavery as part of a broader set of problems threatening the Union.[13]

The District of Columbia emancipation bill revealed how Republicans had to adjust their attitudes toward slavery. In 1861, Ashley introduced a bill to end slavery in the federal enclave, the one area where Republicans could move against the institution without constitutional quibbles. But it passed only after several months and negotiations within the party and between the branches. Secretary of the Treasury Salmon Chase, a fellow Ohioan and radical, asked Ashley to meet with Lincoln, who told him that compensating slave owners in the capital might help him persuade border states to end the institution. When Ashley agreed, Congress approved and Lincoln signed a bill for three hundred dollars per slave to be paid to the affected owner. Even then, displeased conservative Republicans and War Democrats decried its timing and voiced fears that it would compel free blacks to move north.[14]

For a radical to compromise on slavery was unusual, but other factors reveal the measure's significance. Ashley admitted to disagreeing with Lincoln, but the president's radical and moderate support silenced him. Radicals emphasized the result, which thrilled them. The *Detroit Advertiser* said, "That infamy is wiped from the national escutcheon." Indeed, the issue's importance prompted Republicans to ignore what usually divided them. Sumner kept his complaints private when Lincoln delayed signing the bill until a friend removed two elderly slaves from the area to protect them from the vicissitudes of freedom. No Republicans seem to have objected that Lincoln, a supposedly Whiggish executive, directed Ashley to change his bill. The party increasingly saw that power demanded compromise. Whether or not emancipation would be gradual, movement toward it would be, as befit a party adapting to the responsibilities of power and perpetuating both freedom and union.[15]

Confiscation and Conflict

For the party, the limits of power went beyond military action against slavery to confiscating slaves as property. After an earlier bill allowed the seizure of rebel assets used against the Union, Trumbull introduced a broader bill in 1862 for taking rebel property. Radicals were pleased, but conservatives and many moderates doubted its legality, with

Fessenden, usually a Trumbull ally, arguing that Congress had no more power in a war than at other times. Senator Timothy Howe, a Wisconsin moderate, bemoaned the "timid, hesitating and unresolved" conservatives and the "turbulent, passionate and reckless" radicals. Safe from congressional politics, moderate John Bigelow cautioned from Paris against confiscation unless it became "necessary to exterminate the slave holding classes."[16]

Confiscation displayed anew how Republicans differed over means, not ends. An intellectual descendant of the Federalists, Sumner interpreted the Constitution broadly and nationalistically: because Congress had war powers, the Union was at war, and slavery aided the enemy, confiscation was permissible. Wade agreed, but legislative supremacy appealed to him for less ideological reasons than his earlier Whiggery: his disdain for Lincoln. As usual more brutally frank than most Republicans, he also wanted slaves freed and slave owners to suffer: "I care something for the confiscation of the property of the leading rebels; but I do not wish to touch the property of the masses of the people." Yet Montgomery Blair, sharing his bluntness but not his radicalism, wanted to use confiscated slaves to compensate Union slaveholders who lost their property due to the war, and he expected this action to induce Southern unionists to rise against secession to protect their holdings. While similar, these views diverged significantly: they came from personal polar opposites and were rooted in the widely divergent realms of theory and practice. It was the wartime Republicans in microcosm, reaching similar conclusions by unlike reasoning, with the questions of freedom, union, and power at their core.[17]

As politicians reporting to, reflecting, and influencing constituents, Republicans agreed on the need to act by the time Trumbull introduced the bill. Not only had the war gone badly, but they had done little to attack slavery. Confiscation gave them a chance. To Indiana constituents, Colfax admitted divisions on confiscation, but noted signs of a compromise. Radicals could accept it as a war measure rather than going further and seeking emancipation, and conservatives could concede the need to strike at the South. Senator James Grimes, who reflected Iowa's moderation, told Trumbull, "I long ago made up my mind to vote for a law to confiscate all the property of rebels, no matter of what it may consist. . . . and let those who choose to set their faces against it, do so: but mark it, all who do, will be overwhelmed by popular denunciations."[18]

Indeed, congressional debates over confiscation showed the differences over means and people, not goals. Typically, both sides, especially in the Senate, grew personal. When Browning fought the bill, Minnesota radical Morton Wilkinson called him too sensitive to the rebels. Moderates dueled: when Trumbull opposed changes in his bill, Fessenden complained, "Certain gentlemen on this floor seem to think that they are the representatives of all righteousness; that unless we take their opinions we are sure to be wrong, and are threatened with an appeal to the people; that they are the only men who want to put down the rebellion, the only men who have any correct idea of how it shall be done, and that if anybody differs from them he is either a fool or a knave." When Michigan's Jacob Howard said that Congress could act against rebel property owners only through the war power, not its usual powers, an unusual trio—conservatives Browning and James Dixon of Connecticut and radical John Hale of New Hampshire—argued that since secession was illegal, Southerners remained citizens and the government had no right to seize their property. While most War Democrats opposed confiscation on any grounds, Indiana's Joseph Wright wholeheartedly backed it. Finally, the confiscation bill passed Congress, but only after Trumbull disowned many of its new provisions. Thus, Republicans deemed confiscation necessary and constitutional, but by different methods.[19]

However, a key question lingered: Where did Lincoln stand? As the bill moved through Congress, John Forney, a Republican editor with ties to the White House, suspected that Lincoln opposed a strong confiscation policy. Browning met with Seward, decided that they agreed, and expected him to back a veto. The *New York Times,* which often tried to speak for Lincoln, judged confiscation ill advised and premature and urged Congress to concentrate on supporting Lincoln and funding the army. Many Republicans, aware of the ties between Seward and *Times* editor Henry Raymond, were sure that the secretary of state controlled Lincoln and feared the worst.[20]

Lincoln's uncertainty reflected the party's evolution. He stretched the limits of executive and federal power, but objected to the bill as violating a constitutional ban on forfeiting property beyond a traitor's lifetime. As congressional leaders agreed to amend it, conservatives urged him to veto it. Instead he signed the Second Confiscation Act on 17 July 1862—and sent Congress the veto message he had prepared. The act, he said, tested his constitutional scruples. "It is startling to say that congress can free a slave within a state," he said, then admitted that a traitor surrendered ownership to the federal government, eliminating the problem. Nor did he "believe it would be physically possible, for the General government, to return persons, so circumstanced, to actual slavery," but he warned the radicals, "The severest justice may not always be the best policy."[21]

Offering something, and something offensive, for everyone, the message reflected Lincoln's efforts to temper conflicts within his party. Trumbull resented the criticism and changes. *Chicago Tribune* editor Joseph Medill, radical in private but publicly agreeable to Lincoln's moderation, egged on Trumbull; Sumner felt that war allowed for cutting constitutional corners, but legal precedent supported confiscation. Conservative Republicans and War Democrats disagreed with Lincoln but accepted the result out of unionism and their sense that he appreciated their concerns. Accordingly, when Trumbull criticized Lincoln's stand, conservatives rushed to his defense, and radicals helped their occasional supporter restate his position on constitutional rather than political grounds. Republicans took great pains to make sure that the differences they voiced concerned not the ends, but the means of reaching them.[22]

Not long after his confiscation message, Lincoln told Greeley that he would free all or no slaves according to what might save the Union. This letter has received appropriate attention, but the veto message was like it in significant ways. While radicals resented his limited support, they were pleased that he went along with them. In warning conservatives that the federal government soon might free slaves in states, he showed that at least he was aware of their concerns. Congressional leaders lambasted him for interfering and threatening what one Republican called a "back-kitchen style of veto," but in the end he gave House and Senate leaders most of what they wanted. Thus, Lincoln made a statement for executive power at the expense of legislative power, suggested more radical action against slavery, and positioned himself as the obstacle to that action.[23]

It was Lincoln as obstacle who incurred Greeley's displeasure. Greeley had felt unsure of what to do as the war began, but soon he became an ardent emancipationist, unconsciously helping Lincoln prepare public opinion for the proclamation. By October 1861, with the army mired and muddled, he came out for freeing rebel slaves while deferring to the government on the timing and easing the fears of Northern racists by suggesting Florida as a place to send the millions of freedmen. As he said privately, the only way to destroy the slave power was to destroy the institution that empowered it. Tired of what he saw as Lincoln's dawdling, in August 1862 he issued "The Prayer of Twenty Millions," a call for emancipation meant to force Lincoln's hand. The commentary contained little that was new. His prayer inspired a long letter from Lincoln, who began with a telltale comment: "If there be perceptable in it an impatient and dictatorial tone, I waive it in deference to an old friend, whose heart I have always supposed to be right." He understood Greeley's feelings but made clear that he resented his tone—and verged on dishonesty, since he had been privately critical of the editor several times, most notably when Greeley had dabbled with backing Stephen Douglas against Lincoln in Illinois in 1858. As one editor said, Greeley "scolded the President much as a shrewish housekeeper might scold a careless servant. . . . There is not only an assumption of superior wisdom, but a tone of petulant dictation running through it."[24]

What Lincoln's letter said, and left unsaid, offers valuable insight into his and the party's views. He wrote, "What I do about slavery, and the colored race, I do because I believe it helps to save the Union, and what I forbear, I forbear because I do not believe it would help to save the Union." To put the Union above "the colored race" was typical of Lincoln and other Republicans, but while he discussed slavery throughout the letter, that was the lone reference to race. After telling Greeley, "The sooner the national authority can be restored; the nearer the Union will be 'the Union as it was,'" he wrote and deleted, "Broken eggs can never be mended, and the longer the breaking proceeds the more will be broken." As brilliant a writer as he was, as conscious as he was of cadence, no doubt he saw that such homely words would be out of place. But the sentiment was telling: as the war went on, slavery would be increasingly damaged and inevitably destroyed. Since he intended to reassure both radicals and conservatives, Lincoln may have foreseen conservative alarm and edited himself; his reasons are unknowable. But he was bridging a gap between radicals and conservatives, and being coldly calculating in the process.[25]

CRAWLING TOWARD EMANCIPATION

This helps explain the Emancipation Proclamation, the events leading to it, and its character, all of which reflected the ideology of freedom, union, and power. It lacked the beauty of Lincoln's other works: Richard Hofstadter wrote that it had "all the moral grandeur of a bill of lading." But as Phillip Paludan said, "The language of the great deed had to be a lawyer's language because Lincoln was taking legal action. He was placing the great ideal of freedom within the constitutional fabric—the only place that it could have life in a constitutional republic." Eric Foner begins his study of Reconstruction with Lincoln signing the proclamation. Foner says, "For the first time tying Union success to abolition—a commitment from which Lincoln never retreated—it ignored entirely both compensation and colonization, and for the first time authorized the large-scale enlistment of black soldiers," but his subsequent study of American freedom refers sparingly to the proclamation. Other historians have noted that it stirred up antiwar sentiment among westerners who saw it as a step toward racial equality, a claim that Lincoln described as "largely imaginary, if not sometimes malicious." Those who blamed the proclamation for defeats in the 1862 midterm elections included not only conservatives, but Greeley and moderate Senator John Sherman of Ohio. As with historians, so with contemporaries: the proclamation proved to be many things to many people, all connected to Republican ideology.[26]

As 1862 wore on, amid discussion of confiscation and compensated emancipation, more Republicans expected the other shoe to drop. By August radicals had lost patience. Howard asked Trumbull whether it was time for Lincoln "to secure for the union and the government the advantage of so important a step? Is it not certain that one or the other party to this war will emancipate the slaves? If so, why should we lose the golden opportunity—as a war measure?" Then Greeley published his "Prayer" and urged Lincoln to issue a proclamation. To the reply that Kentucky would secede, Greeley said, "The cause of the Union will be stronger if Kentucky should secede with the rest," which showed his awareness of the ties between freedom and union. With similar concerns but a different perspective, Lincoln said, "Oh, I can't think that!"[27]

But Lincoln was thinking about emancipation, and was close to answering Greeley's prayer. Clearly, he understood the radical sentiment expressed by Douglass: "events steadily conspire to make the cause of the slave and the cause of the country identical," another way of declaring freedom and union inseparable. Revoking Hunter's proclamation in May 1862 caused less criticism than the controversy over Frémont, and the language in his order made clear, as Lincoln told Chase, "No commanding general shall do such a thing, upon *my* responsibility, without consulting me." More important, Lincoln's response to Hunter's order said that "whether at any time, in any case, it shall have become a necessity indispensable to the maintenance of the government, to exercise such supposed power." Lincoln was too astute not to sense that the center was moving. As he privately told Chase and publicly told Hunter, he was moving too. He was warning both sides that emancipation might be near.[28]

But how fast Lincoln moved, what he did about freedom, was tied to the state of the Union and its power. A week after Lincoln overruled Hunter, Stanton predicted to Sumner an emancipation proposal within two months. To Sumner, who cultivated good relations with Lincoln and Stanton almost as much as they cozied up to him, that meant it was inevitable, so he was willing to wait. Six weeks later Lincoln told Seward and Welles "that we must free the slaves or be ourselves subdued." By then Union forces were progressing slowly, if at all, but slaves still poured into their lines. For political and military purposes, Lincoln needed to settle on a policy that addressed a problem of logistics and dealt with morale by reinvigorating the war effort against an institution so basically antithetical to freedom.[29]

In July Lincoln showed his proclamation to the Cabinet—not for advice, he said, but for their knowledge. They divided, but unpredictably. Urging immediate emancipation were Stanton, dealing with fugitives inundating the army and headed for radicalism, and Attorney General Edward Bates, a conservative aware that border state men were in a vise. Fearing its effect on Union finances and despite qualms about the military, Chase would leave it up to generals; he expected more public support for emancipation if they did it, and possibly he doubted Lincoln's will. Secretary of the Navy Gideon Welles, Postmaster General Montgomery Blair, and Secretary of the Interior Caleb Smith, all conservatives, were unenthused. Seward shared their concerns but felt that emancipation without victory "would be considered our last shriek, on the retreat"—a shrewd, logical analysis that appealed to the shrewd, logical Lincoln, and in line with the party's ideology of balancing freedom and union with an awareness of the need for the power to achieve those goals. Perhaps more important, while Lincoln acted independently, he had chosen his Cabinet to reflect the varied Republican constituencies. If the most astute politician and the leading radical were dubious while a War Democrat and border state Whig backed it, Lincoln would be wise to wait. The center was moving but had yet to cohere.[30]

Delay was one thing; secrecy and discretion were something else. The Cabinet discussion stayed private, but Lincoln began preparing others for a new departure on slavery. When Massachusetts radical George Boutwell pleaded for emancipation late that summer, Lincoln asked, "Must we not wait for something like a victory?" and shared a letter in which he told a foe of emancipation, "You must not expect me to give up this government without playing my last card." Hindsight may have improved Boutwell's vision, but he was smart enough to see when someone was shifting to his view, and Lincoln was subtle enough to speak carefully. Lincoln also spoke with a Chase ally, New York radical Hiram Barney; New York's radical-conservative split might make his inside knowledge useful later. Better still from Lincoln's perspective, Barney recommended delay for the same reason as Seward, who led the rival faction. Then, on 30 July a call for emancipation appeared in the *Philadelphia Press,* whose editor, Forney, was close to the White House. The party was aware of public opinion and sensitive to the importance of using its power wisely.[31]

While other Republicans discussed rumors and policy, Lincoln spoke to the citizens on whom the proclamation's success depended. When a group of Chicago Christians petitioned for emancipation, his reply revealed that he had pondered it and the ways in which issues of union and power related to freedom: "I do not want to issue a document that the whole world will see must necessarily be inoperative, like the Pope's bull against the comet! Would my word free the slaves, when I cannot even enforce the Constitution in the rebel States?" Without power, a stand for freedom and union would be useless—and, if it cost the Union border state support, dangerous. Yet if he lacked physical, geographical, or political power, he made clear that he had constitutional power as commander-in-chief "to take any measure which may best subdue the enemy." Radicals and conservatives alike could take heart from such a statement.[32]

As usual, and as intended, Lincoln could be read many ways. Referring to measures to encourage rebel slaves to enter Union lines, he asked, "And suppose they could be induced by a proclamation of freedom from me to throw themselves upon us, *what should we do with them?* How can we feed and care for such a multitude?" Suggesting policy was easy, but he saw that with his party in power, suggesting mattered less than doing; the voices raised for emancipation may not have thought beyond the moment. Lincoln reminded visitors that he had no "objections of a moral nature, in view of possible consequences of insurrection and massacre at the South. I view the matter as a practical war measure, to be decided upon according to the advantages or disadvantages it may offer to the suppression of the rebellion." He warned the rebels that emancipation might endanger what they sought to protect, conservatives that he soon might act, and radicals that action against freedom depended on the state of the Union.[33]

On 22 September, five days after Antietam, Lincoln decided that the state of the Union demanded action. Closer than ever to a position of military strength, he told his Cabinet that he was issuing the Preliminary Emancipation Proclamation. This time his ministers were more agreeable, but, granting that he considered it a war measure within his purview as commander-in-chief, his lack of interest in their views demonstrated his view of his powers: this was no meeting of a board of directors in which everybody cast a vote. Yet critics then and historians since have noted the proclamation's fundamentally conservative nature. Cushioning the blow to conservatives, it began by declaring that "hereafter, as heretofore," the war was to restore the Union. Then it offered aid for colonization and compensated emancipation, both of which appealed to unionists uneasy about confiscating slaves and what their freedom meant. Only in the third paragraph did he get to the point: slaves in rebelling states as of 1 January 1863 "shall be then, thenceforward, and forever free."[34]

The proclamation fit neatly into Republican ideology, which obviously appealed to all sides of the party spectrum. After declaring freedom, it said that the government "will recognize and maintain the freedom of such persons, and will do no act or acts to repress such persons, or any of them, in any efforts they may make for their actual freedom," phrasing that left room to maneuver. It offered reminders about not returning fugitive slaves, with references to the Second Confiscation Act, which Lincoln had almost vetoed two months earlier. And, deflecting praise, he doubted its efficacy. "It is known to some that while I hope something from the proclamation, my expectations are not as sanguine as are those of some friends," he told Vice President Hannibal Hamlin, a radical. "The North responds to the proclamation sufficiently in breath; but breath alone kills no rebels." Radicals had demanded such an act, but Lincoln saw it mainly as a policy statement. In reiterating that belief, he reminded them that actions—power—spoke louder than words.[35]

The reaction to the proclamation also suggests how radical it was. Despite wishing that Lincoln had gone further, Greeley hailed him for striking at slavery as the cause of the war and drawing a link between freedom and union that might be beneficial in the future. Whatever Sumner's questions about Lincoln or the document's wording, he was "firmly and sincerely by the side of the President." The *Chicago Tribune* said that it restored the government that the framers had intended: "the home of freedom, the asylum of the oppressed, the seat of justice, the land of equal rights under the law, where each man, however humble, shall be entitled to life, liberty and the pursuit of happiness." The *Peoria Transcript,* an editorial admirer of abolitionist Representative Owen Lovejoy, called the proclamation "as radical as anything Mr. Lovejoy has uttered."[36]

While radicals celebrated, the unfavorable reaction of conservatives and some moderates suggests that they understood the proclamation's meaning all too well. Richard Henry Dana complained that if it failed, the Union would collapse. Other conservatives deemed it unnecessary, since it would take effect as the army rolled on. Still anti-Blair to the core and en route to radicalism, loathe to give Lincoln credit for anything, Henry Winter Davis complained, "These proclamations are powerless but for mischief." Fessenden saw it as likely to do no more than appease radicals. Edward Everett, the old Whig who had joined the Union party but stayed aloof from Republicanism, felt that conservatives would go along with the proclamation as a war measure while radicals would accept it, although it was "not fully up to their standard." But for radicals, it was good enough.[37]

How the Blairs reacted to the proclamation reflected their shrewdness, their conservatism, and their acceptance of Republican ideology. They remained close to McClellan, whom radicals saw as the devil incarnate for his hatred for abolitionism, his Democratic leanings, and his inability or unwillingness to defeat Robert E. Lee. Montgomery Blair told McClellan that "no appreciable portion of the nation will favor the long continuance of slavery after this war is over or will tolerate any guarantees for its perpetuity as the price of peace." Francis Preston Blair, once a member of Andrew Jackson's "Kitchen Cabinet," agreed with his son, expressing hopes that emancipation would be gradual and compensated, and reminding the general that he and the army had to enforce the proclamation for it to be a success. They hoped that McClellan would stand by it, even give it the kind of support that might improve his relationship with Lincoln and the radicals. While the general privately criticized the proclamation and gave it a lukewarm public reception, the Blairs showed that even if they were unenthusiastic, they understood the proclamation and the reasons for it—another sign of the unifying role of Republican ideology.[38]

What conservatives said about the proclamation proved important, as did what they left unsaid. Significantly, few if any suggested that slaves would revert to their old status after the war. Browning opposed the edict, but in the privacy of his diary he wrote that it merely put existing deeds into words; he regretted that the words were more inflammatory—potentially a political danger—and thus ill advised, with midterm voting six weeks away. With a touch of the radicalism he now seemed to lack, Seward put it better. Complimented on his role in the proclamation, he said, "Yes, we have let off a puff of wind over an accomplished fact." He explained that "the emancipation proclamation was uttered in the first gun fired at Sumter and we have been the last to hear it. As it is, we show our sympathy with slavery by emancipating slaves where we cannot reach them and holding them in bondage where we can set them free."[39]

A letter to Seward suggests an answer to the question of whether the proclamation was radical or conservative. As Paris chargé d'affaires, John Bigelow corresponded with radical and conservative friends. Bigelow called the Preliminary Proclamation "improvident as well as impracticable." He told Seward that "to show him the way to take his labor to market on the one hand, and to protect society on the other from the ignorance, the thriftlessness and the vices which the freedman brings with him out of servitude, laws adapted to his peculiar condition should be passed and agents for their administration be appointed"—a primitive forerunner of the Freedmen's Bureau. Suggesting "general laws applicable to all persons answering to his political and social description without reference to race or color," he said, "I see no reason why the Southern lands should not be better tilled, why the supply of labor should not be more regular and less expensive, why the security of property should not be increased, why the thriftlessness and vice of which slavery is the inevitable parent should not gradually diminish." Bigelow was one of the few to address a key issue: What became of the freedmen after emancipation? It was radical for the government to act officially against slavery, given the time and place. Even if it was only a war measure and fell short of what radicals wanted, it surely was more than conservatives wanted.[40]

Because the proclamation fell short of their hopes, radicals feared that Lincoln would fall short of their expectations. The issue had little to do with party ideology. When Republicans suffered rebukes in the midterm elections, some conservatives blamed the proclamation; they hoped that the result would convince Lincoln of their point of view. Emphasizing the Union and believing that freedom would help preserve it, radicals decided that the spread of freedom depended on the Union. This difference was important but surmountable. But late in 1862, they still saw Seward as too influential and expected him to try to change Lincoln's mind about the proclamation. "The President's head is right, God grant he may have the strength to stand up to his convictions and carry them out to the full," Ohio Republican James Garfield said. Reassuring anti-slavery friends on both sides of the Atlantic, Sumner wrote that Lincoln "says that he would not stop the Proclamation if he could, and could not if he would," and, "He said to me that it was hard to move him from a position which he had once taken." Not only did he differ from other radicals, but it was a sign of the stubbornness that would serve Lincoln and the radicals in good stead.[41]

Thus, when Lincoln kept his promise, 1 January 1863 proved to be the day of jubilee for which many Republicans had hoped. The verve of their celebration bespeaks their awareness of the proclamation's importance. Radicals believed not just in the clichés about a new day dawning but that the nation, as Ashley said, was "irrevocably committed to the policy of universal emancipation." Optimism might be expected from radicals, but moderates thought similarly. Massachusetts businessman John Murray Forbes called the proclamation "the turning point in our fate"; Governor Samuel Kirkwood of Iowa told Lincoln that he would never do anything more important—sentiments unlikely to be associated with a temporary or otherwise meaningless measure. Reporting a Cabinet split over gradual or immediate emancipation, the *New York Tribune* noted, "No member harbors for a moment the idea of reconstructing the Union on a basis of Slavery." As Sumner said, "The President is empowered to confer Freedom; but he is impotent to make a slave—so that he cannot undo his own act of Emancipation." Freedom, union, and power had come together.[42]

This collection of opinions suggests that to radicals and moderates, the proclamation set the nation on a course to end slavery. As a document it did no such thing; it freed slaves in rebelling areas. While this accounted for most of the four million slaves in the United States, the proclamation would take effect only where it was unenforceable, at least until Union armies made progress. More important, it changed the Republican party from a coalition opposed to the spread of slavery to an instrument that imminently threatened its survival. Enacting confiscation and the District of Columbia emancipation bill dented slave-owning armor. But despite the debate they caused, these actions were clearly constitutional. No matter how it was couched, the proclamation was the first effort to end bondage by freeing slaves in states by government fiat. It was the perfect enactment of policy based on the Republican ideology merging freedom, union, and power. Thus, "whether there be union or disunion, that decree is eternal for this continent," Boutwell said. Backing away from the proclamation would be as easy as unringing a bell.[43]

Beyond symbolism and statecraft, the proclamation produced tangible results. It limited the South's ability to fight by reducing its labor force: when soldiers in Virginia posted it, one general said that the area, "the heart of aristocratic and wealthy slavery, is alive with a vast hegira of bondmen and bondwomen." It affected the military: while generals such as McClellan voiced distaste for fighting against slavery, confirming Republican fears about the army, the government was committed to a new course that they would have to follow. Overseas, antislavery leaders renewed their support for the Northern cause, and pro-slavery aristocrats saw more clearly what was at stake in the war. To Chase and other Republicans, the proclamation offered a tentative blueprint toward reconstructing the South without slavery.[44]

To many Republicans the proclamation was just that: tentative. Not that they would disown it, but it was a war measure that might require legislation to sustain it. "The original proclamation has no constitutional or legal justification, except as a military measure," Lincoln told Chase, and Fessenden agreed. Consequently, the *Chicago Tribune* said, "legislation of the most effective sort" would be needed to secure emancipation before a pro-slavery Democrat became president. Abolitionist John Jay linked the real and symbolic: "when it is confirmed by Congress, and the freedom of the blacks is solemnly pledged by law, it will seem more like an accomplished fact, never to be undone." In ensuing months, with encouragement from Lincoln, Congress would act as Jay hoped.[45]

Thus, the proclamation accomplished nothing and everything. Greeley's *Tribune* warned, "If the blacks shall now fall asleep in the conviction that the President has given them their liberty, we believe they will awake too late to find themselves in chains for generations." Governments change policies and revolutions may go backward, but the party saw that once some slaves were freed, others would follow and be unlikely to return to their old status. The chance that the proclamation would be rescinded was slim, but there was a chance that it would go no further. Other proclamations and laws would be needed to extend its reach. More than that, it would take Union victories. Lincoln knew that without military success, any proclamation on any issue would be a dead letter. That was his main consideration, as it was for most of his party. He had issued a proclamation of freedom intended to help save the Union; now Union power had to turn the freedom he had proclaimed into a reality.[46]

Changing the Constitution

The Thirteenth Amendment became the party's ultimate declaration for freedom and an apogee for its ideology. For Republicans it represented a result unanticipated when the war had begun and the culmination of a long battle of their own. The few who expected the South's professed goal of saving slavery to lead to its ruin were radicals, although how much of that was wishful thinking is open to debate. The Emancipation Proclamation set slavery on the road to extinction, but it was an act under the war power that might not survive judicial or legislative scrutiny. The amendment cast it in constitutional concrete. Its passage illuminates how the party committed to freedom and union adapted to power.[47]

The road to passing the amendment began in the Senate, with its large Republican majority. Senators received ample advice from constituents and party opinion makers. Governor William Buckingham of Connecticut said, "Slavery is not dead. . . . Let us embrace this opportunity . . . until every man, whether high or low, rich or poor, learned or ignorant, of whatever tribe or race or nation, shall be protected in all the inalienable rights which God has given him, under our national emblem of liberty, union, and power." Former senator Preston King of New York opposed an amendment but told Sherman, "I have believed from an early day that the extinction of slavery was necessary to the extinction of the Rebellion and to the permanent peace and unity of the country." *Forney's War Press* urged the Union party to demand an anti-slavery amendment in its platform. With new territories headed for statehood, the *National Anti-Slavery Standard* said, passing an amendment without the South would be possible. Just in case, some radicals went halfway: Samuel Sewall told Sumner that Congress should compensate loyal slave owners. Radicals had been loath to suggest that, but the political reality was that the anti-slavery amendment lacked sufficient support.[48]

Despite their large majority, steering the measure through the Senate proved difficult. Again, Republican beliefs unified them in the face of personality conflicts and political realities. Sumner proposed a set of measures so elaborate that they could never attract enough votes to pass, nor did his colleagues want to entrust a statement on slavery to a radical. Finally, Trumbull and his Judiciary Committee took a proposal from the House and edited it. Then, when Fessenden stalled debate to bring up a naval appropriation bill, Trumbull demanded immediate action: "It is the most important measure that the American Congress has ever had under consideration. It is a proposition forever to abolish slavery throughout the United States, and to prevent its reestablishment. It is a question believed, as I suppose, by most of us to lie at the foundation of this rebellion." Usually a stalwart realist, Trumbull reflected one of the problems the party unhappily confronted: the need to place the mundane and managerial above the ideological and idealistic.[49]

Despite the delays, the amendment's passage on 8 April 1864 and the reaction to it showed both how much and how little Republicans had changed. The 37-to-6 majority included all Republicans and several War Democrats, reflecting the Union party's success. Calling the margin "unexpectedly decided," an abolitionist admitted his pleasure at listening to those "unaccustomed to making anti-slavery speeches. . . . Such facts assure one that the progress of public sentiment in reference to slavery keeps pace with the war." Gratuitously, since Lincoln supported the measure, he added that "the advance of the people on this great question is so rapid that if the President were a downright Conservative he could not lag behind." The *Sacramento Union* cheered that "we are standing on the verge of the consummation of the entire, perpetual and constitutional freedom of every man, woman, and child beneath the folds of the flag." Despite evolving public opinion, Republicans doubted that they could muster a two-thirds majority in the House and blamed Democrats. Since they claimed that using legislative or war powers to end slavery was unconstitutional, with the amendment introduced, *Forney's War Press* asked, "Will it receive the support of these champions of the Constitution?"[50]

The answer was no: as Republicans feared, the House posed a problem. In June 1864 it approved the measure by a vote of 93 to 65—not the needed two-thirds. Each Republican voted for it and all but four Democrats against it, but the Union coalition was shaky; it was a lot to ask border state congressmen to abolish what their constituents had long supported. Ashley, the amendment's floor manager, chose not to bring it up again in that session. "Those who ought to have been the champions of this great proposition are unfortunately its strongest opponents. They have permitted the golden opportunity to pass," he said of Democrats and border state congressmen. "The record is made up, and we must go to the country on this issue thus presented. When the verdict of the people is rendered next November I trust this Congress will return determined to ingraft that verdict into the national Constitution." Indeed, when Democrat James Brooks of New York declared slavery all but dead anyway, Isaac Arnold of Illinois replied that "we have only to witness the proceedings of the House to know and feel that the institution still lives, and that it has its friends here who are determined that it shall not perish." Slavery remained a partisan issue, a link enhanced by Republican efforts to balance freedom and union.[51]

Thus, Lincoln entered the fray. He may have been behind the Senate's first emancipation proposal, by John Henderson of Missouri, a border state he deemed crucial to ending slavery. He urged Senator Edwin Morgan of New York, keynoting the Union convention, to make the amendment the platform's "key-stone." While its leaders claimed to speak only for the Union, it was the first major party to endorse a constitutional amendment to end slavery, and Republicans, War Democrats, and border state men campaigned for the party in an era in which party platforms mattered far more than they would later. When the party triumphed, whatever the reasons, Lincoln and Congress received a mandate. Indeed, Republicans felt that voters had spoken against slavery and hoped that might induce House Democrats to vote for the amendment, if only to eliminate it as an issue.[52]

That was the Republican plan. Ashley was set to bring the issue before the House after the election, and his arguments echoed those used against its spread. He called slavery morally wrong and antithetical to the wishes of the framers. But only those states then represented in Congress, he argued, had to ratify the amendment for it to take effect—a radical stand redolent of Sumner's claim that states forfeited their rights when they seceded. As if to deflect Democratic or conservative criticism of this kind of argument, the *Washington Chronicle,* which often voiced Lincoln's views, described an amendment as the people's expressed will, and Republicans pointed to the recent election as evidence of that will. Others added that slavery had caused the war and was about to lose; the victor had the right to dispose of it. If moral prodding was needed, Ashley's Ohio provided it: a legislative resolution calling slavery "a violation of the inherent and inalienable rights of men, a crime against justice and humanity, a disturber of the Union and of domestic tranquility, a hindrance to the common defense." But Ashley kept counting noses and found those in the opposition turned up at the thought of voting to end an institution they considered constitutionally protected and entirely up to the states.[53]

In the end, how the amendment passed reflected the party's belief in freedom and union, as well as confidence in its power. That was true of Lincoln, who had no constitutional part to play in the process. Going beyond his role as party leader, he lobbied border state congressmen. He reminded Missouri's James Rollins, who opposed the measure and lost his bid for reelection, of their Whig ancestry. Lincoln cited their admiration for Henry Clay, and "I never had an opinion upon the subject of slavery in my life that I did not get from him." He argued that border state support for slavery helped sustain the rebels. With slavery gone the Southern foundation would crack, and the rest would tumble down. Political careers might fall with it. According to John Alley, a representative from Massachusetts, Lincoln told two wavering congressmen that "two votes must be procured. I leave it to you to determine how it shall be done; but remember that I am President of the United States, clothed with immense power, and I expect you to procure those votes." Whether Lincoln spoke this way matters less than the tale's meaning: Republicans knew how to wield power and were ready to act accordingly.[54]

That included skirting the lines of corruption. Lincoln ordered paroles for prisoners of war related to Democratic congressmen. Probably with Lincoln's tacit approval, agents reporting to Seward apparently promised patronage jobs to recently defeated Democrats or friends of incumbents, who expressed gratitude during the roll call or behind the scenes. As Representative George Julian noted, the amendment's passage "depended upon certain negotiations the result of which was not fully assured, and the particulars of which never reached the public." Proposing more dirty work to Lincoln, Ashley asked him to lobby Sumner for a bill to aid New Jersey financial interests; if satisfied, they might persuade the state's wavering congressmen to back the amendment. Lincoln thought that would backfire: Sumner was "making his history in an issue with me on this very point." His stand showed subtlety in dealing with a difficult radical and less moralistic Republicans.[55]

Nor did he scruple about facts. Amid rumors that rebel commissioners had come to Washington, and aware that the truth might cost their cause several shaky votes, Lincoln told Ashley, "So far as I know, there are no peace commissioners in the city or likely to be in it." That was true: they were just across the city limits. No wonder Stevens said,

"The greatest measure of the nineteenth century was passed by corruption, aided and abetted by the purest man in America."[56]

Perhaps to the amazement of Republicans, Democrats aided their cause. War Democrats had long since accepted the Republican ethos in the Union platform, but those beneath the Democratic banner were another matter. When the amendment failed in June 1864, Republicans surmised that party discipline and the coming election had exacted a toll on Democratic support. After the election several Democrats backed the measure, arguing that they owed no loyalty to the South and that slavery had cost them so dearly that destroying it might help them or avenge their defeat. Other Democrats said that being true to their party's creed required them to vote as the people had done. Thus, Seward went so far as to claim that by rounding up Democrats to vote for the amendment or encouraging its opponents to absent themselves, Samuel "Sunset" Cox deserved the credit for its passage. Blaine later praised "the aid of a minority of the other party." Yet Cox voted against the amendment, despite urging party leaders to back it and remove the albatross of slavery from around their necks. He claimed to see through Lincoln's subterfuge about the rebel commissioners and feared that passing the amendment would ruin any chance for peace. Besides, he said, "I have some relations with Gov. Seward, and can occasionally find out what is up or under."[57]

Thanks to their opponents, Republicans celebrated their achievement. The House passed the amendment 119 to 56 on 31 January 1865; 15 Democrats voted for it, with 8 absent—altogether, it was enough to win a two-thirds majority. Speaker Colfax took the unusual step of asking to be added to the roll call and voting. Congressmen and spectators cheered. Lincoln, Arnold said, "saw in it the complete consummation of his own work, the emancipation proclamation." Garrison called Lincoln "the Presidential chainbreaker for millions of the oppressed." New York's *Evening Post,* which found Lincoln acceptable and Seward intolerable, hailed "those who by a single act . . . emancipated a race and regenerated a nation."[58]

Thus, Republicans worked with some Democrats after the two sides had spent a decade questioning one another's principles and birthright. Not that the two parties now united on slavery. For Cox and other Democrats who had voted or worked for the amendment, it was a way to revive and cleanse their party—to solve a political problem, not a national tragedy. Even some Republicans saw it as political, to bring peace by eliminating the Confederacy's reason for being, not to do what was morally right. But when they went to Hampton Roads to meet with the rebel commissioners, Lincoln and Seward reiterated their commitment to the Emancipation Proclamation and surprised them with news of the amendment's passage. Besides declaring that "he could not recede in the least from what he had publicly said about slavery," Lincoln allegedly told Alexander Stephens, the Confederate vice president and an old Whig friend from the House, that the legislature in his state of Georgia should "ratify this Constitutional Amendment prospectively, so as to take effect—say in five years. Such a ratification would be valid in my opinion." Lincoln had no power to tinker with a proposed amendment's ratification, but he stuck by the amendment and its meaning of freedom as he tried to cobble the Union back together.[59]

The amendment's passage had other meanings. Those involved took great pride in it: many Republicans hailed Ashley for managing it through obstacles in the House; Trumbull, whose committee had written it, later reveled in telling law students, "Gentlemen, this good right hand wrote this Amendment to the Constitution." But early in 1865 the states still had to ratify it, inspiring at least one close Lincoln friend to suggest still more nefarious activities. The minister to Berlin, Norman Judd, told Trumbull that "it would be honest under the circumstances to buy Kentucky and New Jersey—compensation and railroads will do both." And when Democratic state legislators balked at approving the amendment, Republicans resumed partisan sniping. Lieber pointed out to Sumner that the Constitution required further amending to protect black freedom, and the senator agreed. But addressing a crowd gathered to celebrate the amendment, Lincoln reminded his audience of the need for the states to approve it, adding that "this amendment is a King's cure for all the evils [applause]. It winds the whole thing up." To another he said, "The great job is ended."[60]

Of course, the job was far from over. Too many in the party felt that emancipation was all they could or should do for blacks, that freedom was enough and the rest was up to them. This reflected the antebellum free labor ideology: the belief that laborers should be free to reap the benefits of their work. During the war, Republicans extended that thinking to encompass not only the broader idea of freedom but the power to preserve the Union. Whether Republicans would revert or continue and expand upon this thinking would become an issue—and, for the newly freed slaves and their most ardent allies, a bitter disappointment.[61]

But Republicans accomplished more than they had entered the war with any reason to expect. The party that had demanded the constriction of slavery in 1860 choked it to death by 1865. Granted, they received aid from conservatives and War Democrats who joined the Union party, and from a few members of the Democratic opposition. At times their reasons were rooted less in their distaste for the institution and its effects than in pure political calculations. Those who cast the bulk of the votes against slavery during the Civil War and constantly made the case against it were Republicans motivated by a commitment to free labor that became part of a broader awareness of the need to spread freedom across the country—to promote the economic and personal opportunity embodied in the free labor ideology, and because the persistence of slavery threatened the existence of the country. That explained, in part, the Republican belief in the Union and its preservation: the Constitution and the government could jettison the slave power and promote what Lincoln called a new birth of freedom. As the amendment's passage and the events leading up to it show, Republicans understood their power to achieve their goals and perpetuate their power as the party responsible for governance. What they did about slavery, and their success in guiding the North to victory and creating a legacy, would have been impossible without their shared attitudes about freedom, union, and power.

NOTES

1. "First Inaugural Address—Final Text," Lincoln ms, LC, in *CW,* vol. 4, 262–71.

2. Howard, *Religion and the Radical Republican Movement,* 65–66; "Second Inaugural Address," in *CW,* vol. 8, 332–33; "Last Public Address," ibid., 399–405, at 403. On Booth, see Donald, *Lincoln,* 588. My understanding of these issues is influenced by Vorenberg, *Final Freedom.*

3. Foner, *Free Soil,* 261–62 and *passim.* On evolving views of freedom, see Foner, *The Story of American Freedom.* On Lincoln's views, see Don E. Fehrenbacher, "Only His Stepchildren: Lincoln and the Negro," in Fehrenbacher, *Lincoln in Text and Context,* 95–112; George M. Frederickson,

"A Man but Not a Brother: Abraham Lincoln and Racial Equality," *Journal of American History* 41, no. 1 (February 1975): 39–58; and, for a view that puts him closer to the radicals, Oates, *With Malice Toward None.* On Lincoln and slavery, see Eugene Berwanger, "Lincoln's Constitutional Dilemma: Emancipation and Black Suffrage," *Papers of the Abraham Lincoln Association* 5 (1983): 25–38, at 27; Phillip S. Paludan, "Lincoln, Slavery, and the Framers," in Donald G. Nieman, ed., *The Constitution, Law, and American Life: Critical Aspects of the Nineteenth-Century Experience* (Athens: University of Georgia Press, 1992), 20–21, n. 38. More recently, Bennett, *Forced into Glory,* accused Lincoln of racism pure and simple. While Bennett offers, as he has before, a great deal for historians to think about, his interpretation of Lincoln is exceedingly simplistic.

4. "'A House Divided': Speech at Springfield, Illinois," *Illinois State Journal,* 18 June 1858, in *CW,* vol. 2, 461–62; Donald, *Lincoln,* 209; Bancroft, *The Life of William H. Seward,* vol. 1, 458–61. See also Harry V. Jaffa, *Crisis of the House Divided: An Interpretation of the Issues in the Lincoln-Douglas Debates* (Chicago: University of Chicago Press, 1959); and Jaffa, *A New Birth of Freedom: Abraham Lincoln and the Coming of the Civil War* (Lanham, Md.: Rowman and Littlefield, 2000), for an exploration of Lincoln's mind-set and other issues.

5. A fine analysis of these administrative difficulties is Paludan, *The Presidency of Abraham Lincoln,* 3–118.

6. Lockwood, "Garrison and Lincoln," 207; Greeley to Gerrit Smith, 14 August 1861, Greeley ms, LC; Greeley to Beman Brockway, ibid.; Van Deusen, *Horace Greeley,* 284; *Chicago Tribune,* 4 December 1861, in Monaghan, *The Man Who Elected Lincoln,* 264.

7. James M. Ashley, "Address of Hon. J. M. Ashley before the 'Ohio Society of New York,' At its Fifth Annual Banquet, Wednesday evening, February 19, 1890," New York *Evening Post,* ca. 1890, 7–8; Blaine, *Twenty Years of Congress,* vol. 1, 341; Magdol, *Owen Lovejoy,* 284.

8. Donald, *Lincoln,* 314–17; Rolle, *John Charles Frémont,* 190–213.

9. Sumner to Lieber, Boston, 17 September 1861, in Series I, Reel 64, SP; Sumner to Wendell Phillips, Boston, 14 September 1861, Series II, Reel 75, ibid.; George, *Zachariah Chandler,* 53–54; Howard, *Religion and the Radical Republican Movement,* 224, n. 24; *CG,* 37, 2, pt. 2 (7 March 1862), 1, 124; Smith, *Colfax,* 160–61; *Chicago Tribune,* 4–14 September 1861, in Logsdon, *Horace White,* 73–74.

10. Lincoln to Browning, Washington, 22 September 1861, in *CW,* vol. 4, 531–33; Donald, *Lincoln,* 317. On Browning, see Baxter, *Orville H. Browning.*

11. *Chicago Tribune,* 14 September 1861, in Logsdon, *Horace White,* 74; Nicolay, *Lincoln's Secretary,* 124; *New York Tribune,* 22 October 1861; Sumner to John Murray Forbes, Boston, 16 September 1862, in Series II, Reel 76, SP;

Carl Schurz to Sumner, Philadelphia, 16 May 1862, in Reel 75, ibid. On Hunter, see William Pitt Fessenden to Samuel Fessenden, Washington, 24 May 1862, Fessenden Family Papers (Fessenden Family ms), Box 10, Special Collections, Bowdoin College; Chase to Greeley, Washington, 21 May 1862, Greeley ms, Box 3, Folder 11, NYPL; *Sacramento Union,* 19 May 1862.

12. Barnes and Weed, *Life of Thurlow Weed,* 399–402; *New York Times,* 1 April 1862; Curry, *Blueprint for Modern America,* 40; *Philadelphia Press,* 30 July 1862, in Christopher Dell, *Lincoln and the War Democrats: The Grand Erosion of Conservative Tradition* (Rutherford, N.J.: Fairleigh Dickinson University Press, 1975), 146; *Hartford Courant,* 11 October 1861, in James Eugene Smith, *One Hundred Years of Hartford's Courant, from Colonial Times through the Civil War* (New Haven: Yale University Press, 1949), 263.

13. William H. Herndon to Trumbull, Springfield, 20 November 1861, Trumbull ms, Reel 12, LC; Lieber to Sumner, New York, 1 April 1862, in Series II, Reel 75, SP; "The Future of the Abolition Cause," *Douglass' Monthly,* April 1861, in David W. Blight, *Frederick Douglass' Civil War: Keeping Faith in Jubilee* (Baton Rouge: Louisiana State University Press, 1989), 69; Stampp, *And the War Came,* 250.

14. Ashley, "Address of Hon. J. M. Ashley before the 'Ohio Society of New York,'" 12–15; Curry, *Blueprint for Modern America,* 42; Dell, *Lincoln and the War Democrats,* 142; *Sacramento Union,* 7 March 1862; Wait Talcott to Trumbull, Rockford, 9 May 1862, Trumbull ms, Reel 13, LC.

15. William Pitt Fessenden to Samuel Fessenden, Washington, n.p., 29 March 1862, Fessenden Family ms, Box 9, Special Collections, Bowdoin College; John A. Andrew to William Pitt Fessenden, Boston, 6 March 1862, Civil War Miscellaneous ms, Box 1, NYHS; *Chicago Tribune,* 19 April 1862, in Logsdon, *Horace White,* 89; Curry, *Blueprint for Modern America,* 43; Washington, Monday, 14 April 1862, in Pease and Randall, eds., *The Diary of Orville Hickman Browning,* vol. 1, 541. The reference to Whiggishness is easily answered: This was a war issue, and as commander in chief, Lincoln involved himself when Congress confronted such matters. But for a president to call in a congressman to encourage changes in a bill, even related to the war, is hardly Whiggish.

16. Fessenden to William H. Fessenden, n.p., 23 May 1862, Fessenden Family ms, Box 10, Special Collections, Bowdoin College; Fessenden to Samuel Fessenden, 29 March 1862, Box 9, ibid.; Fessenden to Elizabeth C. Warriner, 29 June 1862, Box 10, ibid.; Donald, *Charles Sumner and the Rights of Man,* 60–61; Bigelow to Sumner, Paris, 17 June 1862, Reel 26, SP.

17. Sumner to Lieber, Washington, 25 April 1862, in Series I, Reel 64, SP; Donald, *Sumner and the Rights of Man,* 62; Curry, *Blueprint for Modern America,* 99; Smith, *The Francis Preston Blair Family,* vol. 2, 195–96.

18. *South Bend Register,* 12 and 19 December 1861, in Smith, *Colfax,* 166–67; James W. Grimes to Trumbull, Burlington, 24 October 1861, Trumbull ms, Reel 11, LC.

19. Curry, *Blueprint for Modern America,* 91–92; Bogue, *The Earnest Men,* 231; Dell, *Lincoln and the War Democrats,* 144.

20. Curry, *Blueprint for Modern America,* 86; John Forney to Hannibal Hamlin, Washington, 8 May 1862, Hamlin ms, Reel 1, University of Maine, Orono; Washington, Sunday, 13 July 1862, in Pease and Randall, eds., *The Diary of Orville Hickman Browning,* vol. 1, 558; *New York Times,* 24 April 1862. See also Francis Brown, *Raymond of The Times* (New York: W. W. Norton, 1951).

21. Curry, *Blueprint for Modern America,* 43; *CW,* vol. 5, 328–30.

22. Medill to Trumbull, Chicago, misdated 4 July 1862, with letter of that date, Trumbull ms, Reel 13, LC; Curry, *Blueprint for Modern America,* 87, 91–92; Roske, *His Own Counsel,* 81–94; Donald, *Sumner and the Rights of Man,* 63–64; Dell, *Lincoln and the War Democrats,* 144.

23. *Chicago Tribune,* 9 and 17 July 1862, in Logsdon, *Horace White,* 90.

24. *Indianapolis Daily Journal,* 25 August 1862; *New York Tribune,* 2, 14, 17, and 23 October, and 1 November 1861, and 22 February 1862; Greeley to Brockway, 14 August 1861, Greeley ms, LC; Van Deusen, *Horace Greeley,* 284.

25. Lincoln to Greeley, Washington, 22 August 1862; and *New York Tribune,* 20 and 25 August 1862, in *CW,* vol. 5, 388–89.

26. Hofstadter, *The American Political Tradition,* 132; Paludan, *The Presidency of Abraham Lincoln,* 187–88; Foner, *Reconstruction,* 7; Foner, *The Story of American Freedom, passim;* Donald, *Lincoln,* 417–18; Paludan, *"A People's Contest,"* 100. See especially Vorenberg, *Final Freedom.*

27. Howe to Sumner, Boston, 6 April [1862], in Series II, Reel 75, SP; Jacob M. Howard to Trumbull, Detroit, 16 August 1862, Trumbull ms, Reel 13, LC; Rice, ed., *Reminiscences of Abraham Lincoln,* 87–88.

28. "The War and How to End It," *Douglass' Monthly,* April 1862, in Blight, *Frederick Douglass' Civil War,* 108; Oberholtzer, *Jay Cooke,* vol. 1, 197; Magdol, *Owen Lovejoy,* 337; Lincoln to Chase, n.p., [17 May 1862], *CW,* vol. 5, 219; "Proclamation Revoking General Hunter's Order of Military Emancipation of May 9, 1862," 19 May 1862, ibid., 222–23; Donald, *Lincoln,* 362–63.

29. Sumner to Andrew, Washington, 25 May 1862, in Series II, Reel 75, SP; Donald, *Lincoln,* 362–66.

30. Donald, *Lincoln,* 362–66, summarizes the situation.

31. Rice, ed., *Reminiscences of Abraham Lincoln,* 124–25; "Schuyler," "Memoirs," 14–20, Barney ms, Box 36, HL; *Philadelphia Press,* 30 July 1862, in Harper, *Lincoln and the Press,* 175.

32. "Reply to Emancipation Memorial Presented by Chicago Christians of All Denominations," 13 September 1862, in *Chicago Tribune,* 23 September 1862; and *National Intelligencer,* 26 September 1862, in *CW,* vol. 5, 419–25.

33. Ibid.

34. Preliminary Emancipation Proclamation, 22 September 1862, in *CW,* vol. 5, 433–34. On its conservatism, see Donald, *Lincoln,* 375–76; Paludan, *The Presidency of Abraham Lincoln,* 154–57.

35. Preliminary Emancipation Proclamation, 22 September 1862, in *CW,* vol. 5, 433–36; Proclamation Suspending the Writ of Habeas Corpus, 24 September 1862, ibid., 436–37; "Reply to Serenade in Honor of Emancipation Proclamation," *New York Tribune,* 25 September 1862, ibid., 438–39; Lincoln to Hamlin, Washington, 28 September 1862, ibid., 444. On Lincoln's uncertainty, see Donald, *Lincoln,* 376.

36. *New York Tribune,* 23 and 24 September 1862; *The Independent,* 25 September and 2 October 1862, in Van Deusen, *Horace Greeley,* 287; Donald, *Sumner and the Rights of Man,* 81; *Chicago Tribune,* 24 September 1862; Harper, *Lincoln and the Press,* 177; *Peoria Daily Transcript,* 1 and 6 October 1862, in Magdol, *Owen Lovejoy,* 369; Jacob D. Cox to Chase, Antietam, 26 September 1862, Chase ms, Microfilm Edition, Series 1, Reel 23; Israel Washburn to Seward, Philadelphia, 23 September 1862, Seward ms, Reel 72, UR; Blight, *Frederick Douglass' Civil War,* 108.

37. Richard Henry Dana Jr. to Richard Henry Dana Sr., 1 October 1862, Dana ms, Massachusetts Historical Society, in Samuel Shapiro, *Richard Henry Dana, Jr., 1815–1882* (East Lansing: Michigan State University Press, 1961), 126; Chicago, Tuesday, 14 October 1862, in Pease and Randall, eds., *The Diary of Orville Hickman Browning,* vol. 1, 578–79; Wagandt, *The Mighty Revolution,* 79, n. 34; Fessenden to Grimes, Portland, 25 September 1862, Fessenden Family ms, Box 10, Bowdoin College; Edward Everett to Charles Francis Adams, Boston, 30 September 1862, in Frothingham, *Edward Everett,* 448–49; Henry J. Raymond, *The Life and Public Services of Abraham Lincoln* (New York: Derby and Miller, 1865), 260; Thomas J. Barnett, "Abraham Lincoln, the Peoples' Candidate," speech delivered by Judge T. J. Barnett of New York, in Richmond, Indiana, 6 October 1864, n.p., 6, HL.

38. Montgomery Blair to George B. McClellan, Washington, 27 September 1862, McClellan ms, Series 1, Reel 32, LC; Francis P. Blair to McClellan, Silver Spring, 30 September 1862, ibid.

39. White, *The Life of Lyman Trumbull,* 222.

40. John Bigelow to Seward, Paris, 7 October 1862, in Clapp, *Forgotten First Citizen,* 180.

41. James A. Garfield to Crete Garfield, Washington, 27 September 1862, Garfield ms, Series 3, Reel 5, LC; Sumner to Bright, Boston, 28 October

1862, Series II, Reel 76, SP; Sumner to George Livermore, Washington, 25 December 1862, ibid.; Sumner to Howe, Washington, 28 December 1862, Series I, Reel 64 ibid.; Sumner to Harriet Beecher Stowe, Washington, 25 December [1862], ibid.; Washington, Friday, 5 December 1862, and Washington, Wednesday, 31 December 1862, in Pease and Randall, eds., *The Diary of Orville Hickman Browning,* vol. 1, 592, 607; John W. Forney to Hamlin, Washington, 1 October 1862, Hamlin ms, Supplement 2, Reel 1, University of Maine, Orono.

42. *Toledo Commercial,* 6 January 1863, in Horowitz, *The Great Impeacher,* 84; *South Bend Register,* 8 January 1863, in Smith, *Colfax,* 178–79; Lewis Tappan to Sumner, New York, 9 January 1863, Reel 27, SP; Sumner to Unknown, Boston, 15 October 1864, Series II, Reel 78, ibid.; Sumner to Livermore, Senate Chamber, 9 January 1863, Reel 76, ibid.; Forbes to Fox, Boston, 2 January 1863, Fox ms, Box 6, NYHS; Lathrop, *The Life and Times of Samuel J. Kirkwood,* 204; *New York Tribune,* 13 January and 27 July 1863; Blight, *Frederick Douglass' Civil War,* 108, 115.

43. *CG,* 38, 1, 25 June 1864, 3281.

44. *New York Tribune,* 13 January 1863; *Chicago Tribune,* 2 January 1863, in Monaghan, *The Man Who Elected Lincoln,* 285; William K. Strong to Seward, Headquarters, Dept. of Missouri, 7 February 1863, Seward ms, Reel 75, UR; Howard, *Religion and the Radical Republican Movement,* 68. On the foreign impact, see David Paul Crook, *Diplomacy during the American Civil War* (New York: Wiley and Sons, 1975).

45. Lincoln to Chase, Washington, 2 September 1863, in *CW,* vol. 6, 428–29; *Chicago Tribune,* 6 January 1863, in Logsdon, *Horace White,* 93; Washington, Friday, 28 November 1862, in Pease and Randall, eds., *The Diary of Orville Hickman Browning,* vol. 1, 587–88; Jay to Sumner, New York, 5 January 1863, Reel 27, SP; *Sacramento Union,* 16 March 1864.

46. *New York Tribune,* 1 May 1863; Sumner to Lincoln, Boston, 7 August 1863, in Series II, Reel 77, SP.

47. Washburn to Sumner, Portland, 24 March 1864, Reel 30, SP; Jay to Sumner, New York, 8 March 1864, ibid.; 15 November 1864, Reel 31, ibid.; Lieber to Sumner, New York, 11 December 1864, Series II, Reel 78, ibid.

48. Buckingham, *The Life of William A. Buckingham,* 361; *Ohio State Journal,* 22 March 1864; Preston King to John Sherman, Ogdensburgh, 12 April 1864, Sherman ms, Volume 68, LC; *Forney's War Press,* 20 February 1864; *National Anti-Slavery Standard,* 26 March and 9 April 1864; Samuel E. Sewall to Sumner, Boston, 6 March 1864, Reel 30, SP.

49. Donald, *Sumner and the Rights of Man,* 148–50; *Ohio State Journal,* 22 March 1864; *CG,* 38, 1, 5 April 1864, 1417. Rep. Isaac Arnold wrote, "Be it enacted by the Senate and House of Representatives of the United States in

Congress assembled, That from and after the passage of this act Slavery and Involuntary servitude, otherwise than in the punishment of crime whereof the party shall have been duly convicted, shall be and the same hereby is abolished, and forever prohibited in every state and territory of the United States and every part thereof."

50. *National Anti-Slavery Standard,* 16 April 1864; *Sacramento Union,* 11 May 1864 [Castine, 11 April 1864, Washington]; *Forney's War Press,* 30 April 1864; *Boston Daily Evening Transcript,* 6 April 1864; *CG,* 38, 1, 8 April 1864, 1490.

51. Horowitz, *The Great Impeacher,* 97–98; *CG,* 38, 1, 15 June 1864, 2995; *CG,* 38, 1, 28 June 1864, 3357; *CG,* 38, 1, 29 June 1864, 3399.

52. Paludan, *The Presidency of Abraham Lincoln,* 299–302; Donald, *Lincoln,* 503–4; *Boston Daily Evening Transcript,* 17 and 18 June 1864; James G. Randall and Richard N. Current, *Lincoln the President: The Last Full Measure* (New York: Dodd, Mead, 1956), 307; *Indianapolis Daily Journal,* 5 September 1864; Jay to Sumner, New York, 15 November 1864, in Reel 31, SP; *Sacramento Union,* 10 December 1864.

53. Horowitz, *The Great Impeacher,* 103; *Washington Daily Chronicle,* 11 January 1865, in Randall and Current, *Lincoln the President: The Last Full Measure,* 306; *CG,* 38, 2, 11 January 1865, 225; *CG,* 38, 2, 23 January 1865, 358.

54. Randall and Current, *Lincoln the President: The Last Full Measure,* 309–10; Rice, ed., *Reminiscences of Abraham Lincoln,* 585–86.

55. Berwanger, "Lincoln's Constitutional Dilemma," 34; Randall and Current, *Lincoln the President: The Last Full Measure,* 310; Nicolay, *Lincoln's Secretary,* 220–21.

56. Horowitz, *The Great Impeacher,* 104–5. See also Vorenberg, *Final Freedom;* and Cox and Cox, *Power, Principle, and Prejudice, passim.* Donald, *Lincoln,* 554, mentions Rollins but adds, "If Lincoln used other means of persuading congressmen to vote for the Thirteenth Amendment, his actions were not recorded. Conclusions about the President's role rested on gossip and later recollections." Recollections are part of the historian's craft. While the agents reported to Seward, his relations with Lincoln suggest that he was aware of what was going on or, if he knew nothing, he understood how Seward operated.

57. *CG,* 38, 2, for January 1865; Dell, *Lincoln and the War Democrats,* 317–19, and 323, n. 9; *Chicago Tribune,* 16 and 17 February, 16 and 18 June 1864; Horowitz, *The Great Impeacher,* 104–5; Blaine, *Twenty Years of Congress,* vol. 1, 538–39; *Forney's War Press,* 4 February 1865. See also Samuel S. Cox to Manton Marble, Washington, 7 and 21 December 1864, and 13, 17, 18, and 26 January, and 1 February 1865, Marble ms, Volume 10, LC; Dean Richmond to Marble, Albany, 23 January 1865, ibid.; Samuel S. Cox, *Union—Disunion—Reunion: Three Decades of Federal Legislation* (Providence: J. A. and

R. A. Reid, 1885), 327–29; David Lindsey, *"Sunset" Cox: Irrepressible Democrat* (Detroit: Wayne State University Press, 1959), 93–95.

58. *CG,* 38, 2, 31 January 1865, 531; Randall and Current, *Lincoln the President: The Last Full Measure,* 313; *The Liberator,* 10 February 1865, in Randall and Current, *Lincoln the President: The Last Full Measure*, 314; *New York Evening Post,* 1 February 1865; Medill to Sherman, Chicago, 1 February 1865, Sherman ms, Volume 79, LC.

59. Nicolay to Therena Bates, Washington, 4 February 1865, typescript, Nicolay ms, Box 7, "Jan.–June 1865," LC; Cox and Cox, *Politics, Principle, and Prejudice,* 24; Donald, *Lincoln,* 558; Cox to Marble, Washington, 2 February 1865 [misdated by Cox as 1863], Marble ms, Volume 10, LC.

60. On Ashley and Trumbull, see *National Anti-Slavery Standard,* 11 February 1865; *New York Tribune,* 1 February 1865; Blaine, *Twenty Years of Congress,* vol. 1, 536; Henry Dawes, "Manuscript on the History of the Thirteenth Amendment," Dawes ms, LC; Horowitz, *The Great Impeacher,* 106, 102; Roske, *His Own Counsel,* 109. See Norman B. Judd to Trumbull, Berlin, 5 March 1865, Trumbull ms, Reel 16, LC; *New York Evening Post,* 3 February 1865; *Ohio State Journal,* 6 and 8 February 1865; Lieber to Sumner, New York, 13 December 1864, Series II, Reel 78, SP; *New York Tribune,* 3 February 1865, in *CW,* vol. 8, 254–55; Randall and Current, *Lincoln the President: The Last Full Measure,* 314.

61. Eric Foner, *Nothing But Freedom: Emancipation and Its Legacy* (Baton Rouge: Louisiana State University Press, 1983); Nancy Cohen, *The Reconstruction of American Liberalism, 1865–1914* (Chapel Hill: University of North Carolina Press, 2002).

6

Law and Order: Republicans, the Supreme Court, and the Constitution

ON 9 December 1861, as Congress began the first regular session of the war, Senator John P. Hale introduced a resolution. He was the new chair of the Naval Affairs Committee, but the New Hampshire radical found it hard to adapt to the change from being an opposition voice to becoming a power in the majority. His proposal reflected his problem with adapting to the evolving ideology of freedom, union, and power. He asked the Judiciary Committee to examine "the expediency and propriety of abolishing the present Supreme Court . . . and establishing instead thereof another Supreme Court." Lyman Trumbull of Illinois, the committee's chair, buried the measure. He felt, as most Republicans did, that the trouble lay not with the institution but with its membership, which they expected to change through their new power of appointment. Many Republicans saw that opportunity as crucial, fearing that if the Court had its way, what they did to fight the war or slavery might be held unconstitutional. Nor did a party that had just taken responsibility for preserving the Union wish to suggest or effect that radical a change in the body politic.[1]

This conclusion pained Republicans, and not just because theirs was a reform-minded party. Their members included old Democrats who shared the Court majority's Jacksonian support for democracy and a limited federal government, and Whigs raised to worship the constitutional nationalism of John Marshall and denigrate Andrew Jackson's disobedience of his decisions. But Charles Evans Hughes, a controversial chief justice of the twentieth century, called the *Dred Scott* decision of 1857 a "self-inflicted wound" that not only was bad law but damaged the Court's reputation. With that ruling, an institution Republicans revered turned satanic. As so often happened, Abraham

Lincoln served as a barometer of the middle ground of his party's thought. In 1839 he had called the Court "that tribunal which the Constitution has itself established to decide Constitutional questions." Two decades later, he argued that this view of the Court would lead "to the despotism of an oligarchy." In 1861, echoing Jackson, whom he criticized for such thinking, he said that "if the policy of the government, upon vital questions, affecting the whole people, is to be irrevocably fixed by decisions of the Supreme Court . . . the people will have ceased, to be their own rulers, having, to that extent, practically resigned their government, into the hands of that eminent tribunal."[2]

Lincoln shared his party's reverence for the Constitution, but reverence went only so far when the Constitution might be wrong and need amending. To Republicans this process was an orderly form of governmental change, and order was a key concept. What Robert Wiebe described in his study of the Gilded Age and Progressivism as "the search for order" was part of the Northern ethos during the Civil War. The terms and practices of the war were simpler than those of future decades, but that meant the war created an order in need of further refinement. While prewar Republican ideology—indeed, the dominant Northern view—recognized the right of slavery to exist, the rebellion changed that. The party saw secession as not just a revolution but an act of anarchy prompted by slavery and the South's devotion to it. In this way slavery, rebellion, and anarchy became inseparable in the Republican worldview. Separately and together, they threatened the nation's present and future. Republicans hoped to maintain and extend freedom, preserve the Union, and retain their power while building up that of the government. They believed in the idea of and need for law and order, exemplified by fealty to the Constitution—as they interpreted it. To rebel against the government was to rebel against the Constitution, but to move too fast on the issue of slavery invited disorder and lawlessness. As one editor said, Republicans simply wanted "the authority of the government . . . acknowledged in every State in the Union, and the laws obeyed in every one of the States." They saw that they were in the position to demand and extend that authority.[3]

These views were more complex than they may appear. Before the war the issues had been simpler—and during the war, for some party members, they remained so. Charles Sumner phrased it pithily when he charged that Democratic Senator Reverdy Johnson of Maryland was always "willing to interpret the constitution for slavery. I interpret for freedom." At least on the surface, most Republicans agreed, but different interpretations posed another problem. Party members divided on how and whether the Constitution could be changed with eleven states in rebellion, and on what steps the federal government could take under the Constitution. These were ideological questions, rooted in legitimate arguments over the speed of and responsibility for protecting and expanding freedom, preserving the Union, and using power in their behalf. Those differences concerned the how, when, and whether of such actions, not the actions themselves. Finally, the decisions and members of the Supreme Court lay at the heart of the issue. Republicans were caught between their commitment to the institution and their hatred for some of its members. As with the battles within the Cabinet, so too with their views of the Supreme Court and, to an extent, with issues of law and order themselves: personalities often made the differences seem greater than they were.[4]

The same could be said of the events themselves: they enhanced the appearance of differences. Republicans condoned or advocated suspension of the writ of habeas corpus, defiance of the Supreme Court, suppression of the press, all antithetical to their professed beliefs. There are two keys to understanding these events. One is that their views changed when they took power—but not overnight; they understood that the Union's survival, and theirs as a party, depended on their adaptability. The other is inseparable from the first. This adaptation was rooted in a free labor ideology that retained its resonance even as Republicans faced new issues. Consciously and unconsciously, they met the demand by balancing freedom with the needs of the Union and the requirements of power. Amid the rich historiography on wartime constitutional issues, ideology has been the missing component. In his Pulitzer Prize–winning study of wartime civil liberties, Mark Neely wrote that after Lincoln suspended the writ, his "steadily growing confidence or decisiveness was as much a function of his indifference to constitutional scruple as anything else—except his sure sense of the purpose of the government to win the war and keep the country whole so that democracy could not be said to have failed." The word *indifference* suggests a cavalierness that the writings of Lincoln and other Republicans do not bear out. They thought deeply about what they were doing, and that "sure sense" that Neely correctly refers to was rooted in the party's ideology.[5]

Interpreting the Constitution

Before and during the war, thinking deeply about the words and meaning of the Constitution, Republicans saw it as a sacred document sullied by flawed interpretations and uses. As anti-slavery reformer Robert Dale Owen said, "To the American citizen the Constitution stands in the place occupied, under the monarchical system, by the sovereign in person. It is the highest object of his loyalty." Republicans spoke similarly about the populace and themselves. When Senator William Pitt Fessenden of Maine said, "Men cannot be compelled to yield their views of the Constitution," he spoke for himself and more conservative Republicans loath to expand the Constitution's meaning. From the party's center and right came the argument that the government must protect constitutional rights, even those of the rebels. If the Union and the Constitution were as inseparable as Republicans claimed, that seemed contradictory, but New York's Abraham Olin told the House that "the only theory that can justify the prosecution of this war . . . is that it is a war waged in obedience to the Constitution and the laws."[6]

Conservatives retained such notions. Just as Republicans considered themselves heirs of the Hamiltonians and Jeffersonians, their arguments over the Constitution resolved themselves into a similar debate: should it be strictly or loosely interpreted? For each Republican opposed to change, another was ready to argue that the question was moot; the framers had written the Constitution to be flexibly constructed. "Words receive expansion . . . with time," Sumner said. Ben Wade, the waspish radical senator from Ohio, had no use for those to whom the Constitution was "a stumbling-block," nor did his equally bellicose friend and colleague, Zachariah Chandler of Michigan, cotton to those with "constitution on the brain." Some went further: Representative James Ashley of Ohio dismissed a conservative's concerns by saying, "Sir, we make precedents here," and several radicals declared morality to be above obedience to an immoral law. They reasoned that the framers would never have made provisions to amend the Constitution if they had expected it to be static, nor had they intended their words to keep the government from saving itself and the Constitution from attack.[7]

The same was true of civil liberties, forcing Republicans to reconcile any conflicts in their views of freedom, union, and power by reading the Constitution loosely. To save freedom and union from "the enemy in the rear," Lincoln used freedoms that the party hoped to protect.

The *Chicago Tribune* noted "that a Republican form of government is strong enough to maintain its existence, and need not be so strong as to encroach on the liberties of the people." While Seward cited Hamilton as the basis for a broad view of the Constitution, Lincoln hearkened to John Marshall in *McCulloch v. Maryland* ("We must never forget that it is a *constitution* we are expounding . . . intended to endure for ages to come, and consequently, to be adapted to the various *crises* of human affairs"), acting within its limits—where possible.[8]

But the "Rebellion is beyond the Constitution," which "was not made for such a state of things," Republican legal theorist Francis Lieber said. In those revolutionary times, Congress might have dominated: Lincoln was a minority president who ran behind state tickets electorally. Yet he persevered, triumphing over his party, in a sense, by leading it without becoming a dictator. No dictator would have tolerated an election in 1864, much less planned to accept the result when he seemed likely to lose. Thus, Lincoln and his supporters stretched the Constitution in new directions but retained its basic structure. And that was the work not only of Lincoln, but of his party and the times.[9]

This evolution reflected the changing Republican ideology. In Lincoln's mind the Constitution empowered him to take extraordinary steps to save it, and he did. He sought to act within its strictures. When freedom and union collided, and suppressing free speech or suspending habeas corpus seemed necessary to win a war for the Union and the freedom it would protect and spread, one or the other had to suffer. While the choice was hard, Lincoln and his party believed that freedom required a strong Union. This produced a Constitution different in interpretation and appearance, with the eventual passage of three amendments in five years. Republicans hoped that they would assure that what they did in the war for freedom and union would endure. However, just as those amendments provoked debate for ages to come, Republicans debated the events and issues that led them through the war, and the institutions responsible for equal justice under the law.

Body of Law, Body of Power

The first issue to force the party to face these questions was habeas corpus. The Constitution authorized Congress to suspend the writ and the president to act as needed to protect the people, but it was silent on what happened if Congress was not in session. Lincoln responded by construing it broadly. In April 1861 he ordered General Winfield Scott to quell any uprising in Maryland, including, if necessary, suspending the writ. By October Scott had approval to suspend it along the military line, which Lincoln defined as reaching north to Maine, giving the federal government and himself unprecedented authority. Yet when Seward moved to censor the mail and telegraph, and to arrest those suspected of disloyalty, Lincoln was cautious: "Unless the *necessity* for these arbitrary arrests is *manifest,* and *urgent,* I prefer they should cease." But Lincoln had to think of what was best for the federal government's power and preservation: to lose Maryland and Virginia to secession would isolate Washington. The risk to the Union might outweigh the risk to the Constitution.[10]

More concerned with constitutional power, Chief Justice Roger B. Taney embarked on what Harold Hyman called his "*Merryman* misadventure." In May 1861, military authorities jailed Maryland planter John Merryman for burning bridges and recruiting soldiers for the rebels. Taney issued a writ of habeas corpus. General George Cadwalader refused to bring the prisoner to court, citing Lincoln's order suspending the writ. Taney then ordered Merryman's appearance and claimed that he expected to be imprisoned for doing so. When the marshal reported being denied access to Merryman, Taney ruled for Merryman and accused Lincoln of usurping legislative authority. The Constitution, said Taney, made it clear that only Congress could suspend the writ. If the army "usurped" judicial authority, he warned, "every citizen holds life, liberty and property at the will and pleasure of the army officer in whose military district he may happen to be found."[11]

Understandably, responses to this ruling proved consistent with other reactions to questions of constitutional power. Believers in a restrictive interpretation lauded Taney. These were few among Republicans, who added to the abuse they had heaped upon him for the *Dred Scott* ruling. The *New York Times* expected him to "soil the ermine of justice . . . and go through history as the Judge who draggled his official robes in the pollutions of treason." More radical than the *Times,* the *New York Tribune* and *Chicago Tribune* suggested that he was senile.[12]

However, some Republicans shared his disapproval of Lincoln's action. Radicals were caught between hatred for Taney, their feeling that Lincoln lacked their anti-slavery ardor, and their belief in legislative supremacy. They focused their wrath mainly on Seward, whom Lincoln put in charge of such arrests. Trumbull tried unavailingly to limit Lincoln's authority to make arbitrary arrests. Henry Winter Davis wedded radicalism and Whiggery: "If a discretionary power over the liberty of the citizen . . . is to be tolerated," it was a short step "from the constitutional freedom of America to the . . . despotism of France." Thaddeus Stevens also argued that Lincoln could quash the writ only with Congress in session, and "Congress is the sovereign power of this nation, not the President." Senator Timothy Howe of Wisconsin expressed his fear that suspending the writ might encourage the military to overstep its bounds, while his colleague Orville Browning called "the substitution of military for civil authority . . . virtually an overthrow of the Government."[13]

As if to prove that concerns about the writ knew no ideological bounds, other Republicans defended Lincoln's power to suspend it. Their main concern seems to have been that once Lincoln acted, the party had to stand by him—a political response, rooted in its awareness of and commitment to the perpetuation of power, for itself and the government. They argued that the Constitution allowed for necessity, and the same rule must apply to interpreting it. During a rebellion, Ohio radical John Bingham told the House, "it is no time to be splitting hairs and carping about the question of whether Congress or the President shall first exercise the power." Senator James Doolittle, a Wisconsin conservative, reminded colleagues that some charged Lincoln with going too far, but others assailed his leniency. Henry Wilson of Massachusetts echoed other radicals when he said, "Never since the dawn of creation has any Government menaced by insurrection or rebellion been . . . so forbearing." Nor did Senator Henry Lane of Indiana object to Lincoln's suspension of the writ, for "within the sphere of his powers he is alike independent of Congress and the judiciary, the sole judge of his own powers, accountable only to God and the people."[14]

Lincoln's views were more crucial and potentially more dangerous. He approved the arrests of more rebel sympathizers, ignoring Taney. When Congress met in special session on 4 July 1861, he took pains to explain himself. As he had blamed the South for aggression in his inaugural address, now he blamed Taney: "are all the laws, *but one,* to go unexecuted, and the government itself go to pieces, lest that one be violated?" The answer was clear to him: under the Constitution, the writ could be suspended if a rebellion or invasion endangered the public. That danger obviously existed. Casting a withering editorial glance at Taney, Lincoln said, "Now it is insisted that Congress, and not the Executive, is vested with this power," but "the Constitution itself, is silent as to which, or who, is to exercise the power." He claimed the right to decide, and maintained that the framers had intended it that way for the sake of protecting the Constitution and the republic.[15]

After Merryman, the next controversy over the writ involved the arrest of Clement Vallandigham. Angry at his criticism of the government during his Ohio gubernatorial race, General Ambrose Burnside arrested him in May 1863. Regretting that he had no choice but to back Burnside, Lincoln ordered the copperhead sent to the South; Vallandigham later returned to Ohio and resumed his attacks, but grew more muted. But protests by New York and Ohio Democrats prompted Lincoln to muse about the power to suspend the writ. He told the New Yorkers that secessionists and their sympathizers used the Constitution to their advantage, and he had to act "without ruinous waste of time." Given the expediency and debatable existence of that power, he wrote that the Ohioans asked:

> whether I really claim that I may override all the guarrantied [*sic*] rights of individuals, on the plea of conserving the public safety—when I may choose to say the public safety requires it. This question, divested of the phraseology calculated to represent me as struggling for an arbitrary personal prerogative, is either simply a question *who* shall decide, or an affirmation that *nobody* shall decide, what the public safety does require, in cases of Rebellion or invasion. . . . I think the man whom, for the time, the people have, under the constitution, made the commander-in-chief, of their Army and Navy, is the man who holds the power, and bears the responsibility of making it. If he uses the power justly, the same people will probably justify him; if he abuses it, he is in their hands, to be dealt with by all the modes they have reserved to themselves in the constitution.[16]

Lincoln's comments merit scrutiny for how they reflected and explained the party's ideology. At issue for him was the need to protect freedom and union through the use of power. In the case of the writ, the Republican commitment to freedom and union created a paradox: to abuse individual rights contradicted their belief in freedom, but if the Union collapsed, none of the rights that the Constitution guaranteed would exist. Lincoln argued that he had the power to protect freedom and union, and his words showed his understanding of the need to adapt to circumstance. Whatever he did to the benefit or detriment of those rights reflected his view of the need for Republicans to wield their power wisely. Since Republicans believed that using power wisely would help justify their continuation in office, Lincoln reminded his readers that they still had recourse to the polls, suggesting that he acted only from necessity and not out of dictatorial ambitions.[17]

In the end, Republicans found a happy medium between Lincoln's broader view of power and the more restrictive preferences of his opponents: the Habeas Corpus Act of 1863. Lincoln's power passed into several hands. The law upheld the authority of civilian courts over the military, except in seceded areas where a judicial system no longer existed. The measure assured Lincoln of the power to suspend the writ as he deemed necessary, although the wording could be construed to mean that he had the power anyway, or else Congress magnanimously decided to admit to a reality he had created. Nor, since the arrests continued, did the act prove effective at assuring the protection of individual rights above all else. Its importance lay in its specificity. Republicans turned a broader opinion of executive power into law, and Lincoln could act within it, and possibly outside it.[18]

Clearly, Lincoln and Taney viewed the Constitution and federal power differently. "Had Mr. Lincoln scrupulously observed the Taney policy, I do not know whether we would have had any liberty," Supreme Court Justice Robert Jackson later wrote, "and had the Chief Justice adopted Mr. Lincoln's philosophy as the philosophy of law, I again do not know whether we would have had any liberty." This expressed the certainty of Lincoln and Taney, and the uncertainty of the times. Sticking to precedent, Taney represented a strict construction that dictated against new federal power. In confronting a situation without precedent, Lincoln read the law more broadly. His critics fell somewhere in between, favoring a more flaccid reading but fearing what might be anachronistically called a domino theory of federal power: once centralized under Lincoln, it would be impossible to restore the separation of powers to what it had been. On pure, immobile legal grounds, Taney might justify himself, but necessity put Lincoln in the right. And he found his justification in what his party believed: preserving freedom and union required a liberal yet judicious—meaning flexible but perhaps not most enlightened—exercise of power.[19]

The Constitution and Its Powers

Republicans debated the degree to which that power was used and the person or institution using it, not the need for it. A variety of issues gave them the chance to try to settle this debate, with limited success. As with the Cabinet, the role of personalities, politics, and speed of action showed anew that the party shared general principles. Radicals and conservatives wanted victory for the Union, the party, and themselves in the war over the party's direction. They sought similar ends, but radicals might be described as believing that the ends justified the means; conservatives attached more significance to the means. Moderates moved between both groups, which kept trying to win over Lincoln. This led to a continuous dialogue, but what they said and did about the Constitution was revealing because it was so open to interpretation. With their penchant for animated discussion and personal squabbling, Republicans made the Constitution a key issue in the war for—and within—their party.

The party's evolving views of the Constitution reflected how Lincoln and his administration dealt with legal issues such as the freedoms of the First Amendment. They tried to balance freedom and union, a job made more difficult by the question of who in the government and the party had the right to determine the balance. A notable case, late in 1861, involved General George McClellan's effort to suppress the usually friendly *New York Times,* which he accused of treason for printing a map of his army's works. Editor Henry Raymond countered that the map had appeared in print elsewhere, and some of the information in the story came from McClellan. Nor was McClellan the only critic of an allegedly hostile press: his friend Burnside suppressed the copperhead *Chicago Times,* and a general arrested a critical editor in California and had soldiers destroy his office. While the generals acted on their own, their civilian leader seemed to encourage them. Stanton censored the wires in and out of Washington and threatened to close irksome papers. While admitting the press could be "useful" and "powerful," he called it "subordinate to the national safety," a comment that recurred in future wars. Clearly, Republican views of freedom of the press reflected not radicalism or conservatism, but the issues of how much freedom to surrender for the Union's sake and how draconian the government should be when demanding the surrender of that freedom.[20]

Stanton's admonition, and the discussion these and other cases caused, showed the difficulties in reconciling freedom and union. To those fearful about suspending habeas corpus, the two terms seemed destined to become mutually exclusive. Davis feared creating a precedent: "If men may not advocate what *this* administration dislikes, the *next* will follow the same precedent; & papers may be suppressed for advocating war & opposing peace. To . . . prevent anybody from *thinking & printing anything* is by our constitution *forbidden.*" When Burnside shut down the *Chicago Times,* the party split. Greeley and Browning cheered Lincoln's revocation of the order, but the *Tribune,* the *Times*'s competitor, said, "As the matter stands it is a triumph of treason. Better a thousandfold, in such times as these an occasional exercise of arbitrary power, if directed to the preservation of the Constitution and the enforcement of laws, than a timid, vacillating policy."[21]

If the Union was in danger, so was freedom; if freedom must suffer temporarily for both to endure permanently, most Republicans thought the price worth paying—especially if political power also was at issue. General William T. Sherman seemed to skirmish with reporters almost as much as with the rebels; his brother John, the senator from Ohio, counseled moderation, considering the battle unwise. Since the general claimed to be apolitical and antipolitical, and his brother had navigated the thickets of Ohio politics for half a century, the political implications behind John Sherman's wise advice should be apparent.[22]

Republicans felt similarly, if more dogmatically, about loyalty oaths, which seemed useful during a rebellion but struck at freedom of speech. Debating the oaths in 1863 and 1864, most paid no attention to whether a citizen should be forced to declare allegiance to the Union. Senator Henry Anthony, a Rhode Island moderate, knew of "no form of expression in the language, except the Lord's prayer, that an American citizen can oftener take with advantage to his soul's health than an oath to support the Constitution." Others argued that those refusing to take an oath had no right to take part in the government.

Said Seward, "No one of us ought to object" to the policy of requiring oaths of all Americans seeking passports, "when called upon to reaffirm his devotion to the Union, however unconditionally."

The party seemed unconcerned about whether taking an oath actually proved loyalty, or that the government might fail to distinguish between legitimate criticism and disloyalty. "Whatever of severity, or even of irregularity, may have arisen, will find its justification in the terrible necessity under which the Administration has been called to act," wrote War Democrat Joseph Holt, who had served briefly in Buchanan's Cabinet, was a candidate for Lincoln's, and now worked in the War Department. Necessity indeed demanded action, according to Republicans and their supporters, who accepted that saving the Union and exercising power at times outweighed—or, more accurately, were part of—their obligation to freedom.[23]

With the oath now federal policy, Hyman said, "Congress had had enough of state sovereignty." Battling a rebellion related to states' rights, the party saw federal supremacy as crucial and secession as creating a chance to establish it, through military victory and changes in the law. "There is, and can be, only one paramount sovereign authority," said Governor Austin Blair of Michigan: the federal government. Lieber doubted that "any one, *in America,* still held to that absurdity of individual sovereignty," but that "absurdity" remained potent with Democrats, rebel sympathizers, and Republicans skittish about too much federal power. And radicals sweated details and precedents less than did other Republicans. Thus, when Sumner tried to ban racial bias in calling witnesses at trials, moderate Lafayette Foster of Connecticut replied that states must keep some power. Sumner asked, "Can the Senator forget the character of these local laws: how instinct with barbarism they are; . . . and will he now recognize such a scandal and shame and give them new effect?" Part of their debate was how much change the political and governmental system could absorb.[24]

The Varying Limits of Power

This chest-pounding prompted a question: How much power could the federal government wield for the Union's sake? To Cassius Clay of Kentucky, the Constitution's war powers justified striking at slavery, but he said, "Without law, there is no liberty," which showed that abolitionists who presumably valued results above all sought to maintain a semblance of constitutional order. Republicans used and abused the law—for a purpose. "Much has been said about usurpations of power; but where in history will you find a war against rebellion conducted with such moderation?" a War Democrat asked. The answer was debatable to the engineers who struck the Reading Railroad, which Lincoln seized under emergency war powers; to jailed civilians; and to radicals like Indiana's George Julian, who called him a "virtual dictator." Thomas Jenckes of Rhode Island, his House colleague, disagreed, calling it "a misuse of language." While scholars debate whether he was dictatorial, logic was with Lincoln. Governor Oliver Morton of Indiana found it "absurd" to argue that in fighting the war, "constitutional rights and personal liberty would be endangered, when we know perfectly well that if the rebellion succeeds, civil and religious liberty and constitutional rights . . . will be overwhelmed."[25]

West Virginia gave Republicans an issue for those who prized a changed Union with a more Hamiltonian Constitution, as opposed to those fighting for the Union as it was. Culturally and economically, unionist western Virginia differed from the secessionist east. The result was the birth in May 1862 of a new "state" of Virginia, approved by a state legislature far smaller than that of the old Virginia and composed of western Virginians. For Republicans this created a conundrum: the federal government could carve a new state out of an old one only with the approval of the state that was being split. Amid criticism from Democrats and conservative Republicans, moderates and radicals mulled whether the new state threatened the old order. Representative Schuyler Colfax of Indiana confessed to uneasiness but went ahead. Conservative John Noell of Missouri warned that "we cannot afford, while the nation is trembling upon the brink of destruction, to split hairs on technical constitutional points." From the radical wing, Stevens defined the broader issue: "This talk of restoring the Union as it was under the Constitution as it is, is one of the absurdities which I have heard repeated until I have become about sick of it. This Union can never be restored as it was." Both houses agreed and approved the new state.[26]

What Lincoln would do was uncertain. He asked his Cabinet for opinions on whether statehood was constitutional and expedient. The answers revealed the issues to be more complex than were lines of demarcation between radical and conservative. Yes, said the supposedly conservative Seward, reducing the matter to its barest equation: loyalty took precedence over secession. Secretary of the Treasury Salmon Chase argued that rebels could hardly be the authors of a legitimate government; under the circumstances, admitting a new state set no precedent. Stanton found no violation of the Constitution. Secretary of the Navy Gideon Welles, Postmaster General Montgomery Blair, and Attorney General Edward Bates, all conservatives, disagreed. Blair still deemed the secessionists few in number but momentarily in power; creating another Virginia would dash Southern unionist hopes. Bates saw the Constitution as empowering the people to create a new state, not Congress. A good Jacksonian, Welles doubted that a minority of Virginia voters could speak for the state.[27]

These factors troubled Lincoln, but his ultimate test was not the views of a few Virginians or constitutional theorists; rather, it was his own notion of what was best for the Union, the extension of freedom, and his party's power. His opinion began with the legal issue. He reasoned that those "*who choose to vote* . . . constitute the political power of the state," not simply all of those registered. That a majority of Virginians failed to vote had nothing to do with the decision's legality. More critically, was it constitutional? "Can this government stand, if it indulges constitutional constructions by which men in open rebellion against it, are to be accounted, man for man, the equals of those who maintain their loyalty to it? Are they to be accounted even better citizens, and more worthy of consideration, than those who merely neglect to vote?" he asked. "If so, their reason against the constitution, enhances their constitutional value!" That made no sense to Lincoln, who turned to his next question: If it was constitutional, was it expedient? While this matter was "dreaded as a precedent . . . a measure made expedient by a war, is no precedent for times of peace." It was expedient, he decided, and it was done.[28]

This decision was a turning point for Republicans, although that seems clearer in hindsight than it did at the time. Lincoln took a position more radical than conservative, and constitutionally more expansive than restrictive. Both meant a victory for one wing of his party and a defeat for the other—a minor matter, since each side regularly gained and lost. More important was the reasoning. Lincoln and other Republicans acted according to their wartime beliefs. To allow the anti-slavery—or, at least, less pro-slavery—part of Virginia to form a state was a step toward freedom. To welcome back Virginia's Southern unionists benefited the Union; that was beyond doubt. To permit the process exemplified the Republican view of power. The step was needed for the country and the party to do their duty for freedom and union.

Lincoln's Court: Creating a Republican Institution

Even in extending the Constitution's limits, Republicans still retained respect for such traditional institutions as the Supreme Court. They criticized it and denied its authority, but they wanted to control it, not destroy it. That was ironic, given how ardently they had campaigned against it in 1860; they seemed to attack Taney for *Dred Scott* almost as much as they flayed Democrats. But they adapted, as they often did, according to the precepts of their ideology. What mattered to Republicans was that the Court would uphold legislation or policies they enacted in preserving and perpetuating freedom, saving the Union, and using their powers to do both. Rather than eliminating the Court or creating a new one, which might have encouraged their opponents to assail their radicalism all over again and led to political and constitutional disorder, Republicans simply displayed increased confidence in running the government—and, while they were at it, their convergence on the issues. When it came to choosing Supreme Court Justices, Republicans assumed ideological agreement; they thought in political terms that would aid the party and, by extension, its ideology.

Understanding that their choices would lead to a judiciary that backed their policies, Republicans awaited the chance to appoint new Justices. The *Chicago Tribune* said, "Until a national convention amends the Constitution so as to defeat the usurpations of that body or until the court itself is reconstructed by the dropping off of a few of its members and the appointment of better men in their places we have little to hope for by Congressional action in the way of restricting slavery." Others were less restrained. When Taney was ill early in 1861, Wade "used to pray daily and earnestly that his life might be preserved until the inauguration of President Lincoln, who would appoint a Republican Chief Justice, but when I saw how complete his recovery was and how his life was prolonged, *I began to fear that I had overdone this business.*" Hale said, "I never heard of a judge of the Supreme Court dying, or very rarely, indeed [laughter], and none of them ever resign." But one vacancy enabled Lincoln to make a major change at once: he would pick the successor for Peter Daniel, an ardently racist and states-rights Virginian who died. Then came the resignation of Alabamian John Campbell, who opposed secession but felt that he must secede with his state, giving Lincoln a second appointment that could swing the Court. A third opening, an even trade for the party, followed the death of Senior Associate Justice John McLean, a Jacksonian turned Republican who dissented from the *Dred Scott* ruling.[29]

Whomever Lincoln chose to succeed them would join a Court from another time and perspective. The Associate Justices were Democrats loyal to the Union, but not to the Republican view of it. Two Southerners—James Wayne of Georgia, named in 1835; and Tennessee's John Catron, in 1837—refused to secede. New York's Samuel Nelson had been selected in 1845, Pennsylvanian Robert Grier in 1846, and Maine's Nathan Clifford in 1858. Ambivalent about slavery but pro-Union, they questioned how Republicans could save it, although Nelson and Wayne tried to help as emissaries for the rebels. Grier, a friend of Stanton, urged him to accept his Cabinet post. When Nelson's name surfaced for the Democratic ticket in 1864, Republicans feared that he would be a formidable foe for Lincoln. For one thing, he was from a key state. For another, despite the damage done by *Dred Scott* and their criticism, Republicans still revered the Court as an institution. Worse, Nelson had straddled the issue, arguing that Scott remained a slave but that was the limit of the Court's jurisdiction.[30]

Republican ambivalence about the Court manifested itself in a one-man crusade to restructure it. John Jay had a personal interest in the Court as the grandson of the first Chief Justice. Used to apocalyptic prophecies as an abolitionist, he warned Republicans that the Court might strike down their measures to save the Union and protect freedom. Reminding the party of the Court's disloyalty in *Dred Scott,* Jay fretted that the justices might limit Republican power. The problem was "the profound respect and all but implicit obedience that our people are accustomed to render" to the courts. He sought to reorganize the Court on the basis of population or enlarge it, assuring the North of a majority of its members.[31]

The responses to Jay reflected the party's growing understanding of power. Seward expected Justices to remain loyal and lose influence, both reflecting his belief that Republican values would triumph. Trumbull felt similarly but feared that new Justices might "regard the great end and aim of the constitution to have been the protection of slavery," and throw out the Confiscation Acts. Conservative Boston lawyer Richard Henry Dana urged guarding against that by appointing only Northerners, as Lincoln was likely to do anyway. Virginia abolitionist John Underwood advised Sumner to back bills to pension off senior Justices and to pack the Court with three appointees. To Horace Gray of Massachusetts, later a Justice, "The true remedy for Dredscottitus is in the appointing power." Telling Sumner, "No president since the first has had the opportunity to do so much for the administration of justice," he believed in "weakening and degrading" the Court. Although Republicans cared whether Justices shared their ideological bent, they saw the issue in political terms: they understood one another to be in agreement and grasped the value of their power.[32]

Changing the Court by using political power—and a blatant use it was—began with revamping its circuits. Justices "rode circuit," hearing cases in the regions to which they were assigned. With the South out of power Republicans redrew the map, acknowledging the world the war had created, where the population had grown, and their party's potential to grow with it. The five Southern and border circuits became three, the Old Northwest added a circuit, and Iowa, Kansas, and Minnesota joined new circuits. The South's departure, the West's growth, and political reality dictated that new justices hail from the circuit to which they would be named. Since their selection awaited congressional decisions on which state belonged to which circuit, the decisions were political: who sought appointments, who in Congress had the power to affect the result, and how would the party benefit. With reorganization done, Lincoln could choose the men who would constitute his Court.[33]

His choices similarly reflected politics. Since Republicans agreed on ideology, they could devote themselves to the patronage and back-stabbing of politics. And Lincoln had a pleasure enjoyed by few other presidents: naming a Court majority. How he chose Noah Swayne, Samuel Miller, David Davis, Stephen Field, and Chase demonstrated how the party adapted to the demands of power, saw the need to solidify its base, and agreed enough on the issues not to find them too bothersome. Each was a unionist, including Field, a War Democrat, and likely to uphold Republicans on such issues as emancipation. Each sought the job, reflecting their political experience—a blessing, since they had to adapt to the government's wartime needs, and a curse, since they stayed active politically after donning their robes. By representing areas where the party sought support, each served a purpose geographically. While four were loyal to a party that seemed radical as the war began, and Chase certainly was a leading radical, none wished to rock the boat of business and government. Once appointed, they protected institutions they had criticized in opposition, including the Court. As a Washington observer noted in 1863, "It is easy for the Administration, (or for any administration) to arrange the Supreme Court," and Lincoln demonstrated the possibilities of success and failure in doing so.[34]

Given the Court's geographic balance, it was logical for Lincoln to look first to McLean's Ohio. The favorite was Swayne, a Virginian who moved to Ohio and became active in the anti-slavery movement, an ex-district attorney with a corporate practice. His party orthodoxy was clear, but his connections, and their political and financial implications, mattered more. Ohio hoped to share a circuit with Indiana and Michigan, Governor William Dennison said, to help Swayne's chances and "from the intimacy of business intercourse between the people of the States." As a corporate lawyer, Swayne could be expected to rule in their interests, in keeping with the party's growing coziness with the business community.[35]

While businessmen sought his selection, no one worked harder for it than Swayne, whose efforts showed the party's assumed ideological unity and the primacy of politics as the basis for power. He aided Wade's election and Dennison's war preparations; both responded by urging his appointment. He lobbied Chase, who backed him reluctantly, perhaps due to doubts about his radicalism. Swayne cultivated attorneys outside Ohio, including Senate and court Democrats. He sought aid from a colleague in railroad cases, Democrat Samuel Tilden, who swung the New York bar behind a petition calling for his appointment—an endorsement signed by Democrats whose backing could have been troubling if his Republicanism had been less evident; what mattered now was his political support. When Swayne joined the Court in 1862, he stayed active in Ohio politics and loyal to Lincoln, supporting emancipation and his reelection. As a Republican, though, his beliefs were never in doubt. His importance was political: his selection pleased businessmen the party cultivated and a state whose vote was crucial to the party's continuance in power.[36]

Miller benefited from similar circumstances. Senators James Harlan and James Grimes wanted the ninth circuit for an Iowan: Miller, a lawyer for only twelve years. Lobbied by Governor Samuel Kirkwood, Lincoln said, "I will have to give it serious consideration. I had supposed you wanted me to make some one a Brigadier-General for you." Lincoln sought loyal, geographically correct Justices. Miller fit his needs and Iowans united for him, serving a political purpose. The choice was providential: an Iowa editor said that Miller's "common sense . . . prevents his being overwhelmed by the dust of antiquated precedents or entangled by the cobweb filaments of more modern technicalities," ideal qualities for a Republican Justice ruling on federal powers in an emergency. A throwback to the free labor ideology before its refinement in the quest for business support, Miller lamented Swayne's knee-jerk support for business over labor: "It is vain to contend with judges who have been at the bar the advocates for forty years of railroad companies, and all the forms of associated capital, when they are called upon to decide cases where such interests are in contest."[37]

After more lobbying and debate than Swayne and Miller caused, the next choice proved both simple and political, rooted in the third prong of the ideology of freedom, union, and power. The first problem was the circuits: Illinois and Ohio had to be kept separate to reward the faithful in two key states, especially Illinois, which received less patronage because its man was president. With that done, the front-runner was Illinois judge David Davis, a conservative ex-Whig and one of Lincoln's managers in 1860. Leonard Swett, the other manager, told Lincoln, "If Judge Davis with his tact and force had not lived . . . I believe you would not be sitting now where you are. . . . and you ought in justice to yourself give him this place." By agreeing, Lincoln rewarded a friend and pleased Illinoisans who sometimes felt ignored. Naming someone else might have done no political damage, but losing support in Illinois could and did, when Democrats won the legislature in 1863, embarrass Republicans. Nor did it hurt Lincoln to bring Davis closer to him. Davis was a link to conservatives who saw Lincoln as too radical. As with the other Justices, Davis's presence was meant to help keep Republicans in power.[38]

The next choice reflected similar concerns: geography and extending the party's appeal. Responding to population growth and a need for expertise in land and mining law, Congress added a tenth circuit to give the West a Justice and aid unionist sentiment—and the party that created the justiceship. The front-runner was California's chief justice, Field, a War Democrat. His leading backers were David, his brother, a New York radical; and Governor Leland Stanford, a Republican railroad man who knew him from joint investments in dubious land grants. Lincoln chose Field while Stanford replaced him with Edwin Crocker, whose family was one of his partners in building the transcontinental railroad. The businessmen whom Republicans had been courting were being well served.[39]

These appointments reflected the party's redefined ideology. The best legalist in the West, Field was the ideal choice, but his distant location and Democratic politics would have kept him out of office if the party's ascent and accompanying problems had not broadened its views to enhance their ability to serve and save the Union. The change included Field, a War Democrat and, like Swayne, an ally of business. Davis's Whiggery, judicial record, and ties to Lincoln made him a safe choice. Miller's maverick past could have been troubling, but he would uphold war measures the party deemed necessary.

Lincoln's first four choices owed their selection to the party's beliefs. Pleasing their supporters might help the party. To a Court of dubious reputation, they added men who would uphold their efforts to perpetuate freedom and union. The three Republicans and their unionist ally made clear that they would meet those demands.[40]

Choosing a Chief

Aware that the next Chief Justice would affect their party and ideology, Republicans awaited the chance to replace Taney. Before 1864 only three presidents—Washington, John Adams, and Jackson—had named a Chief Justice. The chief was only first among equals, but his reputation would be that of the Court, as with Marshall and Taney. Thus, Charles Francis Adams said, "The prejudices of thirty years work strongly in me to wish that this Presidential term should not be permitted to pass away without a change of the Chief." When the change came, the process proved similar to the one that produced Lincoln's other Justices, and for the same reason: to expand the party's power to aid freedom and union. Indeed, all Republicans knew the stakes. Sumner foresaw that the court's "old pro-Slavery policy . . . will now tumble. Our new Chief Justice will give a new interpretation to the Constitution." No one knew whether the appointee would be radical or conservative, only that he would be a Republican.[41]

The strands of Republican ideology came together, too. To follow the force behind *Dred Scott,* Republicans sought a Chief Justice who favored emancipation, confiscation, and freedmen's rights. After Taney's carping about the draft and habeas corpus, they wanted his successor to put the Union, and the expansive view of the Constitution needed to save it and perpetuate freedom, above niceties and precedents. He would need mental and physical strength to argue Republican dogma for many years; after all, Marshall spoke for the Federalists long after his party died, and Taney outlived Jackson by two decades. But a presidential election was near, and the appointment might affect the voting. Given their ambitions, their desire to appeal to all regions and leanings, and their hopes for future dominance, Republicans made clear that this appointment involved power for the present and future, and took for granted that whoever they appointed would be an ideological soul mate.[42]

The list of candidates for the job showed its importance and the party's lingering admiration for the Court as an institution. Hale, no longer trying to dismantle it, backed Jay on the grounds that he would be a chief justice "in no respect unequal to the first," Jay's grandfather. Some unionists, aware of Republican efforts to expand their base, pushed Reverdy Johnson, a Democrat from Taney's Maryland. In a similarly political vein, the party invoked regional considerations. New Englanders urged Governor John Andrew of Massachusetts because their lone justice, Clifford, was a Democrat. Yet the Bay State's Nathaniel Banks felt that the chief justice should come from the West and preferred Davis. Swayne denied interest and lobbied furiously. His best chance lay with Lincoln's friendship with Davis, who backed his ambitions, and with Senator Ira Harris of New York, who wanted to be a Justice but had no hope for the center chair; to make him an Associate Justice would require the promotion of a sitting member and would open a Senate seat for ambitious New Yorkers like Greeley, whom Swayne hoped to cultivate. None of these unionists and Republicans mentioned ideology; the title and political implications mattered above all.[43]

More proof of the political implications lay in the Cabinet's role in the discussion. Seward and Weed backed William Evarts, who grasped the job's "political importance over and above its simple judicial authority" and the need for "a bold and competent grasp of the new order of things," suggesting his adaptation to his party's evolving outlook. Hoping to slide him into the War Department, Ben Butler's allies backed Stanton, who was willing; Lincoln told him that he was too valuable to spare. A groundswell bubbled for Fessenden, mainly from allies of Hannibal Hamlin, who wanted the Maine Senate seat that Fessenden hoped to—and did—regain. Bates asked for the Chief Justiceship "as the crowning, retiring honor of my life," but he was too old, conservative, and politically weak for the post.[44]

Conservatism and personality derailed Montgomery Blair's hopes. While radicals found his venomous criticism of them unforgivable, moderate John Murray Forbes called him "the most progressive antislavery man in the Border States" for taking "the side of human freedom . . . when it took great courage and independence." While he tried to convince radical William Cullen Bryant of the *New York Evening Post* that Blair would be a boon for ex-Democrats, the Blair family sought support from old friends. Giving up on Evarts, Seward and Weed swallowed their distaste for Blair, hoping to drive him off the political stage. But, like Bryant, most old Democrats were to the left of Blair, whose family had enough trouble controlling Maryland and Missouri without claiming national consideration. Rumors spread that the Senate would never confirm him. Lincoln respected and liked him, but the chances that he would risk a divisive political firefight were slim indeed.[45]

Besides, one aspirant towered above the rest: Chase. Many expected his appointment. While preferring him for president, Jay called the Court "the place for him. He would restore its dignity and would shape that new course of judicial decision which is to replace the infernal judgments pronounced by the Slavepower in the guise of Justice." Radicals felt that he would be superb, but they regretted the end of his political career. Chase said, "If I know my own heart, a judicial would be more agreeable to my personal feelings than *any* political position." But a judicial post was political, as Lincoln's choices showed. And

Chase had done nothing to win over Lincoln; to the contrary, he had created problems in the Cabinet, stayed in a snit after resigning, and refused to stump for Lincoln's reelection until friends warned that he was damaging his prospects for the position.[46]

When Taney died, Chase and his supporters showed how political power entered into the equation. To say they campaigned is no understatement. The editors of the *Chicago Tribune* and *Ohio State Journal* declared their support. In the Cabinet, Stanton and Dennison backed Chase. Greeley's ally Colfax squelched rumors that Lincoln wanted anyone else. Seward's foes in New York thrilled to the idea of checkmating him with a radical Chief Justice, while his allies hoped that naming Chase would remove him from politics. Massachusetts radicals were vocal, with Sumner in the lead. He reminded Lincoln that he had promised Chase the job. After years of flaying Taney, it was "of inconceivable importance that the Constitution hereafter should be interpreted *always for Freedom,* and I long to have that assurance which can be found only in the appointment of a Chief Justice whose position on this question in all its bearings is already fixed." Sumner told Lincoln, "Our new Chief Justice must believe in Liberty and be inspired by it." Better still, he predicted that choosing Chase would aid Lincoln's election. Even radicals dedicated to freedom understood and accepted political power as a key part of their ideology.[47]

That understanding and acceptance explain Chase's appointment. Conservatives objected that he had been disloyal and was unlikely to give up politics once on the bench—not that his colleagues had. Even radicals feared that he would abandon the post to run for president, and that his unpleasant Cabinet tenure stuck in Lincoln's craw. Colfax fretted when Lincoln "told me of various objections he had heard, which he added, did not influence him, *but he repeated them.*" Indeed, Lincoln was concerned about Chase's ambition, but he deemed Chase the best choice and cited considerations that enveloped the party's ideology: the public expected his selection, and meeting that expectation would enhance Republican power; he would uphold the administration, contributing to the well-being of freedom and union.[48]

Nor did it harm Lincoln to pick a radical for whom he felt little warmth. "Although I may have appeared . . . to have been opposed to Chase's appointment, there never has been a moment since the breath left old Taney's body that I did not conceive it to be the best thing to do . . . and to have done otherwise I should have been recreant to my convictions of duty to the Republican party and the country," he said. That he listed his party first should not go unnoticed. Chase's selection might do more to mend fences between radicals and conservatives than it would affect the Court, because the choice, whoever he would have been, would have been a Republican, and they were sure of one another's beliefs.[49]

Ironically, Chase proved more and less than expected in his new post. Republicans enthused that his selection might mean more in the long run than Lincoln's reelection, both of which were, said William Curtis Noyes, "essential to the complete perfection and success of the great revolution now in progress, by which human freedom and the integrity of the Union are to be secured forever." Chase remained radical, but few cases related to emancipation reached the Court during his tenure. While he kept running for president, he never led the Court. Miller and Field became the Court's dominant thinkers as Chase's colleagues grew annoyed with his electoral pursuits. Disappointing supporters by ruling against wartime actions in *Hepburn v. Griswold* in 1870 and the *Legal Tender Cases* in 1872, Chase accused the federal government, and thus his Treasury Department, of overstepping its bounds by issuing paper money during the war.[50]

As a symbol, Chase succeeded. His appointment revealed how the nation had changed: in 1861 his selection would have seemed revolutionary, but by 1864 any doubts had more to do with personality than ideology. That showed how the party had changed. While conservatives disliked naming a radical to the Court's center chair, the party's views were assumed. They saw the Court's importance; that Chase failed to live up to his billing was due not to the Court or the party, but to Chase. "We have a Supreme Court now, whose distinguished Chief has shown, in another sphere, how well he comprehended the necessities of the times, and whose whole life gives us assurance that constitutional law will now rest upon the foundations of freedom and justice," said one editor, "and will be interpreted in accordance with those principles of government, which we have secured by undying devotion to the Federal authority." The issue had been not just freedom but order, exemplified by obedience of the law; with Chase and the other appointees the Court seemed secure, and Republicans hoped that it would stay that way for a long time.[51]

Cases and Concerns

During and after the war, the Court became more Republican in tone and membership, but not as the party expected. Its rulings showed the value of efforts to control and reconstitute the Court. The first example of the party's success—and evidence of the danger of its position—was the *Prize Cases,* decided in 1863. When the Union seized four ships on the Southern coast in 1861, their owners claimed that Congress had to declare war before Lincoln could enforce the blockade he had proclaimed after the firing on Sumter. Representing the government, conservatives Evarts and Dana argued for the broad application of power, in keeping with the party's ideology. "If the power with which you are at war has such interest in its transit, arrival, or existence, as to make its capture one of the fair modes of coercion, you may take it," Dana said, for war "is a *state of things,* not an act of legislative will," and the president may "repel war with war."[52]

The Court backed the government—barely. By one vote it held that war had existed as of 13 July 1861, when Congress had recognized Lincoln's actions. For the other dissenters—Maine Democrat Clifford and Southern unionists Taney and Catron—Nelson, a War Democrat, argued that the North and South were at war, and that only Congress could declare war; until then Lincoln had no power to act. Five upheld the blockade: Wayne, Grier, Swayne, Miller, and Davis. As senior justice, Wayne wisely assigned the opinion to Grier, the group's only War Democrat, not to himself, a Southerner likely to be more suspect than the Court's conclusion, or to a Lincoln appointee, who might be dismissed as partisan. "A civil war is never solemnly declared," Grier said; to deny its existence would "cripple the arm of the Government and paralyze its power by subtle definitions and ingenious sophisms." These words were agreeable to Republicans. They came from a War Democrat who had joined the *Dred Scott* majority, but at the same time reflected their evolving ethos.[53]

Clearly, the *Prize Cases* were the Court's most crucial wartime ruling. The Court put its imprimatur on Lincoln's powers, but three of the five-member majority were Republicans, highlighting the need for the party's control of the Court and the new seat to which Lincoln named Field. With Wayne and Grier aligned with four new Justices, the majority was solid and would grow as older Justices died. While close, the vote averted another self-inflicted wound and helped the Court rebuild its prestige by proving loyal when it counted most. "Contemplate . . . the possibility of a Supreme Court deciding that this blockade is illegal!" Dana said. "What a position it would put us in before the world whose commerce we have been illegally prohibiting, whom we have unlawfully subjected to a cotton famine and domestic dangers and distresses for two years!"[54]

Given such fears, Republicans were glad that the Court decided little of magnitude, but what it said and did not say proved revealing. The Justices could have ruled on the Legal Tender Act but dismissed the case, which meant that they avoided ruling on the legality of paper money. When New York tried to tax government securities, Nelson's opinion for a unanimous court recalled Marshall's call for federal supremacy in *McCulloch.* On the day it announced the *Prize Cases,* the Court found in *United States v. Castillero* against the claimant of California's New Almaden mine, whose title was confused in the Mexican American War. Lincoln appointees Swayne, Miller, and Davis joined Clifford, Nelson, and Taney in a six-to-three ruling, significant in itself in providing the Union with a source of mercury, possibly reflecting the effort in the *Prize Cases* to buttress the government. The case also helped induce Congress to create the seat for Field, a land and mining law expert—a move expected to help build a Republican or unionist majority.[55]

Further, the wartime Court avoided other constitutional issues, to the relief of Republicans. They had cause for concern: Taney drafted opinions overruling war measures in case he had the chance to rule, and assailed Lincoln in less crucial circuit rulings. In *Ex Parte Vallandigham* the Court could have followed Taney's lead in *Merryman,* but chose not to review the copperhead's trial. No challenge to the draft reached the justices, but Taney had an opinion ready against it. He looked similarly on replacing coin with paper, and Grier opposed it on circuit. Thus, the courts were risky ground for Republicans. Three Republican Justices were on the Court by 1863, but the majority belonged to another party and another time. Yet Taney stalled some of his habeas corpus rulings, aware that they would only provoke confrontations, and the Court sidestepped cases that might limit Lincoln's maneuverability. The Justices seemed to understand that they lacked the power to enforce their rulings and win public opinion to their side. Republicans had that power and would use it.[56]

The Party of Law and Order

These developments had a dual origin. One was the party's commitment to wielding federal power and enhancing political power to aid freedom and union, a creed that Lincoln's appointees followed. The other was the idea of order, which flowed from the party's ideology and reverence for judicial institutions and the law. Yet the idea of order was an entity of its own. Fearing that Republicans would destroy their society by freeing the slaves upon which their social order—indeed, order itself—relied, Southerners claimed to fight for order in rebelling against the Union government and against the new powers Republicans would take for themselves. By contrast, the party saw the survival of freedom and the Union, and the power to assure it, as rooted in law and order, exemplified in obeying the Constitution. To move too fast against slavery invited lawlessness and disorder, especially if that movement was in any way constitutionally questionable. Ignoring or circumventing the Constitution, Republicans felt, was far worse, and that was the sin that the South seemed to them to be committing.

Republicans saw contradictions between what the South said and did, and they were quick to point them out. In his inaugural, Lincoln had said, "Plainly, the central idea of secession, is the essence of anarchy." As bad as its refusal to accept a legally elected government was the South's belief in minority rights. The Declaration of Independence and the Constitution, Lincoln's lodestars, assured majority rule, which he called "the only true sovereign of a free people. Whoever rejects it, does of necessity, fly to anarchy or to despotism." The next day a Vermonter wrote that he wished to know "whether I live under a government of power, or in a state of anarchy." Republicans hoped to prove that they knew how to use power, in this case to repel the anarchy that the South had created. But they would use it wisely: addressing Connecticut legislators in the fall of 1861, Governor William Buckingham posited a "conflict . . . between law and anarchy." He and other Republicans had no doubts about who was on each side, and were ready to accuse others of the same: political opponents among Democrats, and judicial opponents on the Supreme Court.[57]

Indeed, in keeping with their activism, Republicans believed in the need to encourage order and discourage anarchy. According to John Andrew, the government had to welcome responsibility, but not just for the Union and Constitution. "The duty of suppressing the rebellion involves that of restoring and reconstructing order, society, civilization, where treason and slavery have subverted them," he said. Governor Andrew Curtin of Pennsylvania outlined broad federal powers, the first of which was "to stay the progress of anarchy and enforce the laws." That obligation fell to the federal government, because the states lacked the scope and ability to bring that kind of order out of federal chaos.[58]

As so often happened, Republicans saw a problem and a solution, but debated the best route to that solution. Publicly and privately, from conservatives like Bates to radicals like Lieutenant Governor Ignatius Donnelly of Minnesota, they believed that only their party really wanted the triumph of law and order. But how much change would accompany that order was unclear. "Liberty, order, and civilization are staked against a slaveholding despotism and social anarchy," said Frederick Douglass, a radical voice and conscience who saw the issue as "the preservation of society, and nothing worse than anarchy." Conservatives like Weed feared that radicals would "destroy our Government and Union," with "Revolution or Anarchy" resulting if the war lasted long enough for them to achieve their goals.[59]

Order could be hard to define because it depended on which Republican defined it. To radicals, conservatives subscribed to discredited theories of constitutionalism and policy that the war made impossible to maintain; to try to stand by them and refuse to accept any change would keep the government from taking the needed steps to protect its existence and thereby promote disorder. To conservatives, radicals were unreasonably determined to impose their anti-slavery will upon the whole Union, and in doing so endangered the Union's continued survival; disorder inevitably would result. For both sides, order meant obedience to the laws and acceptance of the government's existence. However, they differed in their interpretation of the laws and what the government could or should do. The question of what order really meant mirrored the party's ideology: all Republicans could agree that the growth of freedom, the salvation of the Union, and the retention and use of power were central to their and the nation's success because these issues united them. But how to achieve all of these, and overcome whatever personal differences existed within the party, could and did divide them.

Thus, order could be described as the ribbon that wrapped the package of freedom, union, and power, or as the shadow cast by the three threads of the party's ideology. When Hale tried to dismantle the Supreme Court, he proposed an act of disorder. A party new to power and eager to prove its ability to govern and save freedom and union would avoid that at all costs. When Lincoln chose a railroad lawyer, a doctor turned lawyer, a friend who practiced politics and served as a judge on the side, a mining and railroad lawyer, and a dedicated antislavery lawyer with presidential ambitions pulsing in every vein, and then the Senate confirmed all of them for the Supreme Court, Republicans showed agreement on their beliefs and sought to enhance their political standing—and the power that went with it. They wanted to turn those beliefs into action through the established order. When they jailed or suppressed opponents, they did so in the name of order—and used their power to save the Union. They reconciled taking a step against freedom on the grounds that they acted with the broader goal of saving the Union that would give them the power to protect freedom.

Yet the old order had changed. After Taney died and Chase became chief justice, Sumner took a step that revealed how fully the author of the *Dred Scott* decision had been discredited. He recommended admitting Boston lawyer John Rock to practice before the Supreme Court. Referring to Chase, Rock told Sumner, "We now have a *great* and *good* man for our Chief Justice, and with him I think my color will not be a bar to my admission." Rock was right, and Sumner was jubilant. He wrote to a friend, "You will be interested to know that I moved the admission of a colored person to the bar of the Supreme Court of the U.S.—that very Court which gave the detestable Dred Scott decision." Republicans had used their power to secure the triumph of freedom and union by retaining the old order—by dedicating themselves to order—and converting it into the new.[60]

NOTES

1. *CG,* 37, 2, 9 December 1861, 26–37, 155, and 3 June 1862, 2507; Silver, *Lincoln's Supreme Court,* 42–47; Harold M. Hyman, "Lincoln's Reconstruction: Neither Failure of Vision Nor Vision of Failure," Third Annual R. Gerald McMurtry Lecture, Fort Wayne, Ind., Louis A. Warren

Lincoln Library and Museum of the Lincoln National Life Insurance Foundation, 1980, 10; Baxter, *Orville H. Browning,* 134; Robert Dale Owen, "The Future of the North-West: In Connection with the Scheme of Reconstruction without New England, Addressed to the People of Indiana" (Loyal Publication Society No. 1, New York: Edward O. Jenkins, 1863), 2; Charles Francis Adams to Bird, Washington, 16 February 1861, Adams ms, Reel 164, MHS; Blaine, *Twenty Years of Congress,* vol. 1, 540–42.

2. Harold M. Hyman and William Wiecek, *Equal Justice under Law: Constitutional Development, 1835–1875* (New York: Harper and Row, 1982), 75; "Speech on the Sub-Treasury," 26 December 1839, in *CW,* vol. 1, 171; Paludan, *The Presidency of Abraham Lincoln,* 54–55.

3. Robert H. Wiebe, *The Search for Order: 1877–1920* (New York: Hill and Wang, 1967), *passim; Hartford Courant,* 6 March 1865, in Smith, *One Hundred Years of Hartford's Courant,* 265–66; Phillip S. Paludan, "The American Civil War Considered as a Crisis in Law and Order," *American Historical Review,* 77, no. 4 (October 1972): 1013–34. See also Randall, *Constitutional Problems;* Hyman, *A More Perfect Union;* Paludan, *A Covenant with Death;* Hyman and Wiecek, *Equal Justice under Law;* Neely, *The Fate of Liberty.*

4. Bernard Steiner, *Life of Reverdy Johnson* (Baltimore: Norman, Remington, 1914), 44.

5. Neely, *The Fate of Liberty,* 223–35, is a fine appraisal of the historiography.

6. Robert Dale Owen, *The Wrong of Slavery, The Right of Emancipation, and the Future of the African Race in the United States* (Philadelphia: National Publishing, 1864), 174–75; Bogue, *The Earnest Men,* 192, 224, 307–8; *CG,* 37, 3, 8 January 1863, 241; Hyman, *A More Perfect Union,* 124–40. On worshipping the Constitution, see Michael Kammen, *A Machine That Would Go of Itself: The Constitution in American Culture* (New York: Alfred A. Knopf, 1986).

7. Sumner to Lieber, Boston, 12 October 1865, in Series I, Reel 64, SP; Bogue, *The Earnest Men,* 193, 303–9; Herman Belz, *Reconstructing the Union: Theory and Practice during the Civil War* (Ithaca: Cornell University Press, 1969), 42–43; *CG,* 37, 1, 13 July 1861, 105; Horowitz, *The Great Impeacher,* 74–75; Dale Baum, *The Civil War Party System: The Case of Massachusetts, 1848–1876* (Chapel Hill: University of North Carolina Press, 1984), 58–59; John A. Stevens Jr. to Lieber, New York, 28 March 1863, John A. Stevens ms, 1862–63 Correspondence, NYHS.

8. Oates, *With Malice Toward None,* 235–36; Herman Belz, *Abraham Lincoln, Constitutionalism, and Equal Rights in the Civil War Era* (New York: Fordham University Press, 1998), 17–43; *Chicago Tribune,* 6 July 1861, in Kinsley, *The Chicago Tribune,* vol. 1, 199–200.

9. Lieber to Martin Russell Thayer, New York, 3 February 1864, Lieber ms, HL; Sumner to Lieber, Boston, 12 October 1865, in Series I, Reel 64, SP;

Theophilus Parsons to Sumner, Cambridge, 21 January 1863, Reel 27, ibid.; Benedict, *A Compromise of Principle,* 122; Curry, *Blueprint for Modern America,* 207; Hyman, *Lincoln's Reconstruction,* 14; Fehrenbacher, *Lincoln in Text and Context,* 119–20, 131–32, 138.

10. Lincoln to Winfield Scott, Washington, 25 April 1861, in *CW,* vol. 4, 344; Lincoln to Scott, Washington, 27 April 1861, ibid., 347; "Proclamation Suspending Writ of Habeas Corpus in Florida," Washington, 10 May 1861, ibid., 364–65; Lincoln to Scott, Washington, 14 October 1861, ibid., 554; Oates, *With Malice Toward None,* 235–36. On the writ, see Randall, *Constitutional Problems,* 118–85; Neely, *The Fate of Liberty, passim.*

11. Allan Nevins, "The Case of the Copperhead Conspirator," in Garraty, ed., *Quarrels,* 90–108; Hyman, *Lincoln's Reconstruction,* 12–13; Randall, *Constitutional Problems,* 120–21; Silver, *Lincoln's Supreme Court,* 26–37; Hyman, *A More Perfect Union;* Baker, *The Politics of Continuity,* 59; Paludan, *"A People's Contest,"* 28–29.

12. Roger Taney to Franklin Pierce, Washington, 12 June 1861, Pierce ms, Box 4, NHHS; *New York Times,* 29 and 30 May 1861; *Chicago Tribune,* 30 May 1861; *New York Tribune,* 29 May 1861; Silver, *Lincoln's Supreme Court,* 31–33; John M. Read to Sumner, Philadelphia, 16 September 1861, Reel 23, SP.

13. Fehrenbacher, *Lincoln in Text and Context,* 135; *CG,* 38, 2, 3 March 1865, 1372 (Trumbull); Washington, Monday, 16 December 1861, Pease and Randall, eds., *The Diary of Orville Hickman Browning,* vol. 1, 515; Quincy, Saturday, 23 May 1863, Pease and Randall, eds., *The Diary of Orville Hickman Browning,* vol. 1, 631; Henig, *Henry Winter Davis,* 168–69; Baker, *The Politics of Continuity,* 99; *CG,* 38, 2, 18 January 1865, 318 (Davis); ibid., 37, 3, 8 December 1862, 22; Winter Davis to Trumbull, n.p., 12 July 1862, Trumbull ms, Reel 13, LC; Timothy O. Howe to Seward, Green Bay, 27 September 1863, Seward ms, Reel 80, UR.

14. *CG,* 37, 2, 10 December 1861, 45; *CG,* 37, 3, 8 December 1862, 17–18; 11 December 1862, 62–64; and 22 December 1862, 158–60. James W. Grimes to Unknown, Burlington, 16 September 1861, undated clipping, John Sherman ms, Volume 32, LC; Sumner to Read, Boston, 24 September 1861, in Series II, Reel 75, SP; Sumner to Read, Washington, 1 January 1863 [misdated 1862], Reel 76, ibid.; Frank Freidel, *Francis Lieber: Nineteenth Century Liberal* (Baton Rouge: Louisiana State University Press, 1947), 309–11; Alexander, *A Political History of the State of New York,* vol. 3, 19, n. 7.

15. "Message to Congress in Special Session," 4 July 1861, in *CW,* vol. 4, 430–31. Bates issued an opinion backing Lincoln on 5 July. Lincoln to Bates, Washington, 30 May 1861, in *CW,* vol. 4, 390; Steiner, *Life of Reverdy Johnson,* 50–52; Cain, *Lincoln's Attorney General,* 145.

16. Lincoln to Erastus Corning, et al., Washington, 12 June 1863, in *CW,* vol. 6, 260–69; Lincoln to Matthew Birchard, et al., Washington, 29 June 1863, in *CW,* vol. 6, 300–306. See also Lincoln to Edwin M. Stanton, Washington, 13 May 1863, in *CW,* vol. 6, 215–16; James A. Rawley, "Lincoln and Governor Morgan," *The Abraham Lincoln Quarterly* 6, no. 5 (March 1951): 291–92.

17. Belz, *Abraham Lincoln, Constitutionalism, and Equal Rights,* 17–44, addressing Lincoln as dictator, deals with issues brought up by historians such as Randall and Neely and by popular writers such as William Safire, whose *Freedom: A Novel of Abraham Lincoln and the Civil War* (New York: Doubleday, 1987), belies its title with extended study of the issue of Lincoln's interpretation of the Constitution. Obviously, I subscribe to the theory that Lincoln was no dictator.

18. Randall, *Constitutional Problems,* 130, 163–68; Hyman, *A More Perfect Union,* 245–62; Neely, *The Fate of Liberty,* 68–69, 202–3.

19. Robert H. Jackson, *The Supreme Court in the American System of Government* (Cambridge: Harvard University Press, 1955), 76.

20. James Swinton to Elihu Washburne, New York, 13 July 1863, Washburne ms, LC, typed summary, Nevins ms, Box 5, HL; McClellan to Cameron, Washington, 9 December 1861, copy, Henry J. Raymond ms, NYPL; Raymond to Cameron, New York, 13 December 1861, ibid.; *New York Tribune,* 9 June 1862, in Harper, *Lincoln and the Press,* 132; Shutes, *Lincoln and California,* 76–77; William Henry Smith to John Brough, Indianapolis, 12 June 1864, Smith ms, Box 1, Ohio Historical Society; Neely, *The Union Divided,* 89–117.

21. Buckingham, *The Life of William A. Buckingham,* 184–85; Henig, *Henry Winter Davis,* 164–65; Springfield, Wednesday, 3 June and Saturday, 6 June 1863, in Pease and Randall, eds., *The Diary of Orville Hickman Browning,* vol. 1, 632–33; Greeley to Gerrit Smith, New York, 1 February 1863, Smith Family ms, Box 1, NYPL; *New York Tribune,* 6 June 1863; *Chicago Tribune,* 5 and 6 June 1863, in Harper, *Lincoln and the Press,* 262; Horowitz, *The Great Impeacher,* 87; Neely, *The Union Divided,* 89–117.

22. Stanley P. Hirshson, *The White Tecumseh: A Biography of General William T. Sherman* (New York: John Wiley and Sons, 1997), 146–49.

23. *CG,* 38, 1, 6 January 1864, 106–8; *CG,* 37, 3, 8 January 1863, 235; Harold M. Hyman, *Era of the Oath: Northern Loyalty Tests during the Civil War and Reconstruction* (Philadelphia: University of Pennsylvania Press, 1954), 1–17.

24. Hyman, *Era of the Oath,* 1–2; Magdol, *Owen Lovejoy,* 292; Hesseltine, *Lincoln and the War Governors,* 387–88; Lieber to Sumner, New York, 24, November 1864, in Series II, Reel 78, SP; James G. Randall, *Lincoln the*

Liberal Statesman (New York: Dodd, Mead, 1947), 124; Bogue, *The Earnest Men,* 198–99; *CG,* 37, 3, 4 February 1863, 716 (Senator Jacob Howard of Michigan).

25. Cassius Clay to Anson Burlingame, St. Petersburg, 23 November 1863, Burlingame ms, Box 1, LC; Magdol, *Owen Lovejoy,* 299; James T. Brady, "An Appeal to History," in Loyal Publication Society, No. 61 (New York: Loyal Publication Society, 1864); Fite, *Social and Industrial Conditions,* 203; David Montgomery, *Beyond Equality: Labor and the Radical Republicans, 1862–1872* (New York: Alfred A. Knopf, 1967), *passim;* "George W. Julian's Journal—The Assassination of Lincoln," *Indiana Magazine of History* 11 (1915): 328; *CG,* 38, 2, 11 January 1865, 225; Foulke, *Life of Oliver P. Morton,* vol. 1, 435; Neely, *The Fate of Liberty, passim;* Fehrenbacher, *Lincoln in Text and Context,* 113–15; John L. Blackman Jr., "The Seizure of the Reading Railroad in 1864," *The Pennsylvania Magazine of History and Biography* 111, no. 1 (January 1987): 49–60.

26. Randall, *Constitutional Problems,* 433–77; Paludan, *The Presidency of Abraham Lincoln,* 161–62, 178–79; Foner, *Reconstruction,* 38–39; *CG,* 37, 3, 9–10 December 1862, 37, 43–44, 47–53; Curry, *Blueprint for Modern America,* 51; Washington, Monday, 23 June 1862, Pease and Randall, eds., *The Diary of Orville Hickman Browning,* vol. 1, 553; Friday, 13 June 1862, in Pease and Randall, eds., *The Diary of Orville Hickman Browning,* vol. 1; Trefousse, *Benjamin Franklin Wade,* 193–94.

27. Lincoln to Members of the Cabinet, Washington, 23 December 1862, in *CW,* vol. 6, 17; Randall, *Constitutional Problems,* 457–60. Secretary of the Interior Caleb Smith had recently resigned; John Usher had not yet been named to replace him.

28. Lincoln to Members of the Cabinet, Washington, 23 December 1862, in *CW,* vol. 6, 17; "Opinion on the Admission of West Virginia into the Union," 31 December 1862, ibid., 26–28; Chase to Lincoln, Washington, 4 December 1862, in Chase ms, Microfilm Edition, Reel 24.

29. *Chicago Tribune,* ca. March 1861, in Kinsley, *The Chicago Tribune,* vol. 1, 177; Trefousse, *Benjamin Franklin Wade,* 235; *CG,* 37, 3, 20 January 1863, 396; "Remarks of H. S. Lane at the Bar Meeting called in honor of Judge McLean," n.p., 27 May 1861, typescript, Henry S. Lane ms, IU. On Taney, see Seward to Weed, Washington, 30 November 1860, Weed ms, UR; *Harper's Weekly,* 8 December 1860, 769; Taney to G. S. S. Davis, Washington, 11 July 1863, Taney ms, NYHS; Storey and Emerson, *Ebenezer Rockwood Hoar,* 138–39. On Justices, see Silver, *Lincoln's Supreme Court,* 1–13; John P. Frank, *Justice Daniel Dissenting: A Biography of Peter V. Daniel, 1784–1860* (Cambridge: Harvard University Press, 1964); Francis P. Weisenburger, *The Life of John McLean: A Politician on the United States Supreme Court*

(Columbus: Ohio State University Press, 1937); William Gillette, "John A. Campbell," in Leon Friedman and Fred L. Israel, eds., *The Justices of the United States Supreme Court, 1789–1978: Their Lives and Major Opinions,* 5 vols. (New York: Chelsea House, 1980), 934–39; Bernard Schwartz, *A History of the Supreme Court* (New York: Oxford University Press, 1993), 69–173.

30. Hendrick, *Lincoln's War Cabinet,* 189–200; John V. S. L. Pruyn Journal, 17 December 1860, Pruyn ms, Box 1, New York State Library; John Campbell to Jeremiah Black, Washington, 4 January 1861, Black ms, Reel 17, LC; Adams to Seward, London, 24 March 1864, Adams ms, Series II, Reel 171, MHS; "Memorandum," n.p., ca. April 20, 1864, ibid., Series IV, Reel 569; Seward to Adams, Washington, 8 April 1864, ibid.; Thomas and Hyman, *Stanton,* 137; Cameron to Samuel Corey, Lochiel, 28 July 1863, Ward Lamon ms, Box 15, HL; Winter Davis to Wade, n.p., 3 August 1864, Wade ms, Reel 5, LC; N. L. Hall to Benjamin Curtis, Buffalo, 16 August 1864, Curtis ms, Volume 2, LC; Samuel Nelson to Curtis, Cooperstown, 7 September 1862, ibid.; Alexander A. Lawrence, *James Moore Wayne: Southern Unionist* (Chapel Hill: University of North Carolina Press, 1943); Sumner to Lieber, Senate Chamber, 19 February 1864, Series II, Reel 77, SP.

31. Jay to Sumner, Katonah, 26 March 1861, in Reel 22, SP; Jay to Sumner, Katonah, 12 February 1862, Reel 24, SP; Jay to Sumner, New York, 10 December 1863 and 8 March 1864, Reel 30, SP; Jay to Sumner, Katonah, 28 May 1862, Jay Family ms, CU; Jay to Seward, Katonah, 27 June 1862, ibid.; Jay to Trumbull, Katonah, 5 July 1862, ibid.; Jay to Edward Bates, Katonah, 21 June 1862, ibid.; Jay to William Pitt Fessenden, Katonah, 12 July 1862, Fessenden ms, Box 1, Western Reserve Historical Society; Jay to Seward, Katonah, 23 June 1862, Trumbull ms, Reel 13, LC; Jay to John P. Hale, Katonah, 13 December 1861, Hale ms, Box 13, NHHS.

32. Jay to Trumbull, Katonah, 5 July 1862, Jay Family ms, CU; Trumbull to Jay, Washington, 12 July 1862, ibid.; Richard Henry Dana Jr. to Sumner, Boston, 9 March 1861, in Reel 22, SP; John C. Underwood to Sumner, Alexandria, 3 May 1864, Reel 31, SP; John Appleton to Sumner, Bangor, November 1862, Reel 26, SP; Horace Gray to Sumner, Boston, 27 April 1862, Reel 25, SP; Sam Galloway to Trumbull, Columbus, 10 December 1861, Trumbull ms, Reel 12, LC; *National Anti-Slavery Standard,* 19 December 1863.

33. Silver, *Lincoln's Supreme Court,* 47–50; *CG,* 37, 2, 24 January 1862, 469; Randall and Current, *The Last Full Measure,* 267.

34. T. J. Barnett to S. L. M. Barlow, Washington, 17 August 1863, Barlow ms, Box 45, HL; See also Randall and Current, *The Last Full Measure,* 268.

35. 6 March 1861, in Nevins and Thomas, eds., *The Diary of George Templeton Strong,* vol. 3, 106–7; Carman and Luthin, *Lincoln and the Patronage,* 172–76; William Dennison to Trumbull, Columbus, 10 and 16

December 1861, Trumbull ms, Reel 12, LC; Salmon P. Chase to O. P. Hubbard, Washington, 25 June 1863, "Chase, Letters and Drafts, 1825–1863," Chase ms, HSP; Randall and Current, *The Last Full Measure,* 267; William Gillette, "Noah H. Swayne," in Friedman and Israel, eds., *Justices,* 989–91.

36. Fred Rodell, *Nine Men: A Political History of the Supreme Court from 1790 to 1955* (New York: Random House, 1955), 137; Swayne to Samuel J. Tilden, Columbus, 4 April, 3 July, 27 November, and 28 December 1861, Tilden ms, Box 5, NYPL; "To the President of the United States," New York, 8 April and 6 July 1861, ibid.; Swayne to Thomas Ewing, Columbus, 8 and 9 April 1861, Thomas Ewing and Family Papers (Ewing and Family ms), Box 65, LC; Swayne to Ewing, Columbus, 27 June, and Crestline, 17 November 1861, ibid., Box 66; Swayne to Wade, Columbus, 10 January 1862, Wade ms, Reel 3, LC; Swayne to Wade, Columbus, 30 June 1862, ibid., Reel 4; Gillette, "Swayne," in Friedman and Israel, eds., *Justices,* 991; Carman and Luthin, *Lincoln and the Patronage,* 173–76.

37. Brigham, *James Harlan,* 176; Bogue, *The Earnest Men,* 262–63; Rice, ed., *Reminiscences of Abraham Lincoln,* 378–79; Kasson to Ulysses S. Grant, Des Moines, 10 May 1873, Kasson ms, NYHS; Charles Fairman, *Mr. Justice Miller and the Supreme Court: 1862–1890* (Cambridge: Harvard University Press, 1939), 34–66; Carman and Luthin, *Lincoln and the Patronage,* 178–79; Silver, *Lincoln's Supreme Court,* 74–79; Gillette, "Samuel Miller," in Friedman and Israel, eds., *Justices,* 1011–23.

38. Leonard Swett to Lamon, Bloomington, 6 June 1861, Box 7, Lamon ms, HL; 7 April 1861, Box 4, ibid.; Bloomington, 26 June 1861, Box 12, ibid.; David Davis to Lamon, Urbana, 14 April 1861, Box 5, ibid.; Davis to Lamon, Bloomington, 6 May 1861, Box 6, ibid.; Davis to Lincoln, Bloomington, 29 July 1863, Box 15, ibid.; Davis to Lincoln, Bloomington, 2 June 1864, typescript, Nevins ms, Box 17, HL; Davis to Weed, Washington, 12 February, 14 and 21 March, and 4 April 1864, Weed ms, UR; Van Deusen, *Thurlow Weed,* 264–65; Carman and Luthin, *Lincoln and the Patronage,* 180–83; Silver, *Lincoln's Supreme Court,* 80–82.

39. David Dudley Field to Trumbull, New York, 6 March 1863, Trumbull ms, Reel 14, LC; Edwin Crocker to Chase, Sacramento, 27 June 1863, Chase ms, Reel 20, LC, in Chase ms, Microfilm Edition, Reel 27; Carman and Luthin, *Lincoln and the Patronage,* 184–85; Silver, *Lincoln's Supreme Court,* 88–93; Robert McCloskey, "Stephen J. Field," in Friedman and Israel, eds., *Justices,* 1069–89.

40. Gillette, "Samuel Miller," in Friedman and Israel, eds., *Justices,* 1015.

41. Adams to Dana, London, 5 April 1863, Adams ms, II, Reel 169, MHS; Sumner to Gray, Washington, 30 December 1863, in Series II, Reel 77, SP;

Sumner to Elizabeth, Duchess of Argyll, Washington, 29 December 1863, ibid.; Adams Jr. to Henry Adams, Point Lookout, 15 October 1864, in Worthington C. Ford, ed., *A Cycle of Adams Letters,* 2 vols. (Boston: Houghton Mifflin, 1920), vol. 2, 205–6; Silver, *Lincoln's Supreme Court,* 185–87; Carl B. Swisher, *Roger B. Taney* (New York: Macmillan, 1935), 572–77; Fairman, *Mr. Justice Miller,* 52.

42. Silver, *Lincoln's Supreme Court,* 187–88; Grimes to Fox, Burlington, 19 October 1864, Fox ms, Box 8, NYHS.

43. Trefousse, *The Radical Republicans,* 300; Barlow to George McClellan, New York, 15 October 1864, McClellan ms, LC; Carman and Luthin, *Lincoln and the Patronage,* 315–18; Randall and Current, *The Last Full Measure,* 272–73; Silver, *Lincoln's Supreme Court,* 187–90; Howe to Sumner, n.p., ca. mid-October 1864, in Series II, Reel 78, SP; Sumner to Chase, Boston, 24 October 1864, ibid.; Jay to Sumner, New York, 13 October 1864, Reel 31, ibid.; Bancroft to Sumner, New York, 12 November 1864, ibid.; Banks to Lincoln, unfinished draft, New York, 20 October 1864, Banks ms, Box 35, LC; Swayne to Tilden, Washington, 19 February and 4 December 1864, Tilden ms, Box 6, NYPL; Greeley to Chase, New York, 19 and 30 October 1864, Chase ms, Box 5, HSP; Willard H. King, *Lincoln's Manager, David Davis* (Chicago: University of Chicago Press, 1960), 222; Gillette, "Swayne," in Friedman and Israel, eds., *Justices,* 996–97.

44. William M. Evarts to Charles Francis Adams, New York, 18 October 1864, Adams ms, IV, Reel 572, MHS; Evarts to Edwards Pierrepont, Paris, 8 March 1864, Pierrepont ms, Box 1, Sterling Library, Yale University; Barrows, *William M. Evarts,* 124–26; Carman and Luthin, *Lincoln and the Patronage,* 315–18; Philo Shelton to Weed, Boston, 13 October 1864, Weed ms, UR; Lieber to Sumner, New York, 14 October 1864, in Series II, Reel 78, SP; Hoar to Sumner, Concord, 16 January 1865, Reel 32, ibid.; Greeley to Chase, New York, 13 November 1864, Chase ms, Box 5, HSP; Storey and Emerson, *Ebenezer Rockwood Hoar,* 141–44; Silver, *Lincoln's Supreme Court,* 193–96; Thomas and Hyman, *Stanton,* 336–38; Cain, *Lincoln's Attorney General,* 311–12; Blaine to Fessenden, Augusta, 17 October 1864, Blaine ms, Reel 6, LC; Blaine to Hannibal Hamlin, Augusta, 17 October 1864, Hamlin ms, Reel 1, University of Maine, Orono; Browning to Ewing, Washington, 17 October 1864, Ewing and Family ms, Box 70, LC; Mellen to Chase, Washington, 18 November and 3 December 1864, Chase ms, Box 7, HSP; Greeley to Chase, New York, 13 November 1864, Chase ms, Box 5, HSP; Lieber to Sumner, New York, 15 October 1864, in Series II, Reel 78, SP.

45. Forbes to Bryant, Boston, 21 November 1864, Bryant-Godwin ms, Box 6, NYPL; Francis Preston Blair to Hamlin, Silver Spring, 22 November 1864, Hamlin ms, Reel 1, University of Maine, Orono; King to Blair, Ogdensburgh, 25 November 1864, Blair-Lee Family ms, Box 15, Princeton;

Fox to Butler, n.p., 17 November 1864, Fox ms, Box 8, NYHS; Theodore Tilton to "My Dear Bond," New York, 1 December 1864, Tilton ms, ibid.; Whitelaw Reid to Chase, Philadelphia, 20 November 1864, Chase ms, Box 9, HSP; Carman and Luthin, *Lincoln and the Patronage,* 318; Randall and Current, *The Last Full Measure,* 272–73; Smith, *The Francis Preston Blair Family,* vol. 2, 297–99; Niven, *Gideon Welles,* 487–88; Hendrick, *Lincoln's War Cabinet,* 539–43; Silver, *Lincoln's Supreme Court,* 194–95.

46. Jay to Sumner, New York, 5 January 1864, Reel 30, SP; Chase to Joshua Leavitt, Washington, 7 October 1863, in Jacob W. Schuckers, *The Life and Public Services of Salmon Portland Chase* (New York: D. Appleton and Company, 1874), 393–94; Chase to Greeley, Washington, 19 September 1864, Greeley ms, Box 6, LC; Hart, *Salmon Portland Chase,* 309, 320–21; Stephen Hoyt to Banks, New York, 22 October 1863, Banks ms, Box 29, LC; *New York Tribune,* 24 November 1863; John A. Stevens Jr. to L. E. Chittenden, New York, 5 January 1864, John A. Stevens ms, 1864–68, NYHS; Stevens to Thomas B. Carroll, New York, 11 January 1864, ibid.; Edward L. Pierce to Chase, Boston, 19 September 1864, Chase ms, Box 9, HSP; Horner, *Lincoln and Greeley,* 334; Trefousse, *The Radical Republicans,* 290.

47. *Chicago Tribune,* 15 October 1864, in Harper, *Lincoln and the Press,* 185; *Ohio State Journal,* 21 October 1864; Dennison to Greeley, Washington, 20 October 1864, Greeley ms, Box 3, NYPL; Chase to Greeley, Cincinnati, 21 October 1864, ibid.; Chase to Greeley, Cincinnati, 15 October 1864, Greeley ms, Box 6, LC; Smith, *Colfax,* 201–3; Sumner to Lincoln, Boston, 12 and 24 October, and 20 November 1864, Series II, Reel 78, SP; Sumner to Chase, Boston, 20 November 1864, ibid.; Sumner to Lieber, Boston, 14 October 1864, Series I, Reel 64, ibid.; Lieber to Sumner, New York, 13 October 1864, ibid.; Jay to Sumner, New York, 15 November 1864, Reel 31, ibid.; Greeley to Chase, New York, 19 and 30 October 1864, Chase ms, Box 5, HSP; Colfax to Chase, South Bend, 24 October 1864, ibid.; Colfax to Chase, Quincy, 3 November 1864, ibid.; Colfax to Chase, Washington, 5 December 1864, Chase ms, Box 3, HSP; Fessenden to Chase, Washington, 18 November 1864, Chase ms, Box 4, HSP; Pierce to Chase, Boston, 14 November 1864, Chase ms, Box 9, HSP; Mellen to Chase, Washington, 17 November 1864, Chase ms, Box 7, HSP; Barney to Chase, Washington, 14 October 1864, Chase ms, Box 1, HSP.

48. Colfax to Chase, Washington, 5 December 1864, Chase ms, Box 3, HSP; John Niven, "Lincoln and Chase: A Reappraisal," *Journal of the Abraham Lincoln Association* 12 (1991): 1–2.

49. McClure, *Lincoln and Men of War-Times,* 140–44; Chittenden, *Recollections,* 378–80; Randall and Current, *The Last Full Measure,* 272–74; Rice, ed., *Reminiscences of Abraham Lincoln,* 580–82; Carman and Luthin,

Lincoln and the Patronage, 318–20; Storey and Emerson, *Ebenezer Rockwood Hoar,* 141–43; Silver, *Lincoln's Supreme Court,* 199; Lieber to Sumner, New York, 13, October 1864, Series II, Reel 78, SP; Wilkeson to Greeley, Washington, 18 November 1864, Greeley ms, Box 6, LC.

50. William Curtis Noyes to Chase, New York, 7 December 1864, Chase ms, Box 8, HSP; Montgomery Blair to Barlow, Washington, 9 December 1865, Barlow ms, Box 56, HL; John Sherman to Chase, Cleveland, 31 August 1865, Chase ms, Box 9, HSP; Carman and Luthin, *Lincoln and the Patronage,* 320–21; Horowitz, *The Great Impeacher,* 102; Schwartz, *A History of the Supreme Court,* 149–61; Benedict, *A Compromise of Principle,* 109. On the Court and those who reduced Chase's power, see C. Peter Magrath, *Morrison R. Waite: The Triumph of Character* (New York: Macmillan, 1963). For reaction to the appointment, see *Sacramento Union,* 11 January 1865; *Pittsburgh Gazette,* 8 December 1864, *Brooklyn Union,* 7 December 1864, *Cincinnati Gazette,* 7 December 1864, and *Chicago Tribune,* 7 December 1864, in Reid to Chase, Washington, 9 December 1864, Chase ms, Box 9, HSP; Silver, *Lincoln's Supreme Court,* 206–9.

51. George B. Loring, "The Present Crisis: A Speech Delivered by Dr. Geo. B. Loring, at Lyceum Hall, Salem, Wednesday Evening, April 26, 1865, on the Assassination of President Lincoln. Dr. Loring's Letter to the Salem Gazette, on Reconstruction. Published by Request" (South Danvers, Mass.: Charles B. Howard, 1865), 9, 12; Blaine, *Twenty Years of Congress,* vol. 1, 541; Bryant to Chase, Roslyn, 10 December 1864, Chase ms, Box 2, HSP.

52. Schwartz, *A History of the Supreme Court,* 131; Silver, *Lincoln's Supreme Court,* 104–18; *New York Times,* 24 February 1862; Barrow, *William M. Evarts,* 108–9; Randall, *Constitutional Problems,* 51–59; Shapiro, *Richard Henry Dana, Jr.,* 127.

53. U.S. Supreme Court Report 2 Black 635; Silver, *Lincoln's Supreme Court,* 104–18; Hyman, *A More Perfect Union,* 237–38; Schwartz, *A History of the Supreme Court,* 132; Paludan, *The Presidency of Abraham Lincoln,* 81; Frank O. Gatell, "Robert Grier," in Friedman and Israel, eds., *Justices,* 880–81; Gatell, "Samuel Nelson," in Friedman and Israel, eds., *Justices,* 826–27.

54. Stuart L. Bernath, *Squall across the Atlantic: American Civil War Prize Cases and Diplomacy* (Berkeley: University of California Press, 1970), 31–32; Shapiro, *Richard Henry Dana, Jr.,* 120; Belz, *Reconstructing the Union,* 128; Silver, *Lincoln's Supreme Court,* 117–18; Swisher, *Roger B. Taney,* 564–65.

55. Silver, *Lincoln's Supreme Court,* 144–45, 158–62; Lawrence, *James Moore Wayne,* 188; Gatell, "Nelson," in Friedman and Israel, eds., *Justices,* 827–28; Gillette, "Clifford," in Friedman and Israel, eds., *Justices,* 972.

56. Randall, *Lincoln the President: Springfield to Gettysburg,* vol. 2, 297–98; Swisher, *Roger B. Taney,* 563–72; Fairman, *Mr. Justice Miller,* 86–90; Gatell,

"Grier," in Friedman and Israel, eds., *Justices,* 881; U.S. Supreme Court Report 1 Wallace 243; Paludan, *The Presidency of Abraham Lincoln,* 194.

57. "First Inaugural Address," in *CW,* vol. 4, 268; Paludan, *"A People's Contest,"* 12; C. Coolidge to Justin Morrill, Windsor, 5 March 1861, Morrill ms, Reel 6, LC; Buckingham, *The Life of William A. Buckingham,* 180; Thomas Ewing to Charley Ewing, Washington, 29 December 1860, Thomas Ewing and Family ms, Volume 12, LC.

58. John A. Andrew, "An Address Delivered before the New England Agricultural Society; John A. Andrew, "Address of His Excellency John A. Andrew, to the Two Branches of the Legislature of Massachusetts, January 8, 1864" (Boston: Wright and Potter, State Printers, 1864); William H. Egle, "Curtin's First Administration," in Egle, ed., *Andrew Gregg Curtin: His Life and Public Services* (Philadelphia: G. W. Jacobs, 1895), 120–21; Oberholtzer, *Jay Cooke,* vol. 1, 228.

59. Blight, *Douglass' Civil War,* 61–62, 241–42; Weed to David Davis, New York, 15 March 1864, Davis Family ms, Box 4, Illinois State Historical Library. See also Martin Ridge, *Ignatius Donnelly: The Portrait of a Politician* (Chicago: University of Chicago Press, 1962); Cain, *Lincoln's Attorney General,* 313; *New York Tribune,* 24 September 1862; Evarts to Pierrepont, Paris, 8 March 1864, Pierrepont ms, Box 1, Sterling Library, Yale University; Blaine, *Twenty Years of Congress,* vol. 1, 64–66; *CG,* 37, 2, 25 February 1862, 957.

60. John S. Rock to Sumner, Boston, 17 and 24 December 1864, Series I, Reel 32, SP; Chase to Sumner, Washington, 21 December 1864, ibid.; Chase to Sumner, n.p. [Washington], 23 January 1865, ibid.; Sumner to Elizabeth, Duchess of Argyll, Washington, 7 February 1865, Series II, Reel 79, ibid.; Sumner to Chase, Senate Chamber, 21 December 1864, Reel 78, ibid.

7

The Paradox of Power: Republicans and the Military

ON 26 January 1863, with Union armies mired in the winter muck on the Potomac and the Mississippi, Abraham Lincoln wrote one of his most famous letters. It followed General Joseph Hooker's appointment to lead the Army of the Potomac. As a corps commander, Hooker had been critical of his superiors, George McClellan and Ambrose Burnside. For this and his anti-slavery views, Hooker won support from congressional radicals who pressured generals, especially McClellan, whose commitment to the party's interlocking causes of freedom, union, and power seemed lacking. When Lincoln chose Hooker to succeed Burnside, he told him, "I have heard, in such a way as to believe it, of your recently saying that both the Army and the Government needed a Dictator. Of course it was not for this, but in spite of it, that I have given you the command. Only those generals who gain successes, can set up dictators. What I now ask of you is military success, and I will risk the dictatorship."[1]

As have most of his writings, Lincoln's letter won attention for literary grace and, in addressing the possibility of dictatorship, for his belief in democracy and civil governance. All of that is correct. It also captures the party's ideology as it concerned the military. While their Democratic and Whig background included generals turned politicians such as Andrew Jackson, Winfield Scott, and Zachary Taylor, and while their first presidential candidate had been army explorer John C. Frémont, most Republicans feared the military. They saw it as aristocratic and undemocratic, even antidemocratic, and a threat to freedom; sympathetic toward the South and its way of life, and a threat to the Union; and potentially unwilling to accept civilian authority, and a threat to federal power. For Hooker to speak openly enough about dictatorship for Lincoln to have heard about it symbolized, if not necessarily for the general's Republican supporters, the arrogance that the party expected from the military. While Hooker surely indulged his own arrogance, the exchange demonstrated Lincoln's certainty that even if Hooker won enough battles to achieve his rumored goal, he and the other civilian authorities would be able to handle the problem.

The inescapable irony was that army officers, who seemed to endanger Republicans and republicanism itself, provided the best means for the party to achieve its goals. Republicans saw that there could be no union without freedom, no freedom without union, and neither without power for the government and their party to preserve and perpetuate them. The military was the arm of the government through which they could do all they sought to do, but responsibility for success rested with the party responsible for the government. Thus, Lincoln searched, often fruitlessly and seemingly endlessly, for a commander for the entire army, or at least the Army of the Potomac, who could win without threatening the party and government. He went through an incompetent or underachieving parade—Winfield Scott, Irvin McDowell, McClellan, Henry Halleck, John Pope, Burnside, Hooker, and George Meade—before Ulysses Grant rose to the top and brought William Sherman with him. As the conquerors they became heroes, but still not wholly trustworthy to Republicans. After all, their success resulted not from convincing the North or South of the value of freedom and union, but through using power at its rawest and deadliest.[2]

Indeed, the Republican belief in freedom, union, and power left ample room for varied views of the military and various issues to be resolved. For one thing the war required the army's expansion, fueling debate over the part the military played in a republic. As Sherman, who rose and fell several times in Republican eyes, said, the North had to win and save the Union, "for 'tis not possible that the beautiful fabric of government erected by our forefathers should tumble into anarchy or be rent by schism." But those forefathers had seen a standing army as antithetical to the republic they had created. Republicans had inherited those views, among so many others, from them. Concerned as they were about a powerful military, Republicans had to reconcile their hopes with the power they would have to place in the army's hands to win, their choice of who within the army should hold that power, their belief in how that victory should be won, and their fear that concentrating too much power in the army's hands would threaten the republic and themselves.[3]

However, another aspect of power, combining the military and political, created another conundrum related to Republican ideology. Party leaders understood the need to attract loyal Democrats, to broaden their limited base and to enhance loyalty to the Union they were trying to preserve and the freedom they were trying to protect and perpetuate. One way for them to entice Democrats to enter the Republican tent, as well as serving the country, was to let at least some of the army's power rest in the hands of loyal Democrats. But a general had to be more than a politician or tactician; he had to merge both characteristics without seeming to use his position for advancement or undermine the goals of the civilian authorities. To serve in the military in any capacity connoted a belief in the Union but not necessarily in freedom, and certainly not in expanding the power of the Republican party or the federal government. Republicans doubted that the military could be trusted, and military leaders fed those doubts. Thus, Republicans had to think militarily in their own right, requiring them to find the generals who could and would lead the armies to success—a job for the commander in chief, Lincoln, whom many in his party considered in over his head. How they dealt with battlefields affected what they did in other fields—politics and government, both inextricably linked to power—and their relations with the military forced and encouraged Republicans to think more carefully about their own attitudes regarding freedom, union, and power.

The Wisdom of the Fathers and Their Descendants

Not only did the founding fathers influence their party; Republicans saw themselves as inheriting their mantle. As the framers affected them in so many ways, they warned their Republican descendants about the military. When Jefferson said in 1774 that "a veteran army" would make "the civil subordinate to the military," he referred to a widespread concern about military power that the presence of British soldiers among the rebellious Massachusetts population did nothing to diminish. In 1776, in the Virginia Declaration of Rights, he added, "A well regulated militia, composed of the body of the people, trained to arms, is the proper, natural, and safe defense of a free state . . . standing armies, in time of peace, should be avoided as dangerous to liberty." The militarily more experienced George Washington added, "Men accustomed to unbounded freedom, and no control, cannot brook the Restraint which is indispensably necessary to the good order and Government of an Army." Thus, like the framers, Republicans wanted it both ways. They wanted an army professional enough to win, but amateur enough so that during and after the war, the soldiers would remember that their loyalty was to their country and their civilian pasts, not to a military way of life.[4]

Republicans sought to achieve these goals in three ways: assure that the army resembled the citizenry; maintain a steady drumbeat about the aristocratic pretensions of the army and the institution that trained its leaders, West Point; and guarantee that the large wartime army would be ephemeral. They accomplished the first partly with reminders that the war was fought for free labor by free laborers. Sending an expedition to Texas, they hoped, would regain control of that state and increase emigration; if these plans succeeded, Massachusetts Republican Horatio Woodman said, "the question of conflict of systems of labor, and political power by this barrier of free labor and free territory will be settled forever." A more vociferous Bay State politician, Ben Butler, recounted asking whether anyone in his regiment could fix a railroad engine, and an enlistee replied, "Well, General, I rather think I can. I made that engine." That response showed, the party felt, the equal opportunity that free labor promised. When Congress met for a special session on 4 July 1861, newly elected Speaker Galusha Grow touched on the idea that this was and would be a democratic army of citizens, not aristocrats and career officers: "The merchant, the banker, and the tradesman, with an alacrity unparalleled, proffer their all at the altar of their country, while from the counter, the workshop, and the plow, brave hearts and stout arms, leaving their tasks unfinished, rush to the tented field."[5]

The Republican belief in the superiority of a citizen army translated into an accompanying belief in the inferiority and failings of a professional army trained at West Point. How Republicans viewed West Point revealed their fears and concerns not only about the military, but about taking and keeping power. They argued that the United States Military Academy in New York contributed to the war by reinforcing the South's aristocratic tendencies and its conviction that it was better than the North. Secretary of State William Henry Seward, cautious about too open a stand on most issues, derided the "arrogant assumption of superior valor and heroism which the insurgents had brought into the contest," and other Republicans scoffed at Southern claims of military superiority. When the South seceded, most army officers went with their states, leaving Southerners who put union first but retained pardonable regional sympathies, and Northerners who as cadets had formed lasting friendships with those about to oppose them in battle.[6]

Nor did the party appreciate the pride that West Point instilled in its graduates. They saw themselves as trained professionals and doubted, often with good reason, the ability of equal or superior officers who came armed with enthusiasm for a cause or political connections, not military experience. According to George Templeton Strong, career men were wedded to what they learned at West Point and surer "of the infamy of abolitionism and the provocations of the South, of the worthlessness of volunteer generals . . . and of their excellent but perhaps a little misguided West Point and army friends . . . than of the great national cause."[7]

While Republicans disagreed about individuals and policies, they shared an ideology that fostered doubts about West Point. After all, Southerners lacked proper devotion to freedom and union, but would use and abuse power; so many army officers had been Southerners that the connection seemed clear. While too skeptical to accept this criticism at face value, Lincoln named enough politicians to generalships, if only to win bipartisan support, to show that military education held no charms for him. In the Cabinet, Montgomery Blair was a West Pointer and enough of a democrat and cynic to share Republican reservations, while his brother Frank, a civilian general, said, "The robes of West Point must cease to be sacred and the President must let the Nation go 'on its muscle' and common sense. . . . Alas! those who look only to West Point for chieftains are not likely to have an opportunity to find others or to give an opportunity to others to show themselves"—a classic criticism of the aristocracy of that school and its Southern alumni.[8]

In his first report as secretary of War, Simon Cameron sought to divert attention from his administrative ineptitude by blaming the size and strength of the rebellion on officers who defected to the South after the government trained them at West Point. "The question may be asked, in view of the extraordinary treachery displayed, whether its promoting cause may not be traced to a radical defect in the system of education itself?" His abler successor, Stanton, was sure of the answer, distrusting any general who seemed too confident. But continued exposure to able West Pointers gradually diluted his distaste for their alma mater.[9]

Radicals and conservatives in Congress were more vocal about their concerns regarding the thinking inculcated at West Point. "I do not believe that in the history of the world you can find as many men who have proved themselves utterly faithless to their oaths, ungrateful to the Government that has supported them, guilty of treason and a deliberate intention to overthrow that Government which has educated them and given them its support, as have emanated from this institution," said radical Senator Ben Wade of Ohio. Worse, "the whole principle of it is in opposition to the principle of all our institutions. It is aristocratical; it is exclusive . . . and it stands in the way of merit being advanced." Among those who agreed was John Sherman, Wade's Ohio colleague, who then complained when a civilian appointee won a promotion that he considered more appropriate for his brother, a West Pointer. To his colleague William Pitt Fessenden, "the military education at West Point is of greatest value . . . but I believe the moral education is a very bad one." Indeed, congressional Republicans mustered more support for anti-military legislation than might have been expected, even if they fell short of the needed majority. A quarter of the Senate backed James Lane's proposal to close West Point in 1863. When Representative Abraham Olin of New York proposed requiring West Point cadets to deny state sovereignty and proclaim their allegiance to the Union, the bill sailed to passage.[10]

Buttressing this disdain was public opinion, which the party's orators, press, and pamphleteers affected and reflected. Whatever the Union's military fortunes, most Republicans derided West Pointers. Late in 1862, the *Chicago Tribune* complained that "West Point rules . . . and if it has not yet killed the republic, it has certainly put it in serious jeopardy." While his *New York Tribune* railed at the school, Greeley was blunter in private. He told Charles Halpine, a reporter surprised at how regular army officers accepted him, that "you are not, what most West Pointers are, either a fool or a traitor." While Greeley's daily said, "An army-officer, who goes to the war, pretty well stuffed with Pro-Slavery prejudices, usually has all that nonsense knocked out of him during his first campaign," he and his staff found trained officers suspect and rarely shrank from advising how not only to wage war against the peculiar institution, but also to fight battles properly.[11]

While sharing Greeley's concerns, Republicans offered a militarized free labor ideology. They argued that civilian life provided training that matched or exceeded that of West Point, except perhaps in science, and that equal opportunity in the army would prove them right. Charles Francis Adams argued that "West Point has furnished education, but nothing more. The General is born so. . . . Our West-point graduates appear to have been taught caution in warfare until there is no enterprise left." Nor was this attitude limited to conservatives; all sides voiced a disdain that, as with Adams, had little to do with an understanding of military tactics. Radical New York City mayor George Opdyke said that the Union could "produce from private life ready-made military commanders," but the object of his praise was Butler, a civilian general of little ability. The more common claim was that better generals believed more strongly in the cause. Governor Oliver Morton of Indiana said that he "would rely with infinitely more confidence upon the man of strong intellect, whose head is inspired by his heart, who, although he be unlearned in military science, believes that our cause is sacred," not on a trained soldier "whose sympathies, if he have any, are most likely on the other side."[12]

These views reflected the third prong of the party's theory about the military: the standing army must end with the war. They would return to the citizen militia they believed the founding fathers to have envisioned. The enthusiastic response to the call for men after the firing on Fort Sumter proved, Senator John P. Hale of New Hampshire said, that standing armies were unnecessary, especially with a "republican Government." Lincoln's friend Senator Edward Baker of Oregon called a standing army "always dangerous to liberty, and I believe that the ambition of men, and the interests of men, and the tendency of power to the lust of power, always seeks and finds excuses for the increase and continuance of standing armies in all public emergencies." Although he found it acceptable for the duration, Baker warned, "No standing army ever was raised even in a despotic Government, except under some pretense of maintaining good order or putting down resistance to good government." Others offered more practical reasons, like the cost of maintaining an army. Invoking the founding fathers, moderate Senator James Grimes of Iowa called the army anti-republican and likely to lead the country into wars it could otherwise avoid.[13]

Republicans who preferred only a temporary standing army echoed the framers in citing overseas excesses to help their case. With Republicans aware of his experiences in Europe with monarchy and militarism, Carl Schurz noted that "the army here is not what it is over there. Some day the war will end; the army will disappear and everybody will return to civil life. The so-called regular army will of course remain, but it is a small and exclusive institution." A civilian army not only would prove more committed to the causes of civilian government, but might provide better service. E. L. Godkin, a British-born Republican editor, surmised that since they were less disciplined than professionals, an army of workers would deal better with adversity: "They may be routed, and disorganized, and lose their officers; but as neither the organization nor the officers were ever of much consequence to them, they rally in the first wood they reach and return to the charge."[14]

But a nagging question persisted: Would Republicans dispose of the army as easily as they thought, and, if not, had they overreached in their quest for power? Thaddeus Stevens said that Congress needed only to reduce the army's size. Others were less sure, reflecting the party's concerns about the dangers of wielding too much power, or possibly not enough. Adams in London and John Lothrop Motley in Vienna reported that foreign powers wondered where the reunited nation would turn its strength next, and were relieved at the postwar reduction in the army's size. Financial experts like Secretary of the Treasury Hugh McCulloch fretted about the cost of a large army and hoped for a speedy return to peacetime levels. Political generals feared that in deciding who to muster out and who to keep, West Pointers would protect one another, restoring the army to its antebellum status as an aristocratic group. Worse, Republicans wondered whether Southern intransigence would make it impossible to trim the army: Lincoln expected opposition to emancipation to create problems that only military power could solve, while the *Chicago Tribune*'s Joseph Medill saw the army or the franchise as the only way to protect freedmen in the South. Looking both South and West, conservative Senator Ira Harris of New York sagely predicted in 1861 that with the nation's lengthy frontier, "it will be necessary, for years to come, probably during the whole of our lives, to maintain, at certain important positions, military force." Governing the country might require Republicans to use a force for power that they found frightening simply because it was such a force.[15]

Seeking Explanations

But the dynamic between using and retaining political power and wielding military power seemed contradictory to the party. That Republicans had little faith in military leadership is apparent; they admired and celebrated foot soldiers, but considered most generals dictatorial aristocrats who opposed every concept of freedom for which they stood. If Republicans lacked trust in army leaders, the problem of maintaining an army might go away if their confidence in the soldiers proved well founded. This hope and expectation reflected the ideology with which they entered office: they had a reformist, optimistic plan to spread free labor and improve the country in every imaginable way. While the defeats that slowed and threatened progress could have shattered morale, the Republicans retained a strong belief in human freedom and improvement that they had inherited from the framers, who had drunk deeply at the well of Enlightenment thought on the perfectibility of human nature.

Other events and ideas buoyed Republican hopes for turning theory into practice. The radical wing in particular owed much of its dedication to abolitionism, which had flowed in part from the Second Great Awakening and its concept of building a "heaven on earth." Unsurprisingly, Republicans intended to overcome embarrassments along the Potomac and win the war because they never wavered from the view that their cause was just and their destiny assured. The obstacle, they felt, lay not with right but with might, and the need for the Union to display it—and for them not to shrink from using it.[16]

The power associated with the army and building a war machine might, Republicans hoped, speed the process of achieving or spreading freedom. While even conservatives were hopeful, for radicals the way was clear. By the end of 1861, the *Chicago Tribune* said, "Hereafter this war is to be no longer a velvet-fingered dalliance with slavery, but a struggle honored by men and approved by Heaven. Let the watchword be Liberty and six months will not elapse before peace will smile upon this land guiltless of the ownership of a slave"—an overly optimistic assessment, but a sign of a shift, if tentatively, from the party's old willingness to let slavery wither as free labor constricted it. When the army moved too slowly, the party, seeking to explain why, wondered whether victory must wait until slavery died. "I think we will have to wander in the wilderness a while longer, perhaps like the Israelites till all of that generation who seem bessotted *[sic]* with a superstitious respect for Slavery have died off, before we can hope to be fitted to enter Canaan," John Bigelow said.[17]

Political success and acquiring power require an ability to rationalize failure; if so, Republicans achieved all of these. Some of them deemed victory so elusive because the war had to last long enough for the Union to pay for the sin of slavery. Publicly and privately, Republicans mused that the war had to continue until slavery had been eliminated. These views emanated from behind-the-scenes editors and diplomats such as Bigelow, who wrote to a friend about his "apprehension from time to time that our war in America might end too soon," and more private figures such as Strong, who felt that the long war would make up in some way for the North's long-term failure to stand up to Southern bullying. Even popular politicians such as Governor Richard Yates of Illinois dared to tell an audience that if the Union had won at Bull Run and compelled the South to surrender, "then the Union would have been restored with slavery, but it was not in the counsels of the Almighty that it should be so."[18]

When Republicans found earthly reasons for failure—incompetence—they acted accordingly. Two debacles prompted them to create the Joint Committee on the Conduct of the War. At Bull Run congressmen watched troops scatter as generals bumbled; at Ball's Bluff they lost one of their own, Baker, who probably overdid his orders out of a desire for glory and overconfidence in his ability. Republicans could forgive civilian zeal, but not an error by the army. Senator Zachariah Chandler of Michigan said that Bull Run had been blamed on politicians and civilians, but not on the real culprit: the Union army's leadership, or lack of it. Defeats should be investigated, he said, and "blame should rest where it belongs." Radicals pushed Congress to create the committee to study the military and give Lincoln and his generals the benefit of their counsel. When conservatives opposed it as a potentially unconstitutional check on the commander in chief's power, Owen Lovejoy said, "We have the right to arraign not only our generals, but even the President. We here represent the sovereignty of the people." The result was the committee, chaired by Wade, a radical who saw West Point as a Northern branch office of the Southern aristocracy.[19]

McClellan believed that the committee, especially Wade and Chandler, targeted him. He was right. At first they aided his efforts to force Scott to retire, while he organized the Army of the Potomac and then the whole army. But McClellan's unwillingness to move taxed their patience more quickly than it did Lincoln's, though he more subtly shared their doubts. By October, only weeks after McClellan had taken over, Wade said, "He seems to be determined that his troops shall all be veterans before he permits them to come under fire." McClellan said that he would drive toward Harper's Ferry only after setting up a retreat, to which Wade retorted that if they had to pull back across the river, they should be in coffins. For his part McClellan saw the committee as persecuting him, especially when he was in the field and unable to respond. Had he succeeded in the field, of course, that would have answered them, and his failure simply enhanced the nagging distrust that Republicans felt for anyone of a military background.[20]

As much as the committee hated McClellan, its members loved Stanton. Meeting with him on his first day, Wade, Chandler, and Representative George Julian decided that he was just what the country needed. In turn, Stanton preferred their views to McClellan's and concluded from them and others that McClellan had been ready to move but lacked a plan of action or the desire to attack. His treatment of generals who were McClellan allies or friends could be high-handed in the extreme, but endeared him to the committee. Yet Stanton would go only so far: Wade urged a command for Frémont, a radical of dubious ability, but Stanton never pushed the point with Lincoln and won Frémont's enmity for requiring him to follow orders. But in the end Stanton improved relations between the administration and the committee, which might have been even more of a problem had he failed to earn its respect. To Chandler the problem with the Union war effort lay with "generals who never meant to fight . . . but now thanks be to God the Committee on the Conduct of the War & Secy Stanton these men are all out of command and earnest fighting men in their place."[21]

Whether the committee was as helpful as Chandler said is debatable. Its radical members saved Butler's command several times despite ample evidence of his incompetence, because he shared their views. Indeed, the radical was telling the committee that he had been unfairly blamed for failing to capture the impregnable Fort Fisher when word arrived that it had fallen into Union hands; even then, Chandler said that he had never seen anyone "so thoroughly fortified in my life with official documents, orders, receipts & vouchers as he is. . . . His persecutors are from West Point." Wade and Chandler backed promotions for the incompetent General Daniel Sickles and tried to save Burnside because they were radicals; they pestered Grant, Sherman, and Meade—actually, most West Pointers—because they were not radical. The committee interfered to help radicals rid Missouri of John Schofield, its moderately conservative commander.[22]

The relationship between Lincoln and the Joint Committee reflected differing Republican conceptions of power. Wade believed that his chairmanship gave him power over the army—Lincoln disagreed—and his suggestions often were useless. After probing Frémont's problems in Missouri, where the onetime explorer had overseen a corrupt, high-handed, militarily incompetent operation, Wade said, "His persecution will prove the darkest page in our history and . . . I intend privately to make a full statement of the case to the Secy of War and if possible prevail upon him to restore the Genl to some active and useful command," an effort that failed. When Wade told him to fire McClellan and replace him with "anybody," Lincoln countered, "Wade, anybody will do for you, but not for me. I must have somebody. . . . I must use the tools I have." Wade spent much of the winter of 1863–64 trying to restore Hooker, who had resigned after losing spectacularly to Lee at Chancellorsville, and shove aside Meade, who remained. He welcomed Grant's appointment to overall command, but he had nothing to do with Lincoln's decision to promote him. Whatever else it may have done, the Joint Committee encapsulated party views on whether Lincoln or Congress should wield more power—and, since Lincoln was commander in chief, he simply arrogated the decision to himself, as the committee's displeasure with his decisions showed.[23]

Yet the committee proved useful in other ways. Lincoln agreed on the need for hard fighting, and its attacks on recalcitrant generals provided political backing if he needed to pressure or remove them. While Wade had charged Lincoln with dawdling late in 1861, he blamed McClellan by 1864, when the general was the Democratic presidential candidate—and that could only help Lincoln. The committee sought to reassure the restless public in its reports: "The past, notwithstanding its errors and reverses, is full of encouragement, and gives full assurance of final success. No great war was ever conducted by any people or

Government without great mistakes." Finally, the committee captured the party's distrust of the army and enabled Lincoln to use that distrust when it suited his purposes. If a radical committee and moderate president concurred on the need to watch certain generals, it was a sign of unity based on their ideology.[24]

Accordingly, the Joint Committee reflected its party's views of the slow progress of Union forces. As 1862 began, the *Chicago Tribune* asked what was needed to save the Union and answered, "An Active War." As that summer ended, even moderates and conservatives insisted that the North must "put forth its whole strength." They saw that this strength was considerable. Secretary of the Interior Caleb Smith, one of the party's most conservative members, reminded Chase that if Lincoln's administration failed to use that strength, its members would be held responsible. The obvious implication was that Republicans could expect to lose power—an understandable concern, and Republicans of all kinds were equally sure of how to correct the problem. By the summer of 1864, when Grant seemed mired in the wilderness and Sherman was slowly fighting his way through the deep South, Sumner voiced the conviction of many in his party when he fumed, "If a proper energy—'action'—'action'—'action'—had inspired the Government, it would have been already ended."[25]

Battling Generals, Battling One Another

It was a vicious circle. The shorter the war, the better Republicans looked; the longer the war, the better the chances of ending slavery—and of the rebels winning foreign aid by showing that they had the wherewithal to stave off the North. But the shorter the war, the more likely there was to be a winning general who threatened Republican power and republican government. As the party in power, Republicans were in a bind. They had confidence that their constituents would stand by them and the war as long as the government for which the party was responsible at least made progress. That demanded the kind of military leadership that Republicans feared on the ideological ground that a strong general might threaten the freedom, union, and power they envisioned, and on the political ground that a successful general might become a successful politician who threatened the party's primacy—and the ideology that unified the party.

These concerns manifested themselves in two ways that were largely unrelated, except in their links to the party's ideology. The first was oscillation. Morale varied as the war ebbed and flowed, although Republicans tried to stay optimistic, seeking to reassure the public and themselves, bearing in mind that large armies maneuver and often stay in place. In less than two years, said a Lincoln backer, "We have fought over a hundred battles, and driven the enemy within much narrower limits. We have lost nothing; we have gained much; and we hold all we gain." This pep talk reflected the party's general tendency to look to the future with hope and to the past as an object lesson and as part of a broader picture. In the summer of 1864, Strong observed from a dignified distance in New York, "In July, 1861, a Northern mob and a Southern mob came into collision at Bull Run, and the North was routed. In 1864, Northern veterans are meeting Southern veterans in Georgia and on the Shenandoah, and the case is altered." Yet Republicans wondered whether the government lived up to the faith the people placed in it and waged the war with proper vigor, and thus whether Northerners would stand by the government much longer. Massachusetts conservatives and moderates like Adams and Henry Dawes braced early for a long war, but western radicals like Wade and Chandler expected a quick victory. This belief in Northern potency created false hopes and anger, exactly the reactions that would accompany an unprecedented situation like a civil war, from a party just growing used to wielding power.[26]

The other manifestation of this concern was more complex: strained relations between Republicans and their generals. Of course, Republicans not only understood the political trade but shared views that those in the army hardly could be expected to have developed and refined as carefully or publicly as Republicans had. While they understood that politicians and generals alike hoped to restore the Union, the politicians doubted that the generals were devoted enough to the task to turn their backs on their past—to share the party's beliefs. This colored civil-military relations so much that no matter the circumstances, generals such as McClellan would have been unlikely to close the chasm even if they had wished to do so, which Republicans doubted. Their dealings with military leaders revealed a lot about them and their ideology: how these evolving views enhanced their distrust of the generals on whom so much of their hopes relied.[27]

While generals were generous, if mostly private, in their hatred for politicians, they expressed themselves in inverse proportion to success on the battlefield. This heightened Republican fears. Winning generals went about their business, but those who often lost or proved overrated were quick to project blame. McClellan attacked Lincoln and other Republicans while advising them on policy, creating the not entirely mistaken idea through his actions that he hoped to lead the Democratic opposition. His successor, Halleck, played politics and complained about those who did the same. When Sumner assailed General Charles Stone, accused of treason after the defeat at Ball's Bluff, Stone attacked "the vituperation of a well known coward from a safe distance in the rear." Yet success and disdain could be unrelated. Grant later exaggerated the authority that Lincoln gave him over the Union army, and Sherman could be brutal in describing politicians, even his brother John. Yet the less able William Rosecrans told Lincoln's critics, "He is in his right place. I am in a position to know, and if you live you will see that I am right about him." Some generals saw that they served at the pleasure of politicians, but few liked it. Fewer still seemed to grasp that those politicians wanted to retain power, and that required the kind of action that would please their constituents.[28]

Accordingly, Republicans felt that generals missed the larger meaning of the war and resented it when they tried to make policy on their own. Migrating from the Democrats, Stanton voiced a standard Republican view: "I think the General's true course is to mind his own Department and win a victory. After that all other things will be of easy settlement." Weary of droughts between victories, Republicans had no patience for generals who ignored the pressures the party faced from without and within. These disputes crossed and stayed within ideological and party lines. Radical general David Hunter made known his distaste for the machinations of *New York Tribune* editor Horace Greeley, with whom he often agreed. Hunter failed to grasp that his circulation across the North made Greeley a force for Republicans in the executive and legislative branches to reckon with—and the same was true, to varying degrees, of other editors and politicians. Generals and politicians rarely pleased one another, but Republican leaders were in an especially delicate position. What worked best on the battlefields and most pleased voters might differ entirely, and neither elected officials nor army commanders appreciated it when the other gave orders outside of the ranks. Republicans had won government power and had to expand their political power to keep it. The army would be a bulwark of their success, but even when successful it still seemed somehow untrustworthy to the party in power.[29]

Relations between Republicans and the military also suffered when the generals acted more like politicians than politicians did. Among generals, political machinations ran in three channels, all disturbing to Republicans and either antithetical or seemingly threatening to their beliefs. The first was military: jockeying in the army for position and promotion, and trying to aid their friends. For Scott and McClellan to open themselves to charges of basing military decisions on politics made matters worse. Old foes Thurlow Weed and the Blairs battled over Scott, and Henry Raymond of the *New York Times* accused McClellan of devoting too much time to building political support. Nor did it help that Halleck spent so much time lobbying inside and outside the army for command in the West, nor that McClellan seemed more determined to remove Halleck and Stanton than to defeat the enemy. To explain why the North had trouble subduing the South, Secretary of the Treasury Salmon Chase pointed to "too little scope for honorable ambition to rise" amid the dishonorable ambition that Republicans detected in too many generals. The party was out to refine the government to suit what it considered the goals of the virtuous founding fathers, and to hold onto power while depending for aid on an institution they found as questionable as an army. The back-stabbing in army headquarters seemed unbecoming, even frightening.[30]

What also irked Republicans about military politics was involvement in party politics. They felt that many generals saw the army as the way to a political future—a Democratic future. Ohio conservative Thomas Ewing told his officer son that "you have no right as a military officer to be a political propagandist. . . . The worst evil that could now befall our country were the getting up [of] political positions in the army." This expressed part of their distaste for a standing army, and the risk that Lincoln claimed to take with Hooker. While Republicans across the North warned against generals dallying with politics, especially with Democrats, McClellan constantly received reports from friends about what politicians said about him, and dispensed disdain in equal measure. Whether Republicans understood that generals who indulged in such activities were just acting like politicians mattered less than the threat they perceived in their behavior.[31]

Finally, generals faced the problem of how to handle politicians named to commands in their midst. They preferred to be rid of them—a reaction that was militarily correct, but politically unwise and counter to the channels in which Republican thought ran. Politicians became generals, a Lincoln ally said, "[t]o keep them from fighting against the war with their mouths," and those who stayed out of uniform often seemed to care more about gaining political support than about seeking able commanders. Seward won backing for the party from Irish leaders by asking them for advice on appointments; Sumner urged his Massachusetts colleague, Senator Henry Wilson, for brigadier.[32]

The other issue was whether politicians endangered more lives on the stump or the battlefield. Representative Henry Winter Davis, critical of Lincoln and suspicious of the army, heard rumors that he might be named a general and wrote, "I have a disgust at the thought of undertaking a duty any part of which I can't perform." Greeley's *Tribune* begged Lincoln to choose commanders on the basis of military ability but still pressed him in behalf of radicals of varying competence. Stanton, then outside the Cabinet looking in, wrote in June 1861 that army posts generally went to "persons whose only claim is their Republicanism,—broken-down politicians without experience, ability, or other merit." Strong asked, "Why will men of ability and reputation in civil affairs let themselves be deluded into the notion that they can handle armies?" One answer was that some wanted to help, while others succumbed to ambition. Another was that Republicans wanted to retain and enhance their power, and dispensing military patronage was a way to do it.[33]

Nor did Republicans hesitate to try to proselytize the army with their civilian ideology. Radicals especially worried about whether the military shared their belief in freedom and decided to do something about it. Installing party stalwarts in military posts might be helpful. Abolitionist Wendell Phillips said, "Let me make the Generals, and I don't care who makes the proclamations." In October 1862, Greeley complained, "If the officers who have a thousand times sworn they would resign in case this were made an 'Abolition War,' would only do it," the war would have been won within four months. Part of the problem, they felt, was that politicians appreciated the constitutional process that governed their duties, but the military was anti-constitutional and unfit for a republic. Even when the army pleased radicals—for example,

Hunter's emancipation order, which Lincoln rescinded—Davis denounced such "mischievous usurpations" as "unmilitary, unrepublican & insubordinate." When Yates warned of a likely military dictatorship, he voiced the fears of many Republicans. "The danger of wrecking the Republican institutions of this country in a military despotism is as imminent on the heels of a great success as after great disasters," the *Chicago Tribune* said. Capitalizing "republican" may have been an unintended irony: the rise of an antidemocratic group like the army might wreck the Republicans.[34]

The other irony regarding the party's ideology concerned its agreement on the need for the army to extend its power and reach, just as politicians questioned the wisdom and loyalty of generals from whom they expected such powerful action. When the fighting began, total war was anathema to Union generals. McClellan reminded his men to protect property and let civilians alone. Other generals voiced horror that their rebel counterparts used guerrilla tactics that seemed to violate rules of civilized warfare, rules they expected their men to follow as fighters for the right cause. But Republicans broke with McClellan's view. Irked at slow progress and high costs, they demanded confiscation of property, slaves and otherwise, and retributive justice. A sampling of the thoughts of various Republicans shows similarities in phrasing and attitude, and finally a belief in total war. *Harper's Weekly* deplored the conditions that Union prisoners endured at Richmond's Libby Prison and urged the government to retaliate toward its prisoners. At the crux of these demands was the hope of shortening the war, even solving the problems that caused it. Senator Lyman Trumbull said, "It is only by making this war terrible to traitors that our difficulties can be permanently settled," and his fellow Illinoisan, Yates, sought "stern, relentless, exterminating war." This attitude ranged the ideological spectrum: from radical to conservative, Republicans echoed Yates's demand. Republicans understood that power, in its most terrible form, would be required for the sake of freedom and union.[35]

One exemplar of these views was radical general David Hunter, who advocated emancipation on moral grounds and as a war measure. In April 1863, he complained to Jefferson Davis that the Union's newly enrolled black soldiers "have been cruelly murdered by your authorities, and others sold into slavery. Every outrage of this kind against the laws of war and humanity, which may take place in this Department, shall be followed by the immediate execution of the Rebel of the highest rank in my possession." In declaring all excuses unacceptable, he scorned the Southern defense of its cause. "You say you are fighting for liberty . . . liberty to keep four millions of your fellow-beings in ignorance and degradation . . . liberty to steal the products of their labor, exacted with many a cruel lash and bitter tear,—liberty to seduce their wives and daughters," he wrote, "and to sell your own children into bondage;—liberty to kill these children with impunity, when the murder cannot be proven by one of pure white blood. This is the kind of liberty—the liberty to do wrong—which Satan, Chief of the fallen Angels, was contending for when he was cast into Hell." This screed was radical, but Hunter's tones rang with his party's ideology: it would use its power to defend the government and the party's beliefs.[36]

The Distrusted Exception: Grant

The generals most responsible for the South's defeat and the triumph of Republican ideology demonstrated an irony of that ideology: they were graduates of the detested West Point, and more conservative on issues of importance to Republicans than were many party members. Yet more than any other generals, Ulysses Grant and William Sherman exemplified the kind of leadership and war that Republicans wanted. Grant did his job well and quietly, and rose to the top of the army as Republicans preferred: through demonstrated ability and demonstrable success. By contrast, Sherman had the "hysterical, unscrupulous energy" that Strong saw in the South and waged the total war the party deemed necessary for the Union, and thus freedom and power, to triumph. Between his approach and the instinctive distrust that politicians and generals shared, Sherman represented much that was right and wrong with how Republicans viewed the war and the men who fought it. Deferring to civilian power, he often voiced disdain for those civilians. As editor and politician Alexander McClure noted, Sherman was "one of the very few generals who seldom grieved Lincoln," and "never assumed to be wiser than the government," but he "had the most profound contempt for politicians in and out of the army."[37]

In Grant's case, one battle changed his perception while several altered his reputation. The battle of Shiloh, fought on 6 and 7 April

1862, proved nearly disastrous for the Union, and providential for how the war was fought and Republicans viewed it. Union military leaders—especially Grant as commanding general on the scene and Don Carlos Buell, who headed another army—received heavy criticism for the high death toll and their performance, including the failure to entrench their camp and rumors that they had let the South surprise them. His recent victories at Forts Henry and Donelson had catapulted Grant into national prominence, and certainly into Lincoln's consciousness: under pressure to fire him for the surprise and near-defeat, the president replied, "I can't spare this man; he fights." Almost as important, Shiloh convinced Grant that only the destruction of its armies would subdue the South, not a war of maneuver. After that his policy was to live off the land, supplying his armies with rebel property.[38]

The end came later than Republicans preferred, but the fighting that defeated the South was under the leadership, direct and indirect, of Grant. As a general in the West, first under Halleck and then on his own, he relentlessly pushed ahead and, when stopped at Vicksburg, besieged the enemy to harm the South and keep his army busy. He followed the same precepts as lieutenant-general, pounding the Army of Northern Virginia, forcing Lee to stretch his army to the breaking point. Sherman, Grant's favorite subordinate, acted similarly in destroying Dixie's spirit and resources as he swept through Georgia and up the coast. Yet while Grant was responsible for the army, the military theory came mainly from Lincoln and, to a lesser extent, Republicans who shared his ideas but lacked his power to enforce them.

Lincoln had implored his generals to concentrate on eliminating the rebel fighting force, rather than on a decisive victory that would give the Union control of the capital, Richmond; then, he believed, a Union victory would follow. As had several other generals, Grant planned to focus on Richmond, but Lincoln dissuaded him. Grant agreed, but not necessarily because he shared Lincoln's opinion of the correct strategy. Rather, as he had told another officer, "A sacrifice of my own feelings is no sacrifice when the good of the country calls for it." Grant later gave short shrift to Lincoln's military knowledge, but he never doubted who was commander in chief and who was the subordinate.[39]

Militarily, what Grant said and what both he and Lincoln did reflected Republican thought. Unlike other West Pointers, Grant was deferential. Lacking real military experience, Lincoln studied strategy, because he was commander in chief and shared his party's concerns about the army. He was aware of the need to juggle battlefield needs with the demands of public opinion. As the war went on, his growing confidence was evident in how quickly he fired poor commanders, in his impatience with finger-pointing, and in his habit of planning campaigns that might have worked if properly executed. While too many generals and Republicans targeted Richmond, Lincoln saw that victory would come only when the rebel armies were destroyed. After the disaster at Fredericksburg, he mused that "if the same battle were to be fought over again, every day, through a week of days, . . . the army under Lee would be wiped out to its last man, the Army of the Potomac would still be a mighty host, the war would be over, the Confederacy gone." Historians such as Gabor Boritt rightly cite the economic underpinnings of his strategy—control of the Mississippi, interest in new technology, reliance on the blockade, and the meritocratic rise of Grant and Sherman—but Lincoln believed in the military precept of overwhelming the opposition. That was Grant's strategy, with prodding from Lincoln and his party.[40]

Lincoln's ideas, and how Grant adopted and realized them, are the story of the war after Grant became lieutenant-general in February 1864. These ideas are also crucial to understanding Republican ideology. The party's belief in free labor reflected and affected its view that Northern society was superior to Southern society. The faster growth of the Northern populace was just one example of the proof Republicans could cite. And the war of attrition they practiced—for even if they felt otherwise, that is what it was—reflected their awareness that they could use this power on the South. "With our superiority in numbers and in resources, discipline would make us strong enough to conquer without first-rate generals," Strong said. The equally unmilitary Sumner noted the Army of the Potomac's size early in 1863 and wrote, "Where in history was such a force, thus appointed, gathered together." The Union armies were strong enough to do as Strong suggested and large enough to inspire Sumner's question. Their existence gave Republicans the power to realize their goals, and Lincoln and Grant understood how to use it. Their strategy won the war and was a victory for what Republicans believed. Yet while he did as the party wished, Grant faced distrust over his past: rumors of his drunkenness and his education at West Point. Even the most successful general excited Republican suspicions rooted in concerns about how that great power would be used.[41]

The Distrusted and Distrusting Exception: Sherman

As did most regular army men, and despite his brother John, Sherman provoked Republican distrust. Between his Southern friends from West Point and tenure at a Louisiana military academy, Sherman lacked anti-slavery ardor, which troubled party leaders. He replied that he followed orders, and John Sherman assured Chase that his brother was overcoming his West Point training and changing his opinion of slavery. But Sherman never hid his hatred for politicians. He made no friends when he declined a Blair proposal to become Cameron's aide, nor when he so exaggerated the number of rebels in Kentucky that he left his command and seemed to have suffered a nervous breakdown. The *Chicago Tribune*'s Horace White belittled him as "dyspeptic and laggard," and other editors and politicians assailed him for his part at Shiloh, when rebel forces allegedly surprised him and Grant. But Sherman initially drew little attention from Republicans, except as one of Grant's most trusted subordinates.[42]

Possessing perhaps the army's most original mind, Sherman revealed that he and Republicans were coming together—perhaps a sign of the party's success in broadening its base. From the outset, he marveled at the South's belief that it could "frame a Government better than that of Washington[,] Hamilton & Jefferson." He shared Republican hopes that Southern ardor would cool, but he saw that "the people are generally united in spirit and policy against us," and "the war will soon assume a turn to extermination, not of soldiers alone, that is the least part of the trouble, but the people." Living off the land was the answer, and he cut a swath of destruction across the South—along the Mississippi and on his famous march through Georgia. For Republicans it was an unusual moment: an anti-democratic army destroying the anti-democratic South, and using awesome power as the party wanted.[43]

Republicans admired Sherman's commitment to the Union and hatred for secession and its architects. While Butler created an uproar in New Orleans, Sherman made a similar pronouncement in

Memphis, refusing to "tolerate insults to our country or our cause," but he avoided controversy by declaring simply, "We must bear this in mind, that however peaceful things look, we are really at war; and much that looks like waste or destruction is only the removal of objects that obstruct our fire, or would afford cover to an enemy." In Atlanta, where Sherman's win fired the North's imagination and assured Lincoln's reelection, he replied to rebels seeking a reversal of his order to evacuate the city: "War is cruelty, and you cannot reform it; and those who brought war into our country deserve all the curses and maledictions a people can pour out." As Sherman felt about war, so Republicans felt about the South.[44]

The conservative general who hated politicians resembled Republicans in other ways: they may not have consciously changed, but circumstances forced the party to alter its earlier views and Sherman to overcome his sentimental feelings toward the South. With Sherman's success and how he achieved it came adoration even from Republicans who still doubted the army's loyalty. He was not only a winning general but an avenging angel. Republicans welcomed news that those who threatened their ascent to power, their platform's success, and above all the Union, were paying dearly for their apostasy. Marveling at "this daring and most sagacious chieftain," Motley asked, "Who can doubt that the cause of civilization and of human freedom must triumph under the guidance of such military genius as it now possesses?" Among conservatives, Strong hailed Sherman's actions, and Frank Blair, the general's admiring subordinate, was not alone in believing that "no victory which has been achieved during the war has done them greater damage & given greater prestige to our arms."[45]

This feeling was not mutual; Sherman's dislike for many Republicans and their views may have been due to his cantankerousness, or a sign of the distrust that military leaders felt for politics. Sherman blamed both parties for failing to prepare for war, complicating his work and making the Union look "pusillanimous and cowardly," the kind of rhetoric that Republicans aimed at Democrats but not at themselves. By threatening to quit when he disagreed with the Union's policies, whether on the war or on a command system that sometimes placed him below lesser generals, he acted as Republicans expected. He lamented their efforts to settle on a reconstruction policy when he felt that they should have concentrated on the war. He opposed soldiers electing officers, which

Republicans saw as a way to democratize an undemocratic army, "because an army is not a popular organization." He admired McClellan but dismissed his gentler view of the South: "Cut into them—not talk [to] them, and pursue till they cry enough."[46]

Even while expressing admiration for Sherman, Republicans doubted that he or any general deserved such praise, a sign of their continuing distrust for the army. Rumors spread that Sherman backed McClellan for president in 1864. Resenting his disdain for them, reporters often put him in the worst light. More pertinently, he seemed "very wrong-headed on Slavery," as Sumner lamented. Late in 1862, Chase credited rumors that Sherman had attacked his brother, a moderate, as "one of the—abolitionists who had brought on this war saying that he was ashamed to own you for a brother. Is it possible that the proslavery virus of West Point can have afflicted him in this way?" More confident in Sherman by 1865, Chase still proselytized him on blacks and black suffrage. While the general thanked Chase for his thoughts, he reported that slaves following the army endangered military success and "regard me as a second Moses or Aaron. I treat them as free and have as much trouble to protect them against the avaricious recruiting agents of the New England States as against their former masters." Reassuringly, Sherman held that civilians should decide what to do with ex-slaves, but as usual he had an opinion: he supported freedom but not equality, and doubted black suffrage because he preferred reducing the franchise to extending it, a view more undemocratic and Hamiltonian than racist. "But these are all matters subordinate to the issues of this war, which can alone be determined by war, and it depends on good armies of the best possible material and best disciplined, and these points engross my entire thoughts," he said. That was the kind of thinking that Republicans sought in their generals, partly out of fears of military usurpation, partly because it described themselves. The war had required them to refine their thinking to fit the circumstances.[47]

More important for Republicans, the war's end also ended Sherman's glittering reputation. While Grant voiced Lincoln's generous impulses at Appomattox on 9 April 1865, Sherman went further in talks with rebel General Joseph Johnston after Lincoln's assassination. Lincoln had advised Grant and Sherman not to "exact hard terms," but Sherman misread the changing tenor of the times. While the presidency changed hands smoothly, if violently, the government was in chaos: Lincoln murdered, Seward incapacitated, Stanton paranoid, Andrew Johnson unsure, everyone shocked. Republicans in particular wanted vengeance against the South. Sherman concluded that a few Southerners were creating the problem, and all "men of substance . . . sincerely want peace, and I do not believe they will resort to war again during this century. I have no doubt that they will in the future be perfectly subordinate to the laws of the United States." His agreement with Johnston reflected Appomattox more than the assassination. Conceding that the terms were subject to approval, they included recognition of state governments once their members took an oath, guarantees of their voting and property rights, and an assurance that the government would not "disturb any of the people by reason of the late war, so long as they live in peace and quiet and abstain from acts of armed hostility, and obey the laws in existence at their place of residence."[48]

Stanton was correct in that he had no choice but to overturn Sherman, but his response was undeservedly savage. Sherman's "practical acknowledgment of the rebel government" exceeded his authority. His effort to "re-establish the rebel State governments that had been overthrown at the sacrifice of many thousand loyal lives and immense treasure" might make it possible to restore slavery, protect the rebel debt, challenge loyal governments such as West Virginia, and override the confiscation laws. His terms of surrender "had been deliberately, repeatedly, and solemnly rejected by President Lincoln," and were "better terms than the rebels had ever asked in their most prosperous condition."[49]

For his part, feeling that "four years of patient, unremitting, and successful labor" entitled him to better, Sherman said, "I admit my folly in embracing in a military convention any civil matters; but, unfortunately, such is the nature of our situation that they seem inextricably united, and I understood from you at Savannah that the financial state of the country demanded military success, and would warrant a little bending to policy." When Stanton and Halleck attacked him before the Joint Committee, Sherman called it "a personal insult" and washed his hands of two superiors he had respected. Sherman also returned to one of his old themes, the evils of politicians: "Their minds are so absorbed with the horrid deformities of a few assassins and southern politicians that they overlook the wants and necessities of the great masses." That could have suggested a military presumption of knowing what was best for the Union, confirming civilian concerns that Republicans had voiced about the military throughout the war.[50]

Indeed, the controversy mixed Republican beliefs with the personalities that affected how those beliefs manifested themselves. While Sherman shared Grant's deference to civil authority, he liked to ponder policy, but without his friend's silence and subtlety. Whatever the merit of his ideas, they came from a general, making them suspect. After the war he said, "I don't care who is Governor or Legislator. Indeed, I would rather have a Rebel Governor than a milk and water Union imbecile." But Sherman failed to see his unpopularity with the press and Republican distrust of the army. He said, "I suppose I am too indifferent to newspapers and reporters but can't help it. That they are spies for the enemy, and are catering to the craving appetite of our people for wonders is so manifest that I feel a loathing towards them." Nor did he hesitate to say so. That would have been permissible if he avoided controversy in the aftermath of war, but reporters showed no sympathy and joined the Republican feeding frenzy.[51]

The controversy over Sherman brought all of the party's longstanding fears of military usurpation welling to the surface—especially for radicals who recalled his distaste for abolitionism. Republican criticism verged on the hysterical. In contrast to the disappointment that some expressed, even hardened realists like the moderate Fessenden attacked Sherman's "stupendous behavior"; conservative Senator Jacob Collamer, agreeing that his terms should be rejected, added that "to do it without stating any reasons for it would have been a very dangerous experiment both to the public and to the army." Chandler declared that Sherman "was the coming man of the Copperheads & this blunder had come just at the right time to destroy him," while Sumner believed rumors that Sherman hoped to be the Democratic candidate for president—an odd interpretation of the actions of a general whose main problem seemed to be contempt for politicians.[52]

Neither Sherman nor his defenders helped his cause. When his army joined the grand review in Washington and Sherman approached the stand, Stanton extended his hand. When Sherman snubbed him, Republicans were irate. Trumbull fumed that he would fire him: "As a private individual, General Sherman of course has the right to be discourteous, if such are his tastes, but at the head of his army, in the discharge of official duties, he has no right to vent his spleen towards those in authority." This typified the party's fear of military power and its quest to expand its power, but was an odd view for those who tolerated excesses by radical generals. Even Sherman's brother deemed his terms to Johnston "inadmissible," but his tone with Stanton suggested that Republicans accepted power politics: "I do not wish General Sherman to be unjustly dealt with, and I know that you will not permit it." Even though he was disappointed in all concerned, Grant bristled at the criticism: "It is infamous—infamous! After four years of such service as Sherman has done—that he should be used like this!"[53]

Grant unwittingly captured the significance of the outcry. Both sides were right. Republicans saw a general trying to settle issues better left to civilian leaders; Sherman meant well but failed to consider public opinion and how the unprecedented act of assassination would shift it—as a politician might have. Sherman correctly felt betrayed: after displaying unbending unionism and military genius, he merited better. Ultimately, Republicans lacked abiding faith in the army's loyalty. For every Grant and Sherman, a McClellan had raised doubts. Thus, Secretary of the Treasury Hugh McCulloch saw a higher result than assuring that a deservedly respected general had been cut down to size: "If Gen. Sherman, after his magnificent campaign, can be quietly displaced, I think there will be no doubt resting upon the minds of even the most skeptical, that a government of the people is the strongest government in the world.[54]

That government had indeed proved strong enough to survive a plethora of problems—not only a civil war, but battles between the Republicans in charge of the government and the generals assigned to win that war, and feuds within political and military ranks. In October 1861, War Democrat George Bancroft told soldiers, "Cease to be men of Massachusetts, men of New England, men even of the North—be Americans," and so they became. Although fundamental social and cultural divisions between the North and South persisted, one result of the war was a reconstructed nation without slavery, the key point of disagreement. A related result was the success of the platform on which Lincoln ran and won in 1860—so successful that the country went beyond stopping the growth of slavery and ended it.[55]

The party's belief in freedom and union had spread across the country, and where it had not spread, Republicans were determined to make it so, changing the Constitution and stretching it to new limits, and imposing federal control in ways they had never before suggested. Indeed, Medill, the *Chicago Tribune*'s anti-military radical editor, surveyed Southern intransigence two months after Lincoln died and conceded, "The North must either maintain a large standing army at a heavy cost in that country in order to enforce the laws and support the feeble loyal whites, or it must allow the blacks to support them with their votes. . . . It is a great blunder, and the mischievous fruits will be held to our lips hereafter." For Medill to suggest a standing army shows how much Republicans had changed from the antebellum free labor party that had stood on the cusp of power. Accomplishing their goals as the wartime party responsible for the government had required power, and Republicans had exercised it—at times too cautiously, at times too zealously. Ironically, the crux of that power had been the military, toward which the party often demonstrated contempt and disrespect.[56]

To preserve and perpetuate freedom and union, Republicans required the political power to carry the public with them, the governmental power to make policy, and, at least for the duration of the war, the military power to reunite the divided country and thereby achieve the goals contained within that ideology. They had ardently sought the first of these, welcomed the second despite misgivings about the circumstances surrounding it and the freedom to criticize that they seemed loath to surrender, and feared the third because they doubted that the military sought to do with its power as Republicans wished. That fear manifested itself in the party's response to how the war was fought and who led the fighting of it. Their reaction was inseparable from the party's ideology: Republicans attacked the army and the generals on whom their future and the country's future depended at least in part because of their belief in the importance of freedom, union, and power—all tied together and exercised in the right way, for the right reasons.

Notes

1. Lincoln to Joseph Hooker, Washington, 26 January 1863, in *CW,* vol. 6, 78–79. Historians have pointed out that Lincoln almost certainly never mailed the letter, but resorted to a favorite practice of reading it aloud to the addressee.

2. Don E. Fehrenbacher, "Lincoln's Wartime Leadership: The First Hundred Days," *Journal of the Abraham Lincoln Association* 9 (1987): 11. See

also T. Harry Williams, *Lincoln and His Generals* (New York: Grosset and Dunlap, 1952).

3. William T. Sherman to F. A. P. Barnard, Camp on River, 18 miles from Vicksburg, 28 July 1863, F. A. P. Barnard Papers (Barnard ms), CU.

4. Bailyn, *The Ideological Origins of the American Revolution,* 62–68; Paludan, *"A People's Contest,"* 46–49. My interpretation of the Revolutionary era and the army's role is based largely on Bailyn and three other books: Fred Anderson, *A People's Army: Massachusetts Soldiers and Society in the Seven Years' War* (Chapel Hill: University of North Carolina Press, 1984); Charles Royster, *A Revolutionary People at War: The Continental Army and American Character, 1775–1783* (Chapel Hill: University of North Carolina Press, 1979); Garry Wills, *Cincinnatus: George Washington and the Enlightenment* (Garden City, N.Y.: Doubleday, 1984). My view of Civil War soldiers is based on Reid Mitchell, *Civil War Soldiers* (New York: Viking, 1988), and two works by McPherson: *What They Fought For,* and *For Cause and Comrades.*

5. Horatio Woodman to John A. Andrew, Boston, 15 November 1861, in *Massachusetts Historical Society Proceedings* 57 (October 1924–June 1925): 318–19; Paludan, *"A People's Contest,"* 59, 133–34; *CG,* 37, 1, 4 July 1861, 4–5. See also *CG,* 37, 2, 3 February 1862, 613 (Representatives Frank Blair of Missouri and Owen Lovejoy of Illinois); *CG* 37, 3, 5 January 1863, 187 (Trumbull); William Dennison to John Sherman, Columbus, 17 July 1861, Sherman ms, Volume 30, LC; Stampp, *Indiana Politics,* 119; Albert Gallatin Browne, *Sketch of the Official Life of John A. Andrew as Governor of Massachusetts* (New York: Hurd and Houghton, 1868), 90–94.

6. Seward to Webb, Circular No. 39, Washington, 12 August 1863, Webb Family ms, NYPL.

7. 4 June 1864, in Nevins and Thomas, eds., *The Diary of George Templeton Strong,* vol. 3, 454; *CG,* 37, 1, 13 July 1861, 114 (King); Adams to John Gorham Palfrey, London, 27 November 1862, Adams Family ms, Series II, Reel 168, MHS; Adams to Richard Henry Dana Jr., London, 5 April and 29 July 1863, ibid., Reel 169; William S. McFeely, *Yankee Stepfather: General O. O. Howard and the Freedmen* (New York: W. W. Norton, 1969), 31.

8. Lincoln to Robert H. Milroy, Washington, 29 June 1863, in *CW,* vol. 6, 309; Milroy to Andrew Johnson, Rensselaer, 23 August 1865, typescript, Kenneth Williams ms, Box 1, IU; Barnett to Barlow, Washington, 2 June 1863, Barlow ms, Box 45, HL; Frank Blair to Montgomery Blair, n.p., 13 September 1862, Blair-Lee Family ms, Box 42, Princeton.

9. "Message of the President," Report of the Secretary of War, 1 July 1861, *CG,* 37, 1, Appendix, 12; Chase to Greeley, Washington, 21 May 1862, Greeley ms, Box 3, NYPL; Chase to Robert Denniston, Washington, 25

September 1862, Chase ms, Microfilm Edition, Reel 23; Fischer, *Lincoln's Gadfly,* 114–15; Thomas and Hyman, *Stanton,* 159, 241, 365–66.

10. Paludan, *"A People's Contest,"* 53, 63–64; Nichols, "Sherman," in Wheeler, ed, *For the Union,* 413; *CG,* 37, 1, 11 July 1865, 75; ibid., 12 July 1861, 89; ibid., 18 July 1861, 180; ibid., 37, 2, 23 December 1861, 180; ibid., 38, 2, 3 March 1865, 1384; Hyman, *Era of the Oath,* 16; Trefousse, *Benjamin Franklin Wade,* 149–51, 195, and *passim.*

11. *Chicago Tribune,* 15 September 1862, typescript, Nevins ms, Box 172, CU; Greeley to Charles Halpine, New York, 24 and 31 August 1862, Halpine ms, Box 2, HL; *New York Tribune,* 8 August 1863; *New York Times,* 12 June 1861; Paludan, *"A People's Contest,"* 83–84; Hans L. Trefousse, *Ben Butler: The South Called Him Beast!* (New York: Twayne, 1957), 81; Wheeler, ed., *For the Union,* 341.

12. Charles J. Stille, "How A Free People Conduct A Long War: A Chapter from English History" (Philadelphia: Collins, 1862), 35; Adams to Richard Henry Dana Jr., London, 5 April 1863, Adams Family ms, Series II, Reel 169, MHS; Adams to Palfrey, London, 27 November 1862, ibid., Reel 168; "Speech of the Mayor" (George Opdyke), "Character and Results of the War," 5; Trefousse, *Ben Butler, passim;* Oliver P. Morton to Lincoln, Washington, 7 October 1862, in Foulke, *Life of Oliver P. Morton,* vol. 1, 196–97; Smith, *Colfax,* 166.

13. *CG,* 37, 1, 10 July 1861, 41, 44; 16 July 1861, 141; 15 July 1861, 124–25.

14. *CG,* 37, 1, 6 July 1861, 17; "Message of the President," Report of the Secretary of War, 1 July 1861, *CG,* 37, 1, Appendix, 11; Schurz to Petrasch, Camp near Bridgeport, Alabama, 3 October 1863, and Lookout Valley, 23 December 1863, in Schafer, ed., *Schurz Letters,* 287–88; Schurz to Henry Meyer, Bethlehem, 25 March 1865, ibid., 321–24; Rollo Ogden, *Life of Edwin L. Godkin,* 2 vols. (New York: Macmillan, 1907), vol. 1, 207; Stille, "How A Free People Conduct A Long War," 31.

15. *CG,* 37, 1, 11 July 1861, 72; ibid., 15 July 1861, 124; ibid., 22 July 1861, 221; Adams to Seward, London, 24 March 1865, 908, U.S. Dept. of State, *Foreign Affairs 1865,* vol. 1, 262; John Lothrop Motley to William Hunter, Vienna, 111, 27 June 1865, U.S. Dept. of State, *Foreign Affairs 1865,* vol. 3, 29–30; Hugh McCulloch to Fessenden, Washington, 8 May 1865, Treasury Department Letterbook, March–May 1865, McCulloch ms, IU; McCulloch to John Ross, Washington, 31 July 1865, Treasury Department Letterbook, 23 May–14 August 1865; Samuel R. Curtis to Henry B. Curtis, Milwaukee, 22 May 1865, Samuel R. Curtis ms, Box 2, HL; Nicolay, *Lincoln's Secretary,* 134–36; Logsdon, *Horace White,* 111.

16. King to Doolittle, Ogdensburgh, 22 September 1863, Doolittle ms, NYPL; Bigelow to Kolisch, Paris, 9 April 1863, Bigelow ms, Box 1, ibid.; Greeley to O. D. Case, New York, 1 May 1864, Greeley ms, Box 2, ibid. On reform movements, see especially Walters, *American Reformers.*

17. *Chicago Tribune,* 15 November 1861, in Kinsley, *The Chicago Tribune,* vol. 1, 215–16; Diary of Bigelow, ca. 14 September 1862, Bigelow ms, NYPL.

18. Bigelow to Hargreaves, Paris, 17 July 1862, Bigelow ms, Box 1, NYPL; Bigelow to Miss Bryant, Paris, 22 October 1862, Bryant-Godwin ms, Box 4, ibid.; 31 July 1864, in Nevins and Thomas, eds., *The Diary of George Templeton Strong,* vol. 3, 468–69; *Brooklyn Daily Union,* 4 November 1862, in John H. Krenkel, ed., *Richard Yates: Civil War Governor, by Richard Yates and Catharine Yates Pickering* (Danville, Ill.: Interstate Printers, 1966), 180–81.

19. *CG,* 37, 2, 5 December 1861, 17; ibid., 14 February 1862, 838; ibid., 2 April 1862, 1505; Curry, *Blueprint for Modern America,* 232; Magdol, *Owen Lovejoy,* 312; Trefousse, *The Radical Republicans,* 178 and 252, and chapters 4–6; Trefousse, *Benjamin Franklin Wade,* 151; Chase to James Birney, Washington, 25 October 1861, "Copies of Special Letters, 1861–1865, Bound," Chase ms, HSP; Thurlow Weed to Charles Halpine, Albany, 27 October 1861, Halpine ms, Box 1, HL; A thoughtful rehabilitation of the committee's reputation is Hans L. Trefousse, "The Joint Committee on the Conduct of the War: A Reassessment," *Civil War History* 10, no. 1 (Spring 1964): 5–19. A recent, less complimentary study is Bruce Tap, *Over Lincoln's Shoulder: The Committee on the Conduct of the War* (Lawrence: University Press of Kansas, 1998).

20. Wilmer C. Harris, *Public Life of Zachariah Chandler, 1851–1875* (Lansing: Michigan Historical Bureau, 1917), 57–58; Oates, *With Malice Toward None,* 264–65; McClellan to Halleck, Washington, 3 March 1862, *OR,* I, XI, III, 8; Trefousse, *Benjamin Franklin Wade,* 153, 175; Thomas and Hyman, *Stanton,* 176–77; Samuel G. Ward to Barlow, Washington, 18 March 1862, Barlow ms, Box 44, HL; McClellan to Mary McClellan, Washington, 26 October 1861, George B. McClellan Papers (McClellan ms), LC, in Stephen W. Sears, ed., *The Civil War Papers of George B. McClellan: Selected Correspondence, 1860–1865* (New York: Ticknor and Fields, 1989), 112; ibid., Fairfax Court House, 11 March 1862, 202; ibid., Camp Winfield Scott, 19 April 1862, 244.

21. Thomas and Hyman, *Stanton,* 148, 169–70, 183–84, 260–61; Trefousse, *Benjamin Franklin Wade,* 351–52, n. 15; Ward to Barlow, Washington, 16 March 1862, Barlow ms, Box 44, HL; Hendrick, *Lincoln's War Cabinet,* 347; Blaine, *Twenty Years of Congress,* vol. 1, 395.

22. Chandler to Letitia Chandler, Washington, 16 and 24 January 1865, Chandler ms, LC, in George, *Zachariah Chandler,* 119; Trefousse, *Benjamin*

Franklin Wade, 185–86, 195–203, 208; 22 January 1865, in Nevins and Thomas, eds., *The Diary of George Templeton Strong,* vol. 3, 546–47; Daniel Sickles to Greeley, Washington, 25 April 1862, Greeley ms, Box 3, NYPL; Charles P. Stone to Barlow, Fort Hamilton, 26 June 1862, Barlow ms, Box 43, HL; Barnett to Barlow, Washington, 18 May 1863, Barlow ms, Box 45; Curry, *Blueprint for Modern America,* 232–34; Dell, *Lincoln and the War Democrats,* 138–39; *CG,* 37, 1, 12 July 1861, 89; ibid., 37, 2, 23 December 1861, 162.

23. Wade to Caroline Wade, Washington, 25 October 1861, Wade ms, LC; *Cincinnati Gazette,* 24 October 1864, in Wheeler, ed., *For the Union,* 171; Wade to Dana, Washington, 3 February 1862, Dana ms, LC; Oates, *With Malice Toward None,* 293; Trefousse, *Benjamin Franklin Wade,* 207–14, 353, n. 22; Trefousse, *The Radical Republicans,* 253.

24. Trefousse, *Benjamin Franklin Wade,* 207–14, 353, n. 22; Trefousse, *The Radical Republicans,* 253; Oates, *With Malice Toward None,* 293; Simpson, *Let Us Have Peace,* 63–64; John G. Nicolay, "Lincoln Memoranda," Nicolay ms, Box 10, LC.

25. *Chicago Tribune,* 12 January 1862, in Kinsley, *The Chicago Tribune,* vol. 1, 221; Morrill to Ruth Morrill, Washington, ca. September 1862, in Parker, *The Life and Public Services of Justin Smith Morrill,* 131; Smith to Chase, Bedford Springs, 30 July 1862, Chase ms, Box 10, HSP; Sumner to Lieber, Boston, 19 August 1864, in Series I, Reel 64, SP; Sanford to Webb, Turin, 5 September 1861, Webb ms, Box 7, Sterling Library, Yale University; *CG,* 37, 3, Appendix, "Report of the Secretary of War," 2 December 1862, 30.

26. Charles G. Ames, "Stand by the President! An Address delivered before the National Union Association, of Cincinnati, March 6, 1863" (Philadelphia: King and Baird, 1863), 13; 23 October 1864, Nevins and Thomas, eds., *The Diary of George Templeton Strong,* vol. 3, 505; Adams to Thomas Corwin, London, 1 September 1861, Adams Family ms, Series II, Reel 165, MHS; Dawes to Ella Dawes, Washington, 25 and 26 July 1861, and 27 August 1861, Dawes ms, Box 12, LC; Wade to Chandler, Jefferson, 8 October 1861, Chandler ms, Reel 1, LC; Chandler to Letitia Chandler, Washington, 17 September 1861, ibid.; William Swinton, "The Military and Naval Situation, and the Glorious Achievements of Our Soldiers and Sailors" (Washington, D.C.: Union Congressional Committee, 1864), 13–14.

27. Hendrick, *Lincoln's War Cabinet,* 338.

28. Stone to Sumner, Poolesville, 23 December 1861, in Reel 24, SP; Simpson, *Let Us Have Peace,* 54–55; William T. Sherman, *Memoirs of General William T. Sherman. By Himself,* 2 vols. (New York: D. Appleton and Company, 1875), vol. 1, 185–86; James R. Gilmore, *Personal Recollections of Abraham Lincoln and the Civil War* (Boston: L. C. Page, 1898), 134–47; Horner, *Lincoln and Greeley,* 332; George B. McClellan to Mary McClellan, Washington, 11

October 1861, in Sears, ed., *The Civil War Papers of George B. McClellan,* 106–07, and Berkeley, 17 July 1862, 362–63; McClellan to Stanton, Headquarters Army of the Potomac, Savage Station, 28 June 1862, *OR,* Series I, Volume XI, Section 1, 61; McClellan to Lincoln, Camp near Harrison's Landing, 7 July 1862, ibid., 73–74; Hesseltine, *Lincoln's Plan of Reconstruction,* 70; Halleck to Dix, St. Louis, 25 November 1861, Dix ms, Box 6, CU; Stephen E. Ambrose, *Halleck: Lincoln's Chief of Staff* (Baton Rouge: Louisiana State University Press, 1962), 102, 128, 205–6; Halleck, "Politico-historical argument against disunion," ca. 1861, Eldridge Civil War ms, Box 23, HL.

29. Thomas and Hyman, *Stanton,* 133; David Hunter to Halpine, Washington, 21 July and 1 August 1863, Halpine ms, Box 2, HL; Colfax to Greeley, South Bend, 14 June 1861, Greeley ms, Box 7, LC; McClellan, General Orders, No. 154, Headquarters Army of the Potomac, Camp near Harrison's Landing, 9 August 1862, *OR,* I, XI, III, 364.

30. James E. Harvey to Webb, Lisbon, 12 June 1863, Webb ms, Box 11, Sterling Library, Yale University; Henry Cooke to Jay Cooke, n.p., 2 September 1862, in Oberholtzer, *Jay Cooke,* vol. 1, 202–3; Smith, *The Francis Preston Blair Family,* vol. 2, 279–81; *CG,* 37, 1, 1 August 1861, 386–88 (Frank Blair); Raymond, *The Life and Public Services of Abraham Lincoln,* 316–17; McClellan to Mary McClellan, Camp near Sharpsburg, 20 September 1862, McClellan ms, LC, in Sears, ed., *The Civil War Papers of George B. McClellan,* 473; *New York Times,* 11 April 1865; Simpson, *Let Us Have Peace,* 73–74, 90, 279, n. 13; Chase to Greeley, Washington, 7 September 1862, Greeley ms, Box 3, NYPL; Randall and Current, *The Last Full Measure,* 351–52.

31. Thomas Ewing to Hugh Ewing, Lancaster, 29 November 1861, Hugh Ewing ms, Box 2, Ohio Historical Society; *Cleveland Leader,* 31 March 1862, transcription in Cleveland Newspaper Digest, Ohio Historical Society; McClellan to Mary McClellan, Camp Lincoln, 22 June 1862, McClellan ms, LC, in Sears, ed., *The Civil War Papers of George B. McClellan,* 305; S. L. M. Barlow to McClellan, n.p., 17 June 1862, in Sears, ed., *The Civil War Papers of George B. McClellan,* 306; James B. McPherson to Barlow, Vicksburg, 23 October 1863, Barlow ms, HL, Box 47; Charles P. Stone to Barlow, 1st Brigade, 2d Division, 5th Corps, 5 September 1864, ibid., Box 55; Fitz-John Porter to Barlow, Black Hawk, 3 July and 27 August 1864, ibid., Box 54; McClellan to Barlow, Orange, 13 October 1864, ibid., Box 53.

32. Oates, *With Malice Toward None,* 239; Seward to "My Dear Archbishop," 7 August 1861, H. Browne Papers (H. Browne ms), CU; Henig, *Henry Winter Davis,* 163; Nicolay to Sumner, Washington, 11 September 1861, Reel 23, SP.

33. Henig, *Henry Winter Davis,* 163; *New York Tribune,* 9 May 1863; Stanton to Dix, Washington, 11 June 1861, in George C. Gorham, *Life and*

Public Services of Edwin M. Stanton, 2 vols. (Boston: Houghton Mifflin, 1899), vol. 1, 217–18; Trefousse, *Ben Butler,* 146, 153; Ambrose, *Halleck,* 168, 206; Samuel R. Curtis to Henry B. Curtis, Ft. Leavenworth, 12 December 1864, Curtis ms, Box 2, HL; Grant to Halleck, 1 July 1864, *OR,* I, XL, 2, 558–59; Hunt, *Israel, Elihu, and Cadwallader Washburn,* 360.

34. Bartlett, *Wendell Phillips,* 264; Greeley to H. S. Randall, New York, 2 October 1862, Greeley ms, Chicago Historical Society; Egle, ed., *Andrew Gregg Curtin,* 321–22; Henig, *Henry Winter Davis,* 173; Yates to John Turner, Springfield, 18 September 1862, Turner ms, Box 2, Illinois State Historical Library; Chandler to Chase, Detroit, 13 September 1862, Chase ms, Box 3, HSP; *Chicago Tribune,* 20 September 1862, in Kinsley, *The Chicago Tribune,* vol. 1, 252.

35. McClellan to Lincoln, "Memorandum," 4 August 1861, *OR,* I, V, 6; General Orders, No. 154, Headquarters Army of the Potomac, Camp near Harrison's Landing, 9 August 1862, ibid., XI, III, 364; James H. Lane to General S. D. Sturgis, Headquarters Kansas Brigade, Kansas City, 3 October 1861, ibid., I, III, 516; *Harper's Weekly,* 9 January 1864, 18; White, *The Life of Lyman Trumbull,* 171–72; Yates to Lincoln, Springfield, 11 July 1862, Lincoln ms, LC, in Krenkel, ed., *Richard Yates,* 174–75; *Chicago Tribune,* 31 July 1862, ibid.; Henig, *Henry Winter Davis,* 174–75; *CG,* 37, 3, 9 December 1862, 36 (Doolittle); Norman Graebner, "Conservative Statesman," in Graebner, ed., *The Enduring Lincoln,* 79; "Copy of Speech delivered at White River Junction, July 21, 1863, on my 5th nomination to Congress," Justin S. Morrill ms, No. 1146, Box 1, CR.

36. Hunter to Jefferson Davis, Port Royal, 23 April 1863, in Ira Berlin, et al., eds., *Free at Last: A Documentary History of Slavery, Freedom, and the Civil War* (New York: New Press, 1992), 448–49. See also Edward A. Miller, *Lincoln's Abolitionist General: The Biography of David Hunter* (Columbia: University of South Carolina Press, 1997).

37. 15 August 1861, in Nevins and Thomas, eds., *The Diary of George Templeton Strong,* vol. 3, 175; McClure, *Lincoln and Men of War-Times,* 229; Charles Royster, *The Destructive War: William Tecumseh Sherman, Stonewall Jackson, and the Americans* (New York: Knopf, 1991); and Hirshson, *The White Tecumseh.*

38. Ulysses S. Grant, *Personal Memoirs of U.S. Grant,* 2 vols. (New York: Charles L. Webster, 1885), vol. 1, 368; Mary Drake McFeely and William S. McFeely, eds., *Ulysses S. Grant: Memoirs and Selected Letters; Personal Memoirs of U.S. Grant; Selected Letters, 1839–1865* (New York: Library of America, 1990), 246–47; McClure, *Lincoln and Men of War-Times,* 193–96; Simpson, *Let Us Have Peace,* xvii, 8–9; *Chicago Tribune,* 10 April 1862, in Kinsley, *The Chicago Tribune,* vol. 1, 233; Cadwallader Washburn to Elihu Washburne,

Benton Barracks, 9 April 1862, in Hunt, *Israel, Elihu, and Cadwallader Washburn,* 335; William T. Sherman to Thomas Ewing Jr., copy, Camp Shiloh, 4 April 1862, Thomas Ewing and Family ms, Volume 13, LC.

39. Grant to Brigadier General Benjamin M. Prentiss, Headquarters District of Southeastern Missouri, Cairo, 3 September 1861, *OR,* I, III, 147. John Y. Simon, "Commander in Chief Lincoln and General Grant," in John Y. Simon and Harold Holzer, eds., *The Lincoln Forum: Rediscovering Abraham Lincoln* (New York: Fordham University Press, 2002), 16–33.

40. Barnett to Barlow, Washington, 2 June 1863, Barlow ms, Box 45, HL; Williams, *Lincoln and His Generals, passim;* Oates, *With Malice Toward None,* 219–20, 247; Boritt, *Lincoln and the Economics of the American Dream,* 268–74; Edward Hagerman, *The American Civil War and the Origins of Modern Warfare: Ideas, Organization, and Field Command* (Bloomington: Indiana University Press, 1988), 67; Nicolay, *Lincoln's Secretary,* 181; Herman Hattaway, "Lincoln's Presidential Example in Dealing with the Military," *Papers of the Abraham Lincoln Association* 7 (1985): 19–29; Fehrenbacher, "Lincoln's Wartime Leadership," 11; Thomas and Hyman, *Stanton,* 170–71, 197; "Conversation between President Lincoln and Col. Zagoni," 15 June 1862, Gay ms, Box 76, CU; *New York Tribune,* 28 April 1863.

41. 7 September 1862, in Nevins and Thomas, eds., *The Diary of George Templeton Strong,* vol. 3, 253; Sumner to Lieber, Washington, 23 January 1863, in Series I, Reel 64, SP; Motley to William L. Dayton, Vienna, 8 January 1862, Dayton ms, Box 3, Princeton University; "Suspense," Washington, 23 January 1863, in Peter J. Staudenraus, ed., *Mr. Lincoln's Washington: Selections from the Writings of Noah Brooks, Civil War Correspondent* (South Brunswick, N.J.: Thomas Yoseloff, 1967), 75–76; "No Failure for the North," *Atlantic Monthly,* reprinted as Loyal Publication Society No. 11 (New York: Wm. C. Bryant & Co., 1863), 9–10.

42. John Sherman to Chase, Mansfield, 27 October 1861, and 28 September 1862, Chase ms, Box 9, HSP; Chase to Sherman, Washington, 2 January 1865, "Copies of Special Letters, 1861–1865, Bound," ibid.; *Chicago Tribune,* 22 and 23 January 1862, in Logsdon, *Horace White,* 84; Brigadier General William T. Sherman to Colonel Turchin, Louisville, 15 October 1861, *OR,* I, IV, 307; Sherman to J. H. Hammond, fragment, n.p., ca. 1862, Ewing and Family ms, Volume 15, LC; McFeely, *Yankee Stepfather,* 18–19; Thomas and Hyman, *Stanton,* 343–45; Sherman, *Memoirs,* vol. 1, 171–74, 185–89, 220, 232–33, 249, 267–68, 285; Winfield Scott Kerr, *John Sherman: His Life and Public Services,* 2 vols. (Boston: Sherman, French, 1906), 164–65.

43. Sherman to Thomas Hunton, Memphis, 24 August 1862, in Berlin, et al., eds., *Free at Last,* 68–69; Sherman to Alvin P. Hovey, Memphis, 29 October 1862, Hovey ms, IU; Sherman to Chase, Louisville, 14 October

1861, Chase ms, Box 9, HSP; Sherman to Thomas Ewing Jr., Camp Shiloh, 4 April 1862, Ewing and Family ms, Volume 13, LC; Sherman, *Memoirs,* vol. 1, 171; Sherman to Chase, Memphis, 11 August 1862, ibid., 286; Sherman to Grant, Near Memphis, 10 March 1864, ibid., 428–29; Hagerman, *The American Civil War and the Origins of Modern Warfare,* 207–08.

44. Sherman, *Memoirs,* vol. 1, 300–301, and vol. 2, 583, 593–95, 603–4; McCulloch to Susan McCulloch, Washington, 25 September 1864, McCulloch ms, 1846–65, IU; Sherman to James M. Cahoun, E. E. Rawson, and L. C. Wells, in the field, Atlanta, 12 September 1864, Sherman ms, NYPL; "William T. Sherman to John B. Hood, Headquarters Military Division of the Mississippi and in the Field, Atlanta, September 10, 1864" (New York: Loyal Publication Society, No. 61, 1864).

45. Motley to Seward, Vienna, 15 April 1865, 95, *Foreign Affairs 1865,* vol. 3, 17–18; 9 December 1864, in Nevins and Thomas, eds., *The Diary of George Templeton Strong,* vol. 3, 527; 22 December 1864, ibid., 531; Frank Blair to Francis Preston Blair, near Savannah, 16 December 1864, in Smith, *The Francis Preston Blair Family,* vol. 2, 180; and Fayetteville, 12 March 1865, Blair-Lee Family ms, Box 6, Princeton; Charles L. Wilson to Dudley, Chicago, 12 March 1865, Dudley ms, Box 24, HL; *Chicago Tribune,* 22 February 1865, in Kinsley, *The Chicago Tribune,* vol. 1, 367.

46. Sherman, *Memoirs,* vol. 1, 359, vol. 2, 874, 877; John Sherman to William Sherman, Washington, 16 and 23 February 1863, William T. Sherman ms, LC, in Nichols, "Sherman," in Wheeler, ed., *For the Union,* 413–14; William T. Sherman to McClellan, 11 October 1864, McClellan ms, LC, in Sears, ed., *The Civil War Papers of George B. McClellan,* 604; Ambrose, *Halleck,* 16, 157, 160–61; John Sherman to Chase, Cincinnati, 10 September 1862, Chase ms, Box 9, HSP.

47. Edwin L. Godkin to Frederick Law Olmsted, n.p., 25 December 1864, in Ogden, *Life of Edwin L. Godkin,* vol. 1, 232; Sumner to Elizabeth, Duchess of Argyll, Washington, 7 February 1865, in Series II, Reel 79, SP; Chase to John Sherman, Washington, 20 September 1862, Sherman ms, Volume 52, LC; William T. Sherman to Chase, Savannah, 11 January 1865, Chase ms, Box 9, HSP; Charles James to John Sherman, New York, 2 September 1864, Sherman ms, Volume 73, LC; and 12 September 1864, Sherman ms, Volume 74, LC.

48. Simpson, *Let Us Have Peace,* 78, 98; Sherman to Grant and Halleck, Raleigh, 18 April 1865, in Sherman, *Memoirs,* vol. 2, 842–44; Sherman to Grant, Pocotaligo, 29 January 1865, ibid., 740; Sherman to Chase, Beaufort Harbor, 6 May 1865, Sherman Civil War ms, NYHS; Sherman to Major General Kilpatrick, in the field, Raleigh, 14 April 1865, typescript, Sherman ms, NYPL; Ambrose, *Halleck,* 198–99.

49. U.S. Dept. of State, *Foreign Affairs 1865,* vol. 1, 329–30; Howard to Sherman, 12 May 1865, in Gorham, *Life and Public Services of Edwin M. Stanton,* vol. 2, 198; Thomas and Hyman, *Stanton,* 402–18.

50. Sherman, *Memoirs,* vol. 2, 850–51, 861–62; Ambrose, *Halleck,* 200–202; Sherman to John M. Schofield, Camp near Washington, 6 and 28 May 1865, Barney ms, Box 28, HL.

51. Sherman to James Wilson, Lancaster, 25 June 1865, typescript, Adams Family ms, IV, May–June 1865, Reel 575, MHS; Sherman to Thomas Ewing Jr., copy, Camp Shiloh, 4 April 1862, Ewing and Family ms, Volume 13, LC; John Hayes to Gay, Vicksburg, 26 February 1864, and St. Louis, 8 May 1864, Gay ms, Reel 2, CU; James Swinton to Washburne, New York, 13 July 1863, Washburne ms, LC, summary, Nevins ms, Box 5, HL.

52. Lieber to Sumner, New York, 25 April 1865, in Series II, Reel 79, SP; Sumner to Bright, Washington, 24 April 1865, ibid.; Fessenden to Stanton, n.p., 28 May 1865, in Gorham, *Life and Public Services of Edwin M. Stanton,* vol. 2, 196; Jacob Collamer to Stanton, Woodstock, 14 June 1865, Gorham, *Life and Public Services of Edwin M. Stanton,* vol. 2, 197; Montgomery Blair to Frank Blair, Washington, 22 April 1865, in Smith, *The Francis Preston Blair Family,* vol. 2, 183–84.

53. Sherman, *Memoirs,* vol. 2, 866; Trumbull to Stanton, Chicago, 26 May 1865, in Gorham, *Life and Public Services of Edwin M. Stanton,* vol. 2, 198–99; John Sherman to Stanton, 27 April 1865, in Gorham, *Life and Public Services of Edwin M. Stanton,* vol. 2, 195–96; Simpson, *Let Us Have Peace,* 96–97, 100.

54. McCulloch to S. D. W. Bloodgood, Washington, 28 April 1865, Treasury Department Letterbook, March–May 1865, McCulloch ms, IU.

55. *New York Tribune,* 10 October 1861, in Fred A. Shannon, *The Organization and Administration of the Union Army, 1861–1865* (Cleveland: Arthur H. Clark, 1928), 48.

56. Medill to McCulloch, Chicago, 16 June 1865, McCulloch ms, LC, in Logsdon, *Horace White,* 111; Fite, *Social and Industrial Conditions,* 203.

8

The Republican Party, the Union Party, and Lincoln's Reelection

FRANCIS LIEBER and Thomas Barnett were unlikely compatriots. A legal theorist at Columbia University, Lieber offered radical prescriptions for wartime ailments; Barnett was a government clerk for Secretary of the Interior Caleb Smith, his Whiggish boss, and a friend of S. L. M. Barlow, a Democratic leader and New York lawyer. But their views converged in 1864, Lieber's in a speech and Barnett's in a pamphlet, both calling for Abraham Lincoln's reelection. They also agreed that Democrats had no cause to oppose his reelection, because the party had no reason to exist. "We know of no party in our present troubles. . . . The only line which divides the people of the north runs between the mass of loyal men, who stand by their country, no matter to what place of political meeting they are used to resort," and those "outside of it . . . are traitors to their country in the hour of need," Lieber said. Barnett described the "Opposition Party" as "the only party. In a partizan sense, the supporters of the administration do not deserve to be called a party. . . . Administration men are simply and purely Union men who are in favor of all energetic and lawful measures to put down a wicked revolt, and to establish a healthy peace and a sound Union." But Barnett concluded, "The Republican party has fulfilled a heaven-born and heaven-inspired mission. As a party, its work is done. . . . Henceforth its members are enrolled only under the broad banner of Union."[1]

Unlike Lieber and Barnett, William Seward and Salmon Chase had run for office. Yet the conservative and the radical echoed their views. The secretary of state, speaking near his New York home after the Democratic convention of 1864, accused Democrats of seeking to "subvert the republic." Chase said, "I no longer have any political side save that of my country; and there are multitudes who like me care little for men but everything for measures. I want freedom for all men . . . and I want a currency in which the wages of labor can be received from the Atlantic to the Pacific, . . . and I want a whole Union." In a sense, they described the Union party platform.[2]

Within a year after winning the White House on an anti-slavery, activist platform and confronting Civil War, Republicans had begun to deny that their party still existed. Changing their name to the Union party underscored two points, one intellectual and one blatantly political. The intellectual basis for the change lay in the party's new responsibility for the government and restoring and saving the Union. The political grounds for a new persona were tied to the reputation that Republicans had acquired during their short existence. Governance and what it entailed forced the party to refine its beliefs. Committed to spreading freedom, saving the Union, and perpetuating their and the government's power, Republicans remained too radical for many Democrats and Whiggish conservatives—as Republicans. To call themselves the Union party was a logical appeal for support for the government and a transparent appeal for support for themselves. But whatever their name, their core beliefs stayed the same. The only real alteration, the addition of union and power, was inseparable from freedom. In name and ideology, then, the Union party was politics at its best or worst. Whether the Union party proved beneficial and successful may be judged by the following standard: it helped what had been the Republican party in name win additional support in a time of national trial, and it remained the Republican party in thought and in deed.

But the Democratic party survived the war, and in that regard the Union party failed. Explaining his plans for reconstructing the Union, Thaddeus Stevens, the Pennsylvania radical, said, "Let all who approve of these principles tarry with us. Let all others go with Copperheads and rebels. These will be the opposing parties." The tenor of such comments underscores the problem with determining whether Republicans seriously believed that they could destroy their opposition by creating a Union party and inviting loyalists to join it. To argue that the other party consisted only of traitors seemed demagogic, but it reflected a sincere belief that only one party could be for the Union. Nor was this the first such case. Analyzing the first party system, Stanley Elkins and Eric McKitrick made a point about the founding fathers that may be applied to the Republicans of the Civil War era: "What sets the men of this generation apart from those of any other in American history is that their every response to virtually every question of a public nature was conditioned by their having just been through a revolution," and "in a revolutionary state such parties do not emerge without severe resistance." How the Civil War conditioned the response to partisanship must be viewed through a similar lens. For Republicans, graced with and encumbered by a sense of history, the revolution belonged not to the past but to the present. Opposition could—and, they felt, should—be treasonous. On this belief they would act.[3]

Republicans created a Union party; at least in name, its existence is beyond dispute. They hoped to entice loyal Democrats and Southerners, especially from border states, to join it. Changing the name and offering onetime enemies a voice in party councils would improve their prospects by eliminating the party's seemingly sectional and radical character. A long line of distinguished historians has analyzed the question of what the party system meant to Civil War Republicans. They have left unexplained what Republicans hoped to do to the Democrats. To say that their goal was victory is not enough. Lincoln applied to the opposition the same theory he brought to military operations. Just as he wanted to destroy the South's will to fight by annihilating its army, he and other Republicans hoped to destroy the Democratic party as it existed. The North wished to force the South to renounce secession and return to the Union; Republicans wished to force Democrats to renounce their party, denounce its departure from the unionism that had characterized it since the days of Andrew Jackson's primacy, and accept the one true faith. That faith was rooted in the party's ideology. When historians argue that Republicans found unity in what they were against, they often fail to acknowledge the importance of what they were for. Whatever they called themselves in wartime, they remained committed to perpetuating freedom, union, and power. When the Union party platform of 1864 endorsed the Thirteenth Amendment, it stated what many Republicans had come to understand: saving the Union and extending their own political power required them to eliminate slavery, the gravest threat to achieving those goals. To build a political tent under which everyone could congregate reflected this ideology.[4]

Understanding this requires an analysis based not on the third party system during the Civil War, but on the first and second party systems, those who built them, and how to interpret them in relation to each other. In *The Idea of a Party System: The Rise of Legitimate Opposition in the United States, 1780–1840,* Richard Hofstadter provided a cornerstone for erecting an interpretation of Civil War politics, especially Republicans. Hofstadter assessed the early party system and what participants thought of it. He found that the framers, like most of the British thinkers they read, considered parties a plague to be avoided. None agreed with Edmund Burke, England's leading conservative thinker, who saw that parties might unify disparate elements and serve what he considered the useful purpose of checking radical inclinations. Instead, the leaders of the first two American political parties considered one another treasonous to the principles of the Constitution and the leader of a rabble to be reduced to rubble, leaving one triumphant. While Jefferson's victory in 1800 was their worst nightmare, Federalists expected him to be so incompetent as to require their restoration; in turn, Jefferson anticipated absorbing the Hamiltonians into his party. When the Federalists dissolved in the wake of the War of 1812, the Jeffersonians felt that they had won, but they faced opposition from the party's remnants—not only from John Marshall and his Federalist bastion on the Supreme Court, but from among Jeffersonians who retained or accepted traces of Hamiltonian ideology.[5]

The ideas of Andrew Jackson and his supporters may be traced to many sources, but the leader of the Jacksonians—one might call him the political chief operating officer—was actually Martin Van Buren. Hofstadter credits him with creating the second party system and modern parties as we know them. The key was that in opposing DeWitt Clinton and the Albany Regency in New York, Van Buren expressed himself politically, not personally: as a lawyer, he disagreed with foes in court but they remained friendly adversaries, and he believed the same should be true of politics. He disdained James Monroe's efforts at conciliation, central to the "era of good feelings"; he blamed the 1824 election—with its factious allegations of a "corrupt bargain" between John Quincy Adams and Henry Clay to defeat Jackson—on Monroe's abdication of responsibility and the absence of a party system. Jackson's later success enabled Van Buren to practice what he preached.

The Jacksonian worldview differed from that of Adams, Clay, and the National Republicans, who were part of the Whig party's evolution. Ultimately, Jackson and Van Buren expected to prove more popular than the Whigs, but the expanded franchise they backed meant that the voice of the people would become more discordant, cutting one party's chances of consigning the other to the political or historical scrap heap. Eventually, the Whigs wound up there not because the Democrats destroyed them with the force of their logic, but due to their own ineptitude. When the Whig party disintegrated, many of its Northern members became Republicans, while Southerners chose between the short-lived Know-Nothing and Constitutional Union parties, then ended up with no real means of participating in the newly created third party system.[6]

Those events were beyond the scope of Hofstadter's study, but his concluding analysis put them squarely within the framework of party thought that Van Buren and others of his time erected. Hofstadter pointed out that Republicans "were not hesitant to found their new party upon a firm consciousness of the value of a principled party organization. The Republican remedy for the decayed and obsolescent state of the old parties was not to condemn the party system as such but to form and justify a new party which was portrayed from the outset as ready to take its place among the great parties of the American political tradition." Yet no less august an institution than the Supreme Court held in *Dred Scott* that slavery could spread into the territories; on the legal face of it, Chief Justice Roger Taney had declared the Republican goal unconstitutional.[7]

Politically, Southerners and their sympathizers lumped Republicans with the abolitionist fringe and Democrats piled on, essentially denying that the new party had any reason to be. Complicating matters, as historians have never tired of saying, those who made up the Republican party had been at one another's throats for nearly three decades. And they continued to fight, but over issues of personality and degree, not over the common goals that earlier studies have understated or ignored. One of those goals was to eliminate significant opposition.

Accusing the Opposition

One way to cast doubts on the legitimacy of Democrats was never to miss an opportunity to attack them with the bluntest invective possible. Republicans gleefully took this approach. The emotional, exhausting title of an 1864 pamphlet spoke volumes: *The Chicago Copperhead*

Convention. The Treasonable and Revolutionary Utterances of the Men Who Composed It. Extracts from all the Notable Speeches delivered in and out of the National "Democratic" Convention. A Surrender to the Rebels Advocated—A Disgraceful and Pusillanimous Peace Demanded—The Federal Government Shamefully Villified, and Not a Word Said Against the Cause of Treason and Rebellion.[8] Lincoln lamented "the fire in the rear," or the opposition at home, as a danger equal to that of rebel military victories, and other Republicans went beyond his mildly expressed sentiments. Ex-Democrat William Cullen Bryant's *New York Evening Post* assailed Democrats in 1864 for "hostility to the war," and ex-Whig Horace Greeley saw "no difference between their triumph and that of the outright Rebels." In resolutions written by Lieber, New Yorkers made their feelings clear: "As Macbeth was prompted to treason and murder by the black prophecies of the heath, so the South was instigated to rebellion and usurpation by the darker promises of Northern democrats. And later: Rebellion, staggered by telling blows, revived upon the hope of Opposition gains." The *Chicago Tribune* stated its contempt for opposition criticism with less elegance: "Swine enjoy their own perfume."[9]

Their recourse to these words suggests that Republicans took terms like *treason* and *disloyalty* too lightly. It also means that their comments, especially in private correspondence, transcended the political posturing meant to strike emotional chords for public consumption. It was natural for their constituents to react angrily to critics of a war that endangered their families and friends, and for Republicans to take advantage of any opportunities these sentiments created. Thus, Republicans raised the specter, whatever its legitimacy, of a Democratic plot to overthrow the government. Reports flowed to party leaders, especially Seward, about rumored movements and conspiracies. Republicans fingered such possible leaders as Clement Vallandigham of Ohio and New Yorkers Horatio Seymour and Fernando Wood, with an occasional salvo at McClellan and his friends in the Union army. That several of these men held important posts did nothing to mitigate the charges; if anything, they gave the party visible targets, and showed just how pernicious and tricky Democrats could be in seeking power.[10]

These accusations also spoke volumes about the workings of the Republican mind: from Lincoln to the lowliest loyalist, Republicans feared that Democrats worked not just against them, but against the country. For a party whose members had cut their political eyeteeth on the idea of a slave-power conspiracy, the ground was familiar and comforting, since such notions offered a handy explanation for opposition to their handling of the war. For them the ground was consistent, because it meant that Democrats threatened their quest to spread freedom, preserve the Union, and perpetuate their power.

Had Republicans confined their criticisms to public forums available to all, their sincerity might have been suspect, but their private utterances echoed their public statements, from radical and conservative alike. When Senator Lazarus Powell, a Kentucky Democrat, hailed the 1862 elections, which improved the fortunes of what had seemed like a dying Democratic party, the moderately radical Henry Wilson rose to reply. "All I understand the elections to have settled, is that the Administration party are not strong enough to whip the Southern Democrats who are in rebellion against the country and the Northern Democratic party" together. Conservatives made a similar point: circumspect as always, Seward told his partner, Thurlow Weed, "Factions in the North will co-operate by contrary measures with factions in the South. But we shall survive the combination." Less prominent Republicans, followers with little or no role in forming the party's worldview, felt similarly. "The democrats are organizing to resist the war," said a New Jersey Republican, "and treason is talked as boldly on every street-corner, North, as it ever was at the Confederate Capital."[11]

For Republicans, such treasonous behavior meant that the Democratic party forfeited its right even to exist. "While I think there exist good grounds for a legitimate, noble, decided and patriotic opposition," one pamphleteer wrote, Democrats failed to occupy them. As the war demanded radical anti-slavery measures and a more active federal government, Democrats found themselves in the unaccustomed role of naysayers. Republicans, who once had been in that position, questioned their commitment, and the same writer noted that "it would be far more wise and patriotic to suggest improvements, and to devise better projects, than to indulge in the mere denunciation of bad ones; . . . it would be wiser to exert the utmost efforts to unite and join the people in one whole, rather than to use all endeavors to create wider and more irreconcilable breaches among ourselves." Another Republican explained how Democrats had lost their right to be a legitimate organization: "In a Republic, two parties are well nigh indispensable, and an honest, patriotic Opposition is in the highest degree desirable, but an Opposition which, in a rebellion, takes sides with insurgents, forfeits for the future all claim upon public confidence, and must be content with the contemptuous obscurity accorded to unholy ambition baffled in its wicked schemes."[12]

Republicans found the opposition as a whole to lack legitimacy, but they could also see that some Democrats clearly were on the side of the angels. Thus, hoping to save their political souls and to broaden the Republican base, they tried to entice these right-minded Democrats to follow their path. Massachusetts moderate John Murray Forbes was one of many old Democrats hoping to redeem those who stayed with that party but retained their unionism—"the *true* Democracy" who believed in "democratic *ideas*" that "really conform to republican principles." A New York loyalist told Wisconsin's James Doolittle, an ex-Democrat, that he used "'Democratic' . . . in its broad sense—particularly proper now, when some who profane the name are leaguing with traitors." With a telling double-negative, Doolittle's Senate colleague, Timothy Howe, said that "there are undoubtedly democrats who are not traitors—opponents of the administration who are not aiders of the rebellion. But it is often not a little difficult to discriminate between them." After the 1864 election, the moderate *Springfield Republican* conceded that few Democrats acted disloyally, while ex-Democrats such as Montgomery Blair and War Democrats such as John Dix confessed that a few leaders, lacking loyalty or brains, put the party in an untenable position; most of the rank and file stayed true to the Union. Their reservations about their old party made that a difficult concession for each to make.[13]

One reason for trying to win over their traditional opponents was that Republicans expected the war to kill the Democratic party, and the chance to slip in a knife was irresistible. Seeking cause for optimism after the Union debacle at Chancellorsville in May 1863, a Republican loyalist noted that by opposing the war, Democrats buried themselves. A Union pamphlet attacking the Democratic record argued, "To oppose a successful war . . . is likely, in a Republic, to prove the destruction of any organization guilty of so unpatriotic a blunder, and the Democracy, which has thus proved its faithlessness to the great principles on which it was founded, is now seeking to obliterate the damning record of its course since 1860." Even after the war ended, when

New York Times editor Henry Raymond ran for Congress, young New Hampshire Republican William Chandler, working in the Treasury Department, told him, "We had better have lice and locusts than the revival of the Democratic party." The appearance of disloyalty meant that Democrats could no longer be legitimate opponents, especially for a party that united that union with freedom and power. According to Republicans, Democrats had been untrue to all three of these precepts, and were unworthy of being entrusted with power.[14]

Since the spread of freedom and the enhancement of government power remained more debatable questions, Republicans concentrated on tarring Democrats over opposition to union and denying that any party other than their own had the right to survive the war. In the summer of 1862, the *Sacramento Union* could find "only a single issue before the country—the support of the Government in this war to put down traitors—and upon that there can be but two parties, one for sustaining the Administration in its war policy, and the other opposed to the war and the Administration." Zachariah Chandler, a Michigan radical, told his Senate colleagues, "There are but two parties—patriots and traitors; and none others." Lieber offered a means of judging Democratic loyalty when his pamphlet *No Party Now, but All for Country* devised a litmus test: whether the South should be completely conquered; whether civil liberties could be suppressed; and whether emancipation and the draft were proper. Democrats had every reason to believe that Republicans ultimately sought their extinction.[15]

Making the Union Party

The means to that end, Republicans hoped, would be the Union party. To some historians, its existence suggests that Republicans admitted their divisions and redefined themselves. Actually, the new party combined calculation and intellectual honesty. Republicans understood that old Whigs and Democrats rejected their apparent radicalism, but might join a party that seemed to stand only for the Union. The war gave them a chance to attract new members who might otherwise avoid them. The new party exemplified the Republican belief that the Union was paramount. While that may seem counter to the party's ideology, which merged the Union with other forces and factors, the opposite was true. The free labor ideology with which Republicans had entered the war evolved because of the Union party—partly that it existed, partly that they sought to build it up. Republicans grasped that their responsibilities required them to change. That this requirement suited them politically in no way detracts from the salient fact that it was also what they believed.

Especially just after the firing on Fort Sumter, Republicans pursued a policy of increased tolerance, due to the Northern outpouring of patriotism and because they were just acquainting themselves with power. As the *Indianapolis Journal* said that summer, "It will be time enough to revive the Republican and Democratic parties when we know that we have a government." But as dissatisfaction grew with the war's progress, or the lack of it, Democrats spoke out; Republicans countered with charges of weakness, disloyalty, and treason. Naturally, Democrats disagreed—with good reason, since many of them were as loyal to the Union as Republicans. But peace Democrats made enough noise to allow Republicans to turn the tables, or to return the favor for earlier Democrat charges that they were too rabidly anti-slavery to care about the Union. While both parties always doubted that the other had the best interests of the Union at heart, Republicans could justifiably claim that Democratic policies led to the war and Democratic opposition prolonged it. What began as a Dumasian cry of all for one and one for all degenerated into what it really had been all along: all for one country, yes, but also all for one party.[16]

When the war began, believing the Union's survival to be at stake and still wary of one another, Republicans and Democrats worked together. Even Wood, New York City's ardently Democratic mayor, said, "I know no party now." From Representative Charles Francis Adams, writing in his diary in Boston, to entrepreneur Leland Stanford, addressing Californians as he ran for governor, Republicans claimed to welcome the exchange of partisanship for devout unionism. Across the North they declared the existence of one party only, and for good reason: that was how the North felt. Calling themselves the party of "patriots in a struggle with traitors and the Devil," Maryland unionists said, "One country, one Constitution, and one people now and forever." At the opposite extreme, William Lloyd Garrison advised, "It is no time for minute criticism of Lincoln, Republicanism, or even the other parties, now that they are fusing for a death-grapple with the

Southern slave oligarchy." Abolitionists and the most radical Republicans agreed: secession might breed a greater desire to end the root cause, slavery; achieving freedom might require the growth of federal power beyond anything previously imagined; and the Union would benefit. The whirlwind of unionism that was meant to attract conservatives also caught radicals, and the Republican party's evolving, shared ideology would unite them.[17]

That ideology also helps to explain why this second era of good feelings proved even shorter-lived than the first. "It is certainly proper that Republicans should be preferred in appointment by Republicans—not of course to the exclusion of citizens of different political sentiments specially qualified for particular posts; but so preferred as to satisfy the judgments of reasonable men, who regard party organization as means to the general good of the country," Chase admitted. The Jacksonian spoils system, the Van Burenite view of parties as positive, and even Federalist-era doubts about legitimate opposition merged to make Republicans wary of working closely enough with Democrats to cede too many of the fruits of their victory—and the power that went with it. One of Justin Morrill's Vermont constituents said that for all of the talk "about the 'obliteration of party line' I take it that there is no 'obliteration' so far as Democrats in office are concerned, as long as there are republicans hungering and thirsting for the fat things of the land."[18]

Of course, hungry and thirsty Republicans howled when they believed that Democrats received undue generosity. Nor did old habits die easily. While Republicans spent the late 1850s charging Democrats with every imaginable sin against the framers, against the Constitution, and against humanity in general, Democrats blistered them as wild-eyed radicals guilty of similar transgressions. Both were partisan, with a defined ideology, and unable to change too much, even in wartime.

Thus, by the end of 1861 and for the rest of the war, Republicans felt that there should be only one party: theirs, with Democrats and any like group eliminated. From their perspective, the Republican vision of the nation was the only possible one; after all, Democrats had held power, and the country was reaping what they had sowed. If any party was to give ground to another, it should be the Democrats. The *Chicago Tribune* said, "We thank God that party lines are being obliterated and party prejudices given up, and that people recognize more and more clearly the truth that the only road to success lies in Emancipation"—a linking of freedom and union, with the implication that only Republicans had the power to protect them. The next summer, the *Tribune* saw nothing but victory and disdained partisanship: "The curse of the times . . . is the fact that the partisan journals, the politicians, the members of Congress, the officers of the army, the members of the Cabinet, have each a candidate for the Presidency whose advancement on the road to the White House is nearer to his heart than a victory over the enemy," not that the *Tribune* could be partisan.[19]

Indeed, Republicans were as guilty of partisanship as those whom they attacked for it. On the first anniversary of the firing on Sumter, Morton said that "we know of no party. Parties are unavoidable in free countries, and may be useful if they acknowledge the country far above themselves. . . . But Party has no meaning in far the greater number of the highest and the common relations of human life." Yet after hailing the events of 12 April 1861, because they "had the effect, for the time, to close up the ranks among the people, to heal up the dissensions, and to bring us together," Morton lamented that when the effect wore off, "the demagogues who had been driven into the kennels by the universal outburst of patriotism, came forth and began to do the devilish work of attempting to produce divisions at the North, so as to paralyze the arm of the government." Nor was this attitude confined to Indiana, a presumed hotbed of disloyal groups. Eastern Republicans felt similarly, happily bidding farewell to party because the war's objects were too grave for partisanship, and indulging in partisanship to speed the process—and because it reflected their ideology, which compelled them to question the dedication of others to freedom and union and to assail them as a threat to their power.[20]

Thus, the Union party served, at least for Republicans, as the ideal political organization: partisan in running its own slate of candidates, nonpartisan in having a name inoffensive enough to appeal to politicians of every stripe, and allowing Republicans to be partisan under the cloak of even-handedness. The party did its job. Democrats or Whigs who wanted nothing to do with Republicans could be on the correct (to be charitable) or winning (to be uncharitable) side. Ex-Whig and Constitutional Unionist Edward Everett had so little use for their antislavery ardor that even in Massachusetts, the cradle of abolitionism where he spent his life, he refused to join the party. But he joined the Union party and became one of Lincoln's electors in 1864. Former

Democrat Daniel Dickinson of New York backed the administration to the hilt: "It is not Lincoln and the Republicans we are sustaining. . . . It is the government of our fathers. . . . There is but one side to it." In Maryland the persistence of slavery, Whiggery, and democratic inclinations, and the power struggle between the Blair family and Henry Winter Davis, kept politics in flux, but both sides could claim that Democrats represented "Dixie, Davis (Jefferson, that is), and the devil." As Jean Baker said of Maryland in that era, and could have said of most of the North, "The gravamen of Union charges against the Democrats was quite simple: during the war there could be only two parties—the loyal and the disloyal—and as the Unionists had taken the loyal ground, Democrats were therefore traitors."[21]

Therein lay the problem with eliminating partisanship: Republicans tried, but old habits died hard, especially with the lingering question of whether others would see the dangers they detected. At times they drove home their point more subtly. When Ulysses Grant said in 1864 that the South's "only hope now is a divided North," and the *Albany Morning Express* warned, "None but those whose devotion to party is greater than their love of country will fail to heed his appeal, and history will not be sparing in her condemnation," the target was neither specific nor unfriendly.[22]

But most Republicans had ceased to be subtle or friendly. Instead, they bullied Democrats and denied uttering a partisan word or having a partisan idea. One loyalist told Frederick Seward, "Your father knows no party except his country and its constitution and Laws." Vermont's congressional delegation reportedly urged state and county Union conventions to "take no distinctive Republican ground, at present," while the usually silent John Usher, the secretary of the Interior, told an Indiana rally in 1863, "There is no issue with the government now but the one of its preservation. We are either for it or against it." Other conservatives from Maryland to Massachusetts, where Richard Henry Dana deemed parties "no longer necessary or desirable, or defensible," echoed the "one party" or "no party" theme. They urged Northerners to put aside partisanship, in some cases because fellow Republicans had taken control, but more often out of the sincere belief that dividing along party lines might lead to a divided country. And that could sound the death knell not only of the Union but also of the party's chances of retaining or enhancing freedom and its own power.[23]

Indeed, in pursuing these goals, many Republicans claimed to have been, if anything, too tolerant of opposition—a sign of the illegitimacy they attributed to their political foes. As the 1862 campaign approached, John Jay advocated a general suppression of Democrats; the abolitionist feared their revival because "thousands of weak minded persons are likely to be deceived by the misrepresentation of the President's policy," which revealed more confidence in political trickery than in democracy. After the 1862 election, Doolittle responded to Democratic criticism of arbitrary arrests; the conservative, usually wary of undue federal action, noted that many saw the Lincoln administration as "too lenient towards men who have been notoriously engaged, in sympathy and in act, too, with the traitors against the Government." Two years later, Jacob Howard denied Democratic charges that his party felt "that nothing should be said in opposition to the Administration during a war . . . but I confess at the same time that I have very little charity for those who are the enemies of my country, foreign or domestic." After the election, the *Cincinnati Commercial* pointed out how brutally Democrats had described Lincoln as evidence of Republican openness to dissent, then added that the opposition took advantage of that openness and abused the privilege.[24]

The problem was that the parties' responses to one another created a vicious circle. Democrats began the war believing Republican professions of nonpartisanship for the sake of loyalty. But as the newly ensconced party of government tried to turn theory into practice, Democrats realized that for all of the claims about a Union party, they were very much on the outside looking in. The more Democrats complained, the more convinced Republicans became of their disloyalty. The more Republicans voiced that sentiment, the more critical Democrats became. And when Republicans took a circuitous route to partisan attack, Democrats could hardly miss it. If they did, what Governor Edwin Morgan of New York told political boss Thurlow Weed by way of explanation was, to Republicans, equally true: they missed office, and would do anything to regain it. Republicans were now in office, liked it, and meant to stay in. The way to do that, they felt, was to show that they were the party with the greatest sense of responsibility for the republic's survival. That meant a commitment to the Union, which the party believed to be inextricably linked to a belief in freedom and the growth of their power and the government's power to protect both of them. While it may seem simplistic to say that what Republicans thought motivated what they said, it also is true.[25]

Yet Republicans also distinguished between those Democrats who opposed the war or the administration and those who at long last understood the evil that their party had done. This too was related to party ideology. Republicans clearly and sincerely believed in the importance of freedom, union, and power, and disdained those who disagreed with them. But they also realized that simply to attack those who remained outside their party would do nothing to help them achieve their goal of spreading these views. Simply put, they needed more fellow believers. Thus, the Union party also provided a means by which to broaden their appeal to those who found the Republican commitment to freedom too confining for themselves or too radical for the country.

This could have made the Union organization seem no more than a brazen attempt to trick non-Republicans into joining the Republican party. While that argument contains a degree of legitimacy, it fails to take into consideration that the Union party not only retained Republican ideology, but went beyond it. When Republican wolves donned the clothing of the Union sheep, they remained true to their antebellum ideology of support for free labor and opposition to the slave power. They also won over Democrats who had disagreed with their perceptions of what American society should be, but thoroughly agreed with the need to save the Union. At least for the duration of the war, they brought Democrats into a party committed to saving the Union while also fighting for freedom and for increased power for itself and the government.[26]

What Republicans did in pursuit of Democratic support was and is clear. Both Lincoln and the state governors named a spate of past and present Democrats to high positions, especially in the military. Whether they had been Democrats or nonpartisan opponents of the Republicans seemed immaterial to those responsible for their selection, as long as they were loyal and politically useful. Indeed, their predilections provided an object lesson for other Democrats to emulate. If they supported the war and proved willing to risk their lives in it, their devotion to the Union might, Republicans hoped, move Democrats to support them openly or keep their unhappiness quiet. In either case, Democrats disposed to look unfavorably upon Republicans would find joining the Union party more palatable than switching to the seemingly fanatically anti-slavery Republicans or remaining with the apparently disloyal Democrats.[27]

Amid all of the Democratic generals he appointed, Lincoln's choice of Stanton as secretary of War early in 1862 showed the Republican desire to reach out to the opposition, and how they could broaden their popularity without eroding their ideology. To choose generals who followed orders was one thing; to name the minister who sent or made those orders was very different. Stanton provided the party with a means of bridging the gap to loyal Democrats. In addition to making overtures to Governor Horatio Seymour of New York, whom Lincoln may have seen as a possible successor under the Union umbrella, Stanton induced a War Democrat to run for governor of New Hampshire, drawing away enough votes from the regular Democrat to elect the Republican. But as Stanton grew more radical and disenchanted with Democratic generals like George McClellan, his old party turned on him. His job was never in danger, at least for that reason; the more he differed with Democrats, the more Republicans were likely to support him. But his predicament underscored the problems with creating a Union party: the predominance of Republicans, the Democratic distrust of them, and the old ties that Democrats still found it hard to break.[28]

Welcoming loyalists to the Union party and cause, Republicans toned down their verbiage, swallowed their disdain, and tried to make them feel important. War Democrats like Dickinson, Joseph Holt, and Andrew Johnson, who won Republican admiration for breaking with their party or, in Johnson's case, region, received countless requests to speak at rallies and were often mentioned for Cabinet posts. They also enjoyed political success. Ohio elected War Democrats David Tod and John Brough governor, while the Senate's expulsion of rebel sympathizer Jesse Bright enabled Indiana's Morton to appoint War Democrat Joseph Wright. In each case they strengthened the Union party's standing with Democrats and proved willing to meet Republicans halfway, if not even closer to that party's ideology. By the time the Union won at Gettysburg, Brough warned, "Either slavery must be torn out root and branch, or our Government will exist no longer." While Wright refused to buy the Republican platform lock, stock, and barrel, he made clear that he accepted it. "I am no political friend of this Administration, but in this hour I know no party," he told the Senate, "and if Abraham Lincoln can trust the destinies of this country in the hands of George B. McClellan, Edwin M. Stanton, Halleck, and other men, who differ politically with him, it is as little as I can do to give them my respect and my confidence." The party could hardly have asked for more: a Democrat who supported the war might not be entirely on their side, but he represented another vote for power for Republicans and the Union.[29]

For their part, most Democrats had no interest in adopting Republican views, but to join the Union party was different. It at least suggested an absence of partisanship in the decision, and those who joined it had long since demonstrated a commitment to the Union itself. Holt, a Kentucky Democrat whom Lincoln considered for the war ministry, became a War Department official and Union party stalwart who demanded "the triumph of freedom and civilization and national honor." The 1862 Indiana Union convention chose a slate of Republicans and War Democrats on a platform that ignored slavery in favor of preserving the Union, moving a Democratic state senator to say, "In this meeting we do not abandon our party creeds . . . we do not lose our political identity, we do not adopt each other's supposed political heresies. We waive, for the time, political differences, and suspend mere party warfare for the public good." Even abolitionists like Henry Ward Beecher marveled that War Democrats "formed the band and belt that gave unity to the party of war, and carried the great Democratic party into their ranks." Left unsaid was any reference to the power that Democrats may have wielded. Given the strong resemblance between the Union and Republican platforms, there was little to refer to, and that was how Republicans preferred it.[30]

But some Republicans feared that Democrats would gain too much power in the Union party. In the summer of 1863, Joshua Giddings, a founding father of political anti-slavery, gloomily foresaw "the result of breaking up the republican party and the abandonment of the principles on which it was based. If I mistake not the old Whig dynasty may be said to have been restored," sacrificing "doctrines, principles or character" by making "the Union and the support of the present administration the test question." His radical son-in-law, George Julian, battling Morton for control of the Indiana party, assailed "the 'Morton-Wright' plan of bringing together the fag-ends of all the officeseeking plunder-grabbing cliques of Indiana." Indiana may have been the most divided state, since Caleb Smith and moderately radical Speaker of the House Schuyler Colfax were involved, but Republicans in other states were also concerned. In Ohio, rising young moderate James Garfield condemned Tod's nomination for governor not just because he distrusted War Democrats or because Tod had presided at the convention that had nominated Stephen Douglas in 1860, but because he "made appointments in total disregard of the wishes of both officers or men," and was "an ass, a man destitute of those high qualities of manhood and moral excellence." The uncertainty regarding Democrats reached north and east: Howard urged Governor Austin Blair to ignore Democratic pleas for office in Michigan; New Hampshire's party stuck with Republicans on the theory that only they had the strength to win. Republicans wanted to win, obviously for political reasons, but also to spread their gospel, and they would do what was necessary to achieve their goals.[31]

Republicans enjoyed the convenience of merging theory and reality. For the sake of freedom, union, and power, they surrendered their name but not their beliefs. As a result, they enjoyed at least as much success as they had had when they had been known as Republicans—perhaps more. Not only did they win elections, but they passed even more far-reaching legislation than they had originally proposed. They claimed to do so out of the desire to restore the United States government to the original design of the founding fathers, and they shared the intent of the framers to obliterate all opposition. Both the founding generation and their Republican successors tried to do so, resorting to charges of treason that they sincerely believed. And both failed.

Yet by retaining power and spreading freedom and union, Republicans ultimately were successful. Exemplifying their success were comments by two supporters, neither technically a Republican. Early in the war, an old Jacksonian who wholeheartedly supported the Union put his finger on what Republicans hoped for and believed. According to George Bancroft, "I witnessed the sublimest spectacle I ever knew: the uprising of the irresistible spirit of the people in behalf of law, and order, and liberty." These had been the goals of Republicans who had elected Lincoln in 1860 and then reelected him under the Union party's guise in 1864. They fought for freedom, union, and power, and won the battle and the war. By the end of 1864, with the election of Lincoln and former Democrat Andrew Johnson, it was possible for someone who could only root them on to make the kind of statement that had seemed outlandish when they took office, and merely radical and unlikely when they had kept it. Abolitionist Lydia Maria Child wrote, "I rejoice in having a rail-splitter for President and a tailor for Vice President. I wish a shoe-black could be found worthy to be appointed Secretary of State; and I should be all the more pleased if he were a black shoe-black." If the Union party had not been the Republican party under a different name, support from those who found Child's sentiments horrifying would have been hard to come by; if the Union party had been something other than the Republican party under a different name, Child would have had no reason even to express her hope. Whatever its name, the party that led the nation through the war was the Republican party, and it was guided by the shared ideology of its dominant members, Republicans.[32]

Reelecting Lincoln

In the late summer of 1864, the editors of the *New York Tribune* and the *Chicago Tribune* were upset. By that time displeasure seemed to be their normal state. In New York, Horace Greeley stayed true to the radical faith but varied in his views of Lincoln, his generals, and how they waged war—and, indeed, whether to keep fighting; at times his hatred for bloodshed moved him to suggest peace. In Chicago Joseph Medill maintained more balance, but not easily: a radical at heart, as a leading Republican in Lincoln's Illinois, he saw his paper as an administration voice, meaning that he lacked Greeley's freedom to criticize. In August Greeley sought peace talks with rebel emissaries he mistakenly deemed official enough to effect a truce, and Democrats met in Medill's city for their convention. His paper reacted predictably: "Now let the voice of the loyal Northwest be heard and a tornado of enthusiasm for Union and Liberty will sweep the foul vapor of corrupted Democracy from our political atmosphere."[33]

Greeley's action and Medill's reaction were understandable. Granting that the quixotic Greeley was a trial even to his friends, he was as weary of war as the rest of his party and more convinced than most Republicans not only of the evils of war, but that Lincoln lacked the ability to win it. Thus, his quest to negotiate may be seen as an effort to restore a Union in which Republicans might salvage their power and work to spread freedom; to lose the war and the election might condemn the party to the fate of his old Whig party and the fight against slavery to utter failure. Medill shared Greeley's disgust with military failure and Lincoln's seeming slowness in waging war against rebels and slavery, but his comments were a more common response to Democrats. As did other Republicans, Medill spent much of the war depicting them as disloyal. Both the *New York Tribune* and the *Chicago Tribune* hammered away at Democrats as lacking the legitimacy of a constitutional opposition, and joined the Union party in trying to force them into the margins of American politics. Not only was the war going badly that summer, but Democrats clearly remained strong enough to provide a challenge, even a frightening one, to the renamed Republicans.[34]

The Republican plight was less dire than it seemed. Democrats left Chicago after calling the war a failure, even as Sherman announced the fall of Atlanta. The irony eluded celebrating Republicans: the military power they feared as a threat to freedom made it possible for them to continue to pursue freedom. Yet it was, one historian said, a party divided, doubting Lincoln's ability as a president and potential victor. Since the party was an amalgam of anti-slavery Northern Democrats, Northern Whigs who varied in their hatred for slavery, and old Free-Soilers who were single-minded in opposing the peculiar institution, internal warfare seemed only natural; re-creating it as the Union party and adding Democrats used to fighting Republicans only made the mixture more combustible. But the party was united in more significant ways. Whatever their battles over people and policies, the Republicans—or their cousin, the Union party—agreed on the need to pursue a policy of spreading freedom, saving the Union, and using and enhancing its power. And however grudgingly they accepted him, in the end Lincoln was a central figure in that ideology.[35]

More crucial than the principles that Democrats and Whigs took into the new party, then into the Republican shadow group called the Union party, Lincoln weathered wartime politics. The 1862 midterm elections reduced his majority in Congress. Worse, as Democrats gained seats at state capitals, Republicans seemed determined to cannibalize themselves in a Hobbesian war of all against all. In the race for New York governor radicals chose one of their own, General James

Wadsworth, and blamed his defeat on a lack of support from the conservative machine run by Secretary of State William Seward and Albany editor Thurlow Weed. No evidence suggests open hostility, but they displayed no enthusiasm for the nominee. The Democratic takeover of the Illinois legislature condemned Orville Browning to defeat, but Republicans had no use for him anyway. Such luminaries as Senator Lyman Trumbull and the *Chicago Tribune*'s editors dismissed him as little better than a Democrat. True, Republicans staged a comeback in the 1863 elections, but divisions remained. Whether Lincoln could overcome them remained problematic, but the course he navigated during the war showed that he was above all a survivor.[36]

As the 1864 election neared, party divisions had the potential to affect the war and its outcome; slavery and ideology were not at issue. Radicals made clear that they preferred someone other than Lincoln, but not who it should be and why it should not be him. They rarely, if ever, disagreed substantively with him, reflecting conflicts in personality and approach, the resonance of their ideology, and the weakness of radical opposition. Ironically, abolitionists had grown fonder of Lincoln, whom they saw as headed the right way. He told Frederick Douglass, "I think it cannot be shown that when I have once taken a position, I have ever retreated from it," and similarly reassured Charles Sumner; both were less critical of Lincoln than many Republicans. William Lloyd Garrison, his respect growing, wrote that Lincoln "must be judged by his possibilities, rather than by our wishes, or by the highest abstract moral standard."[37]

While most abolitionists remained detached from the center of power, radicals were another matter. Despite their influence, they seemed more interested in the abstract ideals the president should embody and less in whether those ideals could become reality as easily as they believed. Unlike Garrison, they still lacked confidence in and respect for Lincoln. By 1864, they were tired of the war's length, the military ineptitude that contributed to it, and three years of a president beyond their control. In April 1864, a *Chicago Tribune* correspondent declared it "essential to the success of the Union party at the next election that Mr. Lincoln should cut entirely loose from border state conservatives" like the Blairs. That family's main competitor in Maryland, the increasingly radical Henry Winter Davis, decided that it was too late: Lincoln was "past saving."[38]

Determining the importance of ideology to Lincoln's supporters might seem difficult because they rarely cited one. What shines through their words and deeds is that they assumed the connection. More important to them, Lincoln belonged to their party and was the most popular candidate. As 1864 began, John Kasson, a congressman from Iowa and former deputy to Postmaster General Montgomery Blair, concluded that Lincoln "is already renominated by 9/10ths of the republicans who do not aspire to be political leaders." Schuyler Colfax, close to Greeley but noted for straddling the fence when possible, agreed that his support "comes up from the people, not down from the politicians."[39]

Indeed, even if some questioned his ability, none doubted his desire to succeed—a sign that the party agreed on what it believed, not necessarily on who it considered best suited to achieve its goals. The nonideological cast of Lincoln's backers was clear when they sought early endorsements for his reelection, especially to derail the hopes of his Treasury secretary. Heading Lincoln's campaign in New Hampshire, William Chandler said nothing of Salmon Chase's radicalism or Lincoln's moderation. Objecting to "a corrupt moneyed ring" battling the president, and trying to wrest control of state patronage from radicals, he acted like the professional politician he was. In Chase's home state of Ohio, a friend told James Garfield that "if you have any regard for the popular voice . . . of the State of Ohio you will not waste your powder over Sec. Chase." Across the North Republicans discussed how to win, not Lincoln's commitment or lack of it. Radical or conservative, they cared about winning; finding a candidate who could be elected was more likely to help them perpetuate freedom, union, and power than finding a perfect candidate.[40]

The saga of Chase's abortive presidential campaign in 1864 lends added credence to the key point about wartime Republicans: they differed over personality more than policy, style more than substance. While Chase had disclaimed further ambitions, he continued to pursue the presidency, and the Treasury's vast patronage formed an ideal base. Radicals preferred Chase; he was one of their own, had been a better-known advocate of anti-slavery before the war than Lincoln, and shared their discontent with his slowness on emancipation. In radical minds, what Chase had done before the war outweighed what Lincoln did during the war. Chase's reputation also helped submerge unpleasant memories of his retreat when confronted about his efforts to push Seward from the Cabinet.

More important, other radicals continued to resent the presence of conservatives Seward and Blair, and feared that their influence would somehow assure the survival of slavery. But most Republicans with doubts about Lincoln preferred to exercise caution. Even Greeley, who occasionally abdicated reality for fantasy and called Chase "the ablest man in the country" and "a thorough Radical," refrained from supporting him too openly. The editor who would be a politician told the politician who would be president that he looked askance at those who campaigned for a position that should seek the man.[41]

Yet Chase sought the position, ardently and unwisely. In February 1864 came two circulars deriding Lincoln's abilities and exalting Chase's. Sent out under the franking privileges of allies such as Senator Samuel Pomeroy of Kansas, the guiding spirit behind them, they doubted that Lincoln could suppress the rebellion, restore the Union, and win reelection. Naturally they caused an uproar, with Chase and his friends denying involvement or making an endorsement, and defending themselves. A *New York Tribune* reporter told Greeley, who seemed to be wavering, "It is perfectly idle to go into a contest with Mr. Lincoln for the nomination unless we lay bare temperately, but fearlessly and thoroughly, his incapacity and many failings and failures as the head of this nation at this crisis; and this can be done without in any manner endangering national interests," for "if we allow Lincoln to be *nominated* the Democrats will assuredly elect their candidate, and, perhaps, undo all that we have been doing for three years."[42]

What is crucial about these circulars is not what they said, but what went unsaid. While Lincoln suffered from "indecision," "feebleness," and "want of intellectual grasp," Chase was "a statesman of rare ability, and an administrator of the very highest order." Whatever the value of these claims, they said nothing substantial about the two men's beliefs. Both opposed slavery and endorsed the platform on which Lincoln had become president and Chase had entered the Cabinet. Chase's backers questioned Lincoln's ability, not his commitment; he simply seemed to them to lack the ability to voice or act on it and, more important in their minds, to win reelection. The argument was political, but the ideology of freedom, union, and power was unworthy of discussion because it was assumed. At issue was how to hold onto and expand that power.[43]

The controversy over Chase brought back into sharp relief how the party differed over individuals, not ideology. While Chase denied his candidacy, Lincoln claimed not to have read the circulars and let him stay in the Cabinet. Radical Francis Lieber called Chase's letter of withdrawal "that of a man," but conservatives disagreed. Lincoln's friend David Davis said, "I have heard no one say that Chase's letter was intended as a positive declination. Look at the meanness in not saying one word about Mr. Lincoln." Chase's plan, he said, was for others to attack Lincoln and block his nomination, then offer himself as the compromise candidate. New York conservatives Weed and Senator Edwin Morgan agreed. They were right: Chase mulled his prospects, and Lincoln was renominated.[44]

The National Union convention that June proved two points: whatever its name, it was the Republican party, and Lincoln controlled it. The *Chicago Tribune* said, "From near and from afar the people watch and wait, ready to accept, with a cheer that shall ring throughout the land, the name that stands at the portals of millions of loyal lips—Abraham Lincoln." For him it was more like a coronation: the party chair was Henry Raymond of the *New York Times,* a Lincoln loyalist and Seward-Weed ally; Morgan, his predecessor, was part of the Albany machine; former governor William Dennison of Ohio, who presided, was about to join the Cabinet; and Davis and Leonard Swett, Lincoln's old managers, had no cause for concern and stayed home. At Lincoln's urging, Morgan asked the convention to endorse "such an amendment of the Constitution as will positively prohibit African slavery in the United States." The platform said that "as slavery was the cause, and now constitutes the strength, of this rebellion, and as it must be, always and everywhere, hostile to the principles of republican government, justice and the national safety demand its utter and complete extirpation from the soil of the republic." When the convention chose Lincoln, many Republican editors voiced their optimism: the *Indianapolis Daily Journal* called the combination of his selection and the amendment the "most fatal blow the rebellion" had suffered.[45]

Yet the convention and reaction to it showed that the party still agreed on ends, but not means. Even Lincoln backers like Sumner wanted to delay the gathering because five months remained until the election; given the state of the war, that period might affect what the party should do, how to do it, and with whom to do it. Before the convention met, attuned to its unionist cast, Raymond suggested avoiding discussion of the slavery issue. According to his old *Tribune* foe Charles Dana, now an aide to Secretary of War Edwin Stanton, that would do Lincoln "a great injury, hopelessly alienating the great part of the Radicals." That group opposed admitting delegates from "debatable lands" beginning reconstruction, an issue that Lincoln's allies sought to avoid entirely. Haunted by the carnage, Greeley wanted the party to call for peace but knew that would fail—and the platform approved of "the determination of the Government of the United States not to compromise with rebels, or to offer them any terms of peace, except such as may be based upon an unconditional surrender of their hostility and a return to their just allegiance to the Constitution and laws of the United States." As Republicans or Unionists, they were ready to wield power to the finish for union and freedom.[46]

The rest of the platform combined support for Lincoln and the party with an admission of the rivalries that deeply affected what they and the government did. The Union platform lauded Lincoln for "the practical wisdom, the unselfish patriotism, and the unswerving fidelity to the Constitution and the principles of American liberty" that he displayed. The platform blessed his actions to "defend the nation against its open and secret foes," a reference to the opposition party that Republicans tried to demonize and eliminate. It also supported the Emancipation Proclamation and enrolling black soldiers, both of which reiterated a Republican belief in freedom as the view of what was supposedly no longer the Republican party. The platform resolved "That foreign immigration, which in the past has added so much to the wealth, development of resources, and increase of power to this nation, the asylum of the oppressed of all nations, should be fostered and encouraged by a liberal and just policy," as if to tell the Republican contingent from the nativist Know-Nothings of the 1850s that the past mattered little, if at all. Even if the words were those of the Union party, the melody was resoundingly Republican.[47]

But by the late summer of 1864, with victory seeming nowhere in sight, many Republicans thought that Lincoln would lose. From Buffalo, Greeley's friend Albert Brisbane reported the chilling news that "a strong reaction is setting in, in favor of the Democrats. . . . I have been among the mechanics, and the high price of provisions are driving them to wish a change," meaning that workers to whom the free labor ideology should have been most appealing doubted the party. Raymond urged Lincoln to send peace delegates to Richmond, only to be turned back by the president and three Cabinet members whose views should have convinced any doubters that more unity prevailed than they believed: Seward, wise, conservative, and distrusted by all; William Pitt Fessenden, Chase's successor, shrewdly and grouchily moderate; and Stanton, a War Democrat shifting to the radicals, blunter in his shiftiness than Seward and noisier in his curmudgeonliness than Fessenden. Late in August, despite this heartening and unusual display of cohesion, Lincoln surrendered to melancholy and wrote the "blind memorandum" in which he predicted his defeat, pledged to aid his successor, and ordered his Cabinet to sign it sight unseen. Yet even these contretemps reflected the party's ideology: not only did Lincoln feel free to tell his ministers what to do and receive obedience, but he stayed the course in which his party believed.[48]

That August, sharing Lincoln's concerns and doubting his ability to do anything to improve the situation, New York radicals acted. Greeley and two other editors—Parke Godwin of the *Evening Post* and Theodore Tilton of the abolitionist *Independent*—asked party leaders across the North whether Lincoln could win their state and should remain atop the ticket. The Democratic convention and Sherman's capture of Atlanta affected the replies, which still revealed much about the party and its ideology. Governor John Andrew of Massachusetts felt that "zeal and energy . . . on the part of the faithful who mean to preserve Liberty and Government, will enable our cause to win." Finding Lincoln "lacking in the quality of leadership, which is a gift of God and not a device of man," Andrew called him "an able and devoted magistrate." A change, Governor Samuel Cony of Maine impersonally and pragmatically said, would admit a "weakness not existing and . . . ill advised if not fatal in its consequences." According to Governor Joseph Gilmore of New Hampshire, he "has not run the machine according to God's time-table as I try to run my rail-roads. We want a President who will sacrifice every thing to a permanent, glorious and regenerated Union," an opinion lacking only specifics. Governor Richard Yates of Illinois preached to the converted: "Let our motto be that of Mr. Webster . . . 'Liberty and Union,' now and forever, one and inseperable *[sic]*." Charging them with living in a political vacuum, a West Virginian said that "the masses have an abiding confidence in

Mr. Lincoln's honesty of purpose," and called him "the strongest man . . . named in connection with the Presidency." In each case, including those of the three editors, leadership was at issue, not ideology; no one doubted that Republicans shared the same beliefs, just whether Lincoln was best suited to execute them.[49]

Sumner's position offered another sign that Republicans understood the problems inherent in running the government. An idealist and abolitionist, he seemed likely to be an early addition to the anti-Lincoln bandwagon, unless he was already driving it. But when radicals pressed him to oppose Lincoln, Sumner distanced himself. Fearing the inevitable dissension, he urged postponing all discussion of presidential politics for as long as possible. He admitted to staying aloof from the radical cabal "partly on the ground of my personal relations with the President but more because I was satisfied that it would only endanger the result." Indeed, when he learned of the effort, he told Andrew, "Of course all who wish to preserve the Union and to overthrow Slavery must act together. There must be harmony. . . . I see no way of meeting the difficulties from the candidacy of Mr. Lincoln, unless he withdraws patriotically and kindly, so as to leave no breach in the party. Will he do this?" No, and opposing him would tear at party unity, which "must be had at all hazards and at every sacrifice." Radicals complained that conservatives, namely Seward, controlled Lincoln. If Sumner believed this to be true regarding slavery, he would have joined other radicals; his refusal to do so, despite urgings from his friends, signified his confidence in Lincoln's opposition to slavery, his fear of the possibility that someone worse than Lincoln might end up in office, and his enjoyment at wielding influence. Symbolically a radical leader, Sumner helped torpedo Lincoln's foes with his silence. He showed that even the most radical, seemingly apolitical ideologue and a shrewd moderate could find common ground—in a common ideology.[50]

Lincoln's Ticket and Other Tickets

Andrew Johnson's selection as vice presidential nominee also reflected a political reality related, in an odd way, to party ideology and Sumner's role in it. More accurately, Republicans agreed so thoroughly on the issues that they hardly thought about them. But restoring the nation and creating a union of freedom meant keeping power. They liked Hannibal Hamlin, but he was a radical, and Lincoln and Union party leaders expected radicals to support the ticket; if a more radical candidate materialized, Lincoln's running mate would have no effect on what radicals did anyway. Coming from solidly Republican New England, Hamlin offered no geographic aid. He had been a Democrat—but a radically anti-slavery Democrat who left the party not because it opposed perpetuating the Union and fighting a war for that purpose, but with the others who formed the Republican party in the mid-1850s. Nor did it help his chances of remaining on the ticket that Sumner, a fellow radical, wanted him in the Senate from Maine. He found Hamlin ideologically compatible, but what mattered more to Sumner was that he hated Fessenden and the feeling was mutual. If Lincoln hoped to be reelected and knew that only the strongest ticket would help him, Hamlin was expendable. The grounds were practical, not intellectual.[51]

It was only logical for Lincoln to seek a War Democrat, especially one from a border state, as his running mate. After all, he belonged to the Union party, which had a better chance of winning votes from slave states than did Republicans, and which hoped to broaden the Union coalition. But when the party met in Baltimore Lincoln gave no instructions, presumably leaving the choice to the delegates. His secretary, John Nicolay, attended and told John Hay, "The disposition of all the delegates was to take any War Democrat, provided he would add strength to the ticket. None of the names suggested seemed to meet this requirement, and the feeling therefore is to avoid any weakness. It strikes everybody that Hamlin fills this bill." Opposition to Hamlin came from Sumner's Massachusetts and New York radicals backing War Democrat Daniel Dickinson, who neither wanted the job nor welcomed how Greeley and his allies used his name. Then Weed realized that since two New Yorkers would be unlikely to hold positions in an administration, they were trying to oust Seward, and that spurred him to action. More crucially, the issue was winning, not ideological purity. While old Whigs should have recalled that both of their vice presidents had moved to the White House with disastrous results, the thinking of Lincoln's running mate seemed immaterial. The spread of freedom, union, and power required victory, which meant choosing the best candidate; whether they belonged to the Union or Republican party, they assumed agreement or acceptance.[52]

Thus, the leaders of the sectional, anti-slavery Republican party turned to a slave-owning War Democrat from Tennessee as the vice presidential candidate on a Union ticket committed to defeating Southern secession and ending slavery. Lincoln claimed to have left it to the delegates, but he made clear that he admired Johnson as Tennessee's military governor and the only Southern senator who had refused to secede with his state. As Montgomery Blair told Lincoln, Johnson "was associated with you on the ticket . . . in condemnation of the doctrine of State suicide," Sumner's plan for radical, congressional reconstruction and against Lincoln's quest to restore the South as quickly as possible. But Sumner voiced no objections, since Johnson's selection suited his purpose of making Hamlin available to run for the Senate. More important, picking a Southern unionist made the party seem more like the Union party and less like Republicans without giving a Democrat power: Hamlin's only work as vice president had been to preside over the Senate, choose the Cabinet member from New England (Gideon Welles, whom Lincoln wanted him to select anyway), and discuss emancipation with Lincoln. A Baltimore rally captured Johnson's role by proclaiming, "Lincoln and Johnson—a Free Union—a Free Constitution and Free Labor." This was the kind of enthusiasm in a border state for which Republicans hoped—and that Hamlin was unlikely to inspire.[53]

Indeed, what Johnson was mattered far more than what he believed or might do. He balanced Lincoln on the ticket: a War Democrat with a Whig turned Republican, a slave owner with an anti-slavery politician, a tailor with a rail-splitter or, more accurately, a businessman with a lawyer. But the results fell short of expectations. Thwarting Sumner's plans, Fessenden returned to the Senate. Lincoln won again, but his margin and the reasons for his victory suggest that Johnson's effect was negligible. Yet his presence made the Union party more appealing to Democrats and Unionists—or so Republicans hoped. Johnson did no harm, and if he helped them win votes, he helped them pursue their goals.[54]

While radicals accepted Johnson as Lincoln's running mate, some of them were less sure about Lincoln, prompting still other election issues related more to ambition than to ideology. The key figure was John C. Frémont, who had twice been a major general and twice forced Lincoln to fire him: in Missouri for emancipating slaves without Lincoln's approval, for profligate spending, and for irking the powerful Blairs; and in Virginia for losing to Stonewall Jackson. Yet his exploits as a western explorer made him popular, and his anti-slavery credentials gave him great appeal among radicals, especially the strongly anti-slavery German voters who differed with many Republicans about his work in Missouri and resented Lincoln for demoting him and not promoting other Germans. They shared Frémont's hatred for Lincoln for cashiering him, and rumors spread that he had offered to come to Ohio and attack the treatment of peace Democrat Clement Vallandigham, but Democrats turned him down because they expected him to make a presidential campaign speech for himself instead.[55]

Indeed, Frémont campaigned for himself. In May 1864 his supporters, mostly Democrats grasping at straws and a few ultra-radicals who hated Lincoln, met and chose him on a ticket with Democrat John Cochrane. Most Republicans agreed with the *New York Times,* which called the conclave "a congregation of malcontents" and said, "Hostility to Abraham Lincoln was its mainspring and motive-power." Radicals and moderates lamented that Frémont had become a copperhead tool. If edited slightly, said Governor Oliver Morton of Indiana, his letter of acceptance would read like a Vallandigham screed. Worse, Democratic leaders doubted his choice of associates; if he hurt Lincoln's chances so much the better, but they had no desire to aid Frémont. Republicans agreed with Democrats: they wanted nothing to do with him but feared his German supporters, who "assert that he was laid on the shelf because of his devotedness to the cause of Freedom and Free Labor" and his feud with the Blairs. Whatever the motivations of Frémont and his allies, the question for Republicans was whether they threatened the party's continued success.[56]

Another issue for Lincoln was whether the radical anger that Frémont represented, and from which he hoped to benefit, was broad. This made the Wade-Davis Manifesto significant. When Lincoln proposed letting a Southern state rejoin the Union after 10 percent of its voters in the 1860 election had renounced secession and pledged loyalty to the Union, Davis and Senator Ben Wade of Ohio introduced a more radical reconstruction bill requiring the loyalty of half of the voters. After he let their plan pass without signing it, Lincoln announced that Southerners could choose either set of terms—as though they would prefer the more stringent one. "What an infamous proclamation!

... But what are we to do? Condemn privately and applaud publicly?" Thaddeus Stevens fumed, summing up the radical dilemma. When Wade and Davis issued their manifesto flaying Lincoln, they wound up on a limb, dangling and lonely, as other radicals kept silent. Moderate James G. Blaine of Maine said that the "very strength of the paper was ... its special weakness. It was so powerful an arraignment of the President that of necessity it rallied his friends to his support." Most abolitionists shied away from it; even with Frémont in the race, the choice for president would be between Lincoln and a Democrat, leaving them no choice. Finally, practicality prevailed: radicals may not have loved Lincoln, but he was a Republican. He disagreed with how to get where they wanted to go, but not on whether to head in that direction.[57]

The Benefits of Optimism

A Cabinet reconfiguration afforded another opportunity to examine how radicals viewed Lincoln. The Union convention, controlled by moderates, advised more unity among his advisers. Yet the only minister ditched was the only radical, Chase. In September 1864, aware of radical unhappiness and Frémont's ire at the Blairs, Zachariah Chandler brokered a deal for him to withdraw in return for Blair's ouster. Exiting gracefully, Blair stumped for Lincoln on a Union platform that called for emancipation. Doubting Blair's belief in that cause, radicals were gleeful at his departure. Tilton told a fellow abolitionist, "I have had a waking dream ... that the Angels of Heaven, hearing the other day unusual voices of gratitude ascending from a certain portion of the Earth, looked down with eagerness of curiosity in the direction whence the sounds came, and finally discovered that the spot was My Maryland, and the cause," Blair's removal. Secure in his hatred for "Traitor McClellan," Chandler marveled that Lincoln seemed "infatuated with Seward and Blair." Congratulating his colleague, Wade explained the issue facing radicals: "I can but wish the d—-l had Old Abe. But the issue is now made up and we have either got to take him, or Jeff Davis, for McClellan and all who will support him, are meaner traitors than are to be found in the Confederacy." Since freedom, union, and power required a Republican victory, Wade said, "to save the nation I am doing all for him that I possibly could do for a better man."[58]

The convention also reinvigorated Republicans, now surer than ever of Democratic disloyalty. When Democrats held their convention, Lincoln predicted, "They must nominate a Peace Democrat on a war platform, or a War Democrat on a peace platform." He was right: they called for peace and chose a ticket of McClellan and peace Democrat George Pendleton of Ohio. When McClellan's acceptance letter shied away from the platform, a Republican editor said, "He went to the Chicago gentlemen, and, with the sword given to his valor, loyalty, and fidelity, became their slave. After sealing Faust's bargain with Mephistophiles, he undertook to explain it with a letter." As Blaine said, his party benefited from "the erection of the Rebel Platform at Chicago and the fall of that one at Atlanta." War Democrats complained that their party left them no choice by abandoning the Jacksonian tradition of unionism. Everett, a conservative ex-Whig, held that Democrats lacked the responsibility to govern—a far cry from where the two parties had stood four years earlier. The Union party chose a Republican standard-bearer on a Republican platform, and won support from non-Republicans—with Democratic aid and a Republican ideology.[59]

McClellan's nomination gave Republicans the chance to voice some of their key attitudes: skepticism about the military and its commitment to victory, and certainty of opposition disloyalty. Their views of McClellan ran into four channels. One was that he meant well but lacked the courage to do well: the *Philadelphia Press* explained that he was not treasonous, just afraid to fight. Another, less charitable, cried treason: rumors of incriminating letters from McClellan spread, and some Republicans saw that as typical of a general grasping for power. The third pointed to his failings as a general, implicitly fomenting concerns about his loyalty and his ability to lead: the *Chicago Tribune* called him "the grave-digger of the Chickahominy." Finally came the idea expressed by Charles Francis Adams: "It is no time to change the helm in the midst of a storm." Weed accepted what he saw as too radical a platform, calling McClellan "wholly inexperienced in civic duties." Even then, he added, "Let us not consign all there is left of this priceless government and precious Union to the hands of those who are impatient for an ignominious shameful peace upon the best attainable terms." All reflected the party's belief that Democrats lacked legitimacy as an opposition, and the fear of a general undermining civilian government. What Republicans said reflected the usual give-and-take of politics—it had to—but they also believed in their cause.[60]

Of course, the party reserved venom for Democrats, criticizing them in ways in which it would have been difficult to attack McClellan personally. Republicans accused them of fraud and harped on their treason to the Union and their political heritage. The *Albany Morning Express* said, "We have had factious men clamoring loudly in opposition. The Government has been compelled to confront enemies in the rear as well as enemies in front. Its every step has been vehemently denounced." John Murray Forbes hoped to defuse that kind of criticism and win part of his old party to the Republicans, writing, "I deem it of the greatest consequence to establish closer relations between our administration and the true Democracy"—in other words, the sort of plan to eliminate opposition that the Union party was created to foster. Democrats who joined the party would be seen and described as loyal. Those declining to join would be labeled traitors to the Union, and thus to the freedom and power required for its salvation.[61]

What also helped power the Republican victory was the power the party most feared: the army. If Lincoln and his party needed help understanding the interplay of military and political success, given the results in 1862 and variations in public opinion, the fall of Atlanta in 1864 provided the lesson. Republicans began to breathe easier over Lincoln's chances. In September, General David Hunter, a radical who found him agreeable but slow, said, "Uncle Abe appears full of fun, and I infer that he at least feels well with regard to the result in Nov[ember]." More analytically, Forney's *Philadelphia Press* said, "Sherman's victory will annihilate the Southern Confederacy as surely as it has annihilated the Chicago platform. Its political and military values are incalculable." Similarly, Stevens viewed "Sheridan's speeches," the cavalry commander's work in the Shenandoah Valley of Virginia, as good for the party. Republicans felt queasy about the army's power, but saw that they could use it. Reaping the benefits of military victories merely meant that they must make sure that generals took no unfair advantage of their good fortune.[62]

Whether or not they knew it, though, their fate depended on a general: Ulysses Grant. Logically, they feared that Democrats might nominate him: how better to turn the tide for a party whose loyalty had been questioned than to turn to a war hero? Republicans feared that he might fall for what Medill called a copperhead plot to use him to restore themselves to power. Late in 1863, Cadwallader Washburn told his brother Elihu, the Illinois congressman who had aided in Grant's appointment, "Grant has the prestige of success and so far is the very man, but he is anything but a statesman to say nothing about some other points," and added that "if Grant allows himself to be fooled by the Copperhead Democracy, he is ruined." That effort, such as it was, failed. But one well-connected Republican, Morgan, expected Grant to replace Lincoln as the nominee if he conquered Richmond before the party convention. Morgan made a key, if obvious, point: how Grant fared would decide how the party fared in 1864. Further, Lincoln's need to broaden his support entailed that Grant succeed—and retain inept generals appointed for political purposes. The political and military were part of a coordinated effort to secure success.[63]

At the same time, Republicans depended on the army in another way. If the party lacked confidence in generals, it had faith in soldiers. If they were loyal enough to serve, either voluntarily or by accepting the draft, they were likely to vote for the party of their government, so it was crucial to that party's fortunes for them to vote. This they did, but not without controversy. Democrats objected to the process, arguing that Lincoln had won electoral support in army camps through fraud and threats; William Chandler accused them of knowing that the soldier vote would disprove claims of McClellan's popularity with his former troops. Indeed, retaining their distrust of army officers, Republicans expected McClellan's friends to pressure their men, while McClellan and his party expected Democratic generals such as George Meade and Winfield Scott Hancock, and possibly even Sherman, to take a stand only when they could tell who was likely to win. For Republicans the issue might have seemed unideological: they were trying to win. Given their intellectual adaptation to power and its uses, the question of whether and how soldiers could vote was at the heart of their thought.[64]

Equally clearly, Republicans grasped that without military success, they would probably lose. "The delay in military movements and the postponement by the democrats of their nominating convention," Raymond said in mid-July, "seems to have suspended action and checked enthusiasm in regard to the Presidential canvas throughout the country." Doubting the party's chances if the war was stalemated,

Morton called for more troops yet opposed a draft, sensing that it would hurt the party. He joined Ohio's John Brough and other western governors in a plan to raise more troops in the West. After this effort failed, Lincoln issued another call for soldiers; to his chagrin, Morton expected a draft would be required to fill this call. Throughout the summer these delays created obvious problems for Republicans: the longer the war, the greater the danger to their political fortunes. Before Democrats met in Chicago, one Republican mused that his party's hopes depended on "Grant, Sherman, and Divine Providence." While Lincoln's victory was providential, Grant and Sherman deserved credit, but so did freedom, union, and power. Committed to them all, Republicans did what they had to do to assure their party's success. On 8 November they succeeded, reelecting Lincoln with an electoral majority of 212 to 21.[65]

What Victory Meant

What Lincoln's victory meant depended on the analyst. Republicans saw that War Democrats played a key role. One of them, Dix, told Lincoln that he would be wise to concentrate on keeping their support and using their abilities. In his home state of New York, Dix suggested ignoring Governor Seymour and his "small band of poor politicians and poorer patriots," who would "taint by their narrowness of feeling and want of high principle any organization into which they enter as active elements"—as blunt an anti-Democratic statement as any Republican made. Radical Gustave Koerner of Illinois agreed that "the accession of Democrats to the Republican party gave to it impetus and aggressiveness, which carried the party to victory." Koerner may have suggested that Democratic experience with winning campaigns aided Republicans, who had lived a shorter life as a party and been less successful—and possibly less willing to do whatever it had to do to win.[66]

But even as Republicans impugned their motives, the *Springfield Republican* discerned, "The great body of the Democratic party have meant well for their country in their votes against the Administration. . . . Let their patriotism have generous recognition, and let them still further exhibit and attest it by ready acquiescence in the decision of the majority, and by cordial support of the Administration indorsed so strongly by the people." That Republicans proffered a velvet glove while a War Democrat suggested using an iron fist on his old party may have signified that the opposition, legitimate or not, refused to go away. It might have reflected relief at a hard-fought victory. It also might have been a Republican effort to keep or attract more Democratic support; after all, the party had already done that through the Union party without sacrificing its principles.[67]

Most Republicans preferred Dix's proscription to Bowles's prescription, foregoing magnanimity. Sumner pronounced the Democratic party dead, and Chase suggested investigating McClellan's loyalty. Former senator Preston King of New York blamed the closeness of the vote there on "the shameful and most criminal frauds in the changing of soldiers votes in their envelopes and the manufacture of spurious ones." In the new state of Nevada, a radical wrote, "The 'snakes' are badly whipped every where. . . . Thank God that our country is still safe and treason is dying." Something else was dying, Republicans said: their victory would prove fatal to slavery. The *Springfield Republican* predicted that the approval of the Thirteenth Amendment would prove "even more important in its ultimate consequences than the re election *[sic]* of Mr. Lincoln. It is the crowning glory of the peaceful victory of the day. It is a triumph for all time."[68]

Other Republicans were less sure of what their victory meant. While some radicals muttered that they were stuck with Lincoln for another four years, others in that wing of the party expected him to move in their direction—with good reason, given his support for emancipation. Citing the contribution of War Democrats to the party's victory, conservatives hoped for the opposite, probably in vain, since the Union party had adopted so much of the Republican party's platform and ideology. As for moderates, one of them, Andrew, said, "The vote is an earnest of the virtue and intelligence of the People and a proof that the country is and must hereafter remain true to Liberty, to Democratic ideas, Constitutional, Republican government, to its own honor and renown." Where Lincoln fit into that was uncertain, but Andrew felt that the president was now in a position to retool his Cabinet. Overseas, diplomats Adams in London and John Lothrop Motley in Vienna, a pair of historians from Andrew's Massachusetts, peered into the future and predicted that Lincoln's reelection would drive a stake through the heart of Southern hopes.[69]

Despite their frequent intramural warfare, many Republicans proudly pointed to their nation's ability to hold an election during a civil war. To do so at an unpropitious time, the *Cincinnati Commercial* said, proved "that our form of government is as strong and tenacious of life as any in the world—perhaps the strongest and most vital of them all." Not only did peace Democrats fail, but even amid threats to civil liberties, no one seemed to ponder postponing the vote in wartime, as England did. To do so would have kept Republicans in power through the kinds of methods that they accused the South of employing.[70]

The Union party, then, served its purpose by channeling passion into the cause and uniting disparate elements. Whatever they thought of Lincoln, Republicans could vote for the Union platform. War Democrats could vote for the Union candidate because the rest of their old party lacked the same unifying ideology. Indeed, Democrats proved unable to decide whether to be a war party or a peace party; trying to be both, they proved incapable of being either and lost accordingly. The Union party stood for exactly what its name implied, welcoming those who opposed Republicans into it, but with a platform that completely represented the Republican ethos. Where Republicans found the platform evasive or disagreeable they could agree with Sumner, who deemed it "our plain duty to unite without hesitation against the Chicago-ites. So important is this duty, that . . . we must not stop to debate or wrangle among ourselves."[71]

That this call for party unity came from as uncompromising a radical as could be found in the Republican organization is an irony that should be self-evident. What makes Sumner's statement especially significant is what it signified, what it said and what it did not say. The abolitionist senator from Massachusetts said nothing about the Union party platform's demand for an end to slavery. Reelecting Lincoln mattered more because it assured that Republicans continued in power, empowering them to turn their theories into practice. They believed in a restored Union in which freedom would be guaranteed in the Constitution and their party would have the power to enforce its goals and wishes. Toward that end, Republicans won over some of their old foes, at least for the moment, by changing their name, but not their principles. They united not only their party, but even some of those who had been outside it, and they did it with an ideology: freedom, union, and power.

Notes

1. Francis Lieber, "Address by Francis Lieber. Chairman of the Council's Committee on Addresses, read at the Meeting by Their Request," Rare Books and Manuscripts Library, Columbia University; Barnett, "Abraham Lincoln, the People's Candidate," 17, HL. On Lieber, see Freidel, *Francis Lieber.* See also two collections at the Huntington Library: Lieber's voluminous papers, and Barnett's many appearances as a letter writer to Samuel L. M. Barlow.

2. Baker, ed., *The Works of William H. Seward,* vol. 5, 493; Salmon P. Chase to Hiram Barney, draft, Washington, 24 May 1864, "Chase, Letters and Drafts, 1864–1873," Chase ms, HSP.

3. Thaddeus Stevens, "Reconstruction. Speech of the Hon. Thaddeus Stevens, Delivered in the City of Lancaster, September 7th, 1865" (Lancaster: Examiner and Herald Print, 1865), 8; Elkins and McKitrick, *The Age of Federalism,* 77–78, 263.

4. David Potter, "Jefferson Davis and the Political Factors in Confederate Defeat," in Donald, ed., *Why the North Won the Civil War,* 91–112; Eric L. McKitrick, "Party Politics and the Union and Confederate War Efforts," in Chambers and Burnham, eds., *The American Party Systems,* 117–51; Michael F. Holt, "Abraham Lincoln and the Politics of Union," in Thomas, ed., *Abraham Lincoln and the American Political Tradition,* 111–41; Neely, *The Union Divided.*

5. Richard Hofstadter, *The Idea of a Party System: The Rise of Legitimate Opposition in the United States, 1780–1840* (Berkeley: University of California Press, 1969), 1–211 and *passim;* Stanley M. Elkins and Eric L. McKitrick, "Richard Hofstadter: A Progress," in Elkins and McKitrick, eds., *The Hofstadter Aegis: A Memorial* (New York: Alfred A. Knopf, 1974), 300–68.

6. Hofstadter, *The Idea of a Party System,* 212–71. On the end of the second party system, see Foner, *Free Soil;* Holt, *The Rise and Fall of the American Whig Party;* Gienapp, *The Origins of the Republican Party.*

7. Hofstadter, *The Idea of a Party System,* 268. Fehrenbacher, *The Dred Scott Case,* addresses the ramifications of the case.

8. Congressional Union Committee, "The Chicago Copperhead Convention. The Treasonable and Revolutionary Utterances of the Men Who Composed It. Extracts from all the Notable Speeches delivered in and out of the National 'Democratic' Convention. A Surrender to the Rebels Advocated—A Disgraceful and Pusillanimous Peace Demanded—The Federal Government Shamefully Villified, and Not a Word Said Against the Cause of Treason and Rebellion" (Washington: Congressional Union Committee, 1864).

9. Paludan, *"A People's Contest,"* 231; *New York Evening Post,* 9 February 1863, and 6 October 1864; Horace Greeley to W. O. Bartlett, New York, 30 August 1864, Greeley ms, Box 2, New York Public Library; "Resolutions, presented, at the request of the Committee of Arrangements, at a Union Meeting, held at Cooper Institute, New York, October 29, 1863, on the eve of the New York State Election" (n.p., 1863), 14–15, HL; *Chicago Tribune,* 10 February 1864, in *The Chicago Tribune,* vol. 1, 308; Neely, *The Union Divided,* 40–45; James E. Harvey to William Henry Seward, Lisbon, 26 October 1862, Seward ms, Reel 72, UR.

10. A. "Byington" to Sydney Howard Gay, Washington, 19 July 1863, Gay ms, Reel 1, CU; William H. Kent to Gay, Washington, 21 July and 17 August 1863, Gay ms, Reel 4, CU; *New York Tribune,* 8 October 1862, in Alexander, *A Political History of the State of New York,* vol. 3, 45–46; George R. Sage to Robert Schenck, Lebanon, 17 October 1864, Schenck ms, Hayes Historical Library, Fremont, Ohio; John Jay, "The Great Issue. An Address delivered before The Union Campaign Club, of East Brooklyn, New York, on Tuesday Evening, Oct. 25, 1864" (New York: Baker and Godwin, 1864), 12; Nicolay, *Lincoln's Secretary,* 165; Kinsley, *The Chicago Tribune,* vol. 1, 338; Kelley, "Speeches of Hon. William D. Kelley," 8; M. R. Butz, "Great Speech in Vindication of President Lincoln, delivered at Columbus, Illinois, April 30, 1864" (Quincy, Ill.: Whig and Republican Job Office, 1864), 14–15. For reports and rumors flowing to Seward, see John Livingston to Seward, New York, 4 October 1862, Seward ms, Reel 72, UR; David M. Nagle to Seward, New York, 13 October 1862, ibid.; William M. Burr to Seward, Casenovia, 24 October 1862, ibid.; Jonathan Amory to Seward, Boston, 19 August 1863, ibid., Reel 79, UR; Solomon Caldwell to Seward, Greenwood Lake, 12 October 1863, ibid., Reel 80, UR; Alfred Conkling to Seward, Rochester, 28 November 1863, ibid., Reel 81, UR; Franklin Pierce to Seward, Concord, 7 January 1862, Pierce ms, Box 4, Folder 9, NHHS.

11. *CG,* 37, 3, 9 December 1862, 35, and 7 February 1863, 804; Seward to Thurlow Weed, Washington, 1 April 1862, Weed ms, UR; John Y. Foster to Horace N. Congar, Newark, 4 February 1863, Congar ms, Box 1, NJHS. See also Congar to Marcus L. Ward, Hong Kong, 11 August 1862, Ward ms, Box 2, ibid.; George Gibbs to John A. Stevens, Jr., New York, 5 October 1862, John A. Stevens ms, 1862–63 Correspondence, NYHS; Benson J. Lossing to Gustavus V. Fox, Poughkeepsie, 26 October 1864, Fox ms, Box 9, ibid.; James A. Garfield to Burke Hinsdale, Murfreesboro, 26 May 1863, Garfield ms, Reel 106, LC.

12. Powell, "Extract from a Letter: The Trial of Our Democratic Form of Government, the Great Question now to be solved, is a democratic government a possible thing, or must we have a despotism?" (Philadelphia: C.

Sherman and Son, 1863), HL, 8–9; Henry Charles Lea, "The Record of the Democratic Party, 1860–1865" (Philadelphia: Union League of Philadelphia, 1865), HL, 39. See also Paludan, *"A People's Contest,"* 90–91; Barnett to Barlow, Washington, 6 and 22 June 1863, Barlow ms, Box 45, Huntington Library; Stampp, *Indiana Politics,* 82–83; *CG,* 37, 3, 3 March 1863, 1491 (Trumbull); *CG,* 38, 1, 2 February 1864, 456 (Representative Thomas Davis).

13. John Murray Forbes to William Cullen Bryant, Boston, 30 September 1864, Bryant-Godwin ms, Box 6, NYPL; H. O. Reilly to James R. Doolittle, New York, 1 August 1862, Doolittle ms, Personal Miscellaneous, NYPL; Timothy O. Howe to Seward, Green Bay, 27 September 1863, Seward ms, Reel 80, UR, original in Howe ms, Wisconsin State Historical Society; *Springfield Republican,* 9 November 1864, in Merriam, *The Life and Times of Samuel Bowles,* vol. 1, 362; Montgomery Blair to Barlow, Washington, 29 October 1863, Barlow ms, Box 45, Huntington Library; John A. Dix to Francis Preston Blair, Detroit, 24 September 1864, Blair-Lee Family ms, Box 9, Folder 12, Princeton.

14. George H. Baker to Bayard Taylor, Philadelphia, 20 May 1863, Bayard Taylor Papers (Taylor ms), No. 1169, Box 1, CR; Lea, "The Record of the Democratic Party," 1–2; William E. Chandler to Henry J. Raymond, Treasury Department, 20 October 1865, George Jones Papers (George Jones ms), NYPL; Chandler to Gideon Welles, copy, Concord, 25 February 1865, Chandler ms, Box 12, Folder 6, NHHS.

15. *Sacramento Union,* 17 June 1862, in Clark, *Leland Stanford,* 150; *CG,* 37, 1, 18 July 1861, 193; Paludan, *"A People's Contest,"* 237; Stevens, "Reconstruction," 8.

16. *Indianapolis Daily Journal,* 20 August 1861, in Stampp, *Indiana Politics,* 94–95.

17. Boston, Tuesday, 16 April 1861, Diary of Charles Francis Adams, 10 November 1860–31 December 1861, Adams Family ms, II, Reel 76, MHS; Clark, *Leland Stanford,* 101–02, 117–18; *Cecil Whig,* 29 June, 10 and 31 August 1861, in Baker, *The Politics of Continuity,* 63; *The Liberator,* 19 April 1861; William Lloyd Garrison to Oliver Johnson, Boston, 19 and 23 April 1861, Garrison ms, Boston Public Library, in Lockwood, "Garrison and Lincoln," 211–12; George Livermore to Sumner, Boston, 2 October 1861, Reel 23, SP; Jay to Sumner, Katonah, 28 July 1861, ibid.; Stampp, *Indiana Politics,* 73–75.

18. Chase to W. C. Gould, Washington, 15 July 1861, draft, "Chase, Letters and Drafts, 1825–1863," Chase ms, HSP; Hiram Atkins to Justin Morrill, Bellows Falls, 17 May 1861, Morrill ms, Box 51, LC; William Jayne to Trumbull, Yancton, 15 October 1861, Trumbull ms, Reel 11, LC; James S. Rollins to Frederick W. Seward, Columbia, 27 November 1863, William

Henry Seward ms, Reel 81, UR. See also Carman and Luthin, *Lincoln and the Patronage.*

19. *Chicago Tribune,* 16 October 1861, in Kinsley, *The Chicago Tribune,* vol. 1, 212; *Chicago Tribune,* 10 July 1862, ibid., 241.

20. Loyal National League, "The Sumter Anniversary, 1863. Opinions of Loyalists concerning The Great Questions of the Times; expressed in the speeches and letters from prominent citizens of all sections and parties, on occasion of the inauguration of The Loyal National League, in Mass Meeting on Union Square, New York, on the 11th of April, 1863, the Anniversary of the Attack on Fort Sumter" (New York: C. S. Westcott and Co., 1863), Speech of O. P. Morton, 14, 40–41; George Opdyke to the Common Council, New York, 7 July 1862, in "Proceedings at the Mass Meeting of Loyal Citizens, on Union Square, New York, 15th Day of July, 1862" (New York: George F. Nesbitt and Co., 1862), 6.

21. Paul A. Varg, *Edward Everett: The Intellectual in the Turmoil of Politics* (Selinsgrove, Pa.: Susquehanna University Press, 1992), 210–11 and *passim;* Alexander, *A Political History of the State of New York,* vol. 3, 26; Baker, *The Politics of Continuity,* 128–29.

22. *Albany Morning Express,* 14 September 1864, in Charles E. Smith to Sumner, Albany, 16 September 1864, Reel 31, SP.

23. DeWitt C. Clarke to Frederick W. Seward, Washington, 27 October 1863, William Henry Seward ms, Reel 80, UR; Richard M. Blatchford to William H. Seward, New York, 22 October 1863, ibid.; Theodore M. Pomeroy and Thomas Kirkpatrick to Seward, Auburn, 22 October 1863, ibid.; G. G. Benedict to Morrill, Burlington, 17 June 1862, Morrill ms, Box 51, LC; Richardson and Farley, *John Palmer Usher,* 70–71; Stampp, *Indiana Politics,* 96–97; Dale Baum, *The Civil War Party System: The Case of Massachusetts, 1848–1876* (Chapel Hill: University of North Carolina Press, 1984), 58; Baker, *The Politics of Continuity,* 82, 113.

24. Jay to Sumner, New York, 27 September 1862, Reel 26, SP; *CG,* 37, 3, 8 December 1862, 13; *CG,* 38, 1, 23 June 1864, 3202; *Cincinnati Commercial,* 11 November 1864, copy, Allan Nevins ms, Box 5, HL; Kinsley, *The Chicago Tribune,* vol. 1, 274.

25. Rawley, *Edwin D. Morgan,* 212; Stampp, *Indiana Politics,* 92–99; Paludan, *"A People's Contest,"* 86–87; Baum, *The Civil War Party System,* 70.

26. Foner, *Free Soil, passim;* Paludan, *"A People's Contest,"* 255–56.

27. Yates to Trumbull, Springfield, 12 January 1863, Trumbull ms, Reel 14, LC; Paludan, *"A People's Contest,"* 19.

28. Thomas and Hyman, *Stanton,* 259, 278, 443–45; Merriam, *The Life and Times of Samuel Bowles,* vol. 1, 390–91; John Van Buren to Seward, New

York, 7 May 1863, Seward ms, Reel 77, UR; Edward L. Pierce to Sumner, Boston, 25 January 1865, Reel 32, SP.

29. Richard H. Abbott, *Ohio's Civil War Governors* (Columbus: Ohio State University Press, for the Ohio Historical Society, 1962), 39; *CG,* 37, 2, 10 July 1862, 3220; *CG,* 37, 3, 11 December 1862, 64; *South Bend Register,* 27 February 1862, in Smith, *Colfax,* 170–71; Emma L. Thornbrough, *Indiana in the Civil War Era, 1850–1880* (Indianapolis: Indiana Historical Bureau, 1965), 116; *Indianapolis Daily Journal,* 25 February 1862, in Stampp, *Indiana Politics,* 98.

30. Joseph Holt to James G. Blaine, Washington, 27 July 1863, Blaine ms, Reel 7, LC; Stampp, *Indiana Politics,* 136–37; *New York Tribune,* 5 September 1861, in Alexander, *A Political History of the State of New York,* vol. 3, 17; Everett to Adams, Boston, 11 April 1864, Adams Family ms, IV, March–April 1864, Reel 569, MHS; McCormick, ed., *Memoirs of Gustave Koerner,* vol. 2, 206; Sewell, *John P. Hale,* 192.

31. Joshua R. Giddings to George W. Julian, Montreal, 22 March 1863, Giddings-Julian ms, Volume 5, LC; Stampp, *Indiana Politics,* 134–35; Julian, *Political Recollections,* 223–24 and *passim;* Edward C. Smith, *The Borderland in the Civil War* (New York: Macmillan, 1927), 318–19; Garfield to L. Day, Camp Chase, 30 August 1861, Garfield ms, Series 5, Reel 106, LC; Garfield to J. Q. Smith, Murfreesboro, 30 May 1863, ibid.; Jacob M. Howard to Austin Blair, Washington, 17 May 1862, Blair ms, Burton Historical Collection, Detroit Public Library, typescript, Nevins ms, Box 17, HL; William E. Chandler to "Dear Sir," Concord, 25 November 1862, Chandler ms, Box 12, Folder 4, NHHS.

32. George Bancroft to Dean Milman, Newport, 15 August 1861, Bancroft ms, Box 2, NYPL; Lydia Maria Child to Parke Godwin, Wayland, 13 December 1864, Godwin ms, Box 5, ibid.

33. *Chicago Tribune,* 31 August 1864, in Kinsley, *The Chicago Tribune,* vol. 1, 337, and *passim;* Van Deusen, *Horace Greeley.*

34. The best means of tracing this evolution is through Paludan, *The Presidency of Abraham Lincoln.*

35. See especially Zornow, *Lincoln and the Party Divided,* and Long, *The Jewel of Liberty.*

36. See especially Paludan, *The Presidency of Abraham Lincoln;* Medill to Trumbull, Chicago, 25 June and 4 July 1862, Trumbull ms, Reel 13, LC.

37. Berwanger, "Lincoln's Constitutional Dilemma," 37–38; Lovejoy to Garrison, 22 February 1864, Garrison ms, Boston Public Library, in Magdol, *Owen Lovejoy,* 400; Lockwood, "Garrison and Lincoln," 221–22.

38. *Chicago Tribune,* 4 April 1864, in Kinsley, *The Chicago Tribune,* vol. 1, 316; Winter Davis to Chandler, n.p., 24 August 1864, Chandler ms, Reel 2, LC.

39. Kasson to Greeley, Washington, 24 January 1864, Greeley ms, Box 3, Folder 14, NYPL; Colfax to Gay, Washington, 6 February 1864, Gay ms, Reel 6, CU; Trumbull to H. G. McPike, draft, Washington, 6 February 1864, Trumbull ms, Reel 15, LC.

40. William E. Chandler to Amos Tuck, draft, Philadelphia, 15 December 1863, Chandler ms, Box 12, Folder 5, NHHS; J. Harry Rhodes to Garfield, Cleveland, 4 February 1864, Garfield ms, Reel 12, LC; L. W. Hall to Garfield, Ravenna, 10 January 1864, ibid.; William Claflin to Sumner, Boston, 18 December 1863, Reel 30, SP; John Gorham Palfrey to Charles Francis Adams, Boston, 18 April 1864, Adams Family ms, IV, March–April 1864, Reel 569, MHS.

41. Greeley to Booll, New York, 11 October 1863, J. W. Hill ms, CU; Greeley to Chase, New York, 29 September 1863, Chase ms, Box 5, HSP; Chase to H. S. Bundy, Washington, 20 November 1861, "Copies of Special Letters, 1861–1865, Bound," ibid.; Rufus Spaulding to Chase, Connecticut, 13 August 1863, and Washington, 6 January 1864, Box 10, HSP; Giddings to Chase, Jefferson, 13 January 1863, Box 5, HSP; White to Fessenden, Washington, 2 November 1863, Fessenden ms, Reel 2, LC; Colfax to Greeley, Washington, 24 January 1864, Greeley ms, Box 6, Folder 16, NYPL.

42. White to Greeley, Washington, 13 February 1864, Greeley ms, Box 3, Folder 14, NYPL; A. Byington to Gay, Washington, 28 February 1864, Gay ms, Reel 1, CU.

43. Donald, *Lincoln,* 483.

44. Lieber to Sumner, New York, 16 March 1864, Series II, Reel 78, SP; David Davis to Weed, Washington, 14 March 1864, Weed ms, UR; Morgan to Weed, Washington, 17 March 1864, ibid.

45. *Chicago Tribune,* 7 and 9 June 1864, in Kinsley, *The Chicago Tribune,* vol. 1, 325–26; *Indianapolis Daily Journal,* 11 June 1864, in Stampp, *Indiana Politics,* 225; Davis to Lincoln, Bloomington, 2 June 1864, Davis ms, Chicago Historical Society, typescript, Nevins ms, Box 17, Envelope 1, HL.

46. Dana to Raymond, Washington, 26 July 1864, Jones ms, NYPL; Belz, *Reconstructing the Union,* 213–15; Rawley, *Edwin D. Morgan,* 198; Sumner to Charles Eliot Norton, Senate Chamber, 2 May 1864, Series II, Reel 78, SP; "To the National Executive Committee of the Union and Republican Parties," New York, 26 March 1864, John A. Stevens ms, 1864–68, NYHS; Chandler to Joseph A. Gilmore, Concord, 3 April 1864, Gilmore ms, Box 2, Folder 23, NHHS.

47. On the platform and the machinations behind it, see Zornow, *Lincoln and the Party Divided;* Long, *The Jewel of Liberty;* and Waugh, *Reelecting Lincoln.*

48. Albert Brisbane to Greeley, Buffalo, 2 August 1864, Greeley ms, Box 3, Folder 15, NYPL; Raymond to Cameron, New York, 19 August 1864,

Cameron ms, Reel 10, LC; Nicolay to John Hay, Washington, 25 August 1864, in Nicolay, *Lincoln's Secretary,* 212; Nicolay to Therena Bates, Washington, 28 August 1864, ibid., 213. See Gay to Elizabeth Gay, New York, 6 August 1864, Gay ms, Box 31, CU; Cameron to Francis Preston Blair, Harrisburg, 17 July 1864, Blair-Lee Family ms, Box 8, Folder 4, Princeton; Shelton to Weed, Boston, 25 and 27 August 1864, Weed ms, UR.

49. Greeley to Opdyke, New York, 19 August 1864, John A. Stevens ms, 1864–68, NYHS; Andrew to Greeley, Parke Godwin, and Theodore Tilton, Boston, 3 September 1864, Theodore Tilton Papers (Tilton ms), NYHS; Samuel Cony to Greeley, Godwin, and Tilton, Augusta, 5 September 1864, ibid.; Gilmore to Tilton, Concord, 5 September 1864, ibid.; Yates to Greeley, Godwin, and Tilton, Springfield, 6 September 1864, ibid.; Arthur J. Boreman to Greeley, Godwin, and Tilton, Wheeling, 8 September 1864, ibid.; Thomas Carney to Tilton and others, Leavenworth, 12 September 1864, ibid.; Buckingham to Greeley, Godwin, and Tilton, Norwich, 3 September 1864, ibid.; James Y. Smith to Greeley, Godwin, and Tilton, Providence, 3 September 1864, ibid.; Eugene Pringle to Greeley, Godwin, and Tilton, Jackson, 5 September 1864, ibid.; John Brough to Tilton, Columbus, 5 September 1864, ibid.; J. Gregory Smith to Tilton, St. Albans, 7 September 1864, ibid.; William M. Stone to Greeley and others, Des Moines, 9 September 1864, ibid.; unsigned, apparently Andrew Curtin to Greeley, Godwin, and Tilton, Saratoga Springs, 8 September 1864, ibid.; Stephen Miller to Greeley, Godwin, and Tilton, St. Paul, 9 September 1864, ibid.; Austin Blair to Greeley, Godwin, and Tilton, Saginaw, 11 September 1864, ibid.; William Cannon to Greeley, Godwin, and Tilton, Wilmington, 12 September 1864, ibid.

50. Sumner to Andrew, Boston, 24 August 1864, Series II, Reel 78, SP; also in SP: Sumner to Lieber, Boston, 3 September 1864, Series I, Reel 64; Sumner to Forney, Boston, 6 August 1864, Series II, Reel 78; Sumner to Bright, Boston, 27 September 1864. On postponement, see Sumner to Lieber, Senate Chamber, 15 February 1864, and n.p., ca. May 1864, Series I, Reel 64, SP; Sumner to Brownson, Senate Chamber, 22 March 1864, ibid.; Sumner to Mary Booth, Senate Chamber, 18 March 1864, ibid.; Sumner to Lydia Maria Child, Boston, 7 August 1864, ibid.; Franklin B. Sanborn to Conway, Worcester, 3 May 1864, Conway ms, Box 19, CU.

51. On Sumner and Fessenden, see Sumner to Pierce, Boston, ca. January 1865, Series I, Reel 64, SP; Nicolay, *Lincoln's Secretary,* 207–8; James F. Glonek, "Lincoln, Johnson, and the Baltimore Ticket," *The Abraham Lincoln Quarterly* 6, no. 5 (March 1951): 255–71; Donald, *Lincoln,* 503–7; H. Draper Hunt, *Hannibal Hamlin of Maine: Lincoln's First Vice-President* (Syracuse, N.Y.: Syracuse University Press, 1969), *passim.*

52. Nicolay, *Lincoln's Secretary,* 207–8; Daniel Dickinson to John A. Stevens Jr., Binghamton, 26 August 1864, John A. Stevens ms, 1864–68, NYHS.

53. Belz, *Reconstructing the Union,* 213; Wagandt, *The Mighty Revolution,* 254; *Indianapolis Daily Journal,* 24 February 1864, in Stampp, *Indiana Politics,* 222; Dawes to Ella Dawes, Washington, 9 June 1864, Dawes ms, Box 13, LC; Hamlin to Cameron, Bangor, 18 June 1864, Cameron ms, Reel 10, LC.

54. Fessenden to Israel Washburn, Washington, 18 November 1864, Fessenden ms, Reel 3, LC. On Johnson, see Trefousse, *Andrew Johnson.*

55. On Frémont, see Rolle, *John Charles Frémont.* On his problems, see William H. Kent to Gay, *Tribune* Rooms, 25 February 1864, Gay ms, Reel 4, CU; Medill to Washburne, Chicago, 12 February 1864, Washburne ms, Volume 34, LC; Lieber to Sumner, New York, 26 and 31 January, and 4 February 1864, Series II, Reel 77, SP; H. C. Page to John A. Stevens, New York, 27 May 1864, Stevens ms, 1864–68, NYHS.

56. *New York Times,* 28 May and 3 June 1864; Stampp, *Indiana Politics,* 225; Monroe Porter to Horace Congar, Newark, 1 October 1864, Congar ms, Box 1, NJHS.

57. Thaddeus Stevens to Edward McPherson, n.p., 10 July 1864, Stevens ms, LC; Blaine, *Twenty Years of Congress,* vol. 2, 43–44; Belz, *Reconstructing the Union,* 227–31; *New York Times,* 9 August 1864.

58. Tilton to Judge Bond, New York, 26 September 1864, Tilton ms, NYHS; Chandler to Letitia Chandler, Washington, 2 September 1864, Chandler ms, Reel 2, LC; Wade to Chandler, Jefferson, 2 October 1864, ibid.; Cameron to Francis Preston Blair, Harrisburg, 25, September 1864, Blair-Lee Family ms, Box 8, Folder 4, Princeton.

59. Donald, *Lincoln,* 530; *Philadelphia Press,* 12 September 1864, in Nevins ms, Box 5, HL; Blaine to Raymond, Augusta, 14 September 1864, Jones ms, NYPL; Dix to Blair, Detroit, 24 September 1864, Blair-Lee Family ms, Box 9, Folder 12, Princeton; Varg, *Edward Everett,* 215–16.

60. *Philadelphia Press,* 29 September 1864, Nevins ms, Box 5, HL; Lieber to Sumner, New York, 14 September 1864, Series II, Reel 78, SP; Kinsley, *The Chicago Tribune,* vol. 1, 296; Adams to Everett, London, 16 September 1864, Adams Family ms, II, Charles Francis Adams, Letterbook, 5 March–31 October 1864, Reel 171, MHS; *New York Times,* 17 October 1864; Adams to Motley, London, 7 September 1864, Adams Family ms, II, Charles Francis Adams, Letterbook, 5 March–31 October 1864, Reel 171, MHS.

61. Colfax to Raymond, South Bend, 8 October 1864, George Jones Papers (Jones ms), NYPL; *Philadelphia Press,* 20 September and 13 October 1864, Nevins ms, Box 5, HL; *Albany Morning Express,* 14 September 1864, in Charles E. Smith to Sumner, Albany, 16 September 1864, Reel 31, SP; Forbes to Bryant, Boston, 30 September 1864, Bryant-Godwin ms, Box 6, NYPL.

62. Hunter to Halpine, Washington, 9 September 1864, Halpine ms, Box 3, HL; *Philadelphia Press,* 7 September 1864, Nevins ms, Box 5, HL; Stevens to Morrill, Lancaster, 7 October 1864, Morrill ms, Box 7, LC.

63. Medill to Washburne, Chicago, 30 May 1864, Washburne ms, Volume 38, LC; Cadwallader C. Washburn to Washburne, Carrollton, 5 September 1863, and La Crosse, 21 February 1864, in Hunt, *Israel, Elihu, and Cadwallader Washburn,* 342–43; Alexander McClure to Stevens, Chambersburg, 9 March 1864, Stevens ms, Box 2, LC; *Chicago Tribune,* 23 December 1863, in Kinsley, *The Chicago Tribune,* vol. 1, 297; Rawley, *Edwin D. Morgan,* 197; Simpson, *Let Us Have Peace,* 63–64, 278, n. 77 and *passim.*

64. McClellan to Samuel S. Cox, Orange, 20 October [1864], Thomas F. Madigan ms, NYPL; William E. Chandler, "The Soldier's Right to Vote: Who Opposes It? Who Favors It? Or, the Record of the McClellan Copperheads Against Allowing the Soldier who Fights, the Right to Vote while Fighting" (Washington, D.C.: Lemuel Towers, for the Union Congressional Committee, 1864); Rawley, *Edwin D. Morgan,* 200; E. D. Townsend to August Belmont, Washington, 23 September 1864, Box 55, Barlow ms, HL; McClellan to Barlow, Orange, 13 October 1864, Box 53, ibid.; William Henry Wadsworth to Barlow, Maysville, 24 October 1864, Box 55, ibid.

65. Raymond to Cameron, New York, 17 July 1864, Cameron ms, Reel 10, LC; Stampp, *Indiana Politics,* 227–30; Daniel Porter to Congar, Somerville, 1 September 1864, Congar ms, Box 1, NJHS; Silas Merchant to N. Congar, Newark, 2 September 1864, ibid.; Henry Adams to Charles Francis Adams Jr., London, 8 July 1864, Adams Family ms, IV, July–August 1864, Reel 571, MHS.

66. Dix to Lincoln, Headquarters Department of the East, New York City, 12 November 1864, Dix ms, Box 4, CU; McCormick, ed., *Memoirs of Gustave Koerner,* vol. 2, 206.

67. *Springfield Republican,* 9 November 1864, in Merriam, *The Life and Times of Samuel Bowles,* vol. 1, 362; King to Francis Preston Blair, Ogdensburgh, 25 November 1864, Blair-Lee Family ms, Box 15, Folder 2, Princeton.

68. Neely, *The Union Divided,* 168–72; King to Doolittle, Ogdensburgh, 26 November 1864, Doolittle ms, Personal Miscellaneous, NYPL; North to Ann North, Washoe City, 7 November 1864, North ms, Box 11, HL; *Springfield Republican,* 10 November 1864, in Merriam, *The Life and Times of Samuel Bowles,* vol. 1, 363; Chase to Greeley, Cincinnati, 10 November 1864, Greeley ms, Box 6, LC; George W. Patterson to Trumbull Cary, Westfield, 16 November 1864, Patterson ms, UR.

69. Andrew to Francis Preston Blair, Boston, 13 November 1864, Blair-Lee Family ms, Box 4, Folder 9, Princeton; Adams to Everett, Hanger Hill,

Ealing, 22 November 1864, Adams Family ms, II, Charles Francis Adams, Letterbook, 3 November 1864–10 June 1865, Reel 172, MHS; Adams to Charles Francis Adams Jr., London, 25 November 1864, Adams Family ms, IV, September–December 1864, Reel 572, MHS; Motley to Adams, Vienna, 3 September 1864, ibid.; Shelton to Weed, Boston, 13 September 1864, Weed ms, UR; Ira B. Brown to Hale, n.p., 12 December 1864, Hale ms, Box 14, Folder 17, NHHS.

70. *Cincinnati Commercial,* 11 November 1864, Nevins ms, Box 5, HL; Benjamin Moran to Webb, London, 21 November 1864, Webb ms, Box 14, Folder 146, Sterling Library, Yale University; Paludan, *"A People's Contest,"* 245–46; E. W. Scudder to Dayton, Trenton, 14 December 1864, Dayton ms, Box 3, Folder 8, Princeton.

71. Paludan, *"A People's Contest,"* 258; Sumner to "Dear Madam," Boston, 16 September 1864, Series II, Reel 78, SP.

9

Reforming and Remaking the Nation

WHILE THADDEUS STEVENS seemed to embody radical Republicanism, Thomas Ewing was a quintessential conservative. Known for bitter partisanship, blistering comments about colleagues and issues, and power over House Republicans before the title of majority leader existed, Stevens never hid his desire to free slaves and clothe them with economic and political freedom. A former senator and member of two presidential cabinets, Ewing became a conservative Republican. After joining the new party, the aging politicians retained enough Whiggery to support the internal improvements their old party deemed necessary to developing the nation's economic power. The radical and the conservative endorsed a railroad to the Pacific. "We must either agree to surrender our Pacific possessions to a separate empire or unite them to the Atlantic by a permanent highway of this kind. The Romans consolidated their power by building solid roads from the capital to their provinces," Stevens said. Lobbying for his father and the railroad builders, Thomas Ewing Jr. said, "We are waking up the Abolitionists in favor of the Bill on the ground that the increased demand for labor arising from the contracting for construction will give employ directly and indirectly to tens of thousands of the contrabands, about whom they are greatly troubled."[1]

This strange combination exemplified Republican ideology. Stevens, who later advocated turning plantations over to the ex-slaves who had worked on them and needs no defenders of his support for civil rights, spoke of national power and the need to secure the Pacific to the United States. Never noted for a commitment to black freedom, the Ewings advertised the railroad to radicals as a way to aid black laborers and the free labor cause. They sought basically the same ends through different means. If the radical and conservative somehow seemed to change places, they still occupied Republican ground. They backed a transcontinental railroad as a means of spreading freedom, union, and power. To build it would offer land and opportunity for free labor, bring unionists westward, and aid the power of the party responsible for its construction.

Stevens and Ewing reflected several beliefs that coalesced into the party's ideology. The railroad would be a boon to free labor, opening new vistas for workers. Building and operating it would aid the businessmen whom Republicans cultivated in pursuit of financial and moral support for themselves and the war. Linking East and West with the transcontinental line highlighted their commitment to turning a sectionally divided country into a nation, developing the West, expanding their party, and revising expectations of government. It might seem odd to call the railroad, part of a web of land speculation and political machines, an effort to reform the government and nation. But if what Republicans intended and achieved differed, their achievements and their ideology proved inseparable. Representative Burt Van Horn of New York explained the connection: "The construction of the Pacific Railroad . . . will bear no insignificant part in making this Congress what it really is, the conservator of the highest welfare of the people, and the depository of great trusts faithfully kept and executed." Republicans demonstrated a capacity to govern and vision for the nation's future. To be a part of that future, they would have to realize their vision of perpetuating freedom, the Union, and their own power.[2]

Building Railroads, Building Bridges

As a Republican achievement, the railroad was doubly ironic. Some feared that the iron horse would force adaptation to modern methods, damaging the purity not only of the party but also of the free labor ideals they sought to protect. When its builders later dominated the politics of the last third of the century, the great trust was not what Van Horn had in mind; instead, the great trust proved to be the railroad. A transcontinental line was more than a Republican issue: all parties and regions entered the debate in the 1850s, with nearly everyone for it, but divided over who would build it and where to build it. In 1860, the party's radicals and former Whigs came out strongly for building the line, and Lincoln's election meant that this plan gained a strong backer in the White House. By removing the South from Congress, secession empowered Republicans and shoved easterners into what would be, Republicans hoped, decisive action to keep the West both literally tied to the Union and pleased to realize its desire for a railroad. Constructing the railroad had fit in with the antebellum party's vision of encouraging free labor to spread into the West. It would fit with the wartime party's hopes for enhancing federal power and its own power by spreading its ideology of freedom and union across the country.[3]

As often happened in moving from opposition to power, Republicans had trouble translating goals into reality—at least, the reality they expected. Congress passed the bill easily—79 to 49 in the House, 35 to 5 in the Senate—and Lincoln signed the Pacific Railway Act on 1 July 1862. Later bills cruised to approval, but the road was tortuous. Much depended on events in California, where the Union party was taking over. In 1861 the Central Pacific's organizers included a candidate for governor, Leland Stanford. "A good deal depends upon the election of Stanford, for the prestige of electing a Republican ticket will go a great way toward getting us what we want," Theodore Judah, the road's driving force, said that September in what may be described as a double-edged analysis. The party's quest to broaden its base tended to be all-encompassing, but belonged to the third prong of its wartime ideology; and Republicans understood that their power to govern clothed them with the power to act. With the election the rest of the Big Four—Charles Crocker, Collis Huntington, and Mark Hopkins—was in place, and Stanford was perfectly positioned to aid them. Judah went to Washington, winning over a representative from California as they shared a steamer to Panama, a trip the railroad would eliminate. He obtained patronage jobs for himself on key committees considering the measure, for which he and California's delegation lobbied at every turn.[4]

As the Central Pacific and California urged them on, the eastern portion—the Union Pacific—drew more of the party's attention. This was due in part to being closer to where most Republicans came from, but more to questions tied to building the rest of the line: federal plans for branch roads, and what these policies meant. While John Sherman planned to vote for the Pacific Railway Act, including its branches, he admitted to doubts: "All the other sections of this country have, without the aid of the General Government, or with but the aid of grants of land, constructed their railroads; and there is no propriety in the Government doing anything more than to leap over the desert, which probably will not be peopled for many years." Other Republicans agreed, but their concerns were rooted in politics. Senators Lyman Trumbull of Illinois and Daniel Clark of New Hampshire insisted that the purpose of building branch lines was to serve the interests of those roads and any state officials who might benefit from them. These interests were often in conflict. John Watts, the House delegate for New Mexico territory, complained that some who claimed to back a railroad would never agree on a bill "unless it starts in the corner of every man's farm and runs through all his neighbors' plantations." Republicans wanted to achieve their vision, but that vision also revolved around pure politics, a discovery that displeased some of them.[5]

More vexing was the question of how to divide the work between public and private or where business and the government's business merged. Railroad officials sought favored status, meaning federal aid. They built ties to Republicans such as Representative James Blaine of Maine, whose career suffered amid charges that he profited from his ties to them, and western congressmen whose states became tools of railroad owners. A letter in which Blaine reported to the elder Ewing, whose family invested in Kansas railroads, was instructive. Blaine was a politician of doubtful ethics and great ambition, and, later, a secretary of state with visions of empire—a view that demanded a transcontinental railroad to bind the nation. Ewing appreciated his efforts to win over Justin Morrill, a representative from Vermont. Blaine replied that he served him better by lobbying Fessenden, who was "rancorously hostile to the whole thing—d——d *[sic]* it soundly as a job—extravagant, inopportune and reckless. . . . Had he taken this position in the Senate as Chmn of Finance he would have killed the bill. He was however kept quiet and quasi-acquiescent—if not openly consenting and approving. Herein I served you efficiently." In turn, Ewing's son reported having "friends in all the Delegations. . . . If it passes . . . my interest will be worth a half million of dollars." Republicans like Blaine could seem more interested in building bridges to business than in promoting western settlement or expanding federal power. Ultimately, though, if they were related to expanding Republican and federal power—and they were—these goals were connected to their party's ideology.[6]

But building a railroad through partnership between private enterprise and the government was a big step that Republicans took cautiously. In the House, the otherwise supportive Samuel Shellabarger of Ohio called the road "the means and instrumentality of a large draft upon the Treasury and lands of the Government without resulting in the construction of any continuous line of railroad," with the builders engaged in a massive land grab. Worse, knowing of no proof that a railroad actually could be built to the West, he feared a costly boondoggle. Since the government footed so much of the cost, Senator Jacob Howard of Michigan said, Congress should keep the power to change the railroad's charter. To his Massachusetts colleague Henry Wilson, the national interest was "to induce the capital of this country to go into that road. Every dollar put into that road is so much security to the United States." Thus, the bill provided for the Union and Central Pacific to build a railroad from the Missouri to northern California. The government gave the line public land for a right of way and five alternate sections per mile on each side of track. It made loans to the two companies, through thirty-year bonds at 6 percent interest, of $16,000 to $48,000 a mile, depending on the land. Another act allowed a second mortgage and doubled the land grants. The government eventually provided loans of $60 million and 45 million acres of land, 11.5 million of it in California. This was a massive amount of aid, to be charitable; a silver platter to big business, to be less charitable.[7]

Even as they aided the beneficiaries of a transcontinental line, Republicans never lost sight of the project's deeper meaning. While the Ewings tried to sell abolitionists on the benefits to free labor, other Republicans foresaw benefits to labor and capital. Building the line would encourage agriculture and mining, which would feed the economy, linking the West to the rest of the nation and the nation to the rest of the world. In May 1862, Stevens offered a compendium of ideological and expedient reasons to support the railroad. One was to provide a market for the depressed iron industry, "whose value seems . . . inadequately estimated by many grave legislators," as he, the owner of an iron works, would know. Better still, the timing was right for the Union and free labor: with the Mississippi closed to shipping, the West needed markets, meaning that labor would be cheap and available. Just as crucial, building it would aid the labor and capital of a region, and would provide transportation as part of a world market, so "our

Atlantic sea-ports will be but a resting-place between China, Japan, and Europe." Stevens even tied the road to why he believed the war was fought. After the inevitable defeat and return of the rebels, "we shall find them with the same arrogant, insolent dictation which we have cringed to for twenty years, forbidding the construction of any road that does not run along our southern border," he warned. "The result will be no road. . . . I am, therefore, for passing this law, and making it so irrevocable as to require all the branches of the Legislature to undo it before those halcyon days shall arrive."[8]

For Republicans, the halcyon day was the start of construction. What made the day of the Central Pacific's groundbreaking, the *Sacramento Union* said, was its "patriotic character. . . . the contemplation of the work as a 'bond of union.'" The crowd that day in September 1863 included the builders and Stanford, who was a link between the business that had promised to build it and the government that had encouraged it. He said, "We may now look forward with confidence to the day, not far distant, when the Pacific will be bound to the Atlantic by iron bonds that shall consolidate and strengthen the ties of nationality, and advance with great strides the prosperity of our State and of our country." Stanford elaborated, "The Pacific Railroad will insure still another change; the wealth and the commerce of the East and the West is to float upon its waters, and it is to behold the busy denizens of two hemispheres, in their constant travel over the great highway of nations." Building the railroad would cement ties to foreign lands, enhancing American power and spreading the nation's—and the Republican party's—ideology.[9]

To the east, the celebration resonated with Republican themes. Union Pacific president John Dix, chosen less for financial acumen than for his standing as a civilian general and War Democrat, invited Salmon Chase to write a letter for the groundbreaking in Nebraska. The secretary of the Treasury tied the road to the party mind-set. Private enterprise would build it, "aided by the simple promise of employment and compensation by the Government." With delays lamentable but inevitable, the Thirty-Seventh Congress showed "the stability of the Republic and the worth of Democratic Republican Institutions by taking up this great measure, in the midst of our terrible Civil War, and framing it into a law." That Congress would prove "forever memorable in history as the author of many acts of legislation of transcendent importance and far-reaching consequences," and the railroad bill "one of the most illustrious monuments of the wisdom and courage of its members." Whether the Republican was a hard-headed businessman like Stanford or an ambitious radical like Chase, the vision was the same: the railroad represented a great leap forward for the country, and for the party governing the country.[10]

Republicans agreed on the line's benefits but faced a recurring issue: it cemented ties between government and industry, but which of them would be in control? In 1862 and 1864, Congress approved land grants and subsidies to aid investment and added more government directors to the Union Pacific board to monitor expenditures and repayment. In turn, the Union Pacific issued stock and formed the Credit Mobilier to plow construction profits into paying back stockholders, including congressmen who received shares and made far more from dividends than the pittance they paid. Many Republicans wanted to believe that the railroad would be honestly operated. Iowa's James Grimes accused the Senate of letting investors buy more stock than the law allowed by putting it in other people's names. Trumbull said, "I am not for legislating upon the principle that everybody is dishonest and corrupt. I suppose we want to pass a bill that the capitalists of the country will be willing to take hold of and invest their capital in the construction of this road. What we desire is the construction of the Pacific railroad." Less scrupulous and more realistic, Stevens hoped that the railroad would benefit the government by linking East and West. As Chase told the even more ardent Senator John Conness of California, "The importance to the whole country of the earliest practicable completion of the Pacific Railroad justifies liberal aid . . . to the enterprise." Building a railroad to bring gold East and settlers West fit perfectly with the party's hope that activist government would team with industry to foster power. If Republicans could take drastic action in wartime, other problems would pale in comparison. And they saw that building the road would require them to offer support to the men responsible for investing the time and money—and they would receive support for their goals in return.[11]

But the war bred the future power of railroad owners—indeed, the future changes in the capitalist system. The government awarded large financial and land grants, then adopted a hands-off attitude out of gratitude, inclination, and, in wartime, necessity. To be sure, the party had graver concerns, but when the government did step in, it stepped in to the benefit of the railroad builders. When Native Americans interfered with track laying, the Union Pacific received control of the army, which it used to stop strikes and eject squatters. Not only were grants not repaid, but congressmen sought aid from executives and railroad clerks often wrote reports for federal inspectors. Out of ignorance, apathy, and corruption, and because they left a vacuum that someone had to fill, politicians let businessmen control policy, and they contributed to victory. That seemed a reasonable price to pay for support. Besides, the public-private partnership to build a transcontinental railroad was unique; just as the party had been new to power, it was also new to this kind of activity. In wartime, Republicans looked to the future but had to concentrate on the present. They had little inkling of the seeds they were sowing. But expanding the government's economic role, and the economy with it, meant a more powerful Union for freedom.[12]

Free Soil, Costly Soil

The same was true of the use of public lands: the party's commitment to business and labor mingled with a desire to expand the Republican base, especially in the West. Republican policies revealed a coherent ideology that merged economics and politics while looking to the West as the nation's future. But at times the ideal and the reality failed to mesh. The Homestead Act, passed in May 1862, was a classic example. It offered loyal citizens 160 acres of land if they homesteaded them for five years. Its passage followed through on another plank of the 1860 platform, but only after much debate. One of the act's biggest supporters, Greeley, saw it as central to the free labor ideal. "To throw open all the lands of the republic free of charge, and bid each citizen to help himself to a quarter section, will open a new era in the history of Labor," the *Tribune* said as Congress debated the bill. Speaker of the House Galusha Grow, a Pennsylvania radical who strongly backed the measure, declared, "The long struggle for Land for the landless is at last consummated."[13]

Indeed, Grow articulated the Republican commitment. Taking the dramatic step of leaving the Speaker's chair, he declared from the floor that the bill would "contribute to the greatness and glory of the Republic" and "develop the elements of a higher and better civilization" by encouraging free men to harvest the fruits of their labor. Dismissing claims that the measure would hurt the government's credit by depriving it of the ability to sell the public lands at higher prices, he said: "The capitalists of the country have not been so indifferent spectators of the doings of Congress and the movements of political parties as not to regard the passage of a homestead bill as a foregone conclusion." More important, it would enable the government to sell land to citizens, foiling speculators. Conceding that some of his colleagues sought to make the land available to soldiers as a postwar bounty for them to harvest, Grow referred to the "soldiers of peace—that grand army of the sons of toil, whose lives, from the cradle to the grave, are a constant warfare with the elements, with the unrelenting obstacles of nature and the merciless barbarities of savage life." They were "heroes of the garret, the workshop, and the wilderness home. . . . Such are the men whom the homestead policy would save from the grasp of speculation." It was the kind of free labor tract heard from Republicans before the war, and still part of their belief system, now absorbed into a broader vision.[14]

Other Republicans echoed Grow. Wisconsin's John Potter doubted the wisdom of those who feared removing public land from the market: if enacted earlier, the Homestead Act would have protected the West from land speculators and "the cultivator of the soil from the clog that has been placed upon it by those who have had capital to buy up land in large quantities." Another westerner, Illinoisan Isaac Arnold, added that it would breed immigration and settlement. While Ben Wade of Ohio brought his bluster and radicalism to pushing it through the Senate, another proponent, Kansan Samuel Pomeroy, called it a counter to "unprincipled land monopolies" keeping free farm laborers out of the West: "I am, sir, for opening these lands for the landless of every nation under heaven. I care not whether he comes to us from the populous cities of our older States, or from the enlightened though oppressed nations of Europe." Convinced that the Homestead Act represented the continuation of a march westward that had begun with colonial settlement 250 years earlier, Pomeroy united several threads of Republican ideology—its commitment to free labor, freedom, and union, and to extending these beliefs West, thereby enhancing the power of the party and the government:

> [W]hile this system of small farms of a quarter section of land each will greatly promote the wealth, strength, and glory of the Republic, thus conducing to human happiness, near and remote, now and for all ages,

> still as a consequence and by virtue of the same law, it will secure the entire public domain to human freedom forever! The pioneer struggling amidst many discouragements upon the frontier prairies of the West, comes nearer obeying the divine injunction to "gain his bread by the sweat of his brow," than any other man. The men who have, from their circumstances and education, been inured to self-reliance, can safely volunteer as soldiers of civilization in its onward progress across this continent, from the great valleys of the Mississippi and Missouri to the shores of the Pacific. The man who is able to put all he owns on earth into one canvass-covered wagon, wife, children, household goods, all, and move with slow pace into what has been called "the wilderness of the West," far out upon the frontier, beyond law and civilization, and there plant himself down upon a homestead for life, is doing a work for himself, his family, for civilization, his country, and his God, that can never be fully known, or its influence told, until the final disclosure. Such soldiers of civilization are sentinels, standing as the advance guard on the outposts of civilization, and will yet be high on the page of the world's unwritten history, and will be sure to keep the watch fires of freedom burning conspicuously. Slavery can never extend itself outside and beyond law! It can only follow in the wake of the police regulations that recognize and protect it.[15]

The predictions of Greeley, Grow, and Pomeroy proved both right and wrong. Running for the House in 1862, John Kasson, whose fellow Iowans strongly supported the act, welcomed "free homesteads to the actual settler, instead of the speculator." Oliver Kelley, later a founder of the Grange organization that aided farmers, noted two groups in 1863: homesteaders who would own their farms in five years and absentee speculators. The homesteaders reflected the act's success, the speculators its failure. Yet it was the ultimate exposition of the Jeffersonian side of free labor ideology: according to Greeley, a settler who "transforms by his labor a patch of rugged forest or bleak prairie into a fruitful, productive farm, pays for his land all that we think he ought to pay." Thus, as Republicans promised, the bill provided free land for free labor, and, as they hoped, proved that factory hands could become yeomen. To the West came European immigrants hoping to own farms and emigrants from less affluent and arable parts of New England—farmers and believers in the party creed, claiming more than 25,000 homesteads and presumably sharing the ideology of those who made their homesteads possible.[16]

Peopling the West with Republicans was one thing; understanding the region was another matter. The West's climate was too arid for farms of 160 acres—an "ill-fitted and incongruous" system, wrote Paul Gates, the leading historian of public land policy. Consequently, by the end of the decade speculators had gobbled up 50 million acres, to be tilled by laborers relying on railroads for sustenance and markets. With those lines came their builders, obtaining land from the government and from disgruntled or enterprising homesteaders. While the Homestead Act was Jeffersonian yeomanry writ large, it proved different from what its supporters and opponents had expected. The possibility that it would lead to a massive railroad land grab seems not to have occurred to Republicans, but it should have: railroads even advertised to buy homesteads. Yet the party realized its antebellum goal of settling the West with laborers who shared their views. Republicans also achieved their wartime goal of tying business and industry to the Union cause and to their hopes of retaining and expanding their power by providing railroads with markets and customers—and, it turned out, with more public land than their builders could have expected.[17]

Considering themselves rooted in Jeffersonian ideals, Republicans saw the small producer as central to their ideology, the truly free laborer. Yet Hamilton's ghost loomed larger, in their economic views, than that of Jefferson, whom they invoked more often and admiringly. Hamilton had sired the national bank that Jefferson's political junior partner, James Madison, let die and then revived, only to have Andrew Jackson kill it again. Some future Republicans blamed the ensuing depression, the Panic of 1837, on the avarice of the bank's managers. In power, with new responsibilities and hopes of maintaining that power, Republicans instituted banking reforms, including a national system. They found, as Madison had, that if necessity was the mother of invention, convenience was the father: a war economy would be easier to run with federal controls in place. But even in agriculture Republicans adopted a Hamiltonian approach, linking it to industry and to the national and international economy in ways that Jefferson would have found wanting and frightening.[18]

Secession and war struck Republicans and their agricultural supporters as an opportunity. Federal and state governments, and farming journals and societies, encouraged and educated Northerners to step up production. A Wisconsin Republican editor said, "Let Northern sorghum supersede New Orleans sugar; and Northern flax take the place of Southern cotton, and Northern tobacco drive out 'Dixie's weed,' and three strong points will have been made," although the party preferred to stress the North's ability to feed its armies. More importantly, the president of the Illinois Central Railroad calculated that a quarter of the land in southern Illinois would satisfy all who needed the cotton that rebels saw as crucial to their cause—and added that if radicals "would give up discussing the negro question, and get up a crusade to produce cotton in a free State, they would be better employed." Indeed, paeans from the powerful reminded farmers of their importance to the Union cause and suggested government support, if only moral, for their efforts. Before an agricultural society, Governor John Andrew of Massachusetts welcomed "this becoming and beneficent gathering of the most intelligent yeomanry of New England." Then he waxed rhapsodic and, in his view of farming, Republican: "Here we touch her mother earth, while we join our friendly hands together, in the spirit of a fresh dedication of our powers and hopes to the task of deepening the foundations of her solid fame, of widening the circle of her gracious influence, and brightening the sparkling diadem of her peaceful grandeur."[19]

Acknowledging their devotion to farming and its ties to their ideas about an active government and a growing West, Republicans created a Department of Agriculture. They understood the political wisdom of making farmers feel wanted—Lincoln called agriculture "confessedly the largest interest of the nation"—and they hoped to make the farmer's lot easier in the process. A farm bureau had survived with a small budget and staff in the Patent Office, but Representative Owen Lovejoy, usually associated with the movement for a homestead act and the abolitionist cause in which his brother Elijah had been a martyr, led the charge. While Lincoln and Caleb Smith, his Whiggish Interior secretary, backed a new department in annual messages, Lovejoy's Agriculture Committee complained that eastern manufacturers participated more "in directing and moulding national legislation than all the farming interests in the country." After Congress approved the measure and Lincoln signed it in early 1862, director Isaac Newton promoted scientific farming and a better system of agricultural education to improve production—just as the Morrill Land Grant College Act helped states create schools to teach industrial and agricultural technology, involving the federal government in local life in a variety of new ways.[20]

But this kind of activism had the potential to divide Republicans. They opposed the states' rights rhetoric at the heart of secession, yet many of them expected their yeomen to be happier if left alone; either way, farmers would spread the party's gospel. Accordingly, even farm state Republicans sniped at the new creation, but always lauded the farmers it served—and at times inspired caution. After praising farmers, Senator Henry Lane of Indiana questioned increasing spending on the department, especially when "the individual enterprise of farmers interested in this pursuit would do more to promote agriculture than any fostering care of the Congress." Senator James Lane doubted that the criticism was justified, since the Buchanan administration caused problems for the old bureau. He said, "We are engaged in Kansas now in endeavoring to make that State a cotton-growing free State. We have wrenched it from the iron heel of slavery, and our people are ambitious to prove that this commodity, heretofore grown exclusively by slave labor, can more successfully and more profitably be raised by free labor." Indeed, if Republican praise for farmers was part of their free labor ideology, concern about federal or scientific interference may well have been due in part to their fear that farmers might somehow lose some of that freedom. They never lost sight that either way, they were trying to build support for their ideas.[21]

Yet Republicans wanted farmers to follow in their footsteps and adapt to change. Industry and scientific agriculture helped increase output. Their journals urged farmers to make up for a smaller labor pool and meet the needs of the soldiers; since these publications looked out for the best interests of their readers, this suggested that industry and government supported these efforts. One improvement, the railroad, provided more access to markets and helped farmers sell any surplus or concentrate on one crop; as he became more specialized, whatever a subsistence farmer needed was a train ride away—less, if he went to a nearby storekeeper or banker. Encouraging scientific agriculture, better transportation, and industry, Republicans came closer to their vision of an integrated economy—and sped the decline of the yeomen they celebrated. That system empowered businessmen, as Hamilton wished, putting the farmer at their mercy and, in bringing him into contact with those who controlled or contributed to the market, driving him deeper into debt. Whatever industry produced, "the farmers of the country are the great consumers of all these manufactured articles," and "need protection for the products of their labor," Representative Francis Kellogg of Michigan said; "it is the farming interest which is of the greatest importance in this country. The Government must look to the farmers for its support, and all the wealth and property of the country comes out of the earth to commence with."[22]

Unsurprisingly, farmers feared and hated the manufacturers upon whom they relied. The farmers felt that they had made the manufacturers wealthy and influential, but had received nothing in return. By investing in new machinery, Northern farmers reduced their need for labor and increased costs and acreage. As subsistence farming dwindled, so did mobility for farm workers aspiring to ownership. Yet farmers came out of the Civil War better than they went into it. Through government aid and their own efforts, farmers learned more about their craft and grew more united, enhancing their political power. Markets and the average value of farms increased. Government encouragement of settlement in the West aided this process and fit with what Republicans intended: the spread of the party's gospel. But power bred dependence: the deeper farmers went into markets, the deeper they went into debt, and the angrier they became. The seeds of the Populist revolt in decades to come were being sown.[23]

One key to Populist ideology was hatred for railroads, and Civil War era farmers anticipated the complaints to come. Farmers needed them to take their wares to market, but the railroads charged too much in the West and undercut them by delivering cheaper western products in the East, or so farmers thought. And railroads controlled not only a significant amount of land, but also the water rights; farmers felt squeezed. The combination of farmer complaints and the Republican belief in internal improvements merged in the quest to build canals. When farmers groused that railroad rates ate up 80 percent of the value of wheat and forced them to produce six bushels of grain to pay to ship one, Governor Richard Yates of Illinois called for reopening the Mississippi and backed two canal projects to help shipping: expanding the Erie Canal and deepening the Illinois and Lake Michigan. Agreeing with him, Illinois Central president William Osborn argued that railroads were inundated and backed the building of the Niagara Ship Canal at the "Great Canal Convention" in Chicago. After much debate, the House gave New York $3.5 million to build the Niagara and spent more than $13 million to improve the Illinois and Michigan.[24]

In appropriating funds, Republicans looked beyond sectional and farming interests to define what would aid free labor: farmers and those they supplied. Illinoisan Eben Ingersoll wanted his party to help "the people against the monopolists of the country in giving them a cheap means of communication between the western States and the Atlantic seaboard; by voting this miserable little appropriation, in order that we may have a canal around the falls of Niagara, and be independent of Canada and Great Britain." The canal fit in with "the American character," which he wanted to build up by uniting East and West in every possible way. In the spirit of his namesake, the force behind the Erie Canal, New York's DeWitt Clinton Littlejohn, said that "twenty-five or fifty years hence, from the Atlantic to the Pacific will be a continuous tier of States, members of this Union. . . . Members who reside upon the far western coast have also an interest, then, in this highway." The majority who backed the canal articulated the party's ideology: by connecting regions and aiding industry, Republicans hoped to secure a stronger Union in which they would be strengthened to fight for freedom.[25]

Yet the road to the Niagara bill's passage was arduous, reflecting again how the party could agree on ends but reach them by different means. The plans for that canal were tied to the Illinois canal, which some found too local to merit national action and failed to pass the first time it came up. At that point, House Republicans resorted to arguments they would later use in connection with other measures designed to aid trade. Albert Riddle of Ohio predicted that it would aid "the overburdened lands of the West and reduce transportation costs." That would help the producer and "the sweating worker of the millions of fertile acres in the far-off West, whose products rot and molder away on his hands, or are burned for fuel, offending heaven and the day with the smoke of a blasphemous waste." But it fell to New York's Van Horn, who chaired the committee on the Niagara canal, to weld the many branches of Republican thought on this issue. The House's "devotion to the great interests of our people, its desires to advance their prosperity, develop and expand their great wealth and resources, and lift up to a higher usefulness and grandeur the labor and enterprise of the country," he told his colleagues, demanded passage. Fitting in neatly with the party's ideals, the measure passed.[26]

A Mission to Change

That statement captured the Republican ethos. Written when rebellion seemed implausible to them, the 1860 platform committed them to more than restricting slavery. They proposed a modern version of Henry Clay's American System of internal improvements and government activism, such projects as a transcontinental railroad and a homestead law. The war aided their goals: the departure of Southern congressmen removed an obstacle to what the party desired. An Illinois Republican mixed partisanship, cogency, and rancor in observing that these measures "should have passed years ago, and would have passed, but for a party so vile that no name in our language is sufficient to convey any adequate idea of its damning depravity."[27]

Between the war and their dedication to their beliefs, Republicans changed the government forever. Above all they were reformers. They came together hoping to make the national policy toward slavery reflect their view of slavery. It was natural for them to seek other problems to solve, in war or peace. In keeping with their quest to expand their power and the government's power, it was pragmatic: addressing issues such as transportation and public lands might appeal to those opposed to their view of slavery. But they acted according to their vision of the present and future. When the war began, some of them urged leaders such as Lincoln to postpone any legislative plans other than what was needed to win the war. Others voiced fears that this was just what would happen. Chase's first report as Treasury secretary decried "the criminal insurrection which deranges commerce, accumulates expenditures, necessitates taxes, embarrasses industry, depreciates property, cripples enterprise, and frustrates progress." Greeley lamented that the war "put back by more than fifteen degrees the hand on the dial which marks the progress of mankind toward a wholly Christian Civilization and Social Order; who shall say when it may again move forward?"[28]

Yet some Republicans expected the war to make possible the progress that Greeley expected it to stop. Accused of trying to do too much, they countered that they were obligated to prepare society for the future they envisioned. Indeed, a sense of mission pervaded the party and cannot be separated from any description or analysis of its ideology. Any party committed to confining slavery was engaged in a crusade, and neither the daunting task of assuming the presidency nor a mammoth undertaking like a civil war was likely to change that.

If anything, these new challenges enhanced their missionary zeal. John Greenleaf Whitter, the poetic voice of abolitionism, told Chase three days after Lincoln's election, "God has laid the great responsibility upon us," and many Republicans shared this attitude. "Providence has opened up the way to that higher civilization and purer Christianity which the Republic is to attain," Iowa's James Wilson told the House. "Our Red Sea passage is to be as propitious as that of God's chosen people when the waters parted . . . for their escape from the hosts upon whom those waters closed and effected the burial appointed by Him who declared, 'Let my people go.'" And they acted on this belief: at the end of the activist Thirty-Seventh Congress, which approved the Homestead Act and the transcontinental railroad, among other measures, Sumner looked back and concluded, "Here is enough for an epoch."[29]

Underscoring Sumner's views was how Republicans took advantage of the war: for them it was a social upheaval requiring experimentation, federal activism, and a military machine. They remade the country, especially during the Thirty-Seventh Congress, from 1861 to 1863. Fessenden, the untitled party leader and Senate Finance Committee chair, felt that Congress "discharged its great responsibility . . . with great vigor and devotion. If the country is to be saved (and it is to be) Congress will have saved it." Across Capitol Hill, when Grow bade farewell at the end of the session, the traditionally flowery valedictory reflected the Republican sense of mission, and mission accomplished. He commended the House, which had "contributed not a little to the advancement of the industrial interests and promotion of the greatness and glory of the country."[30]

Republicans faced those issues with a set of related ideas. Some fell flat. Sumner's call for civil service reform took two decades to enact; his view was idealistic, and a realistic plea for the professionalism the party and government needed to wield power wisely. The interests he cited included the federal role in building a railroad to the West, and Republicans even looked to build lines between the North and South. Their leading economic theorist, Henry Carey, wanted to show rebels "that we are preparing to give value to their land, and that our success would add largely to their wealth"; an Ohio railroad executive asked

Sherman, "What stronger tie can there be to hold the North & South together after peace is restored, than this road could furnish—connecting us, as it would with 5,000 miles of Railroad in the South?"[31]

In the 1850s, when mostly conservative Democrats and Whigs had held power, the tradition of limited federal activism had survived. In the 1860s Republicans took over, eager for new policies toward slavery—and farming, railroads, banking, and land. As Republicans grew accustomed to wielding power, they paid less attention to thought and more to action: Trumbull wondered why the Senate should resolve that the government would raise money when "I would much rather manifest my zeal upon practical measures than upon a resolution which amounts to nothing—a mere declaration of what we are going to do." They did a lot, rooted in the party's vision of what the government should be. Once they had been able only to write or talk of their plans; now they could act on them.[32]

The Meaning of Money

Financial necessity inspired Chase to support the Legal Tender Act and a national banking system. These measures forced the party to hone its thinking about the federal role in the economy, and act on it. To regulate banks from Washington was to attack states' rights and state banks—a dream come true for old Whigs but a nightmare for old Jacksonians. "The currency of the country is not a commodity that merely affects the citizens of one state and not those of another. It is not a local matter," the *Philadelphia Press* said. Democrats who had made political capital of a conviction that a national bank was evil before becoming Republicans made clear that new circumstances forced their hands. Defending the bank plan, and federal control of the currency, Wisconsin's James Doolittle reminded the Senate that "for nearly twenty years of my life in political warfare I fought" the national bank because "it created a great monopoly which had control over the whole currency of the country. This system . . . is not giving to a favored few, or any particular few, the control of the banks, the control of the currency; it is opening it to everybody in any State." Nor did a national plan appeal to the financiers whom Chase considered crucial to its passage and crucial to raising funds to fight the war: his chief loan officer, Jay Cooke, opposed federal interference until Chase persuaded him otherwise. Only after Cooke and his brother refined the bill and keelhauled several editors did it pass easily in the spring of 1863.[33]

But the debate continued over the government's role in banking, part of a dialogue over what the government could do to aid freedom, union, and power. As always Republicans knew their goals, and most of them agreed on how to achieve them. In 1864, Congress defeated a bill to let states tax national bank notes. At the heart of this fight lay the war's causes and the changes it prompted. Jacob Howard suggested that John Marshall's edict against state taxation of the national bank in *McCulloch v. Maryland* made the issue moot. Banker Samuel Hooper supported federal control and warned against giving states any power. His fellow congressman from Massachusetts, Henry Dawes, agreed: "If State necessity is to domineer over the national necessities, and that is the generally prevailing Democratic view of the country, tending always to disorganization and the dissolution of the Confederacy, then adopt this amendment." States' rights died hard even among those who supposedly opposed them. Republicans were cautious but convinced that they were correct.[34]

While their success showed that radical stands could be acceptable, Republicans learned that promoting union and freedom required union with the capital that banking provided. The party born to celebrate free labor still did so, and hailed bankers for contributing to the capital employing free laborers. With Lincoln, Chase, and Cooke lobbying Congress, Sherman managed the banking bill in the Senate and pointed out that workers, bankers, and government were often in conflict. The bill would "harmonize their interests; so that every stockholder, every mechanic, every laborer who holds one of these notes will be interested in the government—not in a local bank, but in the Government of the United States." In the House, Colfax paid tribute to banks: "They acted like corporations that had souls. They acted like patriots in their advances to Government in its hour of need." The party honored the worker for his sacrifices but voiced new appreciation for bankers, brokers, and bond sellers whose investments they credited with helping to save the Union. More important, while workers received rhetoric, for financiers they had legislation, which would aid laborers—an embryonic kind of trickle-down economics.[35]

The party's evolving ideology and warm feelings for business merged in the Legal Tender Act of 1863. Before the first year of the war ended, Chase warned the *Chicago Tribune*'s Joseph Medill of the "duty" to provide a national currency and the pressing need to finance the war. Chase conferred with Carey and concluded that with the war depleting the treasury, "Congress must assume the exclusive control of the matter." The resulting bill was the handiwork of Chase and two House financial experts, Hooper and Elbridge Spaulding of New York, bankers on Ways and Means. They worked with the Cookes and a representative of the New York Bank of Commerce, run by John Stevens and his son—radicals and Chase allies. They knew of the financial community's fears about currency problems created by the war and the possibility that printing money would produce rampant inflation, both of which could easily derail Republican plans to maintain their newfound power and their plans to use it.[36]

Yet some Republicans remained doubtful about the measure, deriding the idea of adding greenbacks to the specie used as currency. Printing money would, they feared, weaken the nation at home and abroad. That would lend credence to opponents who charged that Republicans were insanely radical and would reduce the party's chances of retaining its grasp of the federal government. Worse, if the treasury produced unlimited paper and inflation followed, the purpose of greenbacks—to help the Union pay its bills—would defeat itself. From Chicago, Medill alerted Trumbull, "Our country is in as much danger from the bloated degraded currency as from the rebels." From his outpost in Bull's Gap, Tennessee, Jacob Cox of Ohio feared that politics would trump ideology: whether to inflate it further would be up to "a class of men who will hold the balance of power in Congress, and who will plunge the country to ruin rather than vote a taxation which they think may endanger their own seats."[37]

The party also wondered whether legal tender really was legal. While conservative financiers inveighed against it, so did radical William Cullen Bryant's *New York Evening Post,* whose free-tradism put it at odds with businessmen backing a protective tariff. Addressing Lincoln, Bryant said, "The constitution has been violated in its letter by issuing Treasury notes payable on demand. You are now asked to violate its spirit by co-operating to make those notes a legal tender." He implored other radicals to tell Chase that legal tender was a death warrant for the country and his political career. In London, Adams shared Bryant's view and warned that paper money would lead to bankruptcy. But Chase told Sumner and Thaddeus Stevens that while he had hoped "to avoid the necessity of such legislation," it was "indispensably necessary." In a debate redolent of the Federalist belief that the "necessary and proper clause" justified action not specifically addressed in the Constitution, the *New York Times* called the bill a "centralization of power, such as Hamilton might have eulogised as magnificent." And it was for a crucial purpose: George Templeton Strong lamented that printing money would affect his investments but said, "I shall not complain if the nation be saved." Even if Republicans seemed to think of expedience, their belief in freedom, union, and power inspired them to act as needed.[38]

Indeed, the debate over paper extended beyond that issue to the party ethos. Many Republicans could easily support paper money as a means of aiding the war effort, but they were less sure of its postwar effects. When Carey worried that he might contract the money supply to drive out paper, no matter the effect on labor and capital, Hugh McCulloch reassured him that his plans were less draconian. But the Treasury secretary sounded like any other wartime Republican, albeit a more fiscally minded one, when he told Carey that "the specie basis is the only safe and healthy one for business and . . . the interests of capitalists and working-men will be promoted by a return to it . . . without depriving labor of its proper reward." By contrast, one advocate of greenbacks reminded *Cincinnati Gazette* readers that rebuilding the South after the war would help the economies of both regions. "All the worth of the slaves was in their labor, and that will be there when the war closes, to revive industry with greater vigor and production than it ever had before. Then the South will need more money and earn it better than it ever did before. . . . Then the elements of wealth, which nature gave it, will be developed; and the land, which was spewed over with the filth of slavery, will be clean, and industrious, and productive." An Oregon Republican even credited paper for wartime prosperity and predicted that if the government kept printing money, the West would have more currency for building "railroads through our vallies, and for the development of our mineral wealth." At least some Republicans concluded that free labor benefited from greenbacks, which would aid the party in perpetuating its goals.[39]

The ideas powering the greenback debate affected the tariff issue. No economic matter threatened party unity more, especially in protectionist Pennsylvania, which was crucial to Lincoln's victory in 1860. His efforts to pacify the state with a Cabinet post for Cameron had been troubled, and its protectionism made its politicians disagreeable to the party's free-traders. To accede to the state's demands for a protective tariff would please Stevens, Greeley, and the powerful New England delegation, all old bastions of Whiggery. That would anger Chase, Bryant, and their followers—mostly radicals and former Democrats who saw a protective tariff as a Hamiltonian error that no Jeffersonian could tolerate. Yet no Republican influenced the party's economic policies more than Carey, an energetic, eloquent protectionist. Thus, ideology and immediacy intersected. The party's beliefs evolved amid the necessities of governance to look beyond the interests of free labor. While he had that interest at heart, Carey's commitment to protection and the party's need to pacify its large number of followers in Pennsylvania and New England, combined with the power of its northeastern members, pushed Republicans into a stand in behalf of labor and industry that fit with what many of them already believed.[40]

As before the war, Carey pushed for protection with Republicans who influenced financial policy. To him, passing a protective tariff would make one obsolete. This was not a syllogism, but a belief that protected industry would become successful enough to negate a need for a tariff. In turn, free labor and freedom would benefit from a tariff that secured "the right of every man to determine . . . how he will employ his labour, or his capital, or both." Privately, he endorsed secession as a way to avoid more crises and compromises over slavery and the tariff, and hailed Morrill's protectionist tariff as a beacon of prosperity, "a union of the border and Northern states," and a "triumph of freedom." Publicly, he told Seward that secession "left us free to pursue the policy by means of which alone we may repair the damage done, . . . and we shall, one year hence, have reason to return our thanks to heaven for it, as having been the means of saving the Union," since the North then could pass needed legislation.[41]

Carey sought to convert free-traders and win over the undereducated or undecided. He placed Lincoln among the latter: on his way to his inaugural, speaking on the tariff, Lincoln told a Pittsburgh crowd that he would "endeavor to comprehend it more fully." Carey assured him that Clay's tariff policy would have averted secession, and his economic nationalism appealed to old Whigs, especially a Clay worshipper such as Lincoln. Carey proselytized free-traders, warning Chase, "Insidious efforts have been made here and elsewhere recently, to misrepresent your position in regard to one of the great questions of the day, and which we in Pennsylvania regard as vital—I mean protection to American labor," but he knew that the new Treasury secretary would uphold the platform and support protection. In touch with Morrill, whose tariff bore his fingerprints, Carey reported stressing to Chase that the upper South was unionist and more valuable economically than the deep South, and that free trade hampered their development. After meeting with Chase, Morrill told Carey that the Treasury secretary believed in "Free trade . . . but he confessed that in his present agony for money the latter failed"—an admission that the party had found that saving the union and running the government demanded adaptation.[42]

While Carey wrote prolifically, his disciples spread his gospel, extending his influence. In 1861 Sherman, then chair of Ways and Means, helped pass the Morrill Tariff. The two leading financial legislators in Congress, Fessenden and Morrill, were receptive to his ideas. Morrill functioned as the expert and manager on Ways and Means because his friend Stevens, the chair, was busy as an untitled House Republican leader. Worse, the radical Stevens frightened the financial community too much to be trusted with real economic power. Stevens knew it and deferred to Morrill, who called him "a remarkable man, unequalled in a great many respects in the history of the world, but upon business matters he has not the confidence of the House. I have had a good many contests with him, though excellent friends all the time, and have been rarely worsted."[43]

Protectionists like Stevens and Morrill achieved their goals: by 1864, the tariff had doubled from its 1857 levels, providing revenue for what they saw as the inseparable causes of the party and the Union. Nor were they alone. Other Republicans welcomed a higher tariff for compelling political and economic reasons. Senator Timothy Howe of Wisconsin told the Senate that farmers relied on manufacturing and suffered when it was unprotected. Countering Democratic charges that tariffs did nothing to help labor, Pennsylvania's William Kelley replied that reconstructing the Union would be easier with industry protected, built up, and promoted to immigrants. Nor would workers suffer from immigration, because "if we wisely protect our industry we will have emigrants from all parts of the world come and by their labor add to the value of land that now lies valueless because it is uncultivated. Mines now undeveloped will yield their stores, and the growing towns give untold wealth to those who own the land." The *Cleveland Leader* noted the downturns after previous tariff cuts and predicted a disaster if peace led to retrenchment, asking "when have our commercial convulsions and money crises visited our nation, except when labor has not been adequately protected? . . . The Calhoun policy is not the true policy for American Farmers."[44]

The allusions to Calhoun unfurled another thread of party ideology. Believing secessionists to be piqued over higher duties, as they had been in the nullification crisis of the 1820s and 1830s, protectionists tied the tariff to patriotism. While critics complained about the belief of Republicans like Morrill and Greeley in protectionism, the *Tribune* editor shot back that the tariff built confidence in the government. Sumner wrote that the war would end only "by the removal of Slavery. This is the cause and origin of the Rebellion, and nothing else. The Morrill Tariff has had nothing to do with it." For protectionists to agree might seem like an understandable quest for political cover, but given how clearly the South opposed the Republican effort to spread freedom and win power, Sumner's point would also have struck them as obvious.[45]

For Republicans to engage in patriotic breast-beating and question the opposition's loyalty was nothing new, even on the tariff. But they tied protectionism to free labor with a certitude that did Carey proud. "We are a nation of producers, and one of the paramount duties of legislators is to see that producers are profitably employed and have a market for their products," Morrill said. After the war, protectionists begged him to "cut down expenses and abandon extravagance—keep our gold and silver at home—create an American market—regulate our currency by a specie standard—labor hard in all branches of industry, and thoroughly protect all departments of labor," by increasing the tariff. "Every true interest of the farmer, the mechanic, the miner and the manufacturer, demands a judicious embargo on importations. Public and private economy demand it." Thus, Phillip Paludan wrote, "Just as war necessity had brought together hard-money and soft-money Republicans, so it forged unity on the tariff as well. Patriotism diluted the potential economic divisions in the party even as it muted class divisions between labor and capital."[46]

Paludan's analysis is correct, but it fails to take into account the value of ideology for wartime Republicans seeking unity and historians trying to explain their unity. The party split over the tariff. As usual it sought to submerge differences, and passed a protective, revenue-raising tariff. Yet free-traders, tariff backers seeking less draconian taxes for revenue, and some who sought higher rates voiced displeasure. Some of it was personal and political. Hailing Morrill's tariff, Greeley cared little whether foreign powers were offended—unlike Weed, who correctly forecast opposition, fretted about domestic and foreign reaction, and hated to agree with Greeley anyway. Stevens groused that amending Morrill's bill meant "it is no longer a protective tariff. I am obliged to swallow this bill just as it is, or I know it will not be swallowed at all." Favoring a revenue tariff but fearing that it would divide the party, radical New York City mayor George Opdyke called for a tariff that would "produce the needed revenue, meet the expectation of Pennsylvania and other manufacturing states, and at the same time satisfy whatever of free trade sentiment exists in the party"—an impossibility, but a sign of concern. And just as protectionists argued that their methods aided free labor and the party, free-traders were equally convinced that their policies did the same thing.[47]

Although controversial and harmful to party unity, the tariff caused fewer divisions than such issues as slavery and patronage, showing the preeminence and heart of the party ideology. Yet the war forced changes not in Republican economics, but in Republican attitudes about economics. Some still expressed views like that of the *Chicago Tribune,* which called Morrill's tariff "sheer robbery of the poor for the rich, making the poor poorer, and the rich richer, every day that it continues." But the proximity to national business interests that went with power affected Republicans, who had once seemed fanatical, by making them realize the importance of keeping power. The party had to work with business to fund the war and did so under the guidance of Chase, whose political career had been centered on slavery, not finance. In turn, Chase and other Republicans proved ideologically and personally compatible with many bankers, merchants, and financiers, some of whom shared their opposition to slavery but simply concentrated their efforts in a different arena from anti-slavery politics.[48]

In the process Republicans developed a different frame of mind, and perhaps a slightly different view of the life of the mind. Asked to appoint Carey a tax commissioner, McCulloch, a banker, praised his theories but questioned his ability to focus on any issue other than the tariff. Another Carey admirer, William Chandler, a Treasury Department official and New Hampshire Republican, described him as "a very able man, but, after all, a theorist. He has studied the subject of the currency and the Tariff, but has he ever imported a bale of goods or managed a bank?" Their ascent to power presented Republicans with a set of responsibilities unlike any they had known in the opposition. They had to change from the party that had attacked James Buchanan, and even from that which had elected Abraham Lincoln. Their circumstances had changed, and so had those of the country.[49]

Republicans refined their thought; while they sought to reinvent the country, they had no need for a similarly thorough reinvention of themselves. During the war they introduced and passed legislation to aid the growth of business and industry and, they believed, the opportunities available to the free laborers they celebrated. They also advocated and achieved the spread of freedom, the Union's salvation, and the growth of the power of their party and the government.

Republicans divided over a range of issues, from patronage to personalities, from finance to the freedman's fate—if indeed he was to be freed at all. At times they were caught between what they believed and what they could achieve, all mingled with the rivalries at the core of politics. While those jealousies rent the party more than did ideological disputes, regional differences and concerns affected Republican words and deeds—and bred the contradictions inherent in resolving conflicts between what is believed and what must be done to turn those beliefs into reality. One loyalist reflected his party when he wrote, "The mission of the Republican Party is Reform. It cannot begin better than at the root of all evil. Let the People learn through the new organization to detest the Albany Regency maxim that 'to the victors belong the spoils.'" His recipient was *New York Courier & Enquirer* editor James Watson Webb, who was pursuing a patronage job. Republicans spoke of the glories of free labor as they raised taxes on workers they professed to protect and passed laws to make life easier for their employers. If that seems paradoxical, the party could be too. Its members never wavered in their beliefs in freedom and union. But exerting the power to preserve and enhance them meant changes—in how they felt and in the land they found themselves governing—and differences over how to realize their goals, not what those goals should be. Their differences were greater on the outside than on the inside, due to the ideology that united them: freedom, union, and power.[50]

Notes

1. *CG,* 37, 2, 5 May 1862, 1949; Richardson, *The Greatest Nation of the Earth,* 170–75 and *passim;* Thomas Ewing Jr., to Thomas Ewing, Washington, 28 March 1862, Ewing and Family ms, Volume 13, LC; Foner, *Politics and Ideology,* 128–49.

2. *CG,* 37, 3, 9 July 1862, 3162–63.

3. Potter, *The Impending Crisis,* 145–76, explores railroad construction and politics. See Shutes, *Lincoln and California,* 145; David Haward Bain, *Empire Express: Building the First Transcontinental Railroad* (New York: Viking, 1999); Maury Klein, *Union Pacific,* 2 vols. (Garden City, N.Y.: Doubleday, 1987). On propitiating the West, see Henry Adams to Charles Francis Adams Jr., Washington, 22 December 1860, Adams Family ms, IV, Letters Received and Other Loose Papers, August–December 1860, Reel 550, MHS; 22 December 1860, in Nevins and Thomas, eds., *The Diary of George Templeton Strong,* 80; 9 December 1860, ibid., 72; Smith, *The Francis Preston Blair Family,* vol. 2, 133.

4. *CG,* 37, 2, 6 May 1862, 1971; Shutes, *Lincoln and California,* 150–52; Ralph J. Roske, *Everyman's Eden: A History of California* (New York: Macmillan, 1968), 365–66; Clark, *Leland Stanford,* 175–76.

5. *CG,* 37, 2, 18 June 1862, 2784; ibid., 20 June 1862, 2833; ibid., 17 June 1862, 2752; Carter Goodrich, *Government Promotion of American Canals and Railroads, 1800–1890* (New York: Columbia University Press, 1960), 182–83.

6. Blaine to Thomas Ewing, Augusta, 4 July 1862, Ewing and Family ms, Box 67, LC; Blaine to Thomas Ewing Jr., Augusta, 14 June 1861, Box 66, and 13 June 1862, Box 67, LC. On Blaine's career and vision, see Edward P. Crapol, *James G. Blaine: Architect of Empire* (Wilmington, Del.: Scholarly Resource Books, 2000).

7. *CG,* 37, 2, 1 May 1862, 1912; ibid., 18 June 1862, 2779; ibid., 19 June 1862, 2816; Shutes, *Lincoln and California,* 152; Roske, *Everyman's Eden,* 365–66; Younger, *John A. Kasson,* 163.

8. *CG,* 37, 2, 5 May 1862, 1949–50.

9. *Sacramento Union,* 9 September 1863, in Clark, *Leland Stanford,* 185–87.

10. Chase to Dix, Treasury Department, 25 November 1863, Chase Family ms, NHHS.

11. Goodrich, *Government Promotion of American Canals and Railroads,* 184–87; *CG,* 38, 1, 19 May 1864, 2352–53; ibid., 16 June 1864, 3022; Chase to John Conness, Washington, 22 March 1864, "Copies of Special Letters, 1861–1864, Bound," Chase ms, HSP; *Sacramento Union,* 25 April 1863, in Clark, *Leland Stanford,* 195; Merriam, *The Life and Times of Samuel Bowles,* vol. 2, 9–10.

12. Paludan, *"A People's Contest,"* 142–43. On railroads and politics, see Clark, *Leland Stanford,* 208; Paul W. Gates, *Agriculture and the Civil War* (New York: Alfred A. Knopf, 1965), 280–81, 289; David A. Johnson, *Founding the Far West: California, Oregon, and Nevada, 1840–1890* (Berkeley and Los Angeles: University of California Press, 1992), *passim;* Edwin B. Crocker to Chase, Sacramento, Chase ms, Reel 20, LC; Thomas Brown to Chase, New York, 22 May 1863, ibid.

13. *New York Tribune,* 14 May 1862; ibid., 1 February and 7, 9, and 21 July 1862, in Van Deusen, *Horace Greeley,* 288; Grow to Greeley, House of Representatives, 16 May 1862, in *New York Tribune,* 22 May 1862; Gates, *Agriculture and the Civil War,* 272–300; Richardson, *The Greatest Nation of the Earth,* 144–49.

14. *CG,* 37, 2, 21 February 1862, 909–10.

15. *CG,* 37, 1, 18 December 1861, 135–39; ibid., 37, 2, 5 May 1862, 1935–40; Richardson, *The Greatest Nation of the Earth,* 146–49; Robert D. Ilisevich, *Galusha A. Grow: The People's Candidate* (Pittsburgh: University of Pittsburgh Press, 1988), 210–11; Gates, *Agriculture and the Civil War,* 284–85. While it applies mainly to a later period, I have benefited from David M. Wrobel, *Promised Lands: Promotion, Memory, and the Creation of the American West* (Lawrence: University Press of Kansas, 2002).

16. Younger, *John A. Kasson,* 136–37; Gates, *Agriculture and the Civil War,* 283–84, 291; *New York Weekly Tribune,* 14 June 1862; Paludan, *"A People's Contest,"* 167–68.

17. Paludan, *"A People's Contest,"* 135, 166–67; Gates, *Agriculture and the Civil War,* 277–94.

18. The dialogue between Hamilton and Jefferson, and their surrogates, is at the core of Elkins and McKitrick, *The Age of Federalism.* Arthur M. Schlesinger Jr., *The Age of Jackson* (Boston: Little, Brown, 1946), explains the Jacksonians' intellectual debt to the Jeffersonians and the anti-Federalists who opposed the Constitution's ratification.

19. Gates, *Agriculture and the Civil War,* 142; W. H. Osborn to Banks, Chicago, 18 December 1861, Box 17, Banks ms, LC; Osborn to Banks, Chicago, 4 January 1862, Box 13, ibid.; Andrew, "Agricultural Society Address," 5.

20. John A. Klippart to Morrill, Columbus, 21 December 1861, Morrill ms, Box 59, LC; *CG,* 37, 2, Appendix, Lincoln's Message to Congress, 3; Gates, *Agriculture and the Civil War,* 306–09, 321; Isaac Newton to Morrill,

Washington, 31 January 1863, Morrill ms, Box 60, LC; Magdol, *Owen Lovejoy,* 354; Richardson, *The Greatest Nation of the Earth,* 149–60.

21. *CG,* 38, 2, 18 January 1865, 323; *CG,* 37, 3, 2 February 1863, 668–69. See *CG,* 37, 3, 6 January 1863, 210–11 (Representatives Stevens and Lovejoy); Paludan, *"A People's Contest,"* 166–67.

22. *CG,* 38, 1, 25 April 1864, 1856; Gates, *Agriculture and the Civil War,* 129–31, 157, 222, 229.

23. Gates, *Agriculture and the Civil War,* 238–39, 324–25, 374–78. See Lawrence Goodwyn, *The Populist Moment: A Short History of the Agrarian Revolt in America* (New York: Oxford University Press, 1978).

24. Gates, *Agriculture and the Civil War,* 349–50; *CG,* 38, 2, 1 February 1865, 546; Fite, *Social and Industrial Conditions,* 48–53; C. C. Larned to Washburne, Chicago, 18 March 1864, Washburne ms, Volume 36, LC; Isaac Arnold to Samuel B. Ruggles, Chicago, 20 September 1862, Arnold ms, Folder 1, Chicago Historical Society.

25. *CG,* 38, 2, 1 February 1865, 545, 538, and Appendix, 34 (Littlejohn); ibid., 1 February 1865, 543 (Representative Myer Strouse of Pennsylvania).

26. *CG,* 37, 3, 9 February 1863, Appendix, 102; ibid., 7 July 1862, 3162–63.

27. Jesse Stedman to Morrill, Springfield, 14 February 1863, Morrill ms, Box 63, LC.

28. *CG,* 37, 1, "Message of the President, Report of the Secretary of the Treasury," Appendix, 7; *Independent,* 18 April 1861, in Van Deusen, *Horace Greeley,* 270.

29. Hesseltine, *Lincoln and the War Governors,* 92; *CG,* 38, 1, 19 March 1864, 1203; *Indianapolis Daily Journal,* 9 February and 28 June 1864, in Stampp, *Indiana Politics,* 186; Sumner to Elizabeth, Duchess of Argyll, Boston, 11 August 1862, Series II, Reel 76, and Washington, 2 June 1863, Reel 77, SP; Howard, *Religion and the Radical Republican Movement,* 69 and *passim.*

30. Fessenden, *Life and Public Services of William Pitt Fessenden,* vol. 1, 254; *CG,* 37, 3, 3 March 1863, 1552–53. See Curry, *Blueprint for Modern America,* and Richardson, *The Greatest Nation of the Earth,* on this Congress and its activities.

31. Sumner to Lieber, Washington, 15 May 1864, Series I, Reel 64, SP; George W. Smith, *Henry C. Carey and American Sectional Conflict* (Albuquerque: University of New Mexico Press, 1951), 107–9; Gates, *Agriculture and the Civil War,* 295–96.

32. Randall, *Lincoln the Liberal Statesman,* 55–56; *CG,* 37, 2, 17 January 1862, 376.

33. *Philadelphia Press,* 13 February 1863, in Oberholtzer, *Jay Cooke,* vol. 1, 331–36; *CG,* 37, 3, 11 February 1863, 882; Richardson, *The Greatest Nation of the Earth,* 66–102.

34. *CG,* 38, 1, 29 April 1864, 1957; ibid., 6 April 1864, 1451; ibid., 4 April 1861, 1413; Richardson, *The Greatest Nation of the Earth,* 103–38.

35. *CG,* 37, 3, 10 February 1863, 843; ibid., 27 February 1863, 1353. See Paludan, *"A People's Contest,"* 122–23; Nichols, "Sherman," in Wheeler, ed., *For the Union,* 405; Sherman to William T. Sherman, Mansfield, 20 March 1863, William T. Sherman ms, LC, in Wheeler, ed., *For the Union,* 411; Oberholtzer, *Jay Cooke,* vol. 1, 332–33.

36. Chase to Medill, Washington, 16 October 1861, "Copies of Special Letters, 1861–1865, Bound," Chase ms, HSP; Oberholtzer, *Jay Cooke,* vol. 1, 171–73; Garfield to J. Harry Rhodes, Washington, 7 December 1862, Garfield ms, Reel 106, LC; H. A. Vail to John A. Stevens, Washington, 14 and 16 February 1862, Stevens ms, 1862–63 Correspondence, NYHS; P. Perit to Stevens, New Haven, 19 January 1863, ibid.; Maunsell B. Field to Stevens, Treasury Department, 2 October 1863, ibid.

37. Medill to Trumbull, Chicago, 28 January 1863, Trumbull ms, Reel 14, LC; J. D. Cox to Garfield, Bull's Gap, 8 April 1864, Garfield ms, Reel 12, LC; Washington, Wednesday, 12 February 1863, Pease and Randall, eds., *The Diary of Orville Hickman Browning,* vol. 1, 529–30.

38. Robert B. Minturn to Weed, New York, 1 and 8 February 1862, Weed ms, UR; *New York Evening Post,* 17 February 1862, "Newspaper Clippings," Goddard-Roslyn Collection, Bryant-Godwin ms, Box 23, NYPL; Bryant to Sumner, New York, 13 February 1862, Reel 24, SP; Charles Francis Adams to Charles Francis Adams Jr., London, 30 December 1864, Adams Family Papers, IV, September–December 1864, Reel 572, MHS; Chase to Stevens, Treasury Department, 29 January 1862, Morrill ms, No. 1146, Box 1, January–June 1862, CR; Sumner to Lieber, Senate Chamber, 10 February 1862, Series I, Reel 64, SP; *New York Times,* 9 March 1863; 11 January 1862, in Nevins and Thomas, eds., *The Diary of George Templeton Strong,* vol. 3, 201; *CG,* 37, 2, 13 February 1862, 796 (Howard); ibid., 17 June 1862, 2767 (Spaulding).

39. McCulloch to Henry C. Carey, Washington, 4 April 1865, Treasury Department Letterbook, March–May 1865, McCulloch ms, IU; *Cincinnati Gazette,* 23 March 1865, Scrapbook, "Financial," Volume 1, McCulloch ms, IU; *Oregon Statesman,* n.d., ca. 1865, ibid.

40. Stampp, *Indiana Politics,* 138–41; Lee, "Henry C. Carey and the Republican Tariff," 292–94.

41. Lee, "Henry C. Carey and the Republican Tariff," 300–301; Henry C. Carey, *The Past, The Present, and the Future* (New York: A. M. Kelley, 1967; originally published in 1847), 469, 416; Smith, *Henry C. Carey and American Sectional Conflict,* 92–93; *New York Tribune,* 14 February 1861; Stampp, *And the War Came,* 162; Carey to John Sherman, Philadelphia, 27 November 1860, Sherman ms, Volume 17, and 21 December 1860, Volume 18, LC.

42. *Pittsburgh Gazette,* 16 February 1861, in Lee, "Henry C. Carey and the Republican Tariff," 292–97, 301; Carey to Chase, Philadelphia, 16 January and 19 June 1861, Chase ms, Box 3, HSP; Carey to Morrill, Philadelphia, 30 June 1861, Morrill ms, Box 53, LC; Morrill to Carey, Washington, 6 July 1861, Carey ms, HSP; Garfield to Carey, Washington, 20 November 1862, Garfield ms, Reel 106, LC.

43. Lee, "Henry C. Carey and the Republican Tariff," 297–98; Blaine to Morrill, Augusta, 15 November 1865, Morrill ms, Box 52, LC; Morrill to Porter Baxter, n.p., 4 June 1863, Morrill ms, No. 1146, Box 1, 1863–64, CR; Washburne to Morrill, Galena, 30 May 1863, Morrill ms, Reel 6, LC. On Stevens, see Morrill to unknown, n.p., n.d., ca. 1863, Morrill ms, Reel 6, Box 60, LC; Parker, *The Life and Public Services of Justin Smith Morrill,* 115, 165.

44. Paludan, *"A People's Contest,"* 130; *CG,* 37, 2, 27 May 1862, 2372; *CG,* 38, 1, 21 January 1864, 308; *Cleveland Leader,* November 1865, Scrapbook, "Financial," Volume 1, McCulloch ms, IU; *CG,* 38, 1, 2 June 1864, 2681 (Dawes).

45. John Sherman, *John Sherman's Recollections of Forty Years in the House, Senate, and Cabinet,* 3 vols. (Chicago: Werner Company, 1895), vol. 1, 233; *New York Tribune,* 11 April 1861; Sumner to Martin F. Tupper, Boston, 11 November 1861, Series II, Reel 75, SP; Stampp, *And the War Came,* 296–97.

46. *CG,* 38, 1, 27 January 1864, 377; ibid., 4 June 1864, 2750; A. B. Stone, J. E. Williams, H. B. Payne, A. Pope, W. B. Castle, and Daniel P. Rhodes to Morrill, Cleveland, 10 August 1865, Morrill ms, Box 7, LC; Morrill to the Society for the Protection of American Industry, Stratford, 4 September 1865, ibid.; Paludan, *"A People's Contest,"* 130.

47. Van Deusen, *Horace Greeley,* 293, n. 39; Lee, "Henry C. Carey and the Republican Tariff," 299; Parker, *The Life and Public Services of Justin Smith Morrill,* 113; George Opdyke to Trumbull, New York, 30 January 1861, Trumbull ms, Reel 8, LC; Alexander T. Stewart to Weed, New York, 29 January 1861, Weed ms, UR; Weed to Andrew Carrigan, Paris, 3 December 1861, ibid.

48. *Chicago Tribune,* 9 October 1865, in Horace White to Morrill, Chicago, 9 October 1865, Morrill ms, Box 7, LC; Logsdon, *Horace White,* 116–17.

49. McCulloch to James Van Alen, Washington, 10 April 1865, McCulloch ms, Treasury Department Letterbook, March–May 1865, IU; William E. Chandler to Forney, Washington, 21 November 1865, Chandler ms, Treasury Department Letter Book, July 1865–March 1866, NHHS.

50. James A. Hamilton to Webb, Nevis, 25 March 1861, Webb ms, Box 6, Folder 86, Sterling Library, Yale University; Phillip S. Paludan, "Commentary on Lincoln's Economics," in Gabor Boritt, ed., *The Historian's Lincoln* (New York: Oxford University Press, 1996), 120. Webb became minister to Brazil.

CONCLUSION: SUCCESSES AND FAILURES OF REPUBLICAN IDEOLOGY

ON 4 March 1865, Abraham Lincoln delivered a second inaugural address that has become known for its tone of conciliation and rationalization. The conciliation lay in its conclusion, which began, "With malice toward none; with charity for all"—an effort to find room for all to agree on how to restore the Union. As Phillip Paludan wrote, while Lincoln used the occasion to blame the South for the war, he noted "the responsibilities that Northerners shared and that he and Congress and the wider polity must assume." By contrast, Lincoln's leading biographer, David Herbert Donald, described him as absolving himself of responsibility for the war by saying, "The Almighty has His own purposes." Faulting the North and South, Lincoln said, "Both read the same Bible, and pray to the same God; and each invokes His aid against the other. It may seem strange that any men should dare to ask a just God's assistance in wringing their bread from the sweat of other men's faces; but let us judge not that we be not judged." Then came what Donald called "one of the most terrible statements ever made by an American public official": "Fondly do we hope—fervently do we pray—that this mighty scourge of war may speedily pass away. Yet, if God wills that it continue, until all the wealth piled by the bond-man's two hundred and fifty years of unrequited toil shall be sunk, and until every drop of blood drawn with the lash, shall be paid by another drawn with the sword, as was said three thousand years ago, so still it must be said 'the judgments of the Lord, are true and righteous altogether.'"[1]

However terrible—and majestically poetic—the statement, the speech not only illuminates Lincoln's views on Reconstruction, but is a classic exposition of the party's ideology. In no way did Lincoln absolve the South of its sins. Few scholars distinguish between his softer approach to the South in 1861 and his threat to annihilate it in 1865, and that is what he meant by the sword repaying blood drawn with the lash. After the division of the Union that Republicans had been elected to govern, their pursuit of freedom helped extinguish slavery, which they had vowed to protect—until preserving the Union with slavery became impossible. In perpetuating freedom and preserving the Union, Republicans found that their new power could be circular: to expand federal power, they had to retain and enhance their power. They also confronted questions about who would exercise power: the executive or legislature, radicals or conservatives, the federal government or the states. They never fully resolved those questions. By the time hindsight showed them the need to resolve them, it was too late.[2]

A Party without a Leader, a Leader without a Party

The strands of this ideology of freedom, union, and power cohered over Reconstruction. Throughout the war, the overriding issue for Republicans was how to reunite the country. When they began debating Reconstruction is hard to say; after all, when the South left the Union, the North began trying to reconstruct it. The first salvo came on 8 December 1863, when Lincoln proposed a plan of amnesty and reconstruction that came closer to "malice toward none" than "drawn with the sword": when 10 percent of a Southern state's voting populace signed an oath of Union, the state was restored. Hoping that Southerners wanted to avoid the full thrust of Union power, he used his war power to pursue reunion. But his plan was doomed: the rebels were unwilling to return, and most of his party found such easy terms intolerable.

The next summer radicals countered with a program equally in keeping with Republican ideology, and equally doomed. Senator Ben Wade of Ohio and Representative Henry Winter Davis of Maryland pushed through a bill requiring half of the voters to sign on and imposing other restrictions. Lincoln countered by offering rebels a choice between the two plans, prompting Wade and Davis to issue their manifesto accusing him of usurping congressional power. Again the party split over the means of union—the extent of freedom and who would wield power—but not the ends: the continuing movement toward freedom and the exercise of power for the sake of the Union.[3]

The debate continued through the 1864 election and into the spring of 1865. Running for reelection as he ran the Union war machine, Lincoln tried to restore Louisiana to the Union with a new government and constitution. Radicals objected to the lack of legal and political protection for blacks as they tentatively entered a free labor system yet still were required to contract for their labor with their former masters. The Thirteenth Amendment's passage left no doubt that slavery was dying, but the measure said nothing about what would happen to the ex-slaves once they became freedpeople. The plight of black men and women obviously improved during the war, but their rights remained opaque.[4]

Lincoln's plans also were opaque. His second inaugural address could be read several ways, but what proved to be his last speech, on 11 April, showed that he had abandoned the conciliatory nature of his plan of 1863. Indeed, he said, "I presented *a* plan," and admitted to avoiding a hard and fast stand. He sought to reconstruct the Union as speedily and painlessly as he could: "I believe it is not only possible, but in fact, easier, to do this, without deciding, or even considering, whether these states have even been out of the Union," a subtle slap at radical Senator Charles Sumner's "state suicide" theory that Southern states gave up their rights by seceding, and at undue theorizing on the issue. Yet he sought results that gave radicals hope. As for Louisiana's failure to add black suffrage to its constitution, as radicals wanted, he said, "I would myself prefer that it were now conferred on the very intelligent, and on those who serve our cause as soldiers." Although radicals considered this suggestion too limited, it still meant that while Lincoln and the radicals shared an ideology of ends, they had grown closer on the means.[5]

When Lincoln met with his Cabinet on 14 April he felt accommodating toward the South, yet demonstrated that ideologically he also might be hardening. While they discussed ruling the former rebels through military governments, Lincoln said, "We can't undertake to run State governments in all these Southern States. Their people must do that,—though I reckon that at first some of them may do it badly." But he voiced a vision of executive power that certainly would have troubled other ex-Whigs: "If we were wise and discreet, we should reanimate the States and get their governments in successful operation, with order prevailing and the Union reestablished, before Congress came together in December. . . . We could do better, accomplish more without than with them." Whether he planned to use his war powers or saw a chance to enhance executive government, Lincoln was ready to use as much power as he could to restore the Union and promote the freedom that the Thirteenth Amendment promised.[6]

But that night everything changed. With Lincoln's death and the ascent of Andrew Johnson, the party and its ideology were altered irrevocably. The Union party had been no more than Republicans in a different guise, with Johnson on the ticket to appeal to War Democrats and border state unionists. Instead Johnson became president, setting policies based on his background as a Jacksonian agrarian who hated planters for their privileged station, and trying to reap the benefits of the added powers that Lincoln had claimed for himself. As Lincoln had planned, the president took advantage of the absence of Congress to impose his will. By the time Congress convened in December 1865, Johnson had begun issuing pardons and rebels were regaining control of the South.[7]

Not that Republicans took Johnson's policies lying down. Salmon Chase, once secretary of the Treasury and now chief justice, toured the South and touted the freedmen's talents and black suffrage to Johnson; he believed that he was preaching, if not to the converted, then to a willing audience. Sumner wrote letters imploring radicals to stand up to Johnson and moderates to join his crusade; most dismissed his concerns or lamented that they were powerless to act. Republicans had become prisoners of their success. They were achieving freedom and had restored the Union. But the power they had created or enhanced was not only limiting the freedom they had envisioned, but endangering their own power. Johnson was as serious about building a Union party as the Republicans, and, like them, intended to dominate it with his ideology—but his was not a Republican ideology.[8]

Many historians agree that Republicans shared an ideology that helped guide them throughout Johnson's tenure. Aware that he hoped to thwart them, they sought to impose control over the South to stop the restoration of slavery and the destruction of their chance of gaining votes there. They asserted federal power, passing a freedmen's bureau bill to ease the transition to freedom, a civil rights act, and constitutional amendments to define citizenship. Claiming congressional supremacy, they overrode Johnson's vetoes, created the Tenure of Office Act, and used it and other means to impeach him. These events represented a continuation of the Republicans' wartime ideology. They were trying to codify what they fought for: freedom, in this case by assuring the freedmen's civil rights; union, by ruining the South's will or ability to rebel; and their and the government's power to effect both. In this way Republicans changed little, except that losing the White House denied them the executive power they had wielded in wartime.

Given that they had welcomed Johnson into the Union party as a shining example of elusive Southern unionism, it was a bitter pill to swallow. Worse, they proved unable to achieve all they set out to do when he was in office. By the time Ulysses Grant became president in 1869, a kind of national exhaustion with the process had begun to set in, and kept them from holding and using the power they had tasted and savored when Lincoln had been in the White House and Grant had been enacting his will on battlefields across the Confederacy.[9]

Race, Free Labor, and the Fate of Republican Ideology

The war not only promised to regenerate values that Republicans held dear; it also enabled them to achieve their goals. They passed the legislation proposed in their 1860 platform. They realized their hopes of stopping the spread of slavery, and went beyond their wildest dreams by ending it. They showed that a party tarred as fanatical could run the government. When the Union dissolved, Republicans unaccustomed to governance rebuilt the army, managed the executive and legislative branches, and restored the Union. They did all of this despite differences of personality, approach, and degree that often threatened to hobble or even cripple their party. In overcoming these obstacles, their shared ideology was crucial. They believed in freedom, union, and power, and achieved them.

Still, their wartime and postwar achievements differed. Black freedom proved to be "nothing but freedom" or "one kind of freedom," to quote the titles of two books on emancipation. The Union was reunited, but Southern stubbornness meant one of two things. Either the party would have to adopt a completely nationalistic approach that would leave nothing to the states and to chance, or it would continue to believe in a set of admirable ends while battling over the best means to those ends. That battle over means and ends raged on, and no matter how unified the party became, the absence of a Republican from the

White House for four years provided an insurmountable obstacle to fully wielding national power. Thus, the quest for power became more important than its use. Republican power went to less reformist uses than it should have, as the scandals of Grant's presidency and the inability to protect former slaves from injustice show. Why did Republicans fail to meet expectations—their own and those of historians—after the war? The answers all spring from their wartime ideology, which helped produce great results.[10]

The first answer is that the war changed how Republicans saw themselves, not necessarily how they and others saw African Americans. The party's ideological transformation did not extend to color-blindness. To Senator James Doolittle, a Wisconsin conservative, "the question of race is a more troublesome one than the question of condition." But many in his party had no trouble: they considered the freedpeople inferior. Senator Orville Browning of Illinois called them "a debased and degraded race, incapable of making progress because they want that best element and best incentive to progress—social equality—which they never can have here." Willing to end slavery "to save the Government and the Constitution," Frank Blair added, "I am against the social and political equality of the emancipated negro." These men had been Democrats, the party that had countenanced the spread of slavery, or conservative Whigs who had considered their brethren in that organization too radically anti-slavery for the party's good—and seemed to many other Republicans so conservative as to be almost paralyzed.[11]

Yet more enlightened Republicans—or those who claimed to be—lacked either racial tolerance or the ability to put racial tolerance ahead of practical politics. While Horace Greeley disliked William Henry Seward, the *New York Tribune* editor saw no sign of prejudice in him—but when Sumner sought a passport for the son of a black Boston lawyer, Seward said, "It won't do to acknowledge colored men as citizens"; it might cost the party votes. Montgomery Blair, whose family had left the Democrats over slavery, denied differing substantially with the radicals, yet charged that they sought "to make a caste of another color by amalgamating the black element with the free white labor of our land." Conservatives blamed radicals for trying to elevate blacks beyond the level to which they saw them as consigned. Calling the New York City draft riots of 1863 a "crime at which civilization and humanity revolt and shudder," Weed argued that they could have been avoided "but for the stimulants applied by fanatics." His friend Henry Sanford, the minister to Belgium, raised in the North and well educated, told Weed that "we have to fight for the Union—not for the nigger." A less cultured conservative complained that radicals "entertain more hatred to the owners than love for the negro."[12]

For their part, radicals hoped that equal opportunity would allow blacks to prove and protect themselves. George Boutwell, a Massachusetts congressman, argued that blacks should be rewarded for their ability, but added, "It is an imputation on the white people of the country to say that in a fair contest they are not able to maintain, socially, intellectually, and morally, the ascendancy." Samuel Gridley Howe told Sumner, "It would seem to be the purpose of those in power to prevent the black man from vindicating his own cause and showing his capacity for self guidance, by denying him all opportunity of doing any thing for himself." Part of the problem was that even some of those who joined Sumner and Howe in the radical cause doubted that freedpeople could do anything for themselves anyway. To legislators who banned black ownership of guns and intermarriage, James Nye, the governor of Nevada territory and a New York radical transplated to the West, argued, "I do not believe that if the entire energies of the superior race were directed to the elevation of the colored races, it would place them higher in the scale of being than the Creator designed them to occupy."[13]

The issue was equality before the law, and a Republican who never hid his views, Thaddeus Stevens, captured the essence of the party's problem in a speech to the House in January 1864. Assailing Democrats who played on racial fears for political gain, he said, "Our political laws are either to give equal rights to every human being, or they are to crush the one and elevate the other upon his ruin. I do not know that ever I shall come across men of dark color of the same intelligence as white men. I have seen some that I thought not much inferior to most of us." A year later, urged to abandon his demands for black equality, Stevens replied that he meant legal equality, not social equality. While it would be hard to find a more egalitarian politician in his time than Stevens, he proposed turning over confiscated plantations to former slaves, which suggested more than just a laissez-faire attitude toward what would become of the freedmen. A lover of freedom and partisan combat, Stevens made plenty of deals during a long political career—and even he would stop short of declaring that black and white were always and absolutely equal.[14]

These comments run on converging tracks. Republicans seemed to think that blacks needed only freedom and opportunity; then they could prove themselves unequal to the white man. How much of this pandered to the less liberal-minded would be unclear except that these views appeared not only in public, but in private letters in which Republicans had greater freedom to express their views. For every Sumner who believed totally in equality, a Wade voted just as radically yet was racially prejudiced in a way that Sumner never had been. And the chances of finding Sumner or Wade, or those of like mind, in positions of power were smaller than that of finding a moderate Illinoisan, often heralded for his egalitarianism, who had told a delegation of Northern free blacks visiting the White House: "Your race are suffering, in my judgment, the greatest wrong inflicted on any people. But even when you cease to be slaves, you are yet far removed from being placed on an equality with the white race. . . . The aspiration of men is to enjoy equality with the best when free, but on this broad continent, not a single man of your race is made the equal of a single man of ours. Go where you are treated the best, and the ban is still upon you."[15]

What had prompted Lincoln's words was colonization, an issue inseparable from that of equality before the law. Blaming the less advanced, Lincoln argued that the two races simply could not live in harmony and claimed to follow in the footsteps of his idol, Henry Clay, who had seen colonization as the best solution to the race conundrum. And Lincoln was not alone: when he suggested sending black volunteers to Central America, Seward was agreeable, Chase silent and opposed despite an earlier willingness to discuss the subject, Attorney General Edward Bates in favor of ordering them to go, and Secretary of the Interior Caleb Smith for moving freedmen West to build the transcontinental railroad. Granting that all but Chase dwelled in the party's conservative wing, the debate showed that party leaders understood the prejudice that permeated the country and were more interested in eliminating what they saw as the cause of it than in working out a joint solution.[16]

Nor did all Republicans automatically welcome the idea of black soldiers. In the war's first year, they lamented stories of slaves turned away from Union camps and whipped by army officers whose devotion to the cause was already in doubt. But as conservatives flinched, radicals and moderates increasingly argued for black soldiers. Recruiting, paying, and promoting them would strike at Southern claims of racial inferiority and docility. Irked at orders to return fugitives to their masters, more Republicans saw that the Union lost manpower by taking soldiers away from fighting to return slaves who might fight for the Union. And as Frederick Douglass noted, blacks figured to be the most dedicated soldiers imaginable. They were fighting for their lives in more ways than one: victory promised freedom; defeat might mean enslavement or execution.[17]

How radicals and moderates made their case for arming blacks revealed what can only be called the lack of a moral center. According to Senator Henry Wilson of Massachusetts, "We could have employed thousands of colored men at low rates of wages to do the ditching, and thus save[d] the health, the strength, and the lives of our brave soldiers." More radical than Wilson, Zachariah Chandler of Michigan wrote that generals such as George McClellan said no to "Negroes to dig ditches, Cut down timber & do hard work, but will *force* my brave boys to do this menial work & *die in doing it*." As cruel and heartless as it was to suggest that white lives mattered more than black lives, making the case in this way might help overcome conservative leanings and racial prejudices. But this suggested that blacks had the right to move from menial slave labor to menial free labor, a trend that might continue in civilian life. They argued, as abolitionist Joshua Giddings did, that military service "will elevate the negro, teach him the value of freedom and the only mode of defending it."[18]

Yet Republicans were skittish about treating black and white soldiers alike. Tellingly, black soldiers and their supporters had to fight for the same pay and benefits as white soldiers, and succeeded only after long delays and debate. The families of black soldiers fared no better: coming from slave states where black marriages were unsanctioned, widows and children received no federal benefits until late in the war. As always, radicals were at the forefront of such fights, but the federal government's grudging response suggests that even radicals considered these issues dangerous: enough racism existed outside the party, much less inside it, to make it ill-advised to push too hard. As with emancipation, they feared that moving too quickly in the cause of civil rights might harm freed blacks and slaves by setting back the party.

Republicans could hardly aid the freedpeople if they lacked power—as Johnson's actions in the White House showed with dreadful clarity.[19]

But what Republicans would do with that power was unclear. They equated free labor with equality of opportunity, but mainly for whites facing unequal competition from slave laborers. Nor did they doubt that whites would triumph in a competition with blacks; not only did most of them believe in white superiority, but blacks would have to overcome centuries of oppression. That this ideology was attuned more to white concerns and problems was unsurprising; the voters were almost all white, and Republicans knew enough about politics to know that to get ahead of their constituency on issues like race might cost them votes. But to expect more of all Republicans—granting the role of abolitionists like Sumner and Douglass and egalitarians like Stevens—than of the rest of the country at the time is unfair, for to be susceptible to prejudice was hardly unusual then or later. Republicans were advocating that their country change; whether it was going forward or reverting to what they believed the framers of the Constitution to have expected of them, it ultimately meant progress. That progress focused on the existence of slavery, which Republicans began the war viewing as disturbing and by the end of the war had eliminated entirely.

It would be neither overly simplistic nor an exaggeration to say that by eliminating slave labor, Republicans eliminated the antithesis by which they defined free labor. With the war's end and for the rest of the century, Republicans addressed free labor from a different perspective. Workers had the freedom to labor. Whether that extended to the freedom not to labor, to strike and to demand particular wages and hours, was another matter entirely. That affected the concept of order that was so important to the evolution of their ideology—and it affected the free market. Retirement, defeat, or death ended the careers of several leading Republicans not long after the war: William Henry Seward, Salmon Chase, Thaddeus Stevens, and William Pitt Fessenden, to name a few. Whether they would have supported the nascent labor movement of the 1860s and 1870s—or, more accurately, whether they would have significantly affected the Republican response to that movement—is unknowable, of course. What is certain is that Republicans divided in those decades over labor issues, and many of them disagreed with the tactics and actions of workers who felt that the freedom to labor simply was not enough to sustain them.[20]

In some ways, then, the war served as a prelude to the Social Darwinism that Republicans seemed to practice during the Gilded Age. Their anti-slavery beliefs and the responsibilities that the war thrust on them combined to limit too many of them to a myopic view of what to do after slavery ended and set obstacles on the road to genuine freedom. As we have seen, many of them considered blacks, slave or free, inferior. But their fate was up to them, not their emancipators; they would be free laborers, enjoying the freedom to labor, with whatever success or failure might follow. Some Republicans felt differently, but enough agreed, or doubted that helping freedpeople adjust to freedom would do them any good. To assume they would survive if they were fit and die out if not was Darwinism at its rawest, and part of the free labor ideology with which Republicans entered and exited the war. Winning the war demanded a commitment to freedom, union, and power, but so would winning the peace. Not that Republicans reverted to an outdated mode of thought; they adjusted to circumstances but saw that the circumstances had changed again.[21]

Another four score and more years after Lincoln had augured "a new birth of freedom" at Gettysburg, black and white lawyers gathered to plan their argument against school segregation before the Supreme Court. In 1954, when the court ruled unanimously against school segregation, the National Association for the Advancement of Colored People's lead attorney, Thurgood Marshall, predicted a solution to the problem within five years. "In a sense, these men were profoundly naive. They really felt that once the legal barriers fell, the whole black-white situation would change. I was more skeptical, but they were convinced that the relationship between the law and society was the key," said a white historian who consulted with the NAACP and found "that they really believed in the American dream and that it could be made to work for black men, too."[22]

Tragically, nearly a century after the Civil War, those who had been exposed to the most searing racism could cling to their ideals and expectations of social advancement and prove dreadfully wrong. Perhaps, then, the Republicans of the 1860s deserve less condemnation for thinking that emancipation would solve so many of the ills that they hoped to cure. Even at the time many of them agreed that emancipation was not enough, and demanded more for the freedpeople because more was needed. At times they spoke out of true belief, at times out of political calculation, at times out of a combination of both. Whatever their motivations or the basis for them, what matters is that they took a giant step in the right direction, but had trouble deciding whether to take another and how great it should be. That they were less advanced than they should have been had disastrous effects, not only on those whom their policies affected, but also on themselves. That they were divided, given their agreement on general issues and disagreement on specific details, should be no surprise.[23]

More significantly, Republicans retained a significant amount of the idealism and the commitment to using power that had characterized their Civil War ideology. Until the 1890s, the party tried to enforce the voting rights that the Fifteenth Amendment supposedly guaranteed. When they had pondered power during the war—intramural Cabinet warfare, fights over patronage, and the executive fighting the legislature, for example—Republicans also had addressed whether the federal government or the states would predominate. Even if the Civil War seemed to settle the issue in favor of federal supremacy, the states retained some power. Between that and the party's general belief in black inferiority, the federal government would be unlikely to take all necessary steps to protect black suffrage. As Xi Wang, the leading historian of the subject, concluded, "If the Republican party was only partly successful in its all too often halfhearted efforts to protect black political rights in the late nineteenth century, it laid the groundwork for the reenfranchisement of African Americans and a new transformation of American democracy in the twentieth century." Lincoln and then the NAACP were naive about their successes, but what Republicans achieved would enable their colleagues and those who followed to try to rectify their shortcomings.[24]

The Problem of Power—and Unity

Another problem for Republicans was how long they would be able to offer the benefits of their ideology to blacks. They changed their name to the Union party to expand their membership, not to reinvent their ideology. But the party included Democrats whose party had divided in the 1850s, Whigs whose party had dissolved, and Know-Nothings whose party had come and gone. Republicans might face the same fate if they lacked caution. As Mark Neely has pointed out, the idea of a party system during the Civil War exists mainly in the minds of historians and theorists; after so much fluidity, Republicans could hardly be expected to believe that they and their ideas were permanent. One of the unanswerable questions raised by the Union party's creation was whether Republicans foresaw a realignment that would radically alter their party's composition. Complicating the issue is Lincoln's death. He revealed little about his plans, but other Republicans had discussed changing their party either temporarily or permanently, and not just to the Union party. Conservatives mulled building a new organization consisting of like-minded Republicans and Democrats.[25]

The thoughts of Chase and Blair offer a useful window through which to view the party's possible evolution. As usual they disagreed, yet their views were closer than either knew or would have cared to admit. "If, as is given out confidently in some quarters, an attempt shall be made to convert the Republican into the old Whig Party, it will signally fail and the Democratic party will return to power," Chase told another former Democrat, Trumbull, before Lincoln took office. But if the administration were to "represent fully the sense of the Republican Party, there will grow out of this party as out of the party of the same name which achieved a triumph not unlike . . . in 1801 a truly democratic party, which will control the Govt for the next twenty or twenty-four years—or rather until it shall cease to represent the will and instinct of the people." As Chase increasingly soured on Lincoln, he mulled a realignment with a "new party really democratic and really republican." By 1864, out of sorts over his increasingly unhappy relations with Lincoln, he told a radical, "Nothing would gratify me more than to see the Democratic party advance its standard to the full height of a true expression of democratic ideas."[26]

At the same time, Blair contemplated a realignment uniting Republicans he considered conservative—Lincoln, for example, and old Democrats such as his family. Late in 1863, in Maryland, Blair delivered a scorching oration against radical Reconstruction, advocating a smoother path back into the Union and trying to create an issue around which conservatives could coalesce. For the next year Blair engaged in a form of high-minded partisan intrigue, trying to persuade old friends still in the Democratic party to adopt a key provision in the Union platform: a demand for the end of slavery. His arguments to

Democratic leader S. L. M. Barlow, a New York lawyer, were tantalizing. Opposing Lincoln's election would further damage his party because Northerners "are suspicious of opposition to the Govt. especially when the opposition party is composed in part of Peace men and Southern sympathizers." Worse, it would force Lincoln to seek support from Chase and his followers, and, Blair said, neither he nor Barlow wanted that. The answer lay in "giving up the past, considering slavery to be extinct," and "you can make an issue upon which not only the Democracy of the North and South may unite against the Abolitionists, but on which the larger portion of the Republicans will join in sustaining."[27]

Blair sought to block the radicals, and when his effort to sway Barlow failed, he tried another issue: the Thirteenth Amendment. He urged Barlow to swing his party behind it when it came before the House early in 1865, and to support its ratification once it went to the states. Not only would it be good for Democrats, he argued, but parties would regroup "on the Negro question as contradistinguished from the Slave question. This would certainly bring about the Reconstruction of the Union with the rights of the States unimpaired. The Democratic party by this . . . would be the real restorer of the Union," and thereby destroy the radicals. And while Blair felt a great sense of personal and political loss at Lincoln's death, it also accelerated his plans. He hoped to build a coalition of conservative Republicans, border unionists, Southern moderates, and loyal Democrats, with Johnson as leader—a party like the one that Seward envisioned, except that he hoped for a more Whiggish tone than a dedicated Jacksonian such as Blair could abide. Yet when Johnson kept Seward and Stanton in the Cabinet and declined some of Blair's policy suggestions, the former postmaster general refused to despair. He would leave "nothing undone to insure the good relations between the P. and the Democratic party," and unwittingly voiced what Republicans had sought throughout the war: "to inaugurate the Era of Good Feeling" by embracing like-minded Democrats and Republicans in a unionist political party.[28]

In discussing realignment, Chase and Blair sounded both more and less like the ideologues they were. Both wanted their political party based on democratic principles. Both wanted to lead it or share its leadership. Each wanted the party to reflect his worldview. For Chase that meant a belief in civil rights for blacks, including suffrage. For Blair that meant freedom for blacks, but little else; in that way he was the real Democrat, while Chase had both created and imbibed the activism that had permeated the Republican party during the Civil War. But neither Chase nor Blair seems to have worried about what blacks wanted or how they fit into this new structure; what mattered more, even to Chase, was to keep out certain whites. While Chase sincerely advocated civil rights, it seems clear that he fully expected blacks to follow the lead of Republicans like himself who already had done so much to help them and, with their votes, would be in a position to do more. In war and peace, Republicans were more concerned with enhancing freedom, union, and power than with thinking about their effects on those who were new to freedom.

Ideology played a role in their actions and reactions, but so did politics. Republicans hoped to retain and expand their power, requiring them to tread carefully on the issues. But their goal was freedom, however they defined it individually, from limiting the spread of slavery to its total elimination, from keeping blacks on Southern plantations to freeing them to vote and compete with whites. What they wanted to do, and did, followed from what they believed, but it also involved political realities. Not only were they concerned with what they thought they could achieve and how quickly it should be achieved, but they were also concerned with who should achieve it. Thus, the party's wartime ideology was not set in concrete—because ideology itself cannot be concrete, and because it was a work in progress, changing as the circumstances that the party confronted changed, changing as the leaders gave in to their ambitions and dislikes.

Explaining the Transformation

To look to the Civil War for an explanation of Reconstruction and what followed would be counterproductive. In war the past and future matter immensely, but they must still matter less than survival in the present. That is true not only of the soldier but also of institutions such as political parties and their members. Republicans fit this description, as did the nation they had been elected to govern. If they failed so would the Union, and so would any chance of extending freedom beyond its borders at the time. Republicans had to take their newfound power and wield it wisely, forcing them into compromises they would have preferred to avoid. During the war Republicans believed in freedom, union, and power. This was the ideological transformation of the Republican party during the Civil War. When Robert E. Lee handed Ulysses Grant his sword at Appomattox, it meant that the circumstances had changed. When Abraham Lincoln went to the theater five nights later, it meant a change in the party's leadership. The war, the party that fought it, and the ideology that guided it, as Stanton said of Lincoln, now belonged to the ages.

Part of the difficulty with explaining the Republican party's ideology during the Civil War lies in trying to prove a negative. During the war, Republicans wrote far less often about the issues they had discussed before the war. The issues had changed, but so had their responsibilities. They had gone from the opposition to the party in power. They had hoped to stop the spread of slavery; instead they had to deal with the destruction of the Union. They saw themselves as the inheritors and correct interpreters of the founding fathers, and rather than trying to repair the republic that the framers had created, Republicans were forced to save it. The theorizing that had filled their writing before the war was not entirely absent during the war, but thought clearly had to take a back seat to action.

Or did it? The policies that Republicans developed on slavery required much debate and discussion over politics, constitutionalism, and race. In their speeches, editorials, and correspondence, and through their actions, they showed an evolution from opposing the spread of slavery to being convinced that it needed to be eliminated entirely. This was one of the issues that forced them to look both differently and more broadly at the question of freedom—not just at the idea of free soil, free labor, and free men, but also at what they would do for, about, and (if need be) against freedom, which has often been defined in American history by juxtaposing it with slavery. What they would do about slavery and freedom had a great deal to do with the Union: when to act and when not to act to preserve it. That required them to understand power: how to use it, how not to use it, who should use it, and how to keep it.

These questions sometimes tied together easily; sometimes they were contradictory. That forced Republicans to make choices that many of them preferred to avoid, and understandably so. After all, they had campaigned for local and national offices as champions of freedom, then jailed some of their opponents and conducted a long debate over emancipation. They constantly voiced a commitment to the idea of individual, self-sufficient free laborers, but they aided, unwittingly or not, the large accumulation of capital that clothed those who held it with the power to keep free laborers under their thumb. They claimed to believe in the highest ideals and in many ways did, but they engaged in the lowest form of partisan politics. They did all of this in the interests of protecting freedom in the long run, saving the Union for the long term, and wielding power for a long time. If the terminology and meaning of the ideology of freedom, union, and power changed in the years after the Civil War, that does nothing to diminish its importance at the time—and thus for all time.

Notes

1. "Second Inaugural Address," 4 March 1865, in *CW,* vol. 8, 332–33; Paludan, *The Presidency of Abraham Lincoln,* 304–05; Donald, *Lincoln,* 566–68.
2. Paludan, *The Presidency of Abraham Lincoln,* 304–5; Harris, *With Charity for All, passim.*
3. Foner, *Reconstruction,* 35–50, 61–62; Harris, *With Charity for All, passim.*
4. On Lincoln and Louisiana, see LaWanda Cox, *Lincoln and Black Freedom: A Study in Presidential Leadership* (Columbia: University of South Carolina Press, 1981). See also Vorenberg, *Final Freedom.*
5. "Last Public Address," 11 April 1865, in *CW,* vol. 8, 399–405.
6. Donald, *Lincoln,* 589–92; Foner, *Reconstruction,* 74–75.
7. Foner, *Reconstruction,* 176–85. On Johnson, see also Trefousse, *Andrew Johnson,* and McKitrick, *Andrew Johnson.*
8. The Papers of Charles Sumner, a microfilm edition, contain dozens of letters on various reels from 1865. On Chase, see Niven, *Salmon P. Chase,* especially 384–96.
9. Foner, *Reconstruction,* 176–601. See Benedict, *A Compromise of Principle;* Simpson, *The Reconstruction Presidents;* and Hans L. Trefousse, *Impeachment of a President: Andrew Johnson, the Blacks, and Reconstruction* (Knoxville: University of Tennessee Press, 1975).
10. Foner, *Nothing But Freedom;* Roger L. Ransom and Richard Sutch, *One Kind of Freedom: The Economic Consequences of Emancipation* (Cambridge: Cambridge University Press, 1977). See also Wang, *The Trial of Democracy,*

and Heather Cox Richardson, *The Death of Reconstruction: Race, Labor, and Politics in the Post–Civil War North, 1865–1901* (Cambridge: Harvard University Press, 2001).

11. James R. Doolittle to Mrs. James R. Doolittle, Washington, 17 April 1862, James R. Doolittle Papers (Doolittle ms), State Historical Society of Wisconsin, in Curry, *Blueprint for Modern America,* 43; Bogue, *The Earnest Men,* 158; Smith, *The Francis Preston Blair Family,* vol. 2, 216.

12. Horace Greeley, *Recollections of a Busy Life* (New York: J. B. Ford, 1868), 313; Donald, *Charles Sumner and the Rights of Man,* 47; Montgomery Blair, "Speech of the Honorable Montgomery Blair on the Revolutionary Schemes of the Ultra Abolitionists" (New York: D. W. Lee, 1863), 4; Baker, *The Politics of Continuity,* 95; Barnes and Weed, *Life of Thurlow Weed,* 436; Sanford to Weed, Paris, 14 April 1863, Weed ms, UR; Stephen T. Logan to Lamon, Springfield, 12 February 1862, Lamon ms, Box 11, HL. On the draft riots, see Iver Bernstein, *The New York City Draft Riots: Their Significance for American Society and Politics in the Age of the Civil War* (New York: Oxford University Press, 1990). On Sanford, see Joseph A. Fry, *Henry Sanford: Diplomacy and Business in Nineteenth Century America* (Reno: University of Nevada Press, 1982).

13. *CG,* 38, 1, 11 February 1864, 605; Howe to Sumner, Boston, 21 January 1862, in Series II, Reel 75, SP; *New York Evening Post,* 28 October 1862; Elmer R. Rusco, *"Good Time Coming?" Black Nevadans in the Nineteenth Century* (Westport, Conn.: Greenwood Press, 1975), 22–28.

14. *CG,* 38, 1, 7 January 1864, 133; *Sacramento Union,* 21 February 1865; Foner, *Politics and Ideology in the Age of the Civil War,* 128–49; Trefousse, *Thaddeus Stevens.*

15. Trefousse, *Benjamin Franklin Wade;* "Address on Colonization to a Deputation of Negroes," 14 August 1862, in *New York Tribune,* 15 August 1862, in *CW,* vol. 5, 370–75.

16. Donald, *Lincoln,* 166–67, 343–48; Vorenberg, "Abraham Lincoln and the Politics of Black Colonization," 23–45; Smith, *Francis Preston Blair,* 320, 323–24, 331; "Annual Message to Congress," 3 December 1861, in *CW,* vol. 5, 48; Paludan, *The Presidency of Abraham Lincoln,* 130–33; 24 September 1862, in Donald, ed., *Inside Lincoln's Cabinet,* 156–57; "Report of the Secretary of the Interior," *CG,* 38, 1, Appendix, 25–26.

17. Israel Washburn to Hamlin, Augusta, 16 January 1862, Washburn ms, LC; Curry, *Blueprint for Modern America,* 61–62; Sherman to Colonel Turchin, Louisville, 15 October 1861, *OR,* Series I, Volume IV, 307; Blight, *Frederick Douglass' Civil War,* 149–54.

18. Bogue, *The Earnest Men,* 162; Chandler to Letitia Chandler, Washington, 11 July 1862, Chandler ms, LC; Curry, *Blueprint for Modern America,* 62; Giddings to Sumner, Jefferson, 30 July 1863, Reel 29, SP.

19. *Harper's Weekly,* 9 January 1864, 18; Thomas Wentworth Higginson to Fessenden, Headquarters, 1st S.C. Volunteers, Beaufort, 13 February 1864, Higginson ms, NYHS; Garfield to J. Harry Rhodes, Washington, 28 April 1864, Garfield ms, Series 5, Reel 107, LC; Higginson to Sumner, Camp Shaw, Beaufort, 24 November 1863, Reel 29, and 24 June 1863, Series II, Reel 77, SP; Report of the Secretary of War, *CG,* 38, 1, Appendix, 11–12; ibid., 24 June 1864, 3233; ibid., 2, 19 December 1864, 64.

20. I am indebted to Nancy Cohen, *The Reconstruction of American Liberalism,* especially 1–63. See also Amy Dru Stanley, *From Bondage to Contract: Wage Labor, Marriage, and the Market in the Age of Slave Emancipation* (Cambridge: Cambridge University Press, 1998); and, of course, Montgomery, *Beyond Equality.*

21. See especially Hofstadter, *Social Darwinism,* and Richardson, *The Death of Reconstruction.*

22. Richard Kluger, *Simple Justice: The History of Brown v. Board of Education and Black America's Struggle for Equality* (New York: Alfred A. Knopf, 1976), 639, 714.

23. Neely, *The Union Divided,* 187; "Response to a Serenade," *New York Tribune,* 3 February 1865, in *CW,* vol. 8, 254–55.

24. Wang, *The Trial of Democracy,* 266.

25. On the 1850s, see Potter, *The Impending Crisis.*

26. Chase to Trumbull, Columbus, 12 November 1860, Trumbull ms, Reel 7, LC; Chase to Butler, Washington, 14 December 1862, Butler ms, Box 18, LC; Chase to Barney, Washington, 24 and 29 May 1864, draft, "Chase, Letters and Drafts, 1864–1873," Chase ms, HSP.

27. Montgomery Blair to Barlow, Washington, 29 October and 25 December 1863, Box 45, Barlow ms, HL; Blair to Barlow, n.p., 14 January 1864, Box 50, ibid.; Blair to Barlow, Washington, 9 February 1864, Box 56, ibid.; Blair to Barlow, n.p., 27 May 1864, Box 50, ibid.; Blair to Barlow, Washington, 1 May and 15 October 1864, ibid.; Baker, *The Politics of Continuity,* 147.

28. See the following communication from Blair to Barlow, all in Barlow ms, HL: Washington, 20 December 1864, Box 50; Washington, 7 and 12 1865, Box 56; n.p., 16 July 1865; Montgomery County, Maryland, 26 July 1865; Washington, 3 and 11 August, 13 September and 9 December 1865; Baker, *The Politics of Continuity,* 14–51. On political realignment in the year after Lincoln's death, see Cox and Cox, *Politics, Principle, and Prejudice.*

BIBLIOGRAPHY

I. Manuscript Collections

Adams Family Papers, Microfilm Edition, Massachusetts Historical Society

Isaac Arnold Papers, Chicago Historical Society

George Bancroft Papers, Manuscript Division, New York Public Library

Nathaniel P. Banks Papers, Manuscript Division, Library of Congress

Samuel L. M. Barlow Papers, Huntington Library

F. A. P. Barnard Papers, Department of Rare Books and Manuscripts, Butler Library, Columbia University

Hiram Barney Papers, Huntington Library

John Bigelow Papers, Manuscript Division, New York Public Library

Jeremiah S. Black Papers, Microfilm Edition, Manuscript Division, Library of Congress

James G. Blaine Papers, Microfilm Edition, Manuscript Division, Library of Congress

Montgomery Blair Papers, Lilly Library, Indiana University

Blair Family Papers, Manuscript Division, New York Public Library

Blair-Lee Family Papers, Princeton University

Samuel Bowles Papers, Sterling Library, Yale University

Joseph P. Bradley Papers, New Jersey Historical Society

H. Browne Papers, Department of Rare Books and Manuscripts, Butler Library, Columbia University

Orville H. Browning Papers, Illinois State Historical Library

William Cullen Bryant Papers, New-York Historical Society

Bryant-Godwin Papers, New York Public Library

Anson Burlingame Papers, Manuscript Division, Library of Congress

Benjamin F. Butler Papers, Microfilm Edition, Manuscript Division, Library of Congress

Simon Cameron Papers, Microfilm Edition, Manuscript Division, Library of Congress

Lewis Campbell Papers, Ohio Historical Society
Henry C. Carey Papers, Historical Society of Pennsylvania
William E. Chandler Papers, New Hampshire Historical Society
Zachariah Chandler Papers, Microfilm Edition, Manuscript Division, Library of Congress
Salmon P. Chase Papers, Historical Society of Pennsylvania
Salmon P. Chase Papers, Microfilm Edition, Manuscript Division, Library of Congress
Chase Family Papers, New Hampshire Historical Society
Civil War Miscellaneous, New-York Historical Society
Cleveland Newspaper Digest, Ohio Historical Society
Schuyler Colfax Papers, Indiana State Library
Schuyler Colfax Papers, Personal Miscellaneous, Manuscript Division, New York Public Library
Horace Congar Papers, New Jersey Historical Society
Moncure Daniel Conway Papers, Department of Rare Books and Manuscripts, Butler Library, Columbia University
Ezra Cornell Papers, No. 1-1-1, Box 21, Folder 6, Department of Manuscripts and Archives, Cornell University Libraries
Benjamin Curtis Papers, Manuscript Division, Library of Congress
Samuel R. Curtis Papers, Huntington Library
David Davis Papers, Chicago Historical Society
David Davis Papers, Illinois State Historical Library
Henry L. Dawes Papers, Manuscript Division, Library of Congress
William L. Dayton Papers, Princeton University
John A. Dix Papers, Department of Rare Books and Manuscripts, Butler Library, Columbia University
James R. Doolittle Papers, Manuscript Division, New York Public Library
Stephen A. Douglas Papers, Chicago Historical Society
Thomas H. Dudley Papers, Huntington Library
Eldridge Civil War Papers, Huntington Library
Hugh Ewing Papers, Ohio Historical Society
Thomas Ewing and Family Papers, Manuscript Division, Library of Congress
William Pitt Fessenden Papers, Microfilm Edition, Manuscript Division, Library of Congress
William Pitt Fessenden Papers, Western Reserve Historical Society

Fessenden Family Papers, Special Collections, Bowdoin College
Hamilton Fish Papers, Manuscript Division, Library of Congress
George G. Fogg Papers, New Hampshire Historical Society
Gustavus V. Fox Papers, New-York Historical Society
James A. Garfield Papers, Microfilm Edition, Manuscript Division, Library of Congress
Sydney Howard Gay Papers, Department of Rare Books and Manuscripts, Butler Library, Columbia University
Joshua R. Giddings–George W. Julian Papers, Manuscript Division, Library of Congress
Joseph A. Gilmore Papers, New Hampshire Historical Society
Horace Greeley Papers, Chicago Historical Society
Horace Greeley Papers, Manuscript Division, New York Public Library
Horace Greeley Papers, Manuscript Division, Library of Congress
John P. Hale Papers, New Hampshire Historical Society
Charles Halpine Papers, Huntington Library
Hannibal Hamlin Papers, Microfilm Edition, University of Maine, Orono
Stephen S. Harding Papers, Lilly Library, Indiana University
Friedrich Hassaurek Papers, Ohio Historical Society
Thomas Wentworth Higginson Papers, New-York Historical Society
J. W. Hill Papers, Department of Rare Books and Manuscripts, Butler Library, Columbia University
Alvin P. Hovey Papers, Lilly Library, Indiana University
Jay Family Papers, Department of Rare Books and Manuscripts, Butler Library, Columbia University
George Jones Papers, Manuscript Division, New York Public Library
John A. Kasson Papers, New York Historical Society
Ward Hill Lamon Papers, Huntington Library
Henry S. Lane Papers, Lilly Library, Indiana University
Abraham Lincoln Papers, Huntington Library
Robert Todd Lincoln Papers, Microfilm Edition, Manuscript Division, Library of Congress
Charles Maclay Papers, Huntington Library
Thomas F. Madigan Papers, Manuscript Division, New York Public Library
Manton Marble Papers, Manuscript Division, Library of Congress

George B. McClellan Papers, Microfilm Edition, Manuscript Division, Library of Congress
Hugh McCulloch Papers, Lilly Library, Indiana University
Joseph McDonald Papers, Lilly Library, Indiana University
Edward McPherson Papers, Manuscript Division, Library of Congress
Montague Papers, Manuscript Division, New York Public Library
Justin S. Morrill Papers, No. 1146, Box 1, Department of Manuscripts and University Archives, Cornell University Libraries
Justin S. Morrill Papers, Manuscript Division, Library of Congress
Allan Nevins Papers, Department of Rare Books and Manuscripts, Butler Library, Columbia University
Allan Nevins Papers, Huntington Library
John G. Nicolay Papers, Manuscript Division, Library of Congress
John W. North Papers, Huntington Library
George W. Patterson Papers, Department of Special Collections, Rush Rhees Library, University of Rochester
William Pennington Papers, New Jersey Historical Society
Edward L. Pierce Papers, Houghton Library, Harvard University
Franklin Pierce Papers, New Hampshire Historical Society
Edwards Pierrepont Papers, Sterling Library, Yale University
John V. S. L. Pruyn Papers, New York State Library
Charles H. Ray Papers, Huntington Library
Henry J. Raymond Papers, Manuscript Division, New York Public Library
Winfield Scott Papers, Manuscript Division, New York Public Library
William Henry Seward Papers, Microfilm Edition, Rush Rhees Library, University of Rochester
William Henry Seward Papers, Personal Miscellaneous, Manuscript Division, New York Public Library
John Sherman Papers, Manuscript Division, Library of Congress
William T. Sherman Papers, Manuscript Division, Library of Congress
William T. Sherman Papers, Personal Miscellaneous, Manuscript Division, New York Public Library
Gerrit Smith Family Papers, Box 1, New York Public Library
William Henry Smith Papers, Box 1, Ohio Historical Society
Edwin M. Stanton Papers, Manuscript Division, Library of Congress
John Austin Stevens Papers, New-York Historical Society

Thaddeus Stevens Papers, Manuscript Division, Library of Congress
Charles Sumner Papers, Microfilm Edition, Houghton Library, Harvard University
Roger Brooke Taney Papers, New-York Historical Society
Bayard Taylor Papers, No. 1169, Box 1, Department of Manuscripts and University Archives, Cornell University Libraries
Moses Taylor Papers, Manuscript Division, New York Public Library
Samuel J. Tilden Papers, Manuscript Division, New York Public Library
Theodore Tilton Papers, New York Historical Society
Lyman Trumbull Papers, Microfilm Edition, Manuscript Division, Library of Congress
John Baldwin Turner Papers, Illinois State Historical Library
Daniel Ullmann Papers, New York Historical Society
Benjamin F. Wade Papers, Manuscript Division, Library of Congress
Israel Washburn Papers, Manuscript Division, Library of Congress
Elihu Washburne Papers, Manuscript Division, Library of Congress
James Watson Webb Papers, Sterling Library, Yale University
Thurlow Weed Papers, Rush Rhees Library, University of Rochester
Gideon Welles Papers, Manuscript Division, New York Public Library
Kenneth Williams Papers, Lilly Library, Indiana University
L. B. Wyman Papers, New Jersey Historical Society

II. Government Documents

Biographical Directory of the American Congress, 1774–1961. Washington, D.C.: Government Printing Office, 1961.

Congressional Globe, 36th Congress, 2d Session. Washington, D.C.: Government Printing Office, 1861.

Congressional Globe, 37th Congress, 1st Session–3d Session. Washington, D.C.: Government Printing Office, 1861–63.

Congressional Globe, 38th Congress, 1st Session–2d Session. Washington, D.C.: Government Printing Office, 1864–65.

Official Records of the War of the Rebellion. 130 vols. Washington, D.C.: Government Printing Office, 1880–1901.

U.S. Dept. of State, *Foreign Affairs.* 1861 to 1865, 4 vols. each year. Government Printing Office, 1862–66.

III. Published Documents and Contemporary Publications

Ames, Charles G. "Stand by the President! An Address delivered before the National Union Association, of Cincinnati, March 6, 1863." Philadelphia: King and Baird, 1863.

Andrew, John A. "An Address Delivered before the New England Agricultural Society, on Hampden Park, Springfield, Mass., September 9, 1864." Boston: Wright and Potter, 1864.

______. "Address of His Excellency John A. Andrew, to the Two Branches of the Legislature of Massachusetts, January 8, 1864." Boston: Wright and Potter, State Printers, 1864.

______. Letters, *Massachusetts Historical Society Proceedings* 57 (October 1924–June 1925).

Ashley, James M. "Address of Hon. J. M. Ashley before the 'Ohio Society of New York,' At its Fifth Annual Banquet, Wednesday evening, February 19, 1890." New York: *Evening Post,* ca. 1890.

[Atkinson, Edward]. "Cheap Cotton by Free Labor: By a Cotton Manufacturer." Boston: A. Williams and Co. 1861.

Baker, George E., ed. *The Works of William H. Seward.* 5 vols. Boston: Houghton Mifflin, 1853–89.

Bancroft, Frederic, ed. *Speeches, Correspondence, and Political Papers of Carl Schurz.* 6 vols. New York: G. P. Putnam's Sons, 1913.

[Barnard, F.A.P.], "Letter to the President of the United States, by A Refugee." Philadelphia: J. B. Lippincott and Co., 1863.

Barnett, Thomas J. "Abraham Lincoln, the Peoples' Candidate." Speech delivered by Judge T. J. Barnett of New York, in Richmond, Indiana, 6 October 1864. n.p., HL.

Basler, Roy P., Marion Dolores Platt, and Lloyd A. Dunlap, eds. *The Collected Works of Abraham Lincoln.* 9 vols. New Brunswick, N.J.: Rutgers University Press, 1953–55.

Beale, Howard K., ed. *The Diary of Edward Bates, 1859–1866.* Vol. 4 of the Annual Report of the American Historical Association for the Year 1930. Washington, D.C.: Government Printing Office, 1933.

Beale, Howard K., ed. *Diary of Gideon Welles, Secretary of the Navy under Lincoln and Johnson.* 3 vols. New York: W. W. Norton, 1960.

Bigelow, John, *Retrospections of an Active Life.* 5 vols. New York: Baker and Taylor Co., 1913.

Blaine, James G. *Twenty Years of Congress.* 2 vols. Norwich: Henry Bill Publishing Company, 1884–86.

Blair, Frank. "Address of F. P. Blair, Jr. to His Constituents, October 8, 1862." St. Louis: Office of the Daily Union, 1862.

Blair, Montgomery. "Comments on the Policy Inaugurated by the President, in a Letter and Two Speeches." New York: Hall, Clayton and Medole, 1863.

______. "The Principles Involved in the Rebellion. Speech of the Hon. Montgomery Blair, Postmaster-General of the United States, at the Mass Meeting of the Loyal National League, in Union Square, New York, on the Anniversary of the Assault on Sumter, April 11, 1863." New York: C. S. Westcott and Co., 1863.

______. "Speech of the Hon. Montgomery Blair, at the Cooper Institute, N.Y. to Ratify the Union Nominations, September 27th, 1864." New York: Daniel W. Lee, 1864.

______. "Speech of the Hon. Montgomery Blair, on the Causes of the Rebellion and in Support of the President's Plan of Pacification, delivered before the Legislature of Maryland, at Annapolis, On the 22d of January, 1864." Baltimore: Sherwood and Co., 1864.

______. "Speech of the Honorable Montgomery Blair on the Revolutionary Schemes of the Ultra Abolitionists." New York: D. W. Lee, 1863.

Bloodgood, S. Dewitt. "The Crisis. An Economic View of the Present Contest," *American Railroad Journal*, 25 October 1862, in *The Great Questions of the Times, exemplified in the Antagonistic Principles involved in The Slaveholders' Rebellion against Democratic Institutions as well as against the National Union*. New York: C. S. Westcott and Co., 1862.

Boutwell, George S. *Reminiscences of Sixty Years in Public Affairs.* 2 vols. New York: McClure, Phillips and Company, 1902.

Bowles, Samuel. *Across the Continent, A Summer's Journey to the Rocky Mountains, The Mormons, and the Pacific States, with Speaker Colfax.* Springfield, Mass.: Samuel Bowles and Company, 1866.

Brady, James T. "An Appeal to History," in Loyal Publication Society, New York: Loyal Publication Society, No. 61, 1864.

Brooks, James. "The Two Proclamations. Speech of the Hon. James Brooks, before the Democratic Union Association, Sept. 29th, 1862." New York: Constitutional League, 1862.

Brown, Benjamin Gratz. "Address of Col. B. Gratz Brown. Freedom: as Related to Our National and State Administrations. Delived [*sic*] at the Turners' Hall, St. Louis, Mo. on Thursday Evening, August 27th, 1863." n.p., HL.

______. "Freedom and Franchise Inseperable [*sic*]. Letter of the Hon. B. Gratz Brown." Brown to *Missouri Democrat*, Washington, 22 December 1864, published in Washington, D.C.: Gibson Brothers, 1864.

Burlingame, Michael, ed. *An Oral History of Abraham Lincoln: John G. Nicolay's Interviews and Essays.* Carbondale: Southern Illinois University Press, 1996.

Butler, Benjamin F. "Character and Results of the War. A Thrilling and Eloquent Speech by Major-General B. F. Butler." New York: Loyal Publication Society, No. 7, 1863.

Butz, Caspar. "The Wade-Davis Manifesto. A Last Appeal to the Democracy. Printed by order of the Fremont Central Committee." *German American Monthly,* September 1864.

Butz, M. R. "Great Speech in Vindication of President Lincoln, delivered at Columbus, Illinois, April 30, 1864." Quincy, Ill.: Whig and Republican Job Office, 1864.

Carey, Henry C. *The Past, The Present, and the Future.* New York: A. M. Kelley, 1967. Originally published 1847.

Chandler, William E. "The Soldier's Right to Vote. Who Opposes It? Who Favors It? Or, the Record of the McClellan Copperheads Against allowing the Soldier who Fights, the Right to Vote while Fighting." Washington, D.C.: Lemuel Towers, for the Union Congressional Committee, 1864.

Chittenden, Lucius E. *Recollections of President Lincoln and His Administration.* New York: Harper and Brothers, 1891.

Clay, Cassius M. *The Life of Cassius Marcellus Clay. Memoirs, Writings, and Speeches, showing His Conduct in the Overthrow of American Slavery, the Salvation of the Union, and the Restoration of the Autonomy of the States.* Vol. 1. Cincinnati: J. Fletcher Brennan and Co., 1886.

[Conkling, F. A., A. A. Low, William Marvin, John Austin Stevens Jr., Archibald Baxter, and George Opdyke]. "Report of the Special Committee of the Chamber of Commerce of the State of New York, on the Confiscation of Cotton in the Southern States by the Government." New York: John W. Amerman, 1865.

Conness, John. "Speech of Hon. John Conness, delivered at Platt's Hall, San Francisco, on Tuesday Evening, October 18, 1864." n.p., HL.

Congressional Union Committee. "The Chicago Copperhead Convention. The Treasonable and Revolutionary Utterances of the Men Who Composed It. Extracts from all the Notable Speeches delivered in and out of the National 'Democratic' Convention. A Surrender to the Rebels Advocated—A Disgraceful and Pusillanimous Peace Demanded—The Federal Government Shamefully Vilified, and Not a Word Said Against the Cause of Treason and Rebellion." Washington, D.C.: Congressional Union Committee, 1864.

Cony, Samuel. "Address of Governor Cony to the Legislature of the State of Maine, January 5, 1865." Augusta: Stevens and Sayward, 1865.

Cooper, Peter. "The Death of Slavery. Letter from Peter Cooper to Governor Seymour." New York: Loyal Publication Society, No. 28, 1863.

Cox, Samuel S. *Union—Disunion—Reunion: Three Decades of Federal Legislation.* Providence, R.I.: J. A. and R. A. Reid, 1885.

Curtis, George W. "The President: Why He Should be Re-Elected." New York: Daniel W. Lee, 1864.

Davis, Henry Winter. "Speech of Henry Winter Davis at Concert Hall, Philadelphia, September 24, 1863." n.p., n.d., HL.

"Democratic Platform. People's Resolutions. A Republican Form of Government: Definition Manhood Suffrage." New York: C. S. Westcott and Co., 1865.

Dennett, Tyler, ed. *Lincoln and the Civil War in the Diaries and Letters of John Hay.* New York: Dodd, Mead, 1939.

Donald, David, ed. *Inside Lincoln's Cabinet: The Civil War Diaries of Salmon P. Chase.* New York: Longmans, Green, 1954.

Eaton, John. *Grant, Lincoln and the Freedmen.* New York: Negro Universities Press, 1969.

Ellis, George E. "The Nation's Ballot and its Decision: A Discourse delivered in Austin-Street Church, Cambridgeport, and in Harvard Church, Charlestown, On Sunday, Nov. 13, 1864; Being the Sunday following the Presidential Election." Boston: William V. Spencer, 1864.

Foner, Philip S. ed. *The Life and Writings of Frederick Douglass.* 4 vols. New York: International Publishers, 1950–55.

Ford, Worthington C., ed. *A Cycle of Adams Letters.* 2 vols. Boston: Houghton Mifflin, 1920.

Freidel, Frank, ed. *Union Pamphlets of the Civil War.* 2 vols. Cambridge: Harvard University Press, 1967.

Fuller, George N., ed. *Messages of the Governors of Michigan.* 2 vols. Lansing: Michigan Historical Commission, 1926.

Grant, Ulysses S. *Personal Memoirs of U.S. Grant.* 2 vols., New York: Charles L. Webster, 1885.

Greeley, Horace. *Recollections of a Busy Life.* New York: J. B. Ford, 1868.

Hamilton, James A. "The Constitution Vindicated. Nationality, Secession, Slavery." New York: Loyal Publication Society, No. 50, 1864.

Hamilton, John C. "Coercion Completed, Or Treason Triumphant." New York: Loyal Publication Society, No. 66, 1864.

______. "The Slave Power: Its Heresies and Injuries to the American People. A Speech, by John C. Hamilton. November 1864." New York: Loyal Publication Society, No. 74, 1864.

Hasted, Frederick. "Copy of a Letter Written from Buffalo, State of New York, North America, Aug. 25, 1862." n.p., 1863, HL.

Hazard, Rowland G. "Our Resources. A Series of Articles on the Financial and Political Condition of the United States." London: Trubner and Co., 1864.

Heermans, J. "War Power of the President." New York: Loyal Publication Society, No. 32, 1863.

Holmes, Oliver Wendell. "Oration Delivered Before the City Authorities of Boston, on the Fourth of July, 1863." Boston: J. E. Farwell and Company, 1863.

Hyman, Harold M., ed. *The Radical Republicans and Reconstruction, 1861–1870.* Indianapolis, Ind.: Bobbs-Merrill, 1967.

Jay, John. "The Great Issue. An Address delivered before The Union Campaign Club, of East Brooklyn, New York, on Tuesday Evening, Oct. 25, 1864." New York: Baker and Godwin, 1864.

Julian, George W. "George W. Julian's Journal—The Assassination of Lincoln." *Indiana Magazine of History* 11 (1915).

______. *Political Recollections, 1840–1872.* Chicago: A. C. McClurg, 1872.

Kelley, William D. "Speeches of Hon. William D. Kelley. Replies of the Hon. William D. Kelley to George Northrop, Esq. in the Joint Debate in the Fourth Congressional District." Philadelphia: Collins, 1864.

"Letter of Governor Pierpoint to His Excellency The President and the Honorable Congress of the United States, on the subject of Abuse of Military Power in the Command of General Butler in Virginia and North Carolina." Washington, D.C.: McGill and Witherow, 1864.

Lieber, Francis. "A Letter to Hon. E. D. Morgan, Senator of the United States, on the Amendment of the Constitution Abolishing Slavery. Resolutions, Passed by the New York Union League Club, Concerning Conditions of Peace with the Insurgents." New York: Loyal Publication Society, No. 79, 1865.

______. "Amendments to the Constitution, Submitted to the Consideration of the American People." New York: Loyal Publication Society, No. 83, 1865.

______. "The Arguments of Secessionists. A Letter to the Union Meeting, Held in New York, September 30, 1863." Loyal Publication Society, No. 35, New York: Holman, 1863.

______. "Lincoln or McClellan. Appeal to the Germans in America." New York: Loyal Publication Society, No. 67, 1864.

______. "Slavery, Plantations and the Yeomanry." New York: Loyal Publication Society, No. 29, 1863.

Logan, John A. "Speech of Major-General John A. Logan, on Return to Illinois, after Capture of Vicksburg. Reported by 'Mack,' of the *Cincinnati Commercial.*" Cincinnati: Loyal Publications of National Union Association of Ohio, No. 4, Caleb Clark, 1863.

Loring, George B. "The Present Crisis. A Speech Delivered by Dr. Geo. B. Loring, at Lyceum Hall, Salem, Wednesday Evening, April 26, 1865, on the Assassination of President Lincoln. Dr. Loring's Letter to the Salem Gazette, on Reconstruction. Published by Request." South Danvers, Mass.: Charles B. Howard, 1865.

"Loyal Meeting of the People of New-York, to Support the Government, Prosecute the War, and Maintain the Union, held at The Cooper Institute, Friday Evening, March 6, 1863." New York: George F. Nesbitt and Co. 1863.

Loyal National League. "Opinions of Prominent Men concerning The Great Questions of the Times expressed in their letters to the Loyal National League, on occasion of The Great Mass Meeting of the League and Other Loyalists at Union Square, New York, on the Anniversary of Sumter." New York: C. S. Westcott and Co., 1863.

______. "The Sumter Anniversary, 1863. Opinions of Loyalists concerning The Great Questions of the Times; expressed in the speeches and letters from prominent citizens of all sections and parties, on occasion of the inauguration of The Loyal National League, in Mass Meeting on Union Square, New York, on the 11th of April, 1863, the Anniversary of the Attack on Fort Sumter." New York: C. S. Westcott and Co., 1863.

Loyal Publication Society. "The Conditions of Reconstruction, in a Letter from Robert Dale Owen to the Secretary of State." New York: Loyal Publication Society, No. 25, 1863.

______. "Elements of Discord in Secessia." New York: Loyal Publication Society, No. 15, 1863.

______. "Letters of Loyal Soldiers. How Douglas Democrats will Vote. Letters of Generals Wool & Logan." New York: Loyal Publication Society, No. 64, Part 3, 1864.

______. "Letters of Loyal Soldiers. Letter of General Dix, His Opinion of the Chicago Platform." New York: Loyal Publication Society, No. 64, Part 4, 1864.

______. "Opinions of the Early Presidents, and of the Fathers of the Republic, upon Slavery, and upon Negroes as Men and Soldiers." New York: Loyal Publication Society, No. 18, 1863.

______. "Proceedings at the Second Anniversary Meeting of the Loyal Publication Society, February 11, 1865, with the Annual Reports, Prepared by Order of the Society, by the Secretary." New York: Loyal Publication Society, No. 78, 1864.

______. "Rebel Conditions of Peace and the Mechanics of the South." New York: Loyal Publication Society, No. 30, n.d. but presumably 1863.

______. "Results of the Serf Emancipation in Russia." New York: Loyal Publication Society, No. 47, 1864.

______. "William T. Sherman to John B. Hood, Headquarters Military Division of the Mississippi and in the Field, Atlanta, September 10, 1864." New York: Loyal Publication Society, No. 61, 1864.

Marshall, Jessie A., ed. *Private and Official Correspondence of General Benjamin F. Butler during the Period of the Civil War.* 5 vols. Norwood, Mass.: Plimpton Press, 1917.

McClure, Alexander K. *Lincoln and Men of War-Times.* Philadelphia: Times Publishing Company, 1892.

McCormick, Thomas J., ed. *Memoirs of Gustave Koerner, 1809–1896.* 2 vols. Cedar Rapids, Iowa: Torch Press, 1909.

McFeely, Mary Drake, and William S. McFeely, eds. *Ulysses S. Grant: Memoirs and Selected Letters; Personal Memoirs of U. S. Grant; Selected Letters, 1839–1865.* New York: Library of America, 1990.

McKaye, James. "The Mastership and Its Fruits: The Emancipated Slave Face to Face with His Old Master. A Supplemental Report to Hon. Edwin M. Stanton, Secretary of War." New York: Loyal Publication Society, No. 58, 1864.

Miller, Perry, and Thomas H. Johnson, eds. *The Puritans: A Sourcebook of Their Writings.* 2 vols. New York: Harper and Row, 1938.

Minnesota in the Civil and Indian Wars: 1861–1865. Vol. 2, Official Reports and Correspondence. St. Paul: Pioneer Press Company, 1893.

Mitgang, Herbert, ed. *Lincoln as They Saw Him.* New York: Praeger, 1980.

Mordell, Albert, ed. *Lincoln's Administration: Selected Essays of Gideon Welles.* New York: Twayne, 1959.

Nevins, Allan, and Milton Halsey Thomas, eds. *The Diary of George Templeton Strong.* 4 vols. New York: Macmillan, 1952.

"No Failure for the North." *Atlantic Monthly,* reprint. New York: Loyal Publication Society, No. 11, 1863.

Nordhoff, Charles. "America For Free Working Men. Mechanics, Farmers and Laborers, Read! How Slavery Injures the Free Working Man. The Slave-Labor System the Free Working-Man's Worst Enemy." New York: Loyal Publication Society, No. 80, 1865.

"Northern True Men and Southern Traitors. Address and Resolutions of the Connecticut Soldiers. Extracts from Richmond Journals." New York: Loyal Publication Society, No. 6, 1863.

"An Original Republican." "Remarks on the Existing Rebellion: Its Cause—the Duty of Suppressing it—the Object of Suppressing It—A Conservative Movement—the Government to be Preserved—the People to be Compelled to Obey the Laws as Freemen—Disfranchisement of Rebel Masses Impolitic, Unnecessary, Dangerous—A Virtual Abandonment of Liberty—A Setting Up of Arbitrary Government." St. Louis: Dispatch Office, 1865.

Owen, Robert Dale. "The Future of the North-West: In Connection with the Scheme of Reconstruction without New England. Addressed to the People of Indiana." New York: Loyal Publication Society, No. 1, 1863.

______. *The Wrong of Slavery, The Right of Emancipation, and the Future of the African Race in the United States.* Philadelphia: National Publishing, 1864.

Pease, Theodore C., and James G. Randall, eds. *The Diary of Orville Hickman Browning.* 2 vols., Springfield: Illinois State Historical Library, 1925–33.

Pelletan, Eugene. "An Address to King Cotton." New York: Loyal Publication Society, No. 12, 1863.

Perkins, Howard C., ed. *Northern Editorials on Secession.* 2 vols. Washington: American Historical Association, 1942.

Powell, "Extract from a Letter: The Trial of Our Democratic Form of Government, the Great Question now to be solved, is a democratic government a possible thing, or must we have a despotism?" (Philadelphia: C. Sherman and Son, 1863).

"Proceedings at the Mass Meeting of Loyal Citizens, on Union Square, New York, 15th Day of July, 1862, under the auspices of the Chamber of Commerce of the State of New-York, the Union Defence Committee of the Citizens of New-York, the Common Council of the City of New York, and Other Committees of Loyal Citizens. Letters and Speeches." New York: George F. Nesbitt and Co., 1862.

Raymond, Henry J. "Peace and Restoration. Speech of Hon. H. J. Raymond, of New York, in reply to Hon. T. Stevens, of Pennsylvania; delivered in the House of Representatives, December 21, 1865." Washington, D.C.: Congressional Globe Office, 1865.

Schafer, Joseph, ed. *Intimate Letters of Carl Schurz, 1841–1869.* Madison: State Historical Society of Wisconsin, 1928.

Sears, Stephen W., ed. *The Civil War Papers of George B. McClellan: Selected Correspondence, 1860–1865.* New York: Ticknor and Fields, 1989.

Sherman, John. *John Sherman's Recollections of Forty Years in the House, Senate, and Cabinet.* 3 vols. Chicago: Werner Company, 1895.

Sherman, William T. *Memoirs of General William T. Sherman. By Himself.* 2 vols. New York: D. Appleton and Company, 1875.

Smith, Adam. *An Inquiry into the Nature and Causes of the Wealth of Nations.* New York: Modern Library, 1937.

Smith, Gerrit. "Gerrit Smith on McClellan's Nomination and Acceptance." New York: Loyal Publication Society, No. 63, 1864.

Staudenraus, Peter J., ed. *Mr. Lincoln's Washington: Selections from the Writings of Noah Brooks, Civil War Correspondent.* South Brunswick, N.J.: Thomas Yoseloff, 1967.

Stevens, Thaddeus. "Reconstruction. Speech of the Hon. Thaddeus Stevens, Delivered in the City of Lancaster, September 7th, 1865." Lancaster, Pa.: Examiner and Herald Print, 1865.

Stille, Charles J. "How A Free People Conduct A Long War: A Chapter from English History." Philadelphia: Collins, 1862.

Swinton, William. "McClellan's Military Career Reviewed and Exposed: The Military Policy of the Administration Set Forth and Vindicated." Washington, D.C.: Lemuel Towers and the Union Congressional Committee, 1864.

______. "The Military and Naval Situation, and the Glorious Achievements of Our Soldiers and Sailors." Washington, D.C.: Union Congressional Committee, 1864.

Union League of Philadelphia. "The Record of the Democratic Party. 1860–1865." Philadelphia: Union League, ca. 1865.

United States of America. "Report of the Organization and Proceedings of the Union Pacific Railroad Co." New York: Wm. C. Bryant and Co., 1864.

Villard, Henry. *Lincoln on the Eve of '61: A Journalist's Story.* Harold G. Villard and Oswald Garrison Villard, eds. New York: Alfred A. Knopf, 1941.

______. *Memoirs of Henry Villard: Journalist and Financier, 1835–1900.* 2 vols. Boston: Houghton Mifflin, 1904.

Williams, Charles R., ed. *The Diary of Rutherford B. Hayes.* 5 vols. Columbus: Ohio State Archaeological and Historical Society, 1922.

IV. Journals, Newspapers, and Magazines

Albany Evening Journal
Boston Daily Evening Transcript
Chicago Tribune

Forney's War Press
Harper's Weekly
The Independent
National Anti-Slavery Standard
New York Evening Post
New York Times
New York Tribune
Ohio State Journal
Sacramento Union

V. Books

Abbott, Richard H. *Cobbler in Congress: Life of Henry Wilson, 1812–1875.* Lexington: University of Kentucky Press, 1972.

______. *The Republican Party and the South: The First Southern Strategy, 1855–1877.* Chapel Hill: University of North Carolina Press, 1986.

Alexander, DeAlva S. *A Political History of the State of New York.* 3 vols. New York: Henry Holt and Company, 1906–9.

Ambrose, Stephen E. *Halleck: Lincoln's Chief of Staff.* Baton Rouge: Louisiana State University Press, 1962.

Ambrosius, Lloyd E., ed. *A Crisis of Republicanism: American Politics in the Civil War Era.* Lincoln: University of Nebraska Press, 1990.

Anastaplo, George. *Abraham Lincoln: A Constitutional Biography.* Lanham, Md.: Rowman and Littlefield, 1999.

Anbinder, Tyler. *Nativism and Slavery: The Northern Know Nothings and the Politics of the 1850s.* New York: Oxford University Press, 1992.

Auer, J. Jeffrey, ed. *Antislavery and Disunion, 1858–1861: Studies in the Rhetoric of Compromise and Conflict.* New York: Harper and Row, 1963.

Bailyn, Bernard. *The Ideological Origins of the American Revolution.* Cambridge: Harvard University Press, 1967.

Bain, David Haward. *Empire Express: Building the First Transcontinental Railroad.* New York: Viking, 1999.

Baker, Jean H. *Affairs of Party: The Political Culture of Northern Democrats in the Mid-Nineteenth Century.* Ithaca: Cornell University Press, 1983. Reprinted, New York: Fordham University Press, 1998.

______. *The Politics of Continuity: Maryland Political Parties from 1858 to 1870.* Baltimore: Johns Hopkins University Press, 1973.

Bancroft, Frederic. *The Life of William H. Seward.* 2 vols. New York: Harper and Brothers, 1900.

Barnes, Thurlow Weed, and Harriet A. Weed. *Life of Thurlow Weed, Including His Autobiography and a Memoir.* Boston: Houghton Mifflin, 1884.

Barrows, Chester L. *William M. Evarts: Lawyer, Diplomat, Statesman.* Chapel Hill: University of North Carolina Press, 1941.

Barrows, Robert G., and Shirley S. McCord, eds. *Their Infinite Variety: Essays on Indiana Politicians.* Indianapolis, Ind.: Indiana Historical Bureau, 1981.

Bartlett, Irving. *Wendell Phillips, Brahmin Radical.* Boston: Beacon Press, 1962.

Baum, Dale. *The Civil War Party System: The Case of Massachusetts, 1848–1876.* Chapel Hill: University of North Carolina Press, 1984.

Baxter, Maurice G. *Orville H. Browning: Lincoln's Friend and Critic.* Bloomington: Indiana University Press, 1957.

Belz, Herman. *Abraham Lincoln, Constitutionalism, and Equal Rights in the Civil War Era.* New York: Fordham University Press, 1998.

______. *A New Birth of Freedom: The Republican Party and Freedmen's Rights, 1861 to 1866.* Westport, Conn.: Greenwood Press, 1976. Reprinted, New York: Fordham University Press, 2000.

______. *Reconstructing the Union: Theory and Practice during the Civil War.* Ithaca: Cornell University Press, 1969.

Bemis, Samuel Flagg, ed. *The American Secretaries of State and Their Diplomacy.* 12 vols. New York: Pageant Books, 1958.

Benedict, Michael Les. *A Compromise of Principle: Congressional Republicans and Reconstruction, 1863–1869.* New York: W. W. Norton, 1974.

Bennett, Lerone Jr. *Forced into Glory: Abraham Lincoln's White Dream.* Chicago: Johnson, 1999.

Bensel, Richard Franklin. *Yankee Leviathan: The Origins of Central State Authority in America, 1859–1877.* Cambridge: Cambridge University Press, 1990.

Berlin, Ira, et al. eds. *Free at Last: A Documentary History of Slavery, Freedom, and the Civil War.* New York: New Press, 1992.

Bernath, Stuart L. *Squall across the Atlantic: American Civil War Prize Cases and Diplomacy.* Berkeley: University of California Press, 1970.

Bernstein, Iver. *The New York City Draft Riots: Their Significance for American Society and Politics in the Age of the Civil War.* New York: Oxford University Press, 1990.

Billington, Ray Allen, and Martin Ridge. *Westward Expansion: A History of the American Frontier.* 6th ed., Albuquerque: University of New Mexico Press, 2001.

Blair, Harry C., and Rebecca Tarshis. *Lincoln's Constant Ally: The Life of Colonel Edward D. Baker.* Portland: Oregon Historical Society, 1960.

Blight, David W. *Frederick Douglass' Civil War: Keeping Faith in Jubilee.* Baton Rouge: Louisiana State University Press, 1989.

Blue, Frederick J. *Salmon P. Chase: A Life in Politics.* Kent, Ohio: Kent State University Press, 1987.

Bogue, Allen G. *The Congressman's Civil War.* Cambridge: Cambridge University Press, 1989.

______. *The Earnest Men: Republicans of the Civil War Senate.* Ithaca: Cornell University Press, 1961.

Boritt, Gabor. *Lincoln and the Economics of the American Dream.* Memphis: Memphis State University Press, 1978.

———, ed. *The Historian's Lincoln.* New York: Oxford University Press, 1996.

———, ed. *Lincoln, the War President: The Gettysburg Lectures.* New York: Oxford University Press, 1992.

———, ed. *The Lincoln Enigma: The Changing Faces of an American Icon.* New York: Oxford University Press, 2001.

Bradley, Erwin S. *Simon Cameron. Lincoln's Secretary of War: A Political Biography.* Philadelphia: University of Pennsylvania Press, 1966.

Brandon, Mark E. *Free in the World: American Slavery and Constitutional Failure.* Princeton: Princeton University Press, 1998.

Brigham, Johnson. *James Harlan.* Iowa City: State Historical Society of Iowa, 1913.

Brodie, Fawn M. *Thaddeus Stevens: Scourge of the South.* New York: W. W. Norton, 1959.

Brown, Francis. *Raymond of The Times.* New York: W. W. Norton, 1951.

Browne, Albert Gallatin, *Sketch of the Official Life of John A. Andrew, as Governor of Massachusetts.* New York: Hurd and Houghton, 1868.
Bruce, Robert V. *Lincoln and the Tools of War.* Indianapolis: Bobbs-Merrill, 1956.
Buckingham, Samuel G. *The Life of William A. Buckingham: The War Governor of Connecticut.* Springfield, Mass.: W. F. Adams Company, 1894.
Cain, Marvin R. *Lincoln's Attorney General: Edward Bates of Missouri.* Columbia: University of Missouri Press, 1965.
Carman, Harry, and Reinhard Luthin. *Lincoln and the Patronage.* New York: Columbia University Press, 1943.
Catton, Bruce, *Grant Moves South.* Boston: Little, Brown, 1960.
Chambers, William N., and Walter Dean Burnham, eds. *The American Party Systems: Stages of Political Development.* New York: Oxford University Press, 1967.
Cimbala, Paul A., and Randall M. Miller, eds. *An Uncommon Time: The Civil War and the Northern Home Front.* New York: Fordham University Press, 2002.
Clapp, Margaret A. *Forgotten First Citizen: John Bigelow.* Boston: Little, Brown, 1947.
Clark, Dan Elbert. *Samuel Jordan Kirkwood.* Iowa City: The State Historical Society of Iowa, 1917.
Clark, George T. *Leland Stanford, War Governor of California, Railroad Builder, and Founder of Stanford University.* Stanford: Stanford University Press, 1931.
Cohen, Nancy. *The Reconstruction of American Liberalism, 1865–1914.* Chapel Hill: University of North Carolina Press, 2002.
Cole, Arthur C. *The Era of the Civil War, 1848–1870.* Springfield: Illinois Centennial Commission, 1918.
Cox, LaWanda. *Lincoln and Black Freedom: A Study in Presidential Leadership.* Columbia: University of South Carolina Press, 1981.
———, and John H. Cox. *Politics, Principle, and Prejudice, 1865–1866: Dilemma of Reconstruction America.* New York: Macmillan, 1963.
Crapol, Edward P. *James G. Blaine: Architect of Empire.* Wilmington, Del.: Scholarly Resource Books, 2000.
Crook, David Paul. *Diplomacy during the American Civil War.* New York: John Wiley and Sons, 1975.

______. *The North, the South, and the Powers.* New York: John Wiley and Sons, 1974.

Cross, Coy F. II. *Justin Smith Morrill: Father of the Land-Grant Colleges.* East Lansing: Michigan State University Press, 1999.

Current, Richard N. *The Lincoln Nobody Knows.* New York: McGraw-Hill, 1958.

______. *Speaking of Abraham Lincoln: The Man and His Times.* Urbana: University of Illinois Press, 1983.

Curry, Leonard P. *Blueprint for Modern America: Non-Military Legislation of the First Civil War Congress.* Nashville: Vanderbilt University Press, 1968.

Davis, David Brion. *The Slave Power Conspiracy and the Paranoid Style.* Baton Rouge: Louisiana State University Press, 1969.

Davis, Michael. *The Image of Lincoln in the South.* Knoxville: University of Tennessee Press, 1971.

Dell, Christopher. *Lincoln and the War Democrats: The Grand Erosion of Conservative Tradition.* Rutherford, N.J.: Fairleigh Dickinson University Press, 1975.

Donald, David Herbert. *Charles Sumner and the Coming of the Civil War.* New York: Alfred A. Knopf, 1960.

______. *Charles Sumner and the Rights of Man.* New York: Alfred A. Knopf, 1970.

______. *Lincoln.* New York: Simon and Schuster, 1995.

______. *Lincoln's Herndon.* New York: Alfred A. Knopf, 1948.

______. *Lincoln Reconsidered: Essays on the Civil War Era.* 3d ed. New York: Vintage Books, 2001.

———, ed. *Why the North Won the Civil War.* Baton Rouge: Louisiana State University Press, 1960.

Duberman, Martin B. *Charles Francis Adams, 1807–1886.* Boston: Houghton Mifflin, 1961.

Durden, Robert F. *James Shepherd Pike: Republicanism and the American Negro, 1850–1882.* Durham: Duke University Press, 1957.

Egle, William H., ed. *Andrew Gregg Curtin: His Life and Services.* Philadelphia: G. W. Jacobs, 1895.

Elkins, Stanley, and Eric L. McKitrick. *The Age of Federalism: Birth of the Republic, 1788–1800.* New York: Oxford University Press, 1993.

Elliott, Russell R. *Servant of Power: A Political Biography of Senator William M. Stewart of Nevada.* Reno: University of Nevada Press, 1983.

Fairman, Charles, *Mr. Justice Miller and the Supreme Court: 1862–1890.* Cambridge: Harvard University Press, 1939.

Fehrenbacher, Don E. *The Dred Scott Case: Its Significance in American Law and Politics.* New York: Oxford University Press, 1978.

______. *Lincoln in Text and Context.* Stanford: Stanford University Press, 1988.

______. *The Slaveholding Republic: An Account of the United States Government's Relations to Slavery.* Completed and edited by Ward M. McAfee. New York: Oxford University Press, 2001.

Ferris, Norman B. *Desperate Diplomacy: William H. Seward's Foreign Policy, 1861.* Knoxville: University of Tennessee Press, 1976.

______. *The Trent Affair: A Diplomatic Crisis.* Knoxville: University of Tennessee Press, 1977.

Fessenden, Francis. *Life and Public Services of William Pitt Fessenden.* 2 vols. Boston: Houghton Mifflin, 1907.

Field, Phyllis F. *The Politics of Race in New York: The Struggle for Black Suffrage in the Civil War Era.* Ithaca: Cornell University Press, 1982.

Fischer, LeRoy H. *Lincoln's Gadfly, Adam Gurowski.* Norman: University of Oklahoma Press, 1964.

Fite, Emerson D. *Social and Industrial Conditions in the North during the Civil War.* New York: P. Smith, 1930.

Fletcher, George P. *Our Secret Constitution: How Lincoln Redefined American Democracy.* New York: Oxford University Press, 2001.

Foner, Eric. *Free Soil, Free Labor, Free Men: The Ideology of the Republican Party before the Civil War.* New York: Oxford University Press, 1970; 2d ed. 1995.

______. *Nothing but Freedom: Emancipation and Its Legacy.* Baton Rouge: Louisiana State University Press, 1983.

______. *Politics and Ideology in the Age of the Civil War.* New York: Oxford University Press, 1980.

______. *Reconstruction: America's Unfinished Revolution, 1863–1877.* New York: Harper and Row, 1988.

______. *The Story of American Freedom.* New York: W. W. Norton, 1998.

———, and Olivia Mahoney. *A House Divided: America in the Age of Lincoln.* New York: Chicago Historical Society and W. W. Norton, 1990.

Foner, Philip S. *British Labor and the American Civil War.* New York: Holmes and Meier, 1981.

______. *Business and Slavery: The New York Merchants and the Irrepressible Conflict.* Chapel Hill: University of North Carolina Press, 1941.

Forgie, George B. *Patricide in the House Divided: A Psychological Interpretation of Lincoln and His Age.* New York: W. W. Norton, 1979.

Foulke, William Dudley. *Life of Oliver P. Morton: Including His Important Speeches.* 2 vols. Indianapolis, Ind.: Bobbs-Merrill, 1899.

Frank, Allan. *With Ballot and Bayonet: The Political Socialization of American Civil War Soldiers.* Athens: University of Georgia Press, 1998.

Franklin, John Hope. *The Emancipation Proclamation.* Garden City, N.J.: Doubleday, 1963.

Frederickson, George M. *The Black Image in the White Mind: The Debate on Afro-American Character and Destiny, 1817–1914.* New York: Harper and Row, 1971.

______. *The Inner Civil War: Northern Intellectuals and the Crisis of the Union.* New York: Harper and Row, 1965.

Freidel, Frank. *Francis Lieber: Nineteenth Century Liberal.* Baton Rouge: Louisiana State University Press, 1947.

Friedman, Leon, and Fred L. Israel, eds. *The Justices of the United States Supreme Court, 1789–1978: Their Lives and Major Opinions.* 5 vols. New York: Chelsea House, 1980.

Frothingham, P. R. *Edward Everett, Orator and Statesman.* Boston: Houghton Mifflin, 1925.

Fry, Joseph A. *Henry Sanford: Diplomacy and Business in Nineteenth Century America.* Reno: University of Nevada Press, 1982.

Garraty, John A. ed. *Quarrels That Have Shaped the Constitution.* New York: Harper and Row, 1964.

Gates, Paul W. *Agriculture and the Civil War.* New York: Alfred A. Knopf, 1965.

George, Mary K. *Zachariah Chandler: A Political Biography.* East Lansing: Michigan State University Press, 1969.

Gienapp, William E. *The Origins of the Republican Party, 1852–1856.* New York: Oxford University Press, 1987.

______. *Abraham Lincoln and Civil War America: A Biography.* New York: Oxford University Press, 2002.

Gilmore, James R. *Personal Recollections of Abraham Lincoln and the Civil War.* Boston: L. C. Page, 1898.

Goodrich, Carter. *Government Promotion of American Canals and Railroads, 1800–1890.* New York: Columbia University Press, 1960.

Goodwyn, Lawrence, *The Populist Moment: A Short History of the Agrarian Revolt in America.* New York: Oxford University Press, 1978.

Gorham, George C. *Life and Public Services of Edwin M. Stanton.* 2 vols. Boston: Houghton Mifflin, 1899.

Graebner, Norman, ed. *The Enduring Lincoln.* Urbana: University of Illinois Press, 1959.

Greenstone, J. David. *The Lincoln Persuasion: Remaking American Liberalism.* Princeton: Princeton University Press, 1993.

Guelzo, Allen C. *Abraham Lincoln: Redeemer President.* Grand Rapids, Mich.: William B. Eerdmans Publishing, 1999.

Gunderson, Robert G. *Old Gentlemen's Convention: The Washington Peace Conference of 1861.* Madison: University of Wisconsin Press, 1961.

Hagerman, Edward. *The American Civil War and the Origins of Modern Warfare: Ideas, Organization, and Field Command.* Bloomington: Indiana University Press, 1988.

Harper, Robert S. *Lincoln and the Press.* New York: McGraw-Hill, 1951.

Harrington, Fred Harvey. *Fighting Politician: Major General N. P. Banks.* Philadelphia: University of Pennsylvania Press, 1948.

Harris, William C. *With Charity for All: Lincoln and the Restoration of the Union.* Lexington: University Press of Kentucky, 1999.

Harris, Wilmer C. *Public Life of Zachariah Chandler, 1851–1875.* Lansing: Michigan Historical Commission, 1917.

Hart, Albert Bushnell. *Salmon Portland Chase.* Boston: Houghton Mifflin, 1899.

Hendrick, Burton J. *Lincoln's War Cabinet.* Boston: Little, Brown, 1946.

Henig, Gerald S. *Henry Winter Davis: Antebellum and Civil War Congressman from Maryland.* New York: Twayne, 1973.

Hess, Earl J. *Liberty, Virtue, and Progress: Northerners and Their War for the Union.* 2d ed. New York: Fordham University Press, 1997.

Hesseltine, William B. *Lincoln and the War Governors.* New York: Alfred A. Knopf, 1948.

______. *Lincoln's Plan of Reconstruction.* Tuscaloosa: Confederate Publishing, 1960.

Hirshson, Stanley P. *The White Tecumseh: A Biography of General William T. Sherman.* New York: John Wiley and Sons, 1997.

Hochfield, George, ed. *Henry Adams: The Great Secession Winter of 1860–1861 and Other Essays.* New York: Sagamore Press, 1958.

Hofstadter, Richard. *The American Political Tradition and the Men Who Made It.* New York: Alfred A. Knopf, 1948.

______. *The Idea of a Party System: The Rise of Legitimate Opposition in the United States, 1780–1840.* Berkeley: University of California Press, 1969.

______. *The Paranoid Style in American Politics and Other Essays.* New York: Vintage Books, 1967.

______. *Social Darwinism in American Thought.* Rev. ed. Boston: Beacon Press, 1955.

Holt, Michael F. *The Political Crisis of the 1850s.* New York: John Wiley and Sons, 1978.

______. *The Rise and Fall of the American Whig Party: Jacksonian Politics and the Onset of the Civil War.* New York: Oxford University Press, 1999.

Horner, Harlan. *Lincoln and Greeley.* Urbana: University of Illinois Press, 1953.

Horowitz, Robert. *The Great Impeacher: A Political Biography of James Ashley.* Brooklyn: Brooklyn College Press, 1979.

Howard, Victor B. *Religion and the Radical Republican Movement, 1860–1870.* Lexington: University of Kentucky Press, 1982.

Howe, Daniel Walker. *The Political Culture of the American Whigs.* Chicago: University of Chicago Press, 1979.

Hunt, Gaillard. *Israel, Elihu, and Cadwallader Washburn: A Chapter in American Biography.* New York: Macmillan, 1925.

Hunt, H. Draper. *Hannibal Hamlin of Maine: Lincoln's First Vice-President.* Syracuse: Syracuse University Press, 1969.

Hyman, Harold M. *A More Perfect Union: The Impact of the Civil War and Reconstruction on the Constitution.* New York: Alfred A. Knopf, 1973.

______. *American Singularity: The 1787 Northwest Ordinance, the 1862 Homestead and Morrill Acts, and the 1944 G.I. Bill.* Athens: University of Georgia Press, 1986.

______. *Era of the Oath: Northern Loyalty Tests during the Civil War and Reconstruction.* Philadelphia: University of Pennsylvania Press, 1954.

______, and William C. Wiecek. *Equal Justice under Law: Constitutional Development, 1835–1875.* New York: Harper and Row, 1982.

Ilisevich, Robert D. *Galusha A. Grow: The People's Candidate.* Pittsburgh: University of Pittsburgh Press, 1988.

Isely, Jeter Allen. *Horace Greeley and the Republican Party, 1853–1861.* Princeton: Princeton University Press, 1947.

Jackson, Robert H. *The Supreme Court in the American System of Government.* Cambridge: Harvard University Press, 1955.

Jaffa, Harry V. *A New Birth of Freedom: Abraham Lincoln and the Coming of the Civil War.* Lanham, Md.: Rowman and Littlefield, 2000.

______. *Crisis of the House Divided: An Interpretation of the Issues in the Lincoln-Douglas Debates.* Chicago: University of Chicago Press, 1959.

Jellison, Charles. *Fessenden of Maine: Civil War Senator.* Syracuse: Syracuse University Press, 1962.

Johannsen, Robert W. *Stephen A. Douglas.* New York: Oxford University Press, 1973.

Johnson, David A. *Founding the Far West: California, Oregon, and Nevada, 1840–1890.* Berkeley and Los Angeles: University of California Press, 1992.

Jones, Howard. *Abraham Lincoln and a New Birth of Freedom: The Union and Slavery in the Diplomacy of the Civil War.* Lincoln: University of Nebraska Press, 1999.

Kammen, Michael. *A Machine That Would Go of Itself: The Constitution in American Culture.* New York: Alfred A. Knopf, 1986.

Keller, Morton. *Affairs of State: Public Life in Late Nineteenth Century America.* Cambridge: Belknap Press of Harvard University, 1977.

Kelley, Robert. *The Cultural Pattern in American Politics: The First Century.* New York: Alfred A. Knopf, 1979.

Kerr, Winfield Scott. *John Sherman: His Life and Public Services.* 2 vols. Boston: Sherman, French, 1906.

King, Willard L. *Lincoln's Manager, David Davis.* Chicago: University of Chicago Press, 1960.

Kinsley, Phillip L. *The Chicago Tribune.* 3 vols. Chicago: *Chicago Tribune,* 1960.

Klein, Maury. *Union Pacific.* 2 vol., Garden City, N.Y.: Doubleday, 1987.

Klement, Frank L. *The Copperheads in the Middle West.* Chicago: University of Chicago Press, 1960.

______. *Dark Lanterns: Secret Political Societies, Conspiracies, and Treason Trials in the Civil War.* Baton Rouge: Louisiana State University Press, 1984.

Kleppner, Paul. *The Third Electoral System, 1853–1892: Parties, Voters, and Political Cultures.* Chapel Hill: University of North Carolina Press, 1979.

Kluger, Richard. *Simple Justice: The History of Brown v. Board of Education and Black America's Struggle for Equality.* New York: Alfred A. Knopf, 1976.

Knupfer, Peter B. *The Union as It Was: Constitutional Unionism and Sectional Compromise, 1787–1861.* Chapel Hill: University of North Carolina Press, 1991.

Krenkel, John, ed. *Richard Yates: Civil War Governor, by Richard Yates and Catharine Yates Pickering.* Danville, Ill.: Interstate Printers, 1966.

LaFeber, Walter. *The New Empire: An Interpretation of American Expansion, 1860–1898.* Ithaca: Cornell University Press, 1963.

Lathrop, Henry W. *The Life and Times of Samuel J. Kirkwood, Iowa's War Governor, and afterwards a Senator of the United States, and a Member of Garfield's Cabinet.* Chicago: Press of Regan Printing House, 1893.

Lawson, Melinda. *Patriot Fires: Forging a New American Nationalism in the Civil War.* Lawrence: University Press of Kansas, 2002.

Levine, Bruce. *Half Slave and Half Free: The Roots of Civil War.* New York: Hill and Wang, 1992.

Lindsey, David. *"Sunset" Cox: Irrepressible Democrat.* Detroit: Wayne State University Press, 1959.

Logsdon, Joseph. *Horace White: Nineteenth-Century Liberal.* Westport, Conn.: Greenwod Press, 1971.

Long, David E. *The Jewel of Liberty: Abraham Lincoln's Reelection and the End of Slavery.* Mechanicsburg, Pa.: Stackpole Books, 1994.

Luthin, Reinhard H. *The First Lincoln Campaign.* Cambridge: Harvard University Press, 1944.

Magdol, Edward. *Owen Lovejoy: Abolitionist in Congress.* New Brunswick, N.J.: Rutgers University Press, 1967.

Magrath, C. Peter. *Morrison R. Waite: The Triumph of Character.* New York: Macmillan, 1963.

Maltz, Earl. *Civil Rights, the Constitution, and Congress, 1863–1869.* Lawrence: University Press of Kansas, 1990.

Mayer, George H. *The Republican Party, 1854–1964.* 2d ed. New York: Oxford University Press, 1967.

McCrary, Peyton. *Abraham Lincoln and Reconstruction: The Louisiana Experiment.* Princeton: Princeton University Press, 1987.

McFeely, William S. *Grant: A Biography.* New York: W. W. Norton, 1981.

______. *Yankee Stepfather: General O. O. Howard and the Freedmen.* New York: W. W. Norton, 1969.

McKitrick, Eric L. *Andrew Johnson and Reconstruction.* Chicago: University of Chicago Press, 1960.

McPherson, James M. *Abraham Lincoln and the Second American Revolution.* New York: Oxford University Press, 1991.

______. *Battle Cry of Freedom: The Civil War Era.* New York: Oxford University Press, 1988.

______. *For Cause and Comrades: Why Men Fought in the Civil War.* New York: Oxford University Press, 1997.

______. *Ordeal By Fire: The Civil War and Reconstruction.* New York: Alfred A. Knopf, 1982.

______. *The Struggle for Equality: Abolitionists and the Negro in the Civil War and Reconstruction.* Princeton: Princeton University Press, 1964.

______. *What They Fought For: 1861–1865.* Baton Rouge: Louisiana State University Press, 1994.

———, ed. *"We Cannot Escape History": Lincoln and the Last Best Hope of Earth.* Urbana: University of Illinois Press, 1995.

McWhiney, Grady, ed. *Grant, Lee, Lincoln, and the Radicals.* Evansville, Ill.: Northwestern University Press, 1964.

Merli, Frank, and Theodore Wilson, eds. *Makers of American Diplomacy: From Benjamin Franklin to Henry Kissinger.* New York: Scribner, 1974.

Merriam, George S. *The Life and Times of Samuel Bowles.* 2 vols. New York: Century Company, 1885.

Miller, Edward A. *Lincoln's Abolitionist General: The Biography of David Hunter.* Columbia: University of South Carolina Press, 1997.

Miller, Randall M., Harry S. Stout, and Charles Reagan Wilson, eds. *Religion and the American Civil War.* New York: Oxford University Press, 1998.

Mitchell, Reid. *Civil War Soldiers.* New York: Viking, 1988.

Monaghan, Jay. *The Man Who Elected Lincoln.* Indianapolis: Bobbs-Merrill, 1956.

Montgomery, David. *Beyond Equality: Labor and the Radical Republicans, 1862–1872.* New York: Alfred A. Knopf, 1967.

Morgan, Edmund S. *American Slavery, American Freedom: The Ordeal of Colonial Virginia.* New York: Oxford University Press, 1975.

Morrison, Michael A. *Slavery and the American West: The Eclipse of Manifest Destiny and the Coming of the Civil War.* Chapel Hill: University of North Carolina Press, 1997.

Nason, Elias, and Thomas Russell. *The Life and Public Services of Henry Wilson, Late Vice-President of the United States.* Boston: B. B. Russell, 1876.

Neely, Mark E. Jr. *The Fate of Liberty: Abraham Lincoln and Civil Liberties.* New York: Oxford University Press, 1991.

______. *The Union Divided: Party Conflict in the Civil War North.* Cambridge: Harvard University Press, 2002.

Nevins, Allan. *Ordeal of the Union.* 8 vols. New York: Scribner's, 1947–71.

______. *The Statesmanship of the Civil War.* New York: Macmillan, 1953.

Nichols, Roy F. *Blueprints for Leviathan: American Style.* New York: Atheneum, 1963.

______. *The Disruption of American Democracy.* New York: Free Press, 1948.

Nicolay, Helen. *Lincoln's Secretary: A Biography of John G. Nicolay.* New York: Longmans, Green, 1949.

Nicolay, John G., and John Hay. *The Life of Abraham Lincoln.* 10 vols. New York: Century Company, 1890.

Nieman, Donald G., ed. *The Constitution, Law, and American Life: Critical Aspects of the Nineteenth-Century Experience.* Athens: University of Georgia Press, 1992.

Niven, John. *Gideon Welles: Lincoln's Secretary of the Navy.* New York: Oxford University Press, 1973.

______. *Salmon P. Chase: A Biography.* New York: Oxford University Press, 1995.

Oates, Stephen B. *With Malice Toward None: The Life of Abraham Lincoln.* New York: Harper and Row, 1978.

Oberholtzer, Ellis P. *Jay Cooke: Financier of the Civil War.* 2 vols. Philadelphia: G. W. Jacobs, 1907.

Ogden, Rollo. *Life of Edwin L. Godkin.* 2 vols. New York: Macmillan, 1907.

Paludan, Phillip S. *A Covenant with Death: The Constitution, Law, and Equality in the Civil War Era.* Urbana: University of Illinois Press, 1975.

______. *"A People's Contest": The Union and the Civil War, 1861–1865.* New York: Harper and Row, 1988.

______. *The Presidency of Abraham Lincoln.* Lawrence: University Press of Kansas, 1994.

Parker, William B. *The Life and Public Services of Justin Smith Morrill.* Boston: Houghton Mifflin, 1924.

Parrish, William E. *Turbulent Partnership: Missouri and the Union, 1861–1865.* Columbia: University of Missouri Press, 1965.

Pearson, Henry Greenleaf. *James S. Wadsworth of Geneseo: Brevet Major-General of United States Volunteers.* New York: Charles Scribner's Sons, 1913.

Peterson, Merrill D. *The Great Triumvirate: Webster, Clay, and Calhoun.* New York: Oxford University Press, 1987.

______. *Lincoln in American Memory.* New York: Oxford University Press, 1994.

Potter, David M. *The Impending Crisis: 1848–1861.* New York: Harper and Row, 1976.

______. *Lincoln and His Party during the Secession Crisis.* New Haven: Yale University Press, 1942.

Quarles, Benjamin. *Lincoln and the Negro.* New York: Oxford University Press, 1962.

Randall, James G. *Constitutional Problems under Lincoln.* Rev. ed. Urbana: University of Illinois Press, 1951.

______. *Lincoln and the South.* Baton Rouge: Louisiana State University Press, 1946.

______. *Lincoln the Liberal Statesman.* New York: Dodd, Mead, 1947.

______. *Lincoln the President: Midstream.* New York: Dodd, Mead, 1953.

______. *Lincoln the President: Springfield to Gettysburg.* 2 vols. New York: Dodd, Mead, 1945.

———, and Richard N. Current. *Lincoln the President: The Last Full Measure.* New York: Dodd, Mead, 1956.

Ransom, Roger L. and Richard Sutch. *One Kind of Freedom: The Economic Consequences of Emancipation.* Cambridge: Cambridge University Press, 1977.

Rawley, James A. *Abraham Lincoln and a Nation Worth Fighting For.* Chicago: Harlan Davidson, 1996.

______. *Edwin D. Morgan, 1811–1883: Merchant in Politics.* New York: Columbia University Press, 1955.

Raymond, Henry J. *The Life and Public Services of Abraham Lincoln.* New York: Derby and Miller, 1865.

Rice, Allen Thorndike, ed. *Reminiscences of Abraham Lincoln by Distinguished Men of His Time.* New York: North American Publishing Company, 1886.

Richardson, Elmo R., and Alan W. Farley. *John Palmer Usher.* Lawrence: University Press of Kansas, 1960.

Richardson, Heather Cox. *The Death of Reconstruction: Race, Labor, and Politics in the Post–Civil War North, 1865–1901.* Cambridge: Harvard University Press, 2001.

______. *The Greatest Nation of the Earth: Republican Economic Policies during the Civil War.* Cambridge: Harvard University Press, 1997.

Ridge, Martin. *Ignatius Donnelly: The Portrait of a Politician.* Chicago: University of Chicago Press, 1962.

Rodell, Fred. *Nine Men: A Political History of the Supreme Court from 1790 to 1955.* New York: Random House, 1955.

Rolle, Andrew F. *John Charles Frémont: Character as Destiny.* Norman: University of Oklahoma Press, 1991.

Rose, Willie Lee. *Rehearsal for Reconstruction: The Port Royal Experiment.* Indianapolis: Bobbs-Merrill, 1964.

Roske, Ralph J. *Everyman's Eden: A History of California.* New York: Macmillan, 1968.

______. *His Own Counsel: The Life and Times of Lyman Trumbull.* Reno: University of Nevada Press, 1979.

Royster, Charles. *The Destructive War: William Tecumseh Sherman, Stonewall Jackson, and the Americans.* New York: Alfred A. Knopf, 1991.

Rusco, Elmer R. *"Good Time Coming?" Black Nevadans in the Nineteenth Century.* Westport, Conn.: Greenwood Press, 1975.

Safire, William. *Freedom: A Novel of Abraham Lincoln and the Civil War.* New York: Doubleday, 1987.

Salter, William. *The Life of James W. Grimes, Governor of Iowa, 1854–1858; A Senator of the United States, 1859–1869.* New York: D. Appleton and Company, 1876.

Schlesinger, Arthur M. Jr. *The Age of Jackson.* Boston: Little, Brown, 1946.

______, ed. *History of U.S. Political Parties.* 4 vols. New York: Chelsea House, 1973.

______, and Fred L. Israel, eds. *History of American Presidential Elections, 1789–1968.* 4 vols. New York: Chelsea House, 1971.

Schuckers, Jacob W. *The Life and Public Services of Salmon Portland Chase.* New York: D. Appleton and Company, 1874.

Schwartz, Bernard. *A History of the Supreme Court.* New York: Oxford University Press, 1993.

Schwartz, Thomas F., ed. *"For a Vast Future Also": Essays from the* Journal of the Abraham Lincoln Association. New York: Fordham University Press, 1999.

Seward, Frederick W. *Seward at Washington.* 2 vols. New York: Derby and Miller, 1891.

Sewell, Richard H. *John P. Hale and the Politics of Abolition.* Cambridge: Harvard University Press, 1965.

Shannon, Fred A. *The Farmer's Last Frontier: Agriculture, 1860–1897.* New York: Holt, Rinehart, and Winston, 1945.

______. *The Organization and Administration of the Union Army, 1861–1865.* Cleveland: Arthur H. Clark, 1928.

Shapiro, Samuel. *Richard Henry Dana, Jr., 1815–1882.* East Lansing: Michigan State University Press, 1961.

Shutes, Milton H. *Lincoln and California.* Stanford: Stanford University Press, 1943.

Silbey, Joel H. *A Respectable Minority: The Democratic Party in the Civil War Era, 1860–1868.* New York: W. W. Norton, 1977.

______. *The American Political Nation, 1838–1893.* Stanford: Stanford University Press, 1991.

Silver, David M. *Lincoln's Supreme Court.* Urbana: University of Illinois Press, 1956.

Simon, John Y., and Harold Holzer, eds. *The Lincoln Forum: Rediscovering Abraham Lincoln.* New York: Fordham University Press, 2002.

Simpson, Brooks D. *Let Us Have Peace: Ulysses S. Grant and the Politics of Reconstruction, 1861–1868.* Chapel Hill: University of North Carolina, 1991.

______. *The Reconstruction Presidents.* Lawrence: University Press of Kansas, 1998.

Smiley, David L. *Lion of White Hall: The Life of Cassius M. Clay.* Madison: University of Wisconsin Press, 1962.

Smith, Elbert B. *Francis Preston Blair.* New York: Free Press, 1980.

Smith, George W. *Henry C. Carey and American Sectional Conflict.* Albuquerque: University of New Mexico Press, 1951.

Smith, James Eugene. *One Hundred Years of Hartford's Courant, from Colonial Times through the Civil War.* New Haven: Yale University Press, 1949.

Smith, Willard H. *Schuyler Colfax: The Changing Fortunes of a Political Idol.* Indianapolis: Indiana Historical Bureau 1952.

Smith, William E. *The Francis Preston Blair Family in Politics.* 2 vols. New York: Macmillan, 1933.

Stampp, Kenneth M. *America in 1857: A Nation on the Brink.* New York: Oxford University Press, 1990.

______. *And the War Came: The North and the Secession Crisis, 1860–1861.* Baton Rouge: Louisiana State University Press, 1950.

______. *The Imperiled Union: Essays on the Background of the Civil War.* New York: Oxford University Press, 1980.

______. *Indiana Politics during the Civil War.* Indianapolis: Indiana Historical Bureau, 1949.

Steiner, Bernard C. *Life of Reverdy Johnson.* Baltimore: Norman, Remington, 1914.

Stevens, Joseph E. *1863: The Rebirth of a Nation.* New York: Bantam Books, 1999.

Stewart, James Brewer. *Holy Warriors: The Abolitionists and American Society.* New York: Hill and Wang, 1976.

______. *Wendell Phillips: Liberty's Hero.* Baton Rouge: Louisiana State University Press, 1986.

Storey, Moorfield, and Edward W. Emerson. *Ebenezer Rockwood Hoar.* Boston: Houghton Mifflin, 1911.

Summers, Mark W. *The Plundering Generation: Corruption and the Crisis of the Union, 1849–1861.* New York: Oxford University Press, 1987.

______. *Railroads, Reconstruction, and the Gospel of Prosperity: Aid under the Radical Republicans, 1865–1877.* Princeton: Princeton University Press, 1984.

Swisher, Carl B. *Roger B. Taney.* New York: Macmillan, 1935.

______. *Stephen J. Field: Craftsman of the Law.* Washington: Brookings Institution, 1930.

Tap, Bruce, *Over Lincoln's Shoulder: The Committee on the Conduct of the War.* Lawrence: University Press of Kansas, 1998.

Thomas, Benjamin P. *Abraham Lincoln: A Biography.* New York: Alfred A. Knopf, 1952.

Thomas, Benjamin P., and Harold M. Hyman. *Stanton: The Life and Times of Lincoln's Secretary of War.* New York: Alfred A. Knopf, 1962.

Thomas, Emory. *The Confederate Nation: 1861–1865.* New York: Harper and Row, 1979.

Thomas, John L., ed. *Abraham Lincoln and the American Political Tradition.* Amherst: University of Massachusetts Press, 1986.

Thornbrough, Emma L. *Indiana in the Civil War Era, 1850–1880.* Indianapolis: Indiana Historical Bureau, 1965.

Trefousse, Hans L. *Andrew Johnson: A Biography.* New York: Norton, 1989.

______. *Ben Butler: The South Called Him Beast!* New York: Twayne, 1957.

______. *Benjamin Franklin Wade: Radical Republican from Ohio.* New York: Twayne, 1963.

______. *Carl Schurz: A Biography.* Knoxville: University of Tennessee Press, 1982. Reprinted, New York: Fordham University Press, 1998.

______. *The Radical Republicans: Lincoln's Vanguard for Racial Justice.* New York: Alfred A. Knopf, 1969.

______. *Thaddeus Stevens: Nineteenth-Century Egalitarian.* Chapel Hill: University of North Carolina Press, 1996.

Tutorow, Norman E. *Leland Stanford: Man of Many Careers.* Menlo Park: Pacific Coast Publishers, 1971.

Van Deusen, Glyndon G. *Horace Greeley: Nineteenth-Century Crusader.* Philadelphia: University of Pennsylvania Press, 1953.

______. *Thurlow Weed: Wizard of the Lobby.* Boston: Little, Brown, 1947.

______. *William Henry Seward.* New York: Oxford University Press, 1967.

Varg, Paul A. *Edward Everett: The Intellectual in the Turmoil of Politics.* Selinsgrove, Pa.: Susquehanna University Press, 1992.

Vaughan, Alden T. *Roots of American Racism: Essays on the Colonial Experience.* New York: Oxford University Press, 1995.

Voegeli, V. Jacque. *Free But Not Equal: The Midwest and the Negro During the Civil War.* Chicago: University of Chicago Press, 1967.

Vorenberg, Michael. *Final Freedom: The Civil War, the Abolition of Slavery, and the Thirteenth Amendment.* Cambridge: Cambridge University Press, 2001.

Wagandt, Charles L. *The Mighty Revolution: Negro Emancipation in Maryland, 1862–1864.* Baltimore: Johns Hopkins University Press, 1964.

Walters, Ronald G. *American Reformers, 1815–1860.* New York: Hill and Wang, 1978.

Wang, Xi. *The Trial of Democracy: Black Suffrage and Northern Republicans, 1860–1910.* Athens: University of Georgia Press, 1997.

Ward, Geoffrey C., Ric Burns, and Ken Burns. *The Civil War: An Illustrated History.* New York: Alfred A. Knopf, 1990.

Waugh, John C. *Reelecting Lincoln: The Battle for the 1864 Presidency.* New York: Crown Books, 1997.

Wheeler, Kenneth W., ed. *For the Union: Ohio Leaders in the Civil War.* Columbus: Ohio State University Press, 1968.

White, Horace. *The Life of Lyman Trumbull.* Boston: Houghton Mifflin, 1913.

Wiebe, Robert H. *The Search for Order: 1877–1920.* New York: Hill and Wang, 1967.

Williams, Kenneth P. *Lincoln Finds a General: A Military Study of the Civil War.* 5 vols. New York: Macmillan, 1949–59.

Williams, T. Harry. *Lincoln and His Generals.* New York: Grosset and Dunlap, 1952.

______. *Lincoln and the Radicals.* Madison: University of Wisconsin Press, 1941.

Wills, Garry. *Lincoln at Gettysburg: The Words That Remade America.* New York: Simon and Schuster, 1992.

Wilson, Major L. *Space, Time, and Freedom: The Quest for Nationality and the Irrepressible Conflict, 1815–1861.* Westport, Conn.: Greenwood Press, 1974.

Winik, Jay. *April 1865: The Month That Saved America.* New York: HarperCollins, 2001.

Wood, Gordon S. *The Creation of the American Republic, 1776–1787.* Chapel Hill: University of North Carolina Press, 1969.

______. *The Radicalism of the American Revolution.* New York: Vintage Books, 1991.

Wright, John S. *Lincoln and the Politics of Slavery.* Reno: University of Nevada Press, 1970.

Wrobel, David M. *Promised Lands: Promotion, Memory, and the Creation of the American West.* Lawrence: University Press of Kansas, 2002.

Younger, Edward. *John A. Kasson: Politics and Diplomacy from Lincoln to McKinley.* Iowa City: University of Iowa Press, 1955.

Zornow, William Frank. *Lincoln and the Party Divided.* Norman: University of Oklahoma Press, 1954.

VI. Articles and Lectures

Baker, Jean H. "'Not Much of Me': Abraham Lincoln as a Typical American." The Eleventh Annual R. Gerald McMurtry Lecture, Fort Wayne: Louis A. Warren Lincoln Library and Museum, 1988.

Beck, Warren A. "Lincoln and Negro Colonization in Central America." *Abraham Lincoln Quarterly* 6 (September 1950): 162–83.

Belz, Herman. "Lincoln and the Constitution: The Dictatorship Question Reconsidered." The Seventh Annual R. Gerald McMurtry Lecture, Fort Wayne: Louis A. Warren Lincoln Library and Museum, 1984.

______. "The 'Philosophical Cause' of 'Our Free Government and Consequent Prosperity': The Problem of Lincoln's Political Thought." *Journal of the Abraham Lincoln Association* 10 (1988–89): 47–72.

Benedict, Michael Les. "Abraham Lincoln and Federalism." *Journal of the Abraham Lincoln Association* 10 (1988–89): 1–46.

Berwanger, Eugene H. "Lincoln's Constitutional Dilemma: Emancipation and Black Suffrage." *Papers of the Abraham Lincoln Association* 5 (1983): 25–38.

Binder, Frederick M. "Pennsylvania Negro Regiments in the Civil War." *Journal of Negro History* 37, no. 4 (October 1952): 383–417.

Blackman, John L. Jr. "The Seizure of the Reading Railroad in 1864." *The Pennsylvania Magazine of History and Biography* 111, no. 1 (January 1987): 49–60.

Brown, Ira V. "William D. Kelley and Radical Reconstruction." *The Pennsylvania Magazine of History and Biography* 85, no. 3 (July 1961): 316–29.

Cornish, Dudley T. "The Union Army as a Training School for Negroes." *Journal of Negro History* 37, no. 4 (October 1952): 368–82.

Current, Richard N. "Comment." *Journal of the Abraham Lincoln Association* 12 (1991): 43–47.

______. "The Confederates and the First Shot." *Civil War History* 7, no. 4 (December 1961): 357–69.

______. "Lincoln and Daniel Webster." *Journal of the Illinois State Historical Society* 48, no. 3 (Autumn 1955): 307–21.

______. "Unity, Ethnicity, and Abraham Lincoln." The First R. Gerald McMurtry Lecture, Fort Wayne: Louis A. Warren Lincoln Library and Museum, 1978.

Fehrenbacher, Don E. "Lincoln and the Weight of Responsibility." *Journal of the Illinois State Historical Society*, 68, no. 1 (Spring 1975): 45–56.

______. "Lincoln's Wartime Leadership: The First Hundred Days." *Journal of the Abraham Lincoln Association* 9 (1987): 1–18.

Ferris, Norman B. "Lincoln and Seward in Civil War Diplomacy: Their Relationship at the Outset Reexamined." *Journal of the Abraham Lincoln Association* 12 (1991): 21–42.

Fields, Barbara J. "Slavery, Race, and Ideology in the United States of America." *New Left Review* 181, no. 3 (May–June 1990): 95–118.

Foner, Eric. "The Meaning of Freedom in the Age of Emancipation." *Journal of American History* 81, no. 2 (September 1994): 435–60.

Frederickson, George M. "A Man but Not a Brother: Abraham Lincoln and Racial Equality." *Journal of American History* 41, no. 1 (February 1975): 39–58.

Glonek, James F. "Lincoln, Johnson, and the Baltimore Ticket." *The Abraham Lincoln Quarterly* 6, no. 5 (March 1951): 255–71.

Hattaway, Herman, "Lincoln's Presidential Example in Dealing with the Military." *Papers of the Abraham Lincoln Association* 7 (1985): 19–29.

Hubbell, John T. "Abraham Lincoln and the Recruitment of Black Soldiers." *Papers of the Abraham Lincoln Association* 2 (1980): 6–21.

Hyman, Harold M. "Lincoln's Reconstruction: Neither Failure of Vision Nor Vision of Failure." Third Annual R. Gerald McMurtry Lecture, Fort Wayne, Ind., Louis A. Warren Lincoln Library and Museum of the Lincoln National Life Insurance Foundation, 1980.

Lee, Arthur M. "Henry C. Carey and the Republican Tariff." *The Pennsylvania Magazine of History and Biography* 81, no. 3 (July 1957): 280–302.

Lockwood, Theodore D. "Garrison and Lincoln the Abolitionist." *The Abraham Lincoln Quarterly* 6, no. 4 (December 1950): 199–226.

Niven, John. "Lincoln and Chase: A Reappraisal." *Journal of the Abraham Lincoln Association* 12 (1991): 1–15.

Paludan, Phillip S. "The American Civil War Considered as a Crisis in Law and Order." *American Historical Review* 77, no. 4 (October 1972): 1013–34.

Randall, James G. "Lincoln and the Governance of Men." *The Abraham Lincoln Quarterly* 6, no. 6 (June 1951): 327–52.

Rawley, James A. "Lincoln and Governor Morgan." *The Abraham Lincoln Quarterly* 6, no. 5 (March 1951): 272–300.

Roske, Ralph J. "Lincoln's Peace Puff." *The Abraham Lincoln Quarterly* 6, no. 4 (December 1950): 239–45.

Scheips, Paul J. "Lincoln and the Chiriqui Colonization Project." *Journal of Negro History* 37, no. 3 (October 1952): 418–53.

Schlesinger, Arthur M. Jr. "War and the Constitution: Abraham Lincoln and Franklin D. Roosevelt." The 27th Annual Robert Fortenbaugh Memorial Lecture, Gettysburg: Gettysburg College, 1988.

Silbey, Joel H. "'Always a Whig in Politics': The Partisan Life of Abraham Lincoln." *Papers of the Abraham Lincoln Association* 8 (1986): 21–42.

Trefousse, Hans L. "The Joint Committee on the Conduct of the War: A Reassessment," *Civil War History* 10, no. 1 (Spring 1964): 5–19.

Vorenberg, Michael A. "Abraham Lincoln and the Politics of Black Colonization." *Journal of the Abraham Lincoln Association* 14, no. 2 (Summer 1993): 23–45.

Winger, Stewart. "Lincoln's Economics and the American Dream: A Reappraisal." *Journal of the Abraham Lincoln Association* 22 (2001): 51–80.

INDEX

THE NORTH'S CIVIL WAR SERIES
Paul A. Cimbala, series editor

1. Anita Palladino, ed., *Diary of a Yankee Engineer: The Civil War Story of John H. Westervelt, Engineer, 1st New York Volunteer Engineer Corps.*
2. Herman Belz, *Abraham Lincoln, Constitutionalism, and Equal Rights in the Civil War Era.*
3. Earl J. Hess, *Liberty, Virtue, and Progress: Northerners and Their War for the Union.* Second revised edition, with a new introduction by the author.
4. William L. Burton, *Melting Pot Soldiers: The Union's Ethnic Regiments.*
5. Hans L. Trefousse, *Carl Schurz: A Biography.*
6. Stephen W. Sears, ed., *Mr. Dunn Browne's Experiences in the Army: The Civil War Letters of Samuel W. Fiske.*
7. Jean H. Baker, *Affairs of Party: The Political Culture of Northern Democrats in the Mid-Nineteenth Century.*
8. Frank L. Klement, *The Limits of Dissent: Clement L. Vallandigham and the Civil War.* With a new introduction by Steven K. Rogstad.
9. Lawrence N. Powell, *New Masters: Northern Planters during the Civil War and Reconstruction.*
10. John A. Carpenter, *Sword and Olive Branch: Oliver Otis Howard.*
11. Thomas F. Schwartz, ed., *"For a Vast Future Also": Essays from the* Journal of the Abraham Lincoln Association.
12. Mark De Wolfe Howe, ed., *Touched with Fire: Civil War Letters and Diary of Oliver Wendell Holmes, Jr.* With a new introduction by David Burton.
13. Harold Adams Small, ed., *The Road to Richmond: The Civil War Letters of Major Abner R. Small of the 16th Maine Volunteers.* New introduction by Earl J. Hess.
14. Eric A. Campbell, ed., *"A Grand Terrible Dramma": From Gettysburg to Petersburg: The Civil War Letters of Charles Wellington Reed.* Illustrated by Reed's Civil War Sketches.
15. Herbert Mitgang, ed., *Abraham Lincoln: A Press Portrait.*
16. Harold Holzer, ed., *Prang's Civil War Pictures: The Complete Battle Chromos of Louis Prang.*
17. Harold Holzer, ed., *State of the Union: New York and the Civil War.*
18. Paul A. Cimbala and Randall M. Miller, eds., *Union Soldiers and the Northern Home Front: Wartime Experiences, Postwar Adjustments.*
19. Mark A. Snell, *From First to Last: The Lifetime of William B. Franklin.*
20. Paul A. Cimbala and Randall M. Miller, eds., *An Uncommon Time: The Civil War and the Northern Home Front.*
21. John Y. Simon and Harold Holzer, eds., *The Lincoln Forum: Rediscovering Abraham Lincoln.*
22. Thomas F. Curran, *Soldiers of Peace: Civil War Pacifism and the Postwar Radical Peace Movement.*

23. Kyle S. Sinisi, *Sacred Debts: State Civil War Claims and American Federalism, 1861–1880.*
24. Russell Johnson, *Warriors into Workers: The Civil War and the Formation of Urban-Industrial Society in a Northern City.*
25. Peter J. Parish, *The North and the Nation in the Era of the Civil War.* Edited by Adam L. P. Smith and Susan-Mary Grant.
26. Patricia Richard, *Busy Hands: Images of the Family in the Northern Civil War Effort.*